Contextualization of the Gospel

Australian College of Theology Monograph Series

SERIES EDITOR GRAEME R. CHATFIELD

The ACT Monograph Series, generously supported by the Board of Directors of the Australian College of Theology, provides a forum for publishing quality research theses and studies by its graduates and affiliated college staff in the broad fields of Biblical Studies, Christian Thought and History, and Practical Theology with Wipf and Stock Publishers of Eugene, Oregon. The ACT selects the best of its doctoral and research masters theses as well as monographs that offer the academic community, scholars, church leaders and the wider community uniquely Australian and New Zealand perspectives on significant research topics and topics of current debate. The ACT also provides opportunity for contributors beyond its graduates and affiliated college staff to publish monographs which support the mission and values of the ACT.

Rev Dr Graeme Chatfield
Series Editor and Associate Dean

Contextualization of the Gospel

Towards an Evangelical Approach in the Light of Scripture and the Church Fathers

ANDREW JAMES PRINCE

WIPF & STOCK · Eugene, Oregon

CONTEXTUALIZATION OF THE GOSPEL
Towards an Evangelical Approach in the Light of Scripture and the Church Fathers

Australian College of Theology Monograph Series

Copyright © 2017 Andrew James Prince. All rights reserved. Except for brief quotations in critical publications or reviews, no part of this book may be reproduced in any manner without prior written permission from the publisher. Write: Permissions, Wipf and Stock Publishers, 199 W. 8th Ave., Suite 3, Eugene, OR 97401.

Wipf & Stock
An Imprint of Wipf and Stock Publishers
199 W. 8th Ave., Suite 3
Eugene, OR 97401

www.wipfandstock.com

PAPERBACK ISBN: 978-1-5326-1915-1
HARDCOVER ISBN: 978-1-4982-4529-6
EBOOK ISBN: 978-1-4982-4528-9

Manufactured in the U.S.A.   MAY 2, 2017

Contents

Preface | vii
Acknowledgments | ix
Abbreviations | xi

Chapter 1   Introduction | 1
Chapter 2   The Contextualization Debate | 37
Chapter 3   Contextualization in Acts | 72
Chapter 4   Bridging the Gap | 115
Chapter 5   Contextualization in John Chrysostom | 153
Chapter 6   Conclusion | 224

Bibliography | 231

Preface

THIS WORK IS AN attempt to extend and strengthen missiological method from an evangelical perspective in the area of contextualization. My thesis is that a missiological methodology that is governed by Scripture, while also drawing from the church fathers, the social sciences and practical theology, is not only consistent with the nature of evangelicalism but also consistent with the nature of missiology itself. The critical observation that the contextualization debate has been predominantly driven by insights gained from the social sciences (particularly anthropology) and practical theology, with comparatively little insight drawn from Scripture or the writings of the church fathers, has informed this thesis. The investigation here challenges the imbalance of the relative contributions of these four disciplines for contextualization and offers new ways of thinking about mission, with implications for future evangelical missiological praxis. My thesis is tested through an examination of contextualization from missiological, biblical, and historical perspectives, seeking to identify and develop contextual principles that are consistent with the nature of evangelicalism. A survey of the literature on contextualization reveals many contextual principles that have informed missiological praxis since the word was first introduced into missiological vocabulary in 1972. A biblical examination of representative passages from the book of Acts of the early church engaged in contextualization to both Jewish and Gentile audiences reveals various contextual principles which confirm, critique, or are unique to those identified in the literature. Following the establishment of the legitimacy of John Chrysostom informing the contextualization debate, an examination of representative homilies of Chrysostom reveals contextual principles which confirm, critique, or are unique to those identified in the literature or in the study of Acts. The research's conclusion is that an examination of contextualization that draws from biblical studies, the church fathers, the social sciences, and practical theology is consistent with the nature of the discipline of missiology from an evangelical perspective.

Acknowledgments

DEAN FLEMMING'S MONOGRAPH, CONTEXTUALIZATION *in the New Testament*, was a revelation to me. His ability to bring biblical studies and missiology together with such warmth, clarity, and biblical fidelity opened up new vistas that set me on the path of my thesis topic. Professor Flemming has been very generous in his encouragement throughout my research, reading some early chapters, responding to some points of clarification of his book, and making time to meet with me on two different continents. Professor Scott Moreau has likewise been a great source of inspiration, and has also graciously met with me a number of times to discuss my research, and provided support throughout the journey.

That this research has been completed is a tribute to those who have labored patiently with me. My supervisors, Professor Bronwen Neil and Dr. Raymond Laird, have been patient guides, exemplary scholars, and a great source of encouragement. The quality of their feedback would be the envy of many doctoral candidates. I have been very blessed to have had access to such leading patristic scholars. Without them this research would simply not have come to fruition. Dr. Wendy Mayer has been a further source of encouragement, making suggestions for further resources, and also reading through a draft of the thesis and offering constructive feedback. Professor Pauline Allen and those part of the Centre for Early Christian Studies, including Dr. Johan Ferreira, Dr. Geoffrey Dunn, Dr. Chris Hanlon, and Dinah Joesoef, have always been willing to offer advice, wisdom, and resources. Their warmth and professionalism has been both admired and appreciated. Dr. Richard Gibson and Mr. John Coulson from the Brisbane School of Theology have provided feedback on various chapters of the thesis and have been a wonderful source of friendship and support. I am also grateful to the BST Board for granting me a semester of study leave in 2013, which allowed me to dedicate myself completely to crucial areas of the thesis. Many others too numerous to name have contributed their encouragement in the task. A special thanks goes to Verena Adrian and Witali Klein whose fluent German produced some years ago a far better translation of parts of Gustav Warneck's *Evangelische Missionslehre* than I could have achieved alone. It would be extremely remiss of me to fail to give tribute to Susan, my wife. She has been unfailing in her support throughout this whole project and has often carried other aspects of our lives in order to free me up to undertake the research. The encouragement of my father, Barry Prince, has meant an enormous amount too.

Abbreviations

John Chrysostom

Adv. Jud.	*Adversus Judaeos*
Adv. Jud. et Gen.	*Adv. Judaeos et Gentiles demonstratio quod Christus sit dues*
C. Lud. et theat.	*Contra ludos et theatra*
Bab. Jul.	*De Babyla contra Julianum et gentiles*
De beat. Phil.	*De beato Philogonio*
De Comp.	*De compunctione*
De Incomp.	*De incomprehensibili Dei natura*
De Sac.	*De sacerdotio*
De Sac. Lib.	*De sacerdotio libri*
De Stat.	*De Statuis*
Goth. concin.	*Homilia habita postquam presbyter Gothus concionatus fuerat*
In 1 Cor.	*In epistulam i ad Corinthios*
In 2 Cor.	*In epistulam ii ad Corinthios*
In Acta	*In Acta apostolorum*
In Eph.	*In epistulam ad Ephesios*
In Gen.	*In Genesim (homiliae 1–67)*
In Heb.	*In epistulam ad Hebraeos*
In Joan.	*In Joannem*
In Matt.	*In Matthaeum*
In Rom.	*In epistulam ad Romanos*
In Phil.	*In epistulam ad Philippenses*
In Philm.	*In epistulam Philemonem*

In 1 Tim.	*In epistulam i ad Timotheum*
In 2 Tim.	*In epistulam ii ad Timotheum*
In Titum	*In epistulam ad Titum*
Natal.	*In diem natalem Christi*
Virginit.	*De virginitate*

Ps-Martyrius

Orat. Funeb.	*Oratio funebris*

Socrates/Sozomen/Theodoret

Hist. eccl.	*Historia Ecclesiastica*

Reference Books, Monograph Series and Other Source Material

ACU	Australian Catholic University
ANF	Ante-Nicene Fathers
ANTC	Abingdon New Testament Commentaries
BDAG	Bauer, Danker, Arndt, and Gingrich
ECNT	Exegetical Commentary on the New Testament
ECS	Early Christian Studies
EMQ	Evangelical Missions Quarterly
FOTC	Fathers of The Church
GCS NF	Die Griechischen Christlichen Schriftsteller. Neue Folge
HTR	Harvard Theological Review
IBMR	International Bulletin of Missionary Research
IJFM	International Journal of Frontier Missiology
IVP	InterVarsity Press
JBL	Journal of Biblical Literature
NAC	New American Commentary
NIBC	New International Biblical Commentary
NICNT	New International Commentary on the New Testament
NICOT	New International Commentary on the Old Testament
NPNF	Nicene and Post-Nicene Fathers
NTCS	New Testament Commentary Series
NTS	New Testament Studies
PG	Patrologia Graeca, ed., J.-P. Migne

RTR	Reformed Theological Review
SBL	Society of Biblical Literature
TLG	Thesaurus Linguae Graecae
TNAC	The New American Commentary
WBC	Word Bible Commentary
WTJ	*Westminster Theological Journal*

Chapter 1

Introduction

THERE HAS BEEN HEIGHTENED interest in and prolific publication by missiologists about contextualization since the term was first coined in 1972.[1] Various meanings, methods and models of contextualization have since been proposed.[2] Contextualization as a term originated from the conciliar movement of the World Council of Churches leading to an initial mistrust amongst some evangelicals in adopting it for fear of syncretism or compromise.[3] Over time, evangelicals in general have increasingly embraced the term as they have redefined its meaning and contours. There has been ongoing debate, particularly amongst evangelicals themselves, regarding which of these meanings, methods and models of contextualization are acceptable to use.[4] The more recent application of contextualization to Muslim evangelism as part of the Insider Movement has sharpened the debate, with both proponents and detractors arguing that their voice is the one to be heeded.[5] Differing criteria for both the practice and the critique of contextualization

---

1. Theological Education Fund Staff, *Ministry in Context: The Third Mandate Programme of the Theological Education Fund 1970–1977*, 28; Bosch, *Transforming Mission: Paradigm Shifts in Theology of Mission*, 420–32.

2. See Hesselgrave and Rommen, *Contextualization: Meaning, Methods and Models*; Bevans, *Models of Contextual Theology*; Cook et al., *Local Theology for the Global Church: Principles for an Evangelical Approach to Contextualization*; Rommen, *Come and See: An Eastern Orthodox Perspective on Contextualization*.

3. Nicholls, *Contextualization: A Theology of Gospel and Culture*, 21–23.

4. Moreau, *Contextualization in World Missions*, 20.

5. For example, see proponent Travis, "Must all Muslims Leave 'Islam' to Follow Jesus?", 411–5. For a detractor, see Parshall, "DANGER! New Directions in Contextualization," 404–10.

practices have further muddied the waters. There is a need for objective and consistent criteria to be used in the praxis of contextualization. Much of the debate has been carried out by academics and practitioners whose observations and conclusions have been largely shaped by the social sciences and practical theology.[6] In contrast, the disciplines of biblical studies and Christian thought have not featured significantly in the debate.

The purpose of this study is to establish that biblical studies and Christian thought in general (and Scripture and the church fathers in particular) have an essential contribution to make in the contextualization debate and should form part of an evangelical approach to contextualization of the gospel alongside the social sciences, and practical theology.

The hypothesis of this research is that a missiological methodology that is governed by Scripture, while also drawing from the church fathers, the social sciences, and practical theology is not only consistent with the nature of evangelicalism but also consistent with the nature of missiology itself.

1.1 Questions of definition

The missiological framework for this thesis is based on six concepts: evangelical, mission, gospel, contextualization, culture, and syncretism.

1.1.1 Evangelical

The term "evangelical" is one that is used by many Christians from a broad range of theological backgrounds and beliefs.[7] Historically, to be an evangelical meant being a person whose beliefs and life were shaped by the *euangelion*, the gospel of Jesus Christ.[8] Despite the diversity of expression that exists amongst evangelicals, there are five theological convictions that they generally use to characterize their evangelical beliefs:[9]

---

6. Practical theology includes missiology, evangelism, homiletics, spiritual formation, and pastoral theology. The social sciences include anthropology, communications, history, linguistics, education, and sociology.

7. Bebbington, *Evangelicalism in Modern Britain: A History from the 1730s to the 1980s*, 1; Gerstner, "The Theological Boundaries of Evangelical Faith," 21–37, at 22.

8. Gerstner, "The Theological Boundaries," 22–23.

9. Bebbington, *Evangelicalism*, 3. See also Lausanne Committee for World Evangelization, "The Lausanne Covenant," 3–9; Noll, *The Scandal of the Evangelical Mind*, 8; Gerstner, "The Theological Boundaries," 38–67; Stott, *What is an Evangelical?*, 5–14; Phillips and Okholm, *A Family of Faith: An Introduction to Evangelical Christianity*,

First, *the authority of Scripture*. Scripture is regarded as the truthful, reliable, divinely inspired, authoritative source of all doctrine and as the normative guide for Christian belief and practice (2 Tim 3:16–17).[10] The collection of the sixty-six books in the Old Testament and New Testament is the work of the Holy Spirit[11] "who inspired the original writers of Scripture" (2 Pet 1:21).[12] As a divinely inspired text, it stands above all other writings, ecclesiastical traditions and ecclesiastical officials.[13]

Second, *the seriousness of sin*. Since the fall of Adam and Eve all people have been born with a sinful nature which alienates them from God (Gen 3:1–24; Rom 3:1–10, 23; Rom 7:14–24). They are helpless to rescue themselves from their sinful state and face the righteous judgment of God (Rom 7:24; 2 Thess 1:8–9). What they require is forgiveness from and reconciliation to God (Acts 2:37–40; 2 Cor 5:18–20).[14]

Third, *the centrality of the cross of Christ* (Rom 3:21–26; 1 Cor 1:18–19; 2 Cor 5:21; Eph 2:14–18). The problem of sin is only dealt with through the atoning death of the sinless Jesus on humanity's behalf, restoring them to God. Jesus came to seek and save the lost and that is exactly what his death achieved (Mark 10:45; 2 Cor 5:21; Eph 2:4–5, 14–17). The cross is the chief demonstration of God's love for humanity (1 John 4:10). The bodily resurrection of Jesus to new life is God's vindication of the person and work of his Son (Rom 1:4).[15]

Fourth, *the necessity for humanity to respond* to the cross of Christ (Acts 2:38, 40; 2 Cor 5:20). The gospel is not just the great news of God's salvation available through Jesus Christ, but is the great summons to respond to it. Salvation is found in Christ alone: it is not automatically bestowed on a person, nor does it come naturally. Each person needs to appropriate that salvation for themselves by responding in repentance and faith.[16]

15–16; Trinity Evangelical School, "The Evangelical Affirmations," 27–38; Moreau, *Contextualization in World Missions*, 19–20.

10. Stott, "The Authority and Power of the Bible," 33–47, at 33–40; Nicholls, "Theological Education and Evangelization," 634–48, at 635; Phillips and Okholm, *A Family of Faith*, 16, 55–56.

11. Phillips and Okholm, *A Family of Faith*, 56–58.

12. Ibid., 16.

13. Ibid., 16.

14. Milne, *Know the Truth*, 138–46; Phillips and Okholm, *A Family of Faith*, 79–88.

15. Carson, *Scandalous: The Cross and Resurrection of Jesus*, 39–72; Phillips and Okholm, *A Family of Faith*, 103–6.

16. Athyal, "The Uniqueness and Universality of Christ," 49–66, at 50–51, 62–66; Phillips and Okholm, *A Family of Faith*, 16.

Fifth, *the ongoing work of the Spirit in the life of the believer and the means of grace* (Eph 1:13–14; 2:8–10). As a person responds in repentance and faith, they are brought to new life in Christ through the power of the Spirit. The Spirit continues to be at work in the believer's life, engaging in the ongoing work of sanctification (Gal 5:16–26; Rom 12:9–21).[17]

There are a number of implications of these five tenets in relation to developing an evangelical approach to contextualization of the gospel, two of which will be highlighted here. First, for evangelicals, Scripture is the primary and ultimate source of knowledge of God and his world, and is the lens through which all other information is filtered. Contextual principles and practices derived from any source outside of Scripture (e.g., church fathers, social sciences, and practical theology) are secondary and subservient to those found in Scripture.[18] Second, the five basic tenets of evangelicalism above both establish contours and serve as restraints for "determining contextual models and practices that can be identified as distinctly evangelical. They do so [however] without imposing an artificial uniformity on the practitioners [of contextualization] or ensuring agreement among them."[19]

1.1.2 Mission

The word "mission" derives from the Latin words *missio* (sending) and *mittere*—a translation of the Greek verb ἀποστέλλω (to send)[20], and so inherently contains the ideas of "intentionality" and "movement."[21] It was first used by Ignatius Loyola and Jacob Loyner in 1544 to describe the

---

17. Griffiths, "The Power of the Holy Spirit," 239–53, at 239–40, 251.

18. While the word 'principle' can refer to a foundational truth or proposition that is incontrovertible and universally true, that is not how the word is used in this thesis. Rather, 'principle' is used in the sense of a guide that points towards a particular direction. Used in this sense, individual principles can be confirmed or challenged, added or removed, in light of the prevailing data.

19. Moreau, *Contextualization in World Missions*, 20. The two insertions in brackets are my own.

20. Christopher Wright critiques the narrowness of definitions of mission that only emphasize the 'sending' aspect of mission but do not include the broader aspect of what God is doing in the world. Wright, *The Mission of God: Unlocking the Bible's Grand Narrative*, 23.

21. Schnabel, *Paul the Missionary: Realities, Strategies and Methods*, 22–23. By "intentionality" Schnabel means that the sender has a purpose in sending someone and that the person being sent understands the sender's purpose. By "movement" Schnabel means geographical movement between two points. This does not necessarily mean travelling overseas or working cross-culturally.

propagation of the Christian faith, and by the seventeenth century the word "mission" was in common parlance.²²

Until the 1950s the terms "mission" and "missions" were generally used synonymously²³ and had a fairly well-defined set of meanings, namely:

> 1) the sending of missionaries to a designated territory, 2) activities undertaken by such missionaries, 3) the geographical area where missionaries were active, 4) the agency which dispatched missionaries, 5) the non-Christian world or the "mission field", or 6) the centre from which missionaries operated on the 'mission field'.²⁴

Since the 1950s there has been a remarkable expansion in the use of the word "mission" amongst theologians with a subsequent broadening of the traditional understanding of the term in some circles.²⁵ Because of this, some have even questioned whether the word retains any real meaning at all.²⁶ The quest for an agreed definition of mission remains elusive, but there are four definitions that have been particularly influential during the twentieth century:

1. *Mission as missio Dei*. Strongly influenced by Karl Barth's paper read at the Brandenberg Missionary Conference in 1932 (where he expounded mission as an activity of God), Karl Hartenstein, a German missiologist, first introduced the term *missio Dei* in 1934.²⁷ The term *missio Dei* recognizes that all mission is God's mission and that the human activity of mission is predicated on the prior sending of the Son by the Father and the Holy Spirit by the Father and the Son.²⁸

---

22. Ott and Strauss, *Encountering Theology of Mission*, xiv.

23. Moreau et al., *Introducing World Missions: A Biblical, Historical, and Practical Survey*, 16–17.

24. Bosch, *Transforming Mission*, 1.

25. Ibid., 1.

26. Fernando, "Mission: A Problem of Definition," 46–59, at 46. In some missiological circles, a distinction is drawn between 'missions' and 'mission'. 'Mission' is the broader term for what the church does for God in the world (including addressing systemic injustice, political liberation and dialogue with people of other living faiths), while 'missions', as a subset of mission, refers specifically to evangelism, discipleship and church planting. Nevertheless, there is still no clear consensus on the distinction between missions and mission: Moreau et al., *Introducing World Missions*, 70.

27. Bevans and Schroeder, *Constants in Context: A Theology for Mission Today*, 290.

28. Raiter, "'Sent for this Purpose': 'Mission' and 'Missiology' and Their Search for Meaning," 106–49, at 109. For further discussion on the missiological contribution of

At the 1952 International Missionary Council (IMC) Willingen conference, mission as *missio Dei* was further expanded to include the Father, Son and Spirit sending the church into the world.[29] Mission therefore is participating in the sending of God. The concept of *Missio Dei* was introduced as a corrective to the idea that mission is initiated by and centered on the church rather than initiated by and centered on God.[30] Since Willingen, the *missio Dei* concept has, according to David Bosch, been embraced by nearly all Christian persuasions, and represents the broadest understanding of mission.[31]

2. *Mission as liberation.* Strongly influenced by theologians such as Gustavo Gutiérrez, Leonardo Boff, Jon Sobrino, Juan Luis Segundo, and Emilio Castro, mission is defined as faith confronting poverty and oppression.[32] Liberation theology espouses that God favors the poor, that poverty is a scandal and that the poor need to be liberated not just from their poverty but from the root causes of it (which are bound up in unjust societal structures). Gutiérrez writes:

> Development must attack the root causes of the problems and among them the deepest is economic, social, political and cultural dependence of some countries upon others . . . Attempts to bring about changes within the existing order have proven futile . . . Only a radical break from the status quo, that is, a profound transformation of the private property system, access to power of the exploited class, and a social revolution that would break this dependence would allow for the change to a new society, a socialist society.[33]

Mission as liberation, therefore, is fundamentally concerned with proactively seeking to bring about changes so that justice, in all its forms, is brought to oppressed societies.

Karl Hartenstein, see Schuster, "Karl Hartenstein: Mission with a Focus on the End," 53–89.

29. Bosch, *Transforming Mission*, 390.

30. Moreau et al., *Introducing World Missions*, 70–71.

31. Bosch names conciliar Protestantism, Eastern Orthodox, many Evangelicals, and the Catholic Church as having embraced mission as *missio Dei*. Bosch, *Transforming Mission*, 390–1.

32. For some useful introductions to liberation theology, see Gutiérrez, *A Theology of Liberation: History, Politics and Salvation*; Boff and Boff, *Introducing Liberation Theology*; Nunez, *Liberation Theology*.

33. Gutiérrez, *A Theology of Liberation*, 26.

3. *Mission as social action.* This approach identifies mission as social action, alongside the making of disciples.[34] Social action is an imprecise term but is meant to indicate an eminently practical approach, being concerned with the "alleviation of human suffering" in its various forms, such as malnutrition, poor sanitation, disease, inadequate habitation, unemployment, illiteracy and lack of education.[35] Moreau identifies two subgroups under this third approach. One sub-group, of which John Stott is representative, incorporates evangelism and issues of social justice and reconciliation into an integrated, holistic approach. This group sees no dichotomy between evangelism and social responsibility but still places evangelism as ultimately more important.[36] The other sub-group, represented by people such as Ron Sider, C. René Padilla, and Samuel Escobar, go further and say that social justice and evangelism are on equal standing as mission, with neither taking priority over the other.[37]

4. *Mission as the making of disciples.* This definition, which emphasizes the making of disciples as the exclusive content of what constitutes mission, is seen as being most in line with the teaching of Matt 28:19.[38] This view could be misunderstood as a claim that mission is simply about people making decisions for Christ.[39] That, however, is not the case. It recognizes that mission is not just about making converts but making disciples.[40] Matt 28:18–20 contains only one imperative—to make disciples—qualified by three participles (going, baptizing, teaching) which are subject to the imperative. Therefore, the making of disciples is central to the Great Commission.[41] Furthermore, in the ministry of the apostle Paul, disciple-making involved maturation of the believer over a period of time, not simply his or her conversion.

---

34. Ferdinando, "Mission," 52.

35. Ibid., 52.

36. See Stott, "1982: The Grand Rapids Report on Evangelism and Social Responsibility: An Evangelical Commitment," 165–213.

37. Moreau, "Missions and Mission," 636–8, at 637–8. For David Bosch's critique and modification of Stott's view see Bosch, "Evangelism: Theological Currents and Cross-currents Today," 98–103, at 100.

38. Ferdinando, "Mission," 54. See also Egbunu, "To Teach, Baptise, and Nurture New Believers," 25–36.

39. Ferdinando, "Mission," 54.

40. Ferreira, "The Great Commission: Towards a Biblical Theology of Theological Education," 15–32, at 23. See also Wright, *The Mission of God*, 34–35.

41. Ferreira, "The Great Commission," 23–26.

Paul's desire was to see all people, Jews and Gentiles, not only saved but brought to full maturity in Christ (1 Cor 9:19–23).[42] Defining mission in terms of making disciples encompasses not only people being brought to faith but also "fostering their spiritual growth in terms of a relationship with God and his people, and of obedience in all areas of life", and has been the prevalent understanding of mission until recent times.[43]

There is merit in each of these four definitions of mission. For evangelicals, the centrality of the cross, the seriousness of sin, the necessity for human response, and the ongoing work of the Spirit in the life of the believer favor definitions that include the proclamation and ongoing appropriation of these truths as part of disciple-making (e.g., mission as social action, mission as disciple-making). The impact of the gospel should also lead to more just and equitable societies as the gospel truths are appropriated in the lives of individuals (e.g., some elements of mission as liberation). The weakness, however, in defining mission as liberation, social action or disciple-making alone is that each one of them restricts mission to being simply a human activity. Mission certainly does involve human activity (see Matt 28:18–20). Nevertheless, God's chosen way of making disciples is through transformed human agents proclaiming the gospel, which the Holy Spirit applies to the lives of those who receive the gospel. Mission is more than a human activity. The storyline of the Bible, from Genesis to Revelation, shows that mission starts and is driven by God (*missio Dei*). This idea is reflected in Christopher Wright's definition of mission where he stresses both the priority of and the Christian's full participation in God's mission, stating:

> Fundamentally, our mission (if it is biblically informed and validated) means our committed participation as God's people, at God's invitation and command, in God's own mission within the history of the world for the redemption of God's creation.[44]

Wright's definition of mission will have a bearing on my understanding of the nature and contours of missiology and the research method adopted

---

42. Kostenberger and O'Brien, *Salvation to the Ends of the Earth: A Biblical Theology of Mission*, 181.

43. Ferdinando, "Mission," 54–55. Fernando goes on to qualify his thesis by saying that Christian engagement with the world through pursuing justice, the right ordering of society and relieving the plight of the poor and destitute, are still important. He argues that it is inconsistent to proclaim the gospel while being indifferent to these social concerns. But in the interests of clarity he restricts the word 'mission' to the process of making disciples of all nations.

44. Wright, *Mission of God*, 22–23.

(see 1.2 below), but it also serves as an important qualifier. As the various definitions of mission have highlighted, mission has traditionally been conceived as largely a human endeavor. Because mission has been the vehicle through which much of the contextualization debate has been conducted, it is no surprise to find that the discussion of contextualization has focused almost completely on the human side of the activity (e.g., techniques in better communicating the gospel, developing contextualized forms of worship in creative access countries) rather than the place of this human activity in God's mission. In chapters three to five, therefore, I have a strong focus on the human agents in mission—Peter, Stephen, Paul, and John Chrysostom. In as much as these men individually proclaimed the gospel (as defined below) they were engaging in mission, for the gospel cannot be separated from mission. There is, however, a larger context to their missionary activity than simply proclamation or even acts of mercy (e.g., Acts 3:7; 5:15; Chrysostom building hospitals and helping the poor). What needs to be kept in mind is that these people were simply participants in God's mission, the goal of which is the restoration of creation which was marred by the fall (Gen 3:1–19; Ezek 36:28–32; Rom 8:19–23; Rev 22:1–5).[45] God's means of bringing about the restoration of creation is through the gospel—to which we now turn.

1.1.3 Gospel

The word "gospel" (εὐαγγέλιον) is fundamental to the Christian life, frequently the term for just about anything at all related to the Christian faith. Despite its frequent use, there is still significant confusion regarding its meaning.[46] It is an imprecise word that simply means "good news".[47] It has its origins in the Old Testament announcements of God's coming salvation of his people (Isa 40:9; 52:7) and was also used by Jesus (Matt 24:14; 26:13; Mark 8:35; 10:29; 13:10) and the early church (Acts 8:25, 40; 15:8; 20:24; Rom 1:2, 9, 16, 17).[48] It was also regularly used in the Greco-Roman world

---

45. "This mission of God's people within the world is to be understood within an eschatological perspective, that is, it is grounded in the saving events of the gospel and keeps an eye on the final goal—the gathering of men and women from every nation, tribe, people and language before the throne of God and the Lamb." Kostenberger and O'Brien, *Salvation to the Ends of the Earth*, 269.

46. McKnight, *The King Jesus Gospel: The Original Good News Revisited*, 23–27; Wright, *What St Paul Really Said*, 40–41.

47. BDAG, "εὐαγγέλιον," 92. Edwards, *The Gospel According to Mark*, 24.

48. Flemming, *Contextualization in the New Testament: Patterns for Theology and Mission*, 92.

to refer to good news about events such as a military victory, the birthday of an emperor or ascension to the throne.⁴⁹

The origins of the εὐαγγέλιον are in Jesus himself.⁵⁰ The content of the εὐαγγέλιον Jesus announced centered on the immediacy of the arrival of the kingdom of God and the necessary response to that arrival through repentance (μετάνοια) and belief (πίστις) (Mark 1:15).⁵¹ Since εὐαγγέλιον is mostly a Pauline term in the New Testament, the focus of this discussion therefore will be confined to the Pauline literature.⁵²

The apostle Paul regarded the gospel as something that had a specific content, a content briefly summarized in Rom 1:1–5⁵³ and 1 Cor 15:1–8.⁵⁴

i. *Rom 1:1–5*. Having established that the gospel's origin and content is from God and not from humanity (Rom 1:1)⁵⁵ and that the gospel originated in the Old Testament through the proclamation of the prophets (Rom 1:2),⁵⁶ Paul again states that the gospel is all about

---

49. Lane, *The Gospel of Mark*, 42–44; Edwards, *The Gospel According to Mark*, 24.

50. Dumbrell, "The Content of the Gospel and the Implications of that Content for the Christian Community," 33–43, at 33.

51. For a helpful summary on the subject of 'the gospel that Jesus preached', see Snodgrass, "The Gospel of Jesus," 31–44.

52. The noun εὐαγγέλιον appears approximately 60 times and the verb εὐαγγελίζομαι some 21 times in Paul. For further discussion, see Friedrich, "εὐαγγέλιον," 721–36, at 727. On the Pauline gospel: see Ciampa, "Paul's Theology of the Gospel," 180–91; Stuhlmacher, "The Pauline Gospel," 149–72; Wright, *What St Paul Really Said*, 41–62.

53. Gilbert, *What is the Gospel?*, 27–31, finds Rom 1:1–4 as one of the best summaries of the gospel. This is contra McKnight, *The King Jesus Gospel*, 46, 59–60, who critiques Gilbert's understanding of the gospel and also argues for 1 Cor 15:3–5 as the clearest expression of the apostolic gospel, while interpreting passages such as Rom 1:1–4 as part of "God's plan of salvation" rather than gospel summaries. What McKnight fails to take into account, however, are the different contexts in which Paul is delivering his gospel summaries. Ciampa's comment here is apt: "[Paul] never summarizes the gospel the same way twice . . . [His] various articulations of the message reflect his contextualization of the gospel to speak to the issues he faced in his missionary work." Ciampa, "Paul's Theology," 184.

54. Friedrich, "εὐαγγέλιον," 730. For the background to Paul's use of εὐαγγέλιον, see O'Brien, *Gospel and Mission in the Writings of Paul: An Exegetical and Theological Analysis*, 77–81. For a good summary of twentieth-century theological thought on the historical kerygma, see Poe, *The Gospel and its Meaning: A Theology for Evangelism and Church Growth*, 20–52.

55. εὐαγγέλιον θεοῦ is a genitive of origin. Fitzmyer, *Romans*, 232.

56. Witherington III, *Paul's Letter to the Romans: A Socio-Rhetorical Commentary*, 32. Ciampa helpfully demonstrates that Paul's description of the gospel in his epistles either alludes or refers directly to particular Old Testament passages, or to the Old

God's Son, Jesus (Rom 1:3).[57] Jesus was a human being, a descendant of King David, who fulfilled God's promise that there would always be a Davidic king who would reign over his people and his world (Rom 1:4; cf. 2 Sam 7:13). Jesus is the king of the universe because of his resurrection from the dead (cf. Ps 16:10), a resurrection that demonstrates his divinity.[58] Therefore the central theme of the gospel is the declaration of God the Father that his Son, Jesus Christ, is Lord of heaven and earth.[59] Since Jesus is the living Lord of the universe, the appropriate response to the gospel is submission to his lordship, expressed by repentance and faith (Rom 1:5).[60]

ii. 1 Cor 15:1–8. Paul writes to remind the Corinthians of the gospel he had preached to them while he had been with them in Corinth five years earlier, a message which they had received and on which they had taken their stand.[61] The gospel message was the means by which they had been saved and were being saved (1 Cor 15:2).[62] Paul's brief summary of the gospel message of which he was "reminding" them (1 Cor 15:3b–5) had a number of elements. First, Jesus is identified as the Christ, the long-awaited Messiah from God (1 Cor 15:3a).[63] Second, Jesus died, was buried, and rose again to new life (1 Cor 15:3–4). Third, he died for our sins (1 Cor 15:3b): this does not set forth "an explicit theory of the atonement . . . such as penal substitution" but rather refers to the effects of Christ's death for the believer.[64] Fourth,

---

Testament as a whole. Ciampa states, "The term 'gospel' . . . serves as a sort of shorthand for the eschatological message of salvation which is at the core of the prophetic Scriptures." Ciampa, "Paul's Theology," 181.

57. Fitzmyer, *Romans*, 233.

58. Moo, *The Epistle to the Romans*, 48; Fitzmyer, *Romans*, 235. This unbreakable link between Jesus' resurrection and his lordship is similarly expressed in Rom 10:8–9 and provides a succinct summary of the gospel "word of faith" that Paul and his companions were proclaiming. Dodd, *The Apostolic Preaching and its Developments*, 11.

59. For N. T. Wright the "gospel" is simply the announcement that Jesus is Lord. Wright, *What St Paul Really Said*, 55–57, 153.

60. Moo adds that obedience and faith cannot be separated. The Christian faith necessitates obedience to the one in whom that faith is placed. Moo, *Romans*, 53.

61. Barnett, *1 Corinthians: Holiness and Hope of a Rescued People*, 270.

62. The present tense σῴζεσθε indicates the ongoing nature of the salvation and, as a divine passive, it identifies God as the agent who has brought this about. Barnett, *1 Corinthians*, 270.

63. Fee, *The First Epistle to the Corinthians*, 724.

64. Bird, *A Birdseye View of Paul*, 79. Gordon Fee agrees with Bird that no atonement theory is being articulated here but that the concept of atonement underlies

all this happened in accordance with the Scriptures, probably referring not to a particular passage or passages but to the whole of the Old Testament (1 Cor 15:3, 4).[65]

The New Testament writers understood the gospel as having a particular content, something that could be preached (Matt 4:23; 9:35; 24:14; 26:13; Mark 1:15; 8:35; 10:29; 13:10; 14:9; Luke 9:6; 20:1; Acts 5:42; 8:12, 25, 40; 11:20; 13:32; 14:7, 15, 21; 15:7; 16:10; 20:24). The gospel message they proclaimed centered on the kingdom of God (Matt 12:28; 19:24; 21:31; Mark 1:15; 10:25; Luke 4:43; 8:1; Acts 8:12; 14:22; 1 Cor 4:20), Jesus' lordship and kingly rule (Acts 5:42), Jesus as fulfillment of Scripture (Luke 24:27, 45; Acts 2:29–31; 13:32), Jesus' divinity (Acts 2:36; 13:32), his death, his resurrection, (Acts 2:23–24; 3:15), forgiveness of sins, and repentance and faith (Acts 2:21, 38; 3:16, 19–20).

Nevertheless, in the New Testament descriptions of apostolic preaching, we do not discover merely a recitation of facts about Christ's birth, life, atoning death, resurrection and ascension.[66] These facts formed the core of the gospel message, but not their only message. These preachers also declared the *implications* of the gospel for the lives of their hearers,[67] both unbelievers and believers.[68] Paul used the word εὐαγγέλιον "as a label to express in summary fashion the message that he announced to the world of his day."[69] He had been set apart for the gospel in order to preach the gospel (Rom 1:1, 14–15).

Such an understanding of the broader scope of the gospel is reflected in the writings of some of the church fathers. Origen viewed all Christian behavior subsumed under the rubric of the gospel.[70] John Chrysostom

---

the phrase "for our sins." Fee, *Corinthians*, 724. Paul Barnett understands 1 Cor 15:3 to refer directly to Christ's atoning death, saying that Jesus dying for (ὑπὲρ) our sins probably stems from Jesus' words in Luke 23:19: "This is my body, given for (ὑπὲρ) you." Jesus "died for our sins" means that Jesus received the punishment of God that each person deserves. Barnett, 1 *Corinthians*, 273.

65. Bird, *A Birdseye View*, 80; Fee, *Corinthians*, 725; McKnight, *The King Jesus Gospel*, 47–53.

66. Glasser, "The Gospel," 403–4, at 403.

67. For example: unity amongst believers (Eph 4:1–17); how believers are to speak to one another (Eph 4:25, 29); marriage and family life (Eph 5:22—6:4; Col 3:18–22); holy living (1 Thess 4:3–8).

68. Flemming, *Contextualization*, 92. Flemming cites Rom 1:15 where Paul's earnest desire to proclaim the gospel to those who are in Rome is directed not to unbelievers but to Roman Christians.

69. O'Brien, *Gospel and Mission*, 78.

70. Origen, *Against Celsus*, 443.

similarly understood the gospel as a message that impacts every aspect of the life of a believer.[71]

This understanding of the broader scope of the gospel is also reflected in the writings of contemporary theologians. For example, Peter O'Brien argues, both from Romans and Ephesians, that the gospel message is broader than mere facts related to Jesus' life, death and resurrection. It also involves teaching the implications of these facts about Jesus for daily living. The good news about Jesus is "an unfathomable wealth" that calls for careful teaching, instruction and application.[72] Paul's gospel to believers was a "full exposition of the gospel that is designed to edify believers and ground them in the faith."[73]

> Clearly for Paul and his colleagues evangelistic and missionary outreach was not achieved by some superficial presentation about the saving message about Christ to the world; rather, it was effected through warning and intensive teaching in pastoral situations . . . [that is] the ongoing and systematic presentation of Christ as Lord as well.[74]

The comprehensive scope of the gospel, expressed as the lordship of Christ, is echoed by N.T. Wright when he states,

> Preaching the gospel means announcing Jesus as Lord of the world . . . [by which Paul means] that there is no area of existence or life, including no area of human life, that does not come up for critique in the light of the sovereignty of the crucified and risen Jesus.[75]

That the gospel includes not just the events surrounding the cross but also the implications of the cross in the life of the believer forms the basis of Darrell Bock's work, *Recovering the Real Lost Gospel*. Having affirmed Jesus' atoning death for sin as the "hub of the gospel", he adds that it is "*not the entire gospel*" (emphasis his).[76] The good news of the gospel also includes

---

71. For e.g., *Adv. Jud.* 1; PG 48.851, 18–19, 38–40; *Adv. Jud.* 1; PG 48.854, 7–10.

72. O'Brien, *Gospel and Mission*, 62–64. Regarding the gospel summary recorded in 1 Cor 15:3–4, Barnett similarly says, "It is assumed that Paul expanded on these initial summary points in his ongoing pastoral teaching of the congregation." Barnett, *1 Corinthians*, 271.

73. O'Brien, *Gospel and Mission*, 64.

74. Ibid., 64.

75. Wright, *What St Paul Really Said*, 154.

76. Bock, *Recovering the Real Lost Gospel: Reclaiming the Gospel as Good News*, 3.

what results from it, including "access to God's wisdom, righteousness [and] sanctification."[77]

The gospel therefore is defined as the message of God's good news centered on the birth, life, death, resurrection, and ascension of Jesus Christ and the implications of that message for daily life. This definition is critical to my thesis: it is a point of reference when I compare how the term is used in the literature, and it provides contours for the content and scope of the contextualized witness considered in the thesis. Defining the contextualization process, therefore, is our next task.

1.1.4 Contextualization

Just as with the words "mission" and "missiology", there is no agreed definition of "contextualization" amongst evangelicals.[78] Some common definitions include:

1. "Presenting the supracultural message of the gospel in culturally relevant terms."[79]
2. "How the gospel revealed in Scripture authentically comes to life in each new cultural, social, religious and historical setting."[80]
3. "The message (or the resulting church) is defined by Scripture but shaped by culture."[81]
4. "The process whereby Christians adapt the forms, content, and praxis of the Christian faith so as to communicate it to the minds and hearts of people with other cultural backgrounds. The goal is to make the Christian faith *as a whole*—not only the message but also the means of living out our faith in the local setting—understandable."[82]

Implicit in each of the above definitions of contextualization (and many others that have been proposed) are different understandings of the

---

77. Ibid., 3–4. Cf. Packer, "Amsterdam 2000: The Content of the Gospel," 16–17; Ciampa, "Paul's Theology," 186.

78. Hesselgrave and Rommen, *Contextualization*, 35. D. A. Carson adds that the term contextualization is "slippery" and that there is "massive theological disarray in the area." Carson, "Church and Mission: Reflections on Contextualization and the Third Horizon," 213–57, at 219, 221.

79. Hesselgrave and Rommen, *Contextualization*, 1.

80. Flemming, *Contextualization*, 13–14.

81. May, "Ugly Americans or Ambassadors of Christ?", 346–52, at 350.

82. Moreau, *Contextualization in World Missions*, 36. Emphasis his.

relationship between gospel and culture, something that has been a significant part of the contextualization debate.[83] Part of the debate has been whether the starting point for the contextualization process is the gospel or the surrounding culture. The starting point for contextualization that is favored by evangelicals is Scripture, which must then be communicated in ways and thought patterns comprehensible to the receiving culture.[84] This approach takes culture seriously but puts Scripture rather than context as contextualization's starting point. Culture as the starting point has been the favored approach of many conciliar theologians. They consider theology as relative to context and as, in fact, determined by context.[85] The literature often uses the terms "contextual theology" or "local theology" to refer to the development of local theologies, which may or may not be rooted in the gospel.[86] Contextual theology is a way of doing theology that takes not only Scripture and tradition into account (classic theology) but also context.[87] An oft cited definition of contextual theology is that of Stephen Bevans, who says that contextual theology:

> [is] a way of doing theology in which one takes into account four things: (1) the spirit and message of the Gospel; (2) the tradition of the Christian people; (3) the culture of a particular nation or region; and (4) the social change in that culture, due to

83. As will be discussed in chapter 2, conferences such as the 1978 Willowbank conference met exclusively to discuss this issue of the relationship between gospel and culture. See Lausanne Committee for World Evangelism, "1978: The Willowbank Report on Gospel and Culture," 73–113. From an ecumenical perspective, see the consultation held at the Institute for Ecumenical Research in Strasbourg in 1994 whose papers are published in *International Review of Mission* 84, no. 332/333 (Jan/Apr 1995); also, the Conference on World Mission and Evangelism held in Salvador, Brazil in 1996, with papers pre-published in *International Review of Mission* 84, no. 335 (Oct 1995), 85, no. 336 (Jan 1996) and 85, no. 337 (Apr 1996).

84. Nicholls, *Contextualization*, 37–52.

85. Ibid., 24–36. This has led to a proliferation of theologies such as Black theology, Liberation theology, Asian theology, and African theology.

86. See Schreiter, *The New Catholicity: Theology Between the Global and the Local*; Schreiter, *Constructing Local Theologies*; Bevans, *An Introduction to Theology in Global Perspective*; Joseph Spae, "Missiology as Local Theology and Interreligious Encounter," *Missiology* 7 (1979) 479–500.

87. Bevans, *Models of Contextual Theology*, 3–4. For helpful introductions to the background of the contextual theology debate from an evangelical perspective, see Fleming, *Contextualization of Theology: An Evangelical Assessment*; Conn, "Contextualization: Where Do We Begin?", 90–119. For more on contextual theology, see Cortez, "Context and Concept: Contextual Theology and the Nature of Theological Discourse," 85–102; Cortez, "Creation and Context: A Theological Framework for Contextual Theology," 347–62; Matheny, *Contextual Theology: The Drama of Our Times*.

both technological advances on the one hand and struggles for justice and liberation on the other.[88]

Former professor of systematic theology and philosophy of religion at Trinity Evangelical School, Paul Feinberg, contrasts these different starting points or approaches to the contextualization task:

> The inspired and inerrant Scriptures constitute the normative pole from which, as evangelicals, all theologizing is to be done... This is of crucial importance because biblical revelation abides as the only guide to Christ's work in the past and God's activity in contemporary history. The culture or context is the second pole. Because cultures are so diverse and because they are changing, this must be seen as the relative pole. Nevertheless, culture is very important because it is an avenue through which God reveals Himself.[89]

In this thesis I adopt an evangelical approach that takes Scripture as the normative pole for contextualization. While it is possible that contextualizing the gospel and contextual theology could refer to the same basic task, in practice this is generally not the case. In addition, to speak only of contextualizing "theology" seems to limit the task of contextualization, which concerns how we practice and live out the gospel, as well as how we think about it. Therefore, I will regularly use the term 'contextualization of the gospel' for the sake of clarity,[90] so as to differentiate it from the broadly used term 'contextual theology.'[91] Throughout the course of the contextualization debate, many different definitions, models and applications of contextualization have been proposed (see chapter two). The definition of contextualization of the gospel adopted for this research is: the activity of explaining and applying the gospel message, centered on Jesus Christ, in ways and categories that are relevant and understandable to the receiving culture. What is meant by culture will now be considered.

---

88. Bevans, "Models of Contextual Theology," 185–203, at 186.

89. Feinberg, "An Evangelical Approach to Contextualization of Theology," 7.

90. Following Flemming, *Contextualization*.

91. I am indebted to Professor Dean Flemming who helped clarify the difference between "contextualisation of the gospel" and "contextual theology" through personal correspondence.

1.1.5 Culture

"Culture" is one of the most complicated English words in existence, making it a challenging and elusive concept to define.[92] Sir Edmund Burnet Tylor, the "father of modern anthropology,"[93] is thought to have offered the first recognized definition, stating that culture is "that complex whole which includes knowledge, belief, art, law, morals, custom, and any other capabilities and habits acquired by man as a member of society."[94] Hundreds of definitions have been proposed since then.[95] Richard Niebuhr understood culture as an "artificial" construction comprising "language, habits, ideas, beliefs, customs, social organization, inherited artefacts, technical processes and values."[96] Harvey Conn defines culture as "the common ideas, feelings and values that guide community and personal behaviour, that organize and regulate what the group thinks, feels and does about God, the world, and humanity."[97] Paul Hiebert states that culture is "the more or less integrated system of ideas, feelings and values and their associated patterns of behaviour and products shared by a group of people."[98] Clifford Geertz similarly states that culture "denotes a historically transmitted pattern of meanings embodied in symbols, a system of inherited conceptions, expressed in symbolic form by means of which men communicate, perpetuate, and develop their knowledge about and attitudes towards life."[99] Each of these definitions reflects a similar understanding of culture, namely, a collection of distinctive shared patterns of behavior, beliefs and ways of thinking of a particular group of people.[100]

---

92. Williams, quoted in Roger Silverstone, "The Power of the Ordinary: On Cultural Studies and the Sociology of Culture," 991–1001, at 991.

93. Luzbetak, *The Church and Cultures: New Perspectives in Missiological Anthropology*, 134.

94. Tylor, *Primitive Cultures: Researches into the Development of Mythology, Philosophy, Religion, Art and Custom*, 1. For a helpful introduction to the history of anthropological thought concerning culture, see Chris Jenks, *Culture*, 6–24.

95. Anthropologists Alfred Kroeber and Clyde Kluckholm found over 200 definitions in their literature review in 1952, most of them variations of Tylor's definition. Silverstone, "The Power of the Ordinary," 991; Luzbetak, *The Church and Cultures*, 134.

96. Niebuhr, *Christ and Culture*, 32.

97. Conn, "Culture," 252–5, at 252.

98. Hiebert, *Anthropological Insights for Missionaries*, 30.

99. Geertz, *The Interpretation of Cultures*, 89.

100. Robert Redfield emphasizes the shared components of culture when he defines culture as "the shared understandings made manifest in act and artefact." Cited by Carson in *Christ and Culture Revisited*, 2. See also Lingenfelter and Mayers, *Ministering Cross-Culturally*, 17–18.

Cultures are not random collections of isolated ideas or ways of thinking but rather integrated, holistic patterns of ideas structured around the meeting of basic human needs. In 1944, anthropologist Bronislaw Malinowski famously proposed his *Permanent Vital Sequence* in which he identified seven basic needs common to all human beings (metabolism, reproduction, bodily comforts, safety, movement, growth, and health) and defined culture as the human response to those seven needs.[101]

In sum, I propose that there are three main aspects to culture. First, it is always social, bound up with an individual's life in society. Second, it is bound up in human achievement, the work of humanity's thoughts and actions, and therefore includes speech, education, tradition, myth, science, art, philosophy, government, law, rite, beliefs, interventions, technologies. Third, it is concerned with the formation and preservation of values, particularly those which are good for humanity.[102] Nevertheless, cultures are not merely an accumulation of traits but rather an organic whole which is greater than the sum total of its parts.[103] A dynamic in human cultures never allows cultures to be complete, closed entities. The gaps and inconsistencies in cultures provide opportunities for change, modification, decline, and growth. This means that culture is not static but, as it is acquired by a generation, it interacts with the social forces impacting that current generation and their synthesis is then passed to the next generation.[104]

Anthropologist Paul Hiebert identifies culture as having three layers or levels, starting from the surface level and working down to the deeper structural level. First, at the surface *sensory* level is the material culture, patterns of behavior, signs, and rituals. Second, at the middle *explicit* level are the belief systems. Third, the deep *implicit* level is the level of worldviews.[105] Hiebert defines worldview as "the most encompassing view of reality we share with other people in a common culture. It is what we think with, not what we think about. It is the mental picture of reality we use to make sense of the world around us."[106]

---

101. Bronislaw Malowinski, quoted in Grunlan and Mayers, *Cultural Anthropology*, 40–50.

102. Niebuhr, *Christ and Culture*, 32–39.

103. Nida, *Customs and Cultures: Anthropology for Christian Missions*, 30.

104. This echoes the view of Lamin Sanneh, who defines culture as, "all learned behaviour, which is socially acquired and passed from one generation to the next." Sanneh, *Translating the Message: The Missionary Impact on Culture*, 239–40.

105. Hiebert, *The Gospel in Human Contexts: Anthropological Explorations for Contemporary Missions*, 153–9.

106. Hiebert, *The Gospel*, 158. For further discussion on worldviews see, Sire, *The Universe Next Door: A Basic Worldview Catalog.*; Goheen and Bartholomew, *Living*

Both Niebuhr and Conn believe the closest New Testament approximation to the concept of culture is the word κόσμος—but only when it refers to organized, language-bound human life (e.g., 1 Cor 14:10)—or the system of values, traditions and social structures that have been affected by sin.[107] Flemming disagrees with Niebuhr and Conn, equating Paul's use of κόσμος with the modern notion of culture because cultures are "the arena of God's gracious activity" and are capable of being transformed. He further asserts that the evil forces that make up the κόσμος constantly resist the saving purposes of God and so are doomed to destruction under God's judgment.[108] Not only can cultures be changed, but changed positively, by the gospel.

The issue of culture has been an inextricable part of the debate about contextualization, as the proclamation of the gospel message cannot be separated from the culture in which that message is proclaimed.[109] Although I take the view that the gospel takes precedence over culture, it does not view culture negatively nor consider it unimportant. Rather, in defining culture as the shared ideas, feelings, values, and patterns of behavior of a group of people which allow them to live their lives, I take a positive view of culture and a positive view of the changes that the gospel can bring to culture. Peripheral changes can end up being merely cultural conversion rather than conversion to Christ, while the goal of mission must be one that seeks to bring cultures into conformity with the kingdom of God. As Harvey Conn concludes, "The whole of cultural life ought to be subjected to the royal authority of him who has redeemed us by his blood (Matt 28:18–20)."[110]

1.1.6 Syncretism

One final term that is essential to the subject of contextualization is "syncretism". Non-Christian religions pose a challenge in many missiological areas, including that of syncretism.[111] Syncretism has been defined differently by

---

at the Crossroads: An Introduction to Christian Worldview; Eckman, *The Truth About Worldviews: A Biblical Understanding of Worldview Alternatives*; Naugle, *Worldview: The History of a Concept*.

107. Conn, "Culture," 253; Niebuhr, *Christ and Culture*, 32, 45–49.

108. Flemming, *Contextualization*, 139.

109. Lausanne Committee for World Evangelism, "1978: The Willowbank Report on Gospel and Culture," 77.

110. Conn, "Culture," 254.

111. Moreau et al., *Introducing World Missions*, 18, 289. Jackson Wu distinguishes between *cultural syncretism* (where the cultural context is emphasized over the biblical text) and theological syncretism (where the gospel is confused with a missionary's

the disciplines of anthropology, psychology, philosophy, and theology.[112] Theological syncretism has been variously defined as:

1. "The mixing of elements of two religious systems to the point where at least one, if not both, of the systems lose basic structure and identity."[113]

2. "The replacement of core or important truths of the gospel with non-Christian elements."[114]

3. "The blending of Christian beliefs and practices with those of the dominant culture so that Christianity loses its distinctiveness and speaks with a voice reflective of its culture."[115]

4. "A message that has lost the heart of the gospel."[116]

5. Where "the biblical message is made to harmonize so closely with a given culture (or subculture) that the biblical truth is compromised."[117]

Inherent in the above definitions is the idea that syncretism can be said to have occurred when critical and basic elements of the gospel are lost or are blended or replaced by religious elements from another religious or cultural group.[118] While evangelicals have been generally unified in their call for syncretism to be avoided in the contextualization process, achieving an agreed definition of syncretism, and, in particular, finding agreement regarding at what point contextualization ceases and syncretism begins has proved more challenging. While each of the above definitions views syncretism negatively, as has been the traditional stance, there are many modern scholars who view it more positively, including broadening the meaning to a neutral meaning of conflation of multiple paradigms.[119] The Scriptures,

theological traditions); Wu, *One Gospel for All Nations: A Practical Approach to Biblical Contextualization*, 11.

112. Vroom, "Is not all Contextual Understanding of the Gospel Contextual?," 274–87, at 277.

113. Schreiter, *Constructing Local Theologies*, 98–99.

114. Moreau et al., *Introducing World Missions*, 18.

115. Van Rheenen, "Syncretism and Contextualization: The Church on a Journey Defining Itself," 1–29, at 7–8.

116. Hiebert, "Syncretism and Social Paradigms," in *Contextualization and Syncretism: Navigating Cultural Currents*, 44.

117. Wu, *One Gospel*, 10.

118. For example, see Bradshaw, "The Gospel, Contextualization and Syncretism Report,"; Moreau, "Syncretism," 924–5; Vanhoozer, "One Rule to Rule them All? Theological Method in an Era of World Christianity," 85–126, at 102.

119. Schreiter, *Constructing Local Theologies*, 144; Moreau, "Syncretism," 924–5, at 924; Robbins, "Crypto-Religion and the Study of Cultural Mixtures: Anthropology,

however, reveal God's strong opposition to his people engaging in the practice of syncretism. The Old Testament records God choosing the nation of Israel and setting it apart to be his chosen nation, solely serving him (Exod 19:1–6), in contrast to the idolatrous practices of the nations that surrounded Israel, with which Israel was to have nothing to do (Exod 20:1–7; 23:23–33; Deut 4:1–4; 18:10–14).[120] Israel refused to obey God's word and practiced idolatry, intermarriage, and cult prostitution alongside their worship of Yahweh (2 Kgs 17:41; Zeph 1:5).[121] In the face of polytheism and the "syncretistic forms and practices" of the first-century Hellenistic world,[122] the New Testament proclaims the uniqueness of Jesus Christ as the only way to the Father (John 3:36; 14:6): worship of him is not to be combined with worship of any other deity or their associated religious practices (e.g., Eph 1:20–21; Col 2:6, 13–19).[123]

Syncretism cannot be divorced from contextualization. Rather, they can be viewed as a continuum, with contextualization on one end of the spectrum and syncretism the other. Where the line is drawn between where contextualization ends and syncretism begins, who determines that line, and based on what criteria, continues to be debated.[124] A case in point is Messianic Judaism, which is a variegated rather than singular movement that has evolved over time, particularly since the 1970s.[125] While initially fashioned as a movement of Jewish converts to Christianity seeking to proselytize Jews and convert them to Christianity (e.g., "Jews for Jesus"), it has now splintered to include Messianic Jewish groups who are ethnically Jewish, vibrant followers of Yeshua and "dedicated to practicing Judaism within a Christian theological framework."[126] It also includes Gentiles who participate in various Jewish holidays, festivals, dietary restrictions, dress

---

Value and the Nature of Syncretism," 408–24; Goosen, "Syncretism and the Development of Doctrine," 137–50, at 140.

120. Moreau et al., *Introducing World Missions*, 289; Van Rheenen, "Syncretism and Contextualization," 3, 11; Poston, "'You Must not Worship in their Way': When Contextualization Becomes Syncretism," 243–63, at 243.

121. Moreau et al., *Introducing World Missions*, 18, 289–90; Van Rheenen, "Syncretism and Contextualization," 11–12.

122. Schnabel, *Paul the Missionary*, 362.

123. Moreau et al., *Introducing World Missions*, 290.

124. Van Rheenen, "Syncretism and Contextualization," 3, 9–11; Vroom, "Contextual Understanding," 276–7; Greenspahn, "Syncretism and Idolatry in the Bible," 480–94, at 488.

125. Power, "Blurring the Boundaries: American Messianic Jews and Gentiles," 69–91, at 69–71, 83–85.

126. Ibid., 71.

code, and commitment to the Torah.[127] Messianic Judaism is essentially a blending of two religions, Christianity and Judaism, to form a new and distinct religious movement, occupying a "liminal space between two institutionalised religions."[128] The end result of this movement is a syncretistic or "hybrid-blend" where neither of the two religions are distinct, and it has been rejected as apostate and heretical by both the American Jewish community and many evangelical Gentile churches.[129] A second example is that of Insider Movements (IM).[130] IM proponents view the movement as groups of Muslim background believers who choose to remain within the Muslim community as followers of Jesus the Messiah (rather than of Mohammed). IM detractors (within both the Christian and Muslim communities), however, generally view IM as a syncretistic combination of Christianity and Islam and not an authentic expression of either religion.[131] The core element of syncretism is the incorporation of non-Christian elements into the Christian faith resulting in the formation of a new entity which is no longer Christian, and this is the definition I adopted in this thesis.

While contextualization carries the inherent risk of syncretism, Dean Flemming posits that a failure to contextualize may pose "an even *greater* risk of syncretism" occurring.[132] Where the Christian message that has been imported into a culture fails to address particular issues pertinent to the worldview of that culture (e.g., health, evil spirits, ancestor worship), converts can easily reach back and adopt various practices from their former (or another) religious heritage in order to fill the void.[133]

The priority that evangelicalism gives to Scripture rather than to culture leads Paul Hiebert to conclude that Scripture is the primary check

---

127. Ibid., 81.

128. Ibid., 81.

129. Ibid., 70.

130. For discussion of Insider Movements, see 2.4.1.

131. Lewis, "Insider Movements: Honouring God-Given Identity and Community," 33–36; Higgins, "Beyond Christianity: Insider Movements and the Place of the Bible and the Body of Christ in New Movements to Jesus," 12–13; Corwin, "Insider Movements and Outsider Theology," 10–11; Tennant, "Followers of Jesus (Isa) in Islamic Mosques: A Closer Examination of C5 "High Spectrum" Contextualization," 101–15.

132. Flemming, "Paul the Contextualizer," in *Local Theology for the Global Church: Principles for an Evangelical Approach to Contextualization*, 18 (emphasis his); Ott and Strauss, *Encountering Theology*, 266–7; Whiteman, "Contextualization: The Theory, the Gap, the Challenge," 2–7, at 5.

133. Flemming, "Paul the Contextualizer," 18–19; Schreiter, *Constructing Local Theologies*, 98–99.

against syncretism, followed by the work of the Holy Spirit in the "hermeneutical community" of the church.[134] Importantly for this thesis, Hiebert explains that by church he means not only the twenty-first-century church, but the collective church since the time of the first-century apostles. Scripture, and the wisdom of Christians down through the centuries (including the church fathers) provide significant checks and balances in the evaluation of a contextual approach for signs of syncretism.[135]

Having defined evangelical, mission, gospel, contextualization, culture, and syncretism, I will draw on these definitions to outline the research methodology adopted by the thesis.

1.2 Research Methodology

In this thesis I develop an evangelical approach to the contextualization of the gospel that is biblically sound, internally coherent, and consistent with the nature of the discipline of missiology itself. I will do this through focusing on the respective disciplines of biblical studies and Christian thought. This is a different approach to the issue of contextualization of the gospel than is normally taken. As will be demonstrated in chapter two below, much of the theoretical reflection on contextualization of the gospel, as it has been conducted by missiologists, has drawn predominantly upon models from the social sciences (particularly linguistics, anthropology, cross-cultural communication and contextual theology) and practical theology.[136] As insightful as these some of these approaches have been, there have been at least two very significant weaknesses. First, reflection on the primary source documents of Scripture in general and the New Testament in particular, has been lacking.[137] Second, there has also been scant consideration given to how the church fathers contextualized the gospel in the light of Scripture. In fact, I have been unable to find any sustained treatment of contextualization

---

134. Hiebert, "Syncretism and Social Paradigms," 44. Dean Flemming acknowledges the difficulty at times in determining the point at which contextualization becomes syncretism, but emphasizes the role of the Holy Spirit in helping the Christian church determine when syncretism is occurring. Flemming, "Paul the Contextualizer," 18.

135. Hiebert, "Syncretism and Social Paradigms," 44.

136. Flemming, *Contextualization*, 14.

137. Flemming, *Contextualization*, comments that, in terms of looking at biblical precedents for contextualization, while there are a number of articles and book chapters on the topic, none of them go beyond a preliminary level of discussion. He lists these main books and articles on p. 15n2. In p. 25n1, he lists books that look particularly at contextualization in Acts.

of the gospel from an evangelical perspective that has engaged the works of the church fathers to any great extent, so my work in this area will be original.[138]

Any missiological research needs to be informed and shaped by the nature of the discipline itself. What I have found surprising is how little has been written specifically on the subject of missiological methodology. While there are many books written on the general subject of research methods, the only book specifically on missiological method I have identified is Edgar J. Elliston, *Introduction to Missiological Research Design*.[139] As Elliston states, "as an academic discipline missiology does not have a unique or distinctive methodology."[140] In general terms, missiological research is divided into two broad categories: academic missiology and applied missiology. A subject such as contextualization of the gospel can naturally be examined as applied missiology due to its immediate and practical nature.[141] In terms of more specific missiological methodologies, the discipline is lacking.

For any evaluation of an issue to be considered both valid and reliable, the methodology chosen needs to be consistent with the nature and contours of the discipline itself. In the case of a missiological issue, such as

---

138. One notable monograph on contextualization that engages significantly with a wide range of church fathers, written from an Eastern Orthodox perspective, is Rommen, *Come and See*, 2013. By this stage Rommen had moved from the evangelical position he held when he co-authored *Contextualization: Meaning, Methods, and Models*,1989, to one of Eastern Orthodoxy. In *Come and See*, xiii, Rommen argues that his 1989 book "made little use of the idea of the church's tradition, and . . . did not ask about the ways in which it might limit or facilitate the process of contextualization"—something he sets out to address in his 2013 publication. In *Come and See*, 194–6, he lists seven basic principles of Eastern Orthodox contextualization that can be drawn from his study: a. The gospel is a person; b. The evangelistic task is to introduce the person of Jesus Christ; c. The church is the focal point of that activity; d. The sacraments are the privileged place of Christ's presence in the world today; e. The core invitational context needs to be established; f. The invitational context has to be projected onto fields of human presence; g. The witness needs to be "spiritualized." Interestingly, while Rommen quotes the church fathers extensively throughout the book, at no point does he say that he views the church fathers as having engaged in the task of contextualization, or examine the writings of the church fathers looking to evaluate if they contextualized the gospel in their contexts. My thesis will, however, will take such an approach, even further distinguishing it from Rommen's engagement with patristic sources.

139. Elliston, *Introduction to Missiological Research Design*. Paul Hiebert has two chapters which discuss missiological method in Hiebert, *The Gospel in Human Contexts*, 36–57, 160–73. See also Wan, "Rethinking Missiological Research Methodology."

140. Elliston, *Introduction*, 1.

141. Ibid., 5–6, where he lists contextualization as a category of research under "applied missiology."

contextualization of the gospel, a valid and reliable evaluation requires a methodology shaped by the history, nature and contours of the discipline of missiology. It is to this task that I now turn.

Missiology is a relatively new discipline in theological education, having only formally come into existence in the latter part of the nineteenth century. Since then it has become a legitimate and important discipline in its own right. Missiology is the formal, academic study of missions and of missionary activity, including "biblical, theological, historical, contemporary, and practical reflection and research."[142] Its approach as a discipline is critical and interdisciplinary.[143] It aims to be systematic and critical and starts from a positive affirmation of the legitimacy of the Christian missionary task as a central part of the church's existence.[144] Missiology has three main concerns: the nature of mission; the goal of mission; and, the method of mission.[145] Activities subsumed under the discipline include research, teaching and publication about mission. Yet, as Johannes Verkuyl pertinently notes, missiology as a discipline does not exist for its own insular purposes but for the purposes of participation and action.[146]

Missiology is an interdisciplinary approach to the practice of mission, combining the insights from the disciplines of biblical studies, Christian thought, practical theology and the social sciences.[147] Paul Hiebert states

142. Wright, *The Mission of God*, 25. James Scherer states that there is no agreed definition of missiology—most likely because there is no agreed definition of mission. His conclusion is that this has left the whole discipline "in a state of flux and ferment," still searching for an agreed definition of both mission and missiology. Scherer, "Missiology as a Discipline and What It Includes," 173–87, at 175.

143. Verkuyl, *Contemporary Missiology*, 5; Scherer, "Missiology as a Discipline," 175.

144. Escobar, *The New Global Mission: The Gospel from Everywhere to Everyone*, 21.

145. Moreau et al., *Introducing World Missions*, 19.

146. Verkuhl, *Contemporary Missiology*, 8.

147. Different authors propose similar but not identical lists of which disciplines constitute missiology, each author having nuanced understandings of what they mean by the different discipline headings. For example, Scherer lists missiology comprising biblical studies, church history, systematic theology, social sciences, and world religions: Scherer, "Missiology as a Discipline," 179–83. Verkuyl lists biblical studies (which include exegesis and hermeneutics), systematic theology, ethics, church history, ecumenics, and science of religion. Verkuyl, *Contemporary Missiology*, 9–10. Escobar lists biblical studies, history, the social sciences, and systematic theology. Escobar, "Mission Studies: Past, Present, and Future," 3–29, at 7. Hiebert lists Scripture, theology, church history, and anthropology. Hiebert, *The Gospel in Human Contexts*, 33, 35. In these lists the various disciplines mentioned would all be seen to inform missiological "praxis." There is enough consensus in these lists to conclude that missiology

that the central question missiology seeks to answer is: "how can the gospel of Jesus Christ be incarnated in human contexts so that people understand and believe, societies are transformed, and the kingdom of God is made manifest on earth as it is in heaven?"[148] The way missiology seeks to answer this central question is to integrate data drawn from these different disciplines, with Scripture the central point through which the data from these other disciplines is evaluated.[149]

While missiology as a theological discipline only formally came into being in the late nineteenth century, its roots extend much further back in history. While missionary activity and thinking have been part of Christianity since its inception, Majorcan Raymond Lull (ca. 1235–1315) is considered the first missiologist in Christian history. As well as publishing over 300 works, he established a missionary training school in Majorca in 1276 for the purpose of linguistic and theological preparation of missionaries to Jews and Muslims.[150] Other Catholic missiologists include Jose de Acosta (1540–1600), author of *On Procuring the Salvation of the Indians* (1588), and Thomas a Jesus (1564–1627), author of *On Procuring the Salvation of All Men* (1613).[151] Catholic missiological reflection, after such a promising start, slowed significantly during the eighteenth century.[152]

Protestant missiological reflection began to develop through the work of Hadrianus Savaria (1531–1613) and Justus Heurnius (1587–1652) during this same period.[153] But the most influential missiologists were Gisbert Voetius (1589–1676), professor at Utrecht, who produced the first systemization of Protestant missiology, and one of his students, Johannes Hoornbeeck, who argued the case for the church to be sending out missionaries.[154] During the seventeenth and eighteen centuries some of the

---

is constituted by biblical studies, Christian thought (which includes church history and systematic theology), social sciences, and practical theology, all of which inform missiological praxis. Cf. Priest and DeGeorge, "Doctoral Dissertations on Mission: Ten Year Update, 2002–2011," 195.

148. Hiebert, *The Gospel*, 33.

149. Ibid., 33–35. In Hiebert, *The Gospel*, 38–57, he elaborates on this methodology and gives two examples of how missiological praxis is informed by such an approach.

150. Moreau et al., *Introducing World Missions*, 99–101.

151. Neely, "Missiology," 633–6, at 633; Bavinck, *An Introduction to the Science of Missions*, xiii.

152. Anderson, "The Great Century and Beyond," 199–218, at 193.

153. Moreau, "Missiology," 780–4, at 780.

154. Myklebust, *The Study of Missions in Theological Education*, vol. 1, 40–41; Moreau, "Missiology," 780. Gisbert Voetius worked very hard at elucidating his principles of mission directly from the Bible and shaped his missiological thinking

important precursors of contemporary missiologists included: August Herman Franke (1633–1727), who established a missions curriculum at the University of Halle in the early 1700s;[155] Reformed theologian, Jonathan Edwards (1703–58); Baptist missionary, William Carey (1761–1834), whose *Inquiry into the Obligations of Christians to Use Means for the Conversion of the Heathen* (1792) refuted the common view of the time that the Great Commission was only for the apostles, and who initiated the establishment of missions societies; and renowned theologian, Friedrich Schleiermacher (1768–1834), "[who] proposed integrating mission study into the discipline of practical theology."[156] These men all contributed to a change in attitude towards missions to the point that missions began being considered more seriously as an academic discipline.[157] Despite these positive changes, little progress was made during this time in establishing missionary training programs in European or American universities.

The situation changed during the nineteenth century. Princeton University elected Charles Breckenridge (1797–1841) as Professor of Practical Theology and Missionary Instruction (1836), the first such position in the world. Scottish missionary to India, Alexander Duff, developed a systematic theory of missions and in 1867 was appointed to a new position as chair of Evangelistic Theology at St Andrew's, Scotland.[158] Following Alexander Duff's appointment in 1867, there was an increasing interest in some of the European universities for lectures and conferences on the subject of mission.[159] Further university professorships were also established.[160] However, it was Gustav Warneck (1834–1910), regarded as the "father of missiology,"

---

accordingly. Bavinck, *An Introduction*, xiii–xiv.

155. Myklebust, *The Study of Missions*, vol. 1, 50–51.

156. Moreau, "Missiology," 780; Bavinck, *An Introduction*, xiii–xiv.

157. Neely, "Missiology," 633.

158. For an excellent treatment of Duff's tenure as chair of Evangelistic Theology see, Myklebust, *The Study of Missions*, vol. 1, 158–242. See also Walls, "Alexander Duff," 187–8.

159. In the 1870s mission lectures were delivered at the University of Berne (by F. Nippold), the University of Strasbourg (K. W. A. Schmidt), Norway (Tønder Nissen) and Denmark (C. Kalkar). In 1877 the Dutch universities of Utrecht, Leiden and Groningen recognized missions as a stand-alone subject. Early in the 1880s mission lectures were given in every Swiss university (e.g., by R. Stähelin and W. Bornemann) as well as in Oxford, Cambridge and Dublin universities. Myklebust, *The Study of Missions*, vol. 1, 304–49.

160. University of Utrecht (E. H. Lasonder, 1878), Cumberland University (H. Bell, 1884), Southern Baptist Theological Seminary (W. O. Carver, 1899), Chicago University Divinity School (A. K. Parker, 1901). Myklebust, *The Study of Missions*, vol. 1, 304–34, 376–84.

who established missiology as a legitimate and accepted academic discipline.[161] Installed at the University of Halle, Germany, as the Professor of the Science of Missions, in 1897, he was first to elaborate a systematic missiology, most famously in *Evangelische Missionslehre*.[162]

In *Evangelische Missionslehre* Warneck establishes that Christianity by nature is a missionary religion and, driven by the Great Commission, has been engaged in mission since the time of the apostles, except for a few "periodical interruptions."[163] But it had not developed into a systematic discipline. This had, he wrote, not been to missiology's detriment though because,

> Mission collected a wealth of practical experience during this time and this experience becomes for a developing academic discipline of mission what experiments and observations are in science. The more clarified these experiences, the more ready mission is for an academic approach.[164]

Mission is not just ready for such an academic approach, Warneck argued:

> [M]issionary work as such needs a systematic formation and standardisation, the complicated practical mission work needs an academic justification and representation: which means a theory. Just as the practical work that constitutes the local church ministry has found its theoretical approach in the academic discipline of practical theology, so the practical activities that constitute mission work need to find a theoretical approach as an academic discipline of mission theology. This theory of missionary activities is best called missiology, which means doctrine of mission: its justification as well as its task, its goal and its work at home and abroad.[165]

Warneck articulated his understanding of the major divisions of missiology:

> The scientific doctrine of mission therefore divides into two major areas: history of mission and theory of mission—of missiology. The latter, because of its wealth of content and its work

---

161. Myklebust, *The Study of Missions*, vol. 1, 280.

162. Henkel, "German Centres of Christian Research," 103–10, at 103.

163. Warneck, *Evangelische Missionslehre: Ein Missionstheoretischer Versuch*, 9, 21.

164. Ibid., 9. The translations from *Evangelische Missionslehre* are my own, with the help of Witali Klein and Verena Adrian [in the Acknowledgements].

165. Ibid., 17.

for a systematic design with an academic justification, qualifies just as much as history of mission does.¹⁶⁶

Warneck subsequently provided a more comprehensive definition of missiology:

> Missiology is what we interpret as the scientific understanding about mission work as a whole, and therefore all that involves the constitution as well as the practical implementation of mission so its goal can be reached.¹⁶⁷

Thus, it is important to note that from its origin as a theological discipline, missiology has been interdisciplinary. Historically, the Bible has been the foundation of missiology, whose gospel message is centered on God's Son, Jesus, who was sent by God for the "salvation of all humanity."¹⁶⁸ It is this same gospel message that "has to be proclaimed to the entire world" as Jesus commanded in the Great Commission, through "human vessels."¹⁶⁹ The sent Son sends these redeemed human vessels with the message of the Son embodied in Scripture.¹⁷⁰ This message has been proclaimed over the past 2,000 years and so the writings of the church over that time, particularly as they have reflected on Scripture, along with the accounts of the practice of mission entailed in mission history, make Christian thought an essential part of missiology. But since "the academic discipline of mission has to operate from an extensive knowledge of mission experience,"¹⁷¹ practical theology is the third essential element in developing missiological praxis.¹⁷²

Missiology continued to develop not just in the academy but outside of it as well through the development of a number of Student Missionary Associations,¹⁷³ and eventually the formation of the global World Student Christian Federation (WSCF).¹⁷⁴ The WSCF, through leading figures J. H.

---

166. Ibid., 17. On p. 21 he adds that by the "theory of missions" he means "mission principles and mission methods."

167. Ibid., 18.

168. Ibid., 21.

169. Ibid., 21.

170. Ibid., 21.

171. Ibid., 9.

172. Bavinck similarly summarizes Warneck's tripartite structure of missiology. Bavinck, *An Introduction*, xix–xxi.

173. For example, Uppsala (1884), Lund (1886), the universities of Oxford, Cambridge, Durham and Dublin, and the Free Church colleges in Edinburgh, Glasgow, and Aberdeen. Myklebust, *The Study of Missions*, vol. 1, 339–41.

174. In 1895 the World Student Christian Federation was formed, with John R.

Oldman and John R. Mott, played a significant role in the development of the International Missionary Conference in Edinburgh, 1910.[175] The conference met to investigate eight missionary problems, each overseen by a Commission.[176] There were many significant outcomes for mission from this unique conference, two of which had direct impact on the developing discipline of missiology.[177] First, there was an increased ecumenical spirit post-Edinburgh, which encouraged the subsequent creation of "worldwide Christian fellowships, confessional and ecumenical."[178] The Universal Christian Council for Life and Work (world meetings in Stockholm, 1925; Oxford, 1937), and the World Conference on Faith and Order (world meetings in Lausanne, 1927; Edinburgh, 1937) joined in the 1930s to become the World Council of Churches (officially constituted in 1948).[179] Second, missiology became an increasing part of the curricula of North American and European seminaries and universities, evidenced by the establishment of many mission professorships and scholarships.[180]

The issue of missiological education in places outside of North America and Europe (such as Africa, Asia and Latin America) rose to the fore at the 1938 World Missionary Conference in Tambaram, India.[181] While the impetus was interrupted by World War II, it was not lost, and the 1958 Ghana Conference began to deliver what Tambaram had asked, through the establishment of the Theological Education Fund (TEF). The initial aim of the TEF was to raise the standards of approximately twenty centers of theological training to that of the best of North American and European, including significant investment in the production of new literature and upgrade of libraries.[182] The work of the TEF (particularly from 1958–1977) has played a significant and strategic role in the development of missiology as an important discipline and the strengthening of theological education in the Third World.[183]

Mott as General Secretary. Myklebust, *The Study of Missions*, vol. 1, 340–4.

175. Myklebust, *The Study of Missions*, vol. 2, 23; Stanley, *The World Missionary Conference, Edinburgh 1910*, 23–26.

176. Stanley, *The World Missionary Conference*, 32–33.

177. See ibid., 303–24.

178. Myklebust, *The Study of Missions*, vol. 2, 14.

179. Ibid., 164–7.

180. Ibid., 71–160; Stanley, *The World Missionary Conference*, 317.

181. Newbigin, "Theological Education in World Perspective," 18–25, at 18.

182. Ibid., 18.

183. The First Mandate of PTE 1978, "Theological Education—An Ongoing Concern of the Churches now an Integral part of the WCC," 25.

Roman Catholic missiological studies have followed much the same trend as those of Protestants since the time of Johann Baptist von Hirscher (1788–1865), a Catholic theologian who urged that missiology be accepted as a legitimate theological discipline in its own right.[184] Some outstanding Catholic missiologists since Hirscher include Robert Streit (1875–1930), the "father and founder of Catholic missiology" Joseph Schmidlin (1876–1944), Wilhelm Schmidt (1868–1954), Pierre Charles (1883–1954), John J. Considine (1898–1982) and Stephen Bevans (1944–).[185]

One of the more significant developments in the discipline of missiology since the 1950s has been that it has increasingly drawn on the methods and insights of the social sciences, to the point where the social sciences are considered a key component in any missiological discussion.[186] Debate has centered on whether Scripture is still the legitimate starting point and driver in determining missiological praxis or whether the social sciences (particularly anthropology and linguistics) or practical theology more broadly have assumed that mantle.[187] Having just surveyed the history of missiology, it is my conclusion that, while the social sciences and practical theology are important components in missiology, they are not the central components. As Moreau et al. states, "The foundations of missiology are grounded in biblical and theological studies."[188] Valuable insights can be gained from the social sciences and from practical theology, but these must all be "filtered through the grid of Scripture."[189] Michael Raiter argues that in recent decades missiology has pushed what has traditionally been at the center of missiology (biblical studies and Christian thought) to the margins of missiological thought. Concurrently, those disciplines entailed in the social sciences, which should rightly be consulted but are "unworthy of any authoritative

---

184. Neely, "Missiology," 634.

185. Ibid., 634; Moreau, "Missiology," 781. Bosch argues that Josef Schmidlin is regarded as the founder of Catholic missiology. Bosch, *Transforming Mission*, 5. Prominent Protestant missiologists in the twentieth century include Stephen Neill, Lesslie Newbigin, David Bosch, Donald McGavran, David Hesselgrave, Samuel Escobar, Ralph D. Winter, Paul Hiebert, and Charles Kraft.

186. Pocock, "Introduction: An Appeal for Balance," 7–18, at 10–11; Moreau, Corwi, and McGee, *Introducing World Missions*, 71.

187. For a useful summary of this debate, see Rommen and Corwin, *Missiology and the Social Sciences*. The contributing authors argue that the social sciences are a legitimate part of missiology but are subservient to Scripture. The Gospel and Culture conference in Willowbank, 1987, brought together missionaries, theologians and anthropologists in an attempt to bridge the gap between these groups. Discussion papers from that conference appear as Lausanne Occasional Paper 2 (LOP 2).

188. Moreau et al., *Introducing World Missions*, 71.

189. Raiter, "Sent for This Purpose," 140.

status," have been moved to the center of missiological thought and become the "pillars and agenda-setters for the study and practice of mission."[190]

In summary, missiology is the formal, critical and interdisciplinary study of mission. Missiology draws primarily from four fields: biblical studies, Christian thought, the social sciences and practical theology. However, it does not draw from these fields equally. Since the inception of missiology, Scripture has been the foundation of the discipline. Scripture is authoritative, and the considerations drawn from any other source are relative to and constrained by Scripture. In the study of any missiological topic, the starting point for the missiologist is the careful exegesis of Scripture.[191] Missiology is also firmly grounded in Christian thought. Missiologists must understand the historical framework and background to contemporary issues as well as gleaning the lessons and reflections that have been hammered out and "refined in the fires of previous missionary practice."[192] Missiology is also inherently practical as its aim is the making of disciples of all nations. Therefore, further insights are brought in from the area of the social sciences and practical theology. The cumulative reflections from the four disciplines are synthesized and used to inform and shape missiological praxis.[193]

A multidisciplinary approach is one that is already well recognized and accepted in missiological research.[194] In fact, because of the complexities of missiological subjects, multidisciplinary perspectives are often required.[195] Based on the multidisciplinary nature of missiology, it is necessary to take such a multidisciplinary approach, bringing together the four key components of missiology: biblical studies, Christian thought, the social sciences, and practical theology, in order to develop an evangelical approach to contextualization of the gospel which can contribute to the global debate.[196] Here I will achieve this through a twofold process. First, important

190. Ibid., 140–1.

191. Ibid., 140; Bavinck, *An Introduction*, xv.

192. Ott and Strauss, *Encountering Theology*, xxiii.

193. Bavinck, *An Introduction*, xviii–xix; Hesselgrave and Rommen, *Contextualisation*, 1–26; Hiebert, *The Gospel in Human Contexts*, 32–53; Bevans, *Models of Contextual Theology*, 25; Verkuyl, *Contemporary Missiology*, 6–11; van Engen, *Mission on the Way*, 22–25; Wright, *The Mission of God*, 25; Ott and Strauss, *Encountering Theology*, xxi–xxiii.

194. Elliston, *Introduction*, 62.

195. Ibid., xxii, xxvii, 1.

196. Hiebert states that to leave out any one of these four components of missiology would be "to omit an essential dimension of the gospel." Hiebert, *The Gospel in Human Contexts*, 51 (see p. 161). The methodological approach of this thesis is similar to the methodological approach Paul Hiebert advocates for any missiological issue. He

principles of contextualization from cultural anthropologists and practical theologians will be highlighted in the literature review throughout chapter two. The second step will then be to focus on the two areas where the contextualization debate has been deficient, namely Scripture and the writings of the church fathers, with the principles discovered compared with those in chapter three. The end result will be contextual principles that reflect a balanced whole, representative of missiology's multidisciplinary nature.

1.3 Thesis Structure

Each chapter is designed to build on the previous one and contribute to the next as I seek to present a new approach to evangelical contextualization of the gospel.

The second chapter will review the literature on contextualization of the gospel: its origins in the Conciliar movement of the World Council of Churches in 1972 and its relationship to the missionary approaches of the previous 150 years; evangelical reactions to the introduction of contextualization; clarification and redefinition of the term, both from evangelical and conciliar perspectives; models of contextualization; the interaction between gospel and culture; and the current state of the debate, including the issues of contextual theology, the Insider movement, and evangelical parameters for contextualization. This review will highlight the dominance of contributions from the social sciences and practical theology and the relative paucity of contributions from the disciplines of biblical studies and Christian thought. Having highlighted these lacunae, I address them in the subsequent three chapters.

The third chapter will examine contextualization of the gospel from the perspective of biblical studies, focusing particularly on the New Testament book of Acts. I will begin by examining four literary, hermeneutical, and contextual issues that confront the reader of Acts: contextualization in the New Testament; authorship, audience, and purpose of Luke–Acts; rhetoric in the New Testament; and the nature of the speeches in Acts. The majority of the chapter, however, will focus on the book of Acts. Due to limitations of space, Acts has been chosen as a representative example from

---

states that the first step is *phenomenological* whereby the specifics of the issue at hand are studied using the tools of the social sciences, especially anthropology. The second step is *ontological*, whereby the results of the phenomenological study are checked in the light of Scripture and Christian thought. Thirdly, the phenomenological and ontological steps are brought together to produce a *missiological* course of action—that is, to shape the praxis. Hiebert, *The Gospel in Human Contexts*, 47–53.

Scripture because, as well as being a contextualized document in its own right, it also records many examples of the early church engaged in contextualizing the gospel. Four speeches in the book of Acts where the gospel is contextualized both to Jews (Acts 2:1–40; 7:1–60; 13:13–47) and Gentiles (Acts 17:16–31) will be examined, compared and contrasted, with conclusions drawn regarding principles of contextualization. These principles will confirm, critique or add to some of the contextualization principles uncovered in the literature review of chapter two, and will form a strong basis for establishing evangelical contours for contextualization.

As this chapter examines Acts from a biblical studies perspective an evangelical exegetical approach to interpretation based on the historical-critical method will be adopted that takes the intention of the biblical writer or author of Acts as the starting point for interpretation, along with the historical context from which the text of the book of Acts emerged.[197] Therefore, in terms of the book of Acts, this approach takes the view that the history that the author of Acts presents is actual history.[198] Furthermore, the chapter, and thesis as a whole, adopts a biblical theology hermeneutic that emphasizes both the unity and diversity of Scripture, with each text of Scripture interpreted in the light of the divine revelation as a whole.[199]

The fourth and fifth chapters will consider contributions from the discipline of Christian thought, focusing on the works of one of the church fathers, John Chrysostom.

The fourth chapter will examine the case for appropriating the works of the church fathers in general (and John Chrysostom in particular) for the contextualization debate. Beginning with various issues that make bridging the gap between the church fathers and the twenty-first century challenging, criteria will be established by which the suitability of a church father to inform the contextualization debate can be measured. The works of John Chrysostom will then be measured against these criteria in order to evaluate his potential contribution to the contextualization debate. The chapter will conclude by considering a number of other historical, hermeneutical, and contextual issues in his homilies that will be important in the interpretation of Chrysostom homilies in chapter five.

---

197. Thistelton, *Hermeneutics: An Introduction*, 20.

198. Fee and Stuart, *How to Read the Bible for all its Worth*, 109–10, 118–25. For further on my hermeneutical approach, including justification for considering Acts as apologetic history, the use of rhetoric in Acts by both its author and its recorded speakers, and the historicity of the speeches in Acts, see 3.2–3.4.

199. Goldsworthy, *Christ-Centred Biblical Theology: Hermeneutical Foundations and Principles*, 40.

The fifth chapter will examine a selection of homilies of John Chrysostom, and consider how he sought to contextualize the gospel in light of his reflection on Scripture. Chrysostom's theology and praxis of contextualization of the gospel will be the focus of the study. Chrysostom has been chosen as a representative example of a church father for several reasons. First, he is universally regarded as a significant figure in church history and as one of the Greek church fathers.[200] Second, he is significant for the area of mission. Third, he has written a significant amount of material that is still available for examination.[201] Fourth, he fulfills the criteria established in chapter four for a church father who could potentially contribute to the contextualization debate. As part of this chapter there will be a consideration of the background and context of a selection of Chrysostom's homilies as a point of reference for his contextualization of the gospel.

The sixth chapter draws together the findings on contextualization of the gospel developed throughout the thesis and synthesizes them in order to suggest an alternative approach to evangelical contextualization of the gospel. In doing so, I affirm the importance and relevant contribution of both biblical studies and Christian thought to the contextualization debate. Furthermore, I will make suggestions regarding missiology and missiological research methods, and suggest further avenues for research on contextualization.

1.4 Significance

The significance of the research is the demonstration that an exploration of both Scripture and the church fathers, neither of which is definitive or all-embracing, points to the challenge posed to current missiological theory and praxis. Furthermore, such an approach argues the benefits of taking greater consideration of both these components in the future. The main purpose of the research, therefore, is to test the hypothesis that adding the contribution of Scripture and the church fathers to that of the social sciences and practical theology is both meaningful and consistent with an evangelical approach to missiology, and offers new ways of thinking about

---

200. As evidenced by the fact that there are collections of his writings in the *Nicene and Post-Nicene Fathers*, 1st series (vols. 9–14), he has a reputation for oratory comparable only to that of the great Augustine, and is the most admired of the Eastern writers. Quasten, *Patrology*, 429–30.

201. Chrysostom has left the greatest literacy legacy of any of the Greek Fathers. See ibid., 429.

contextualization, with implications for future evangelical missiological praxis.

I do not claim in my research on contextualization to test this hypothesis comprehensively. The research is limited in its scope. It does not examine all of Scripture, but focuses on just one book—Acts. It does not examine all the material that is considered part of Christian thought, but some of the works of one representative church father—John Chrysostom. The research's scope is further restricted in that it seeks to develop an evangelical approach to contextualization of the gospel, not a general model. Nevertheless, within these parameters, the study seeks to prove the hypothesis and make a claim within evangelical contextual missiology for both Scripture and the church fathers. Therefore, I am not seeking to provide a definitive evangelical approach to contextualization of the gospel, but rather an approach that is consistent with the tenets of evangelicalism and consistent with the discipline of missiology itself. Other models have been and could be developed that would also constitute an evangelical approach to contextualization of the gospel.

In developing an evangelical model of contextualization of the gospel with a focus on Scripture and the church fathers, I will do five things. First, the research will provide input into the debate regarding the essence of missiology and missiological research methods. Second, it will provide a deeper appreciation of the place of Scripture in contextualization of the gospel and its necessary contribution to the contextualization of the gospel debate. Third, it will highlight the importance and value of the writings of one church father, John Chrysostom, and the place of Christian thought more generally in contextualization of the gospel, thus providing a more comprehensive framework and stronger theological base for contextualizing the gospel in the twenty-first century. Fourth, it will provide an answer to the question: how might Scripture and the church fathers contribute to an evangelical model of contextualization of the gospel? Fifth, it will contribute to the discussion regarding the nature, content and communication of the gospel.

The next chapter will summarize the debates of approximately the last forty-five years up to the present, highlighting contextual principles that have been developed over that period. Having highlighted some of the lacunae in the debate, I will then discuss these gaps in chapters three, four, and five.

Chapter 2

The Contextualization Debate

THE TERM CONTEXTUALIZATION HAS been the subject of vigorous missiological debate both in ecumenical and evangelical circles since it was first introduced as a neologism in 1972. This chapter has two aims. First, it will answer the question: how have evangelicals gone about the task of developing an evangelical approach to contextualization? Second, it will demonstrate that, in fact, the disciplines of anthropology and practical theology have dominated the contextualization debate, while the disciplines of biblical studies and Christian thought have made relatively minor contributions.

In order to address these aims, this chapter will review the history of the contextualization debate since 1972.[1] There has been a vast amount written about contextualization since that time, so the focus of this chapter will be in reviewing the literature that will assist in addressing the two aims raised above.

The contextualization debate can be organized into three chronological stages subsequent to its introduction as a new missiological term. The first stage (1972–1979) was dominated by the evangelical reaction to contextualization in light of its origin within the ecumenical World Council of Churches (WCC). The second stage (1980–1992) was a period of consolidation of the concept, since it had been widely accepted by evangelicals. It was during this stage that evangelicals developed distinct methods, models and approaches to the actual task of contextualization. The third stage

---

1. For summaries of the contextualization debate, see Moreau, *Contextualization in World Missions*, 32–36; Kraft, "The Development of Contextualization Theory in Euroamerican Missiology," 15–34; Ahonen, *Transformation Through Compassionate Mission: David J. Bosch's Theology of Contextualization*, 28–39; Hesselgrave and Rommen, *Contextualization*, 28–35.

(1993-2015) has seen a splintering of the debate into a variety of foci in which the most significant areas of development have been in approaches to Muslim evangelism and the continued development of evangelical principles and parameters of contextualization.

The current state of the contextualization debate is not solely the culmination of four decades of missiological discussion but of almost two centuries of missiological reflection and practice. It is necessary to be aware that the introduction of the neologism was a reaction to some of the missionary practices of the previous 150 years, particularly those characterized by the approach known as indigenization.

Indigenization is a term that has been used predominantly in Protestant mission and is most clearly exemplified in the "three-self" principle which Henry Venn and Rufus Anderson developed in the mid-1800s regarding the establishment of indigenous churches.[2] Their goal was for every indigenous church to become self-governing, self-supporting and self-propagating.[3] The indigenization approach to missions continued for most of the following 150 years, and provided the tinder which was subsequently ignited by the WCC's introduction of the term contextualization.[4]

2.1 Contextualization as a neologism

In 1972, Dr Shoki Coe, who had formerly been the principal of Tainan Theological College in Taiwan, was the director of the Theological Education Fund (TEF), an agency established by the WCC during the International

---

2. Henry Venn was secretary of the London Church Missionary Society from 1841 to 1873. Rufus Anderson was a Congregational minister and foreign secretary of the American Board of Commissioners for Foreign Missions from 1832 to 1866. Shenk, "Rufus Anderson and Henry Venn: A Special Relationship?", 168-9.

3. Beyerhaus and Lefever, *The Responsible Church and Foreign Missions*, 27-30, 33; Nicholls, *Contextualization*, 20.

4. Roman Catholic scholarship has traditionally preferred the terms "adaptation" and "accommodation" to indigenization. Luzbetak, *The Church and Cultures*, 67-69; Moreau, "Contextualization: From an Adapted Message to an Adapted Life," 321-48, at 326. Adaptation refers to adapting the message and practices of the church to fit in with the culture in which the missionary is working. Schineller, *A Handbook on Inculturation*, 16. Accommodation refers to the incorporation of practices, rituals, and behaviors into the Christian community from the host culture that are not Christian but are consistent with the gospel. Luzbetak, *The Church and Cultures*, 67-68; Moreau, "Contextualization: From an Adapted Message," 326. As missiological approaches, both adaption and accommodation have been rejected by many Catholic scholars. Schreiter, *Constructing Local Theologies*, 9-16; Gallagher, "Inculturation: Some Theological Perspectives," 171-80, at 172-3.

Missionary Council Assembly in Ghana in 1957–1958.[5] The fund's particular concern was the advancement of "theological education in Africa, Asia and Latin America."[6]

During its first mandate period (1960–1964) the fund's emphasis was on raising the level of academic scholarship and increasing the level of excellence in theological training in the Majority World (although "excellence" was still largely defined by western educational standards).[7] The fund's emphasis during its second mandate (1965–1970) was upon raising this excellence in theological education by the use of resources developed by Majority World educators. This included the redefinition of excellence as that which leads to "a real encounter between the students and the gospel in terms of his own forms of thought and culture."[8] The fund's emphasis during its third mandate period (1970–1977) was renewal and reform of theological education in the Majority World by taking their respective contexts into account, including experiments with theological curriculum, teaching methodology, and seminary structure.[9] By doing so it gave churches and theological institutions "the capacity to respond meaningfully to the Gospel within the framework of [their] own situation."[10]

In 1972 the fund published a report titled *Ministry in Context: The Third Mandate Programme of the Theological Education Fund (1970–1977)*. The third mandate was driven by a central concept—"contextuality."[11] Dr Coe explained what the term contextualization implied:

> It means all that is implied in the familiar term "indigenization" and yet seeks to press beyond. Contextualization has to do with how we assess the peculiarity of Third World contexts. Indigenization tends to be used in the sense of responding to the

---

5. Werner, "Letter from Staff," 3–4, at 3.

6. Ranson, "The Theological Education Fund," 432–38, at 432; see also the excerpt of the Minutes of the Assembly of the IMC, Ghana, 28 December 1957 to 8 January 1958, published by the Ecumenical Theological Education, "The Establishment of the Theological Education Fund (TEF) During the IMC Assembly in Ghana, 1957/1958," 12–14, at 12–13; TEF Staff, *Ministry in Context*, 12, 29; Coe, "Contextualizing Theology," 19–24, at 19–20.

7. TEF Staff, *Ministry in Context*, 12. Despite the TEF document using the term "Third World," as do some other authors, throughout this research I will use the term "Majority World."

8. Ibid., 12–13, 29.

9. Ibid., 14.

10. Ibid., 19. Cf. Ecumenical Theological Education, "Contextualization in Theological Education," 15–17, at 15.

11. TEF Staff, *Ministry in Context*, 19.

Gospel, in terms of traditional culture. Contextualization, while not ignoring this, takes into account the process of secularity, technology, and the struggle for human justice, which characterize the historical moment of nations in the Third World.[12]

Whereas indigenization was a process primarily driven by the dominant (usually Western) culture, contextualization was a process primarily driven by each local culture itself. Whereas indigenization more often referred to taking the gospel to static, colonialized communities, contextualization usually referred to theologising in communities facing rapid change and social upheaval. Furthermore, whereas indigenization sought to produce churches that were self-governing, self-supporting, and self-propagating, contextualization aimed to produce churches that were also self-theologising.[13] Therefore, at the core of contextualization (when first coined by the TEF) was the belief that in communicating the gospel the local context must be taken into account in the development of theology and ministry practice.

2.2 Stage 1: Evangelical reaction to and interaction with contextualization (1972–1979)

The relationship between gospel and culture had previously been explored in H. Richard Niebuhr's seminal work, *Christ and Culture*. Niebuhr, a North American, identified five main ways that Christianity understood its relationship with culture. His five models were opposition ("Christ against culture"), agreement ("Christ of culture"), fulfillment ("Christ above culture"), polarity and tension ("Christ and culture in paradox"), and conversion ("Christ the transformer of culture").[14]

---

12. TEF Staff, *Ministry in Context*, 20.

13. Hiebert, "Critical Contextualization," 104–11, at 106. For further on the distinction between indigenization and contextualization, see Haleblian, "The Problem of Contextualization," 95–111, at 98.

14. Niebuhr, *Christ and Culture*, 40–43. Cf. Ahonen, *Transformation*, 31. Two recent critiques question the current validity of Niebuhr's typologies: i) D. A. Carson argues from a biblical theology perspective. Rather than continuing to use Niebuhr's models as "alternative models" from which to choose, Carson argues that a more integrative approach should be taken whereby each of the five models are emphasized at different times, depending on the particular context. Carson, *Christ and Culture Revisited*, 31–65; ii) Carter, *Rethinking Christ and Culture: A Post-Christendom Perspective*, argues that Niebuhr's work "belongs to the passé era of Christendom," whereas today's western society is post-Christian (p. 53). In rendering Niebuhr's typology "inadequate" he proposes his own post-Christendom models: "Christ legitimizing culture," "Christ

The relationship between gospel and culture, which is at the heart of the contextualization debate, continued being discussed by missiologists throughout the rest of the 1970s. The evangelical community was slow to adopt contextualization as a term because of its ecumenical origin.[15] Evangelicals were particularly concerned that contextualization appeared to mark a move away from the authority of Scripture, towards one where context was the governing framework for determining theology.[16] During the 1970s the evangelical community discussed, debated and sought to clarify its own understanding of contextualization through various consultations and publications.

The first significant evangelical response to contextualization came through the International Congress on World Evangelization (ICWE), held in Lausanne, Switzerland from July 16-25, 1974.[17] During the congress, participants discussed and sought to clarify an evangelical understanding

---

separating from culture," "Christ humanizing culture," and "Christ transforming culture" (pp. 111-96). Carter's models share many similarities with those of Niebuhr's and are not as distinct as he tries to make out, despite his post-Christendom hermeneutic. Seeking to label historical figures and more recent figures as representative of one of his typologies (e.g., Tertullian's approach as "Christ against culture") is too simplistic. Carson's more integrative approach better approximates how people operate in their lives. For further discussion on Niebuhr's, see Yoder, "How H. Richard Niebuhr Reasoned: A Critique of Christ and Culture," 31-90; Friesen, "A Discriminating Engagement of Culture: An Anabaptist Perspective," 145-56.

15. Buswell III, "Contextualization: Theory, Tradition and Method," 87-111; Buswell III, "Reply," 126. For a helpful discussion regarding the growing ecumenical/evangelical divide on the nature of Scripture, theology, and mission that had been occurring over the preceding decades of the twentieth century see, Fleming, *Contextualization of Theology*, 1-32.

16. In Buswell's reply to three respondents to his paper, "Contextualization," he acknowledged the reservations evangelicals had about contextualization, simply because it was proposed in a conciliar context. He subsequently offered a challenge to evangelicals to be more willing to evaluate theories and methods that may result in more effective communication of the gospel, no matter from which theological perspective they arise. Buswell, "Reply," 126.

17. Kinsler, "The Current Debate about Contextualization," 23-29, at 23. The ICWE papers and proceedings are in *Let the Earth Hear His Voice: Official Reference Volume—Papers and Responses.*

of the terms: gospel,[18] culture,[19] contextualization,[20] and syncretism.[21] Even at this early stage the ICWE was distancing itself from the ecumenical definition of contextualization outlined by the TEF document. Whereas for the TEF contextualization was a process primarily driven by each local culture, for the ICWE contextualization was a process primarily driven by Scripture, with Scripture critiquing and interpreting culture. Whereas for the TEF contextualization was primarily concerned with developing local theologies, for the ICWE contextualization was primarily about the transmission of the gospel message in the context of evangelism.[22] The ICWE was focused on differentiating the gospel "core" from the gospel's "clothing" (i.e. on differentiating form and meaning), with contextualization being the attempt to change the form but ensure that the original meaning is preserved and communicated.[23]

Various other papers were presented at the congress in an initial attempt to illustrate what contextualization of the gospel might look like in practical terms in Africa, Asia, Latin America, Europe, and the Anglo-Saxon world.[24] There were at least two pertinent principles that arose from these papers. First, "People can become Christians in their own culture, with a minimum of social dislocation. Cultural adaptation is acceptable, but

---

18. The ICWE defined the gospel as the good news of Jesus (Acts 8:35) which includes the gospel events, the gospel witnesses, the gospel promises, and the gospel demands. Stott, "The Biblical Basis of Evangelism," 65–78, at 70–71. Cf. Stott, "The Lausanne Covenant," 3–9, at 3–4. This definition of the gospel is consistent with the one adopted in this thesis but is still just one definition among many that Christians have adopted.

19. The ICWE described culture as both positive and flawed, needing redemption through the gospel, with the gospel itself not belonging to any one culture. Evangelism should enrich and transform rather than destroy culture. "The Lausanne Covenant," 6–7; Kato, "The Gospel, Cultural Context and Religious Syncretism," 1216–23, at 1216.

20. The ICWE defined contextualization as making the unchanging Word of God understandable and relevant through changing the mode of expression to suit the context without falling into syncretism. Contextualization can occur in many areas of life including "liturgy, dress, language, church service, and any other form of gospel truth." Kato, "The Gospel," 1217.

21. While the ICWE was unable to agree on a definition for syncretism it surmised that "[s]yncretism might be said to occur when critical and *basic elements* of the Gospel are lost in the process of contextualization and are replaced by religious elements from the receiving culture." Bradshaw, "The Gospel," 1227. Emphasis his.

22. Kato, "The Gospel," 1224.

23. Ibid., 1224, 1226.

24. See *Let the Earth Hear His Voice*, 1229–93.

should not lead to syncretism of any kind."[25] Second, "Cultural pressures must not permit a change of emphasis in the purity and demands of the New Testament Gospel and discipleship."[26] These papers, along with the introductory paper on contextualization and syncretism, were populated with biblical references and reflections on those passages, and overall provided some initial biblical basis for their conclusions. There was, nevertheless, no systematic biblical treatment of contextualization at this evangelical conference, despite the fact the term had already been in use for two years.

The next significant evangelical assessment of contextualization occurred when Trinity Evangelical School held the Consultation of Theology and Mission, March 22-25, 1976. Part of the 1976 consultation focused on the theme "The Contextualisation of Theology," with contrasting papers delivered by Norman R. Ericson and James O. Buswell III.

Ericson favored the use of contextualization as a term, arguing that the New Testament is itself a contextualized document and contains examples and patterns of contextualization which act as signposts for the contours of acceptable contextualization.[27] Following brief comments on four New Testament passages, which he cited as examples of contextualization,[28] he drew three contextual principles from them. First, the gospel is centered on the life, death, and resurrection of Jesus and forms the core body of truth by which societies and their respective cultures and ideas are to be evaluated. Second, meaning usually takes precedence over form, although Christians need to take care that the culturally appropriate meaning is communicated by the form. Third, the gospel, as it is communicated verbally and behaviorally, must be communicated in a way that makes sense to its hearers.[29] Furthermore, Ericson posits general criteria for "acceptable" contextualization and contextual limits. His criteria are:

(1) The core: revelation and salvation effected in Jesus Christ; (2) The substance: the gospel tradition in apostolic transmission;

---

25. Chan, "How to Evaluate Cultural Practices by Biblical Standards in Maintaining Cultural Identity in Asia Report," 1249-50, at 1249.

26. Moreas, "How to Evaluate Cultural Practices by Biblical Standards in Maintaining Cultural Identity in Latin America Report," 1263-6, at 1264.

27. Ericson, "Implications from the New Testament for Contextualization," 71-85, at 71.

28. Acts 15:1-29; 1 Cor 8:1—10:22; 1 Cor 5:1-8; Col 3:18-21. Ericson, "Implications," 74-79.

29. Ericson, "Implications," 79-80.

(3) The application: exhortations addressed to particular people;
(4) The expression: quality of life in a cultural setting.[30]

Buswell's rebuttal to Ericson's paper (against also Shoki Coe,[31] Byang Kato,[32] and Bruce Nicholls[33]) was that the introduction of the term contextualization was unnecessary. He argued that the existing terms inculturation, indigenization, translation, and ethnotheology sufficiently described all that was entailed in the neologism contextualization.[34] Buswell's response contained no biblical justification to substantiate his argument.

The interrelationship between gospel and culture had already been a subject of interest at the Lausanne 1974 World Congress. That congress was the catalyst for the Lausanne Committee's Theology and Education Group convening a consultation devoted to the topic "Gospel and Culture," from January 6–13, 1978 in Willowbank, Bermuda.[35] The result was the production of a report—*Lausanne Occasional Paper 2: The Willowbank Report: Consultation on Gospel and Culture*.[36] Significantly, theologians and evangelical anthropologists were brought together to discuss contextualization with the view to their coming to some measure of consensus. Previous to the consultation, theologians and anthropologists were seen as being in opposition to one another over the issue.

The 1978 Willowbank consultation positively affirmed the relationship between gospel and culture and the need for contextualization, as had

30. Ibid., 83.
31. TEF Staff, *Ministry in Context*, 20.
32. Kato, "The Gospel," 1217.
33. Nicholls, "Theological Education," 637.
34. Buswell, "Contextualization," 88–99.

35. This Consultation also firmly built on the work of another Lausanne-sponsored conference, *The Colloquium on the Homogenous Unit Principle*, held 31 May to 2 June 1977 in Pasadena, California, resulting in the "Pasadena Statement on the Homogenous Unit Principle." See LCWE, "1977: Pasadena Statement on the Homogenous Unit Principle," 59–71. Four significant statements regarding the relationship between gospel and culture are reflected in the Pasadena Statement: First, it recognizes and celebrates cultural diversity (p. 63). Second, it highlights the need for the gospel to preserve, not destroy, this cultural diversity (p. 63). Third, it affirms the validity and importance of churches being "rooted in the soil" of their local culture (p. 63). Fourth, it acknowledges the effect that the fall (Gen 3) has had on culture (p. 65).

36. LCWE, "The Willowbank Report," 73–112. The stated goals of the Consultation included: developing a biblical understanding of the relationship between gospel and culture; critically reflecting on the implications of this relationship for gospel proclamation; identifying how the gospel could be more adequately communicated; and sharing the results of the Consultation with the wider Christian body. LCWE, "The Willowbank Report," 77.

previously been agreed upon at the 1974 congress.[37] It also concluded that no Christian could hope to interpret Scripture or effectively proclaim the gospel, centered on Jesus Christ, unless they took the cultural context seriously.[38] The 1978 consultation also suggested further contextual principles. First, it placed limits on the practice of contextualization, reiterating that, in the translation and proclamation of Scripture across cultures, the essential meaning of the text must be retained, with consideration given to changing some of the original forms to express the meaning.[39] Second, the consultation also rightly affirmed that the primary drivers of the contextualization process needed to be indigenous churches themselves.[40] The consultation affirmed that "[t]he church must be allowed to indigenize itself, and to 'celebrate, sing and dance' the gospel in its own cultural medium."[41] Third, the danger of syncretism was highlighted, both in Majority World churches as well as in Western churches, and was to be avoided in the contextualization process. Few guidelines, however, (biblical or otherwise) were given as to how to avoid syncretism.[42] While the report contained no reflections on the works of patristic or medieval theologians, it did acknowledge the importance of Christian theology and of listening to the voices of the saints throughout the history of the church in a general sense when it stated that "[n]o group of believers can disregard this heritage without risking spiritual impoverishment."[43]

The Willowbank Report is deficient nonetheless in at least one significant area. While the report does contain some biblical reflection on the nature of culture, the nature of the gospel, and the communication of the gospel, it lacks an accompanying detailed biblical justification for its conclusions.

Concurrent with the Lausanne Committee's "Consultation on Gospel and Culture," *Evangelical Missions Quarterly* devoted its entire January

---

37. LCWE, "The Willowbank Report," 78–82.

38. Ibid., 84, 86. Don Richardson's *Peace Child* is a positive example of the culture being taken seriously. In this book he describes how he used the Sawi tribe's practice of the offering of a peace child to explain and illustrate the incarnation of Jesus and the atonement brought about through Jesus' sacrifice.

39. LCWE, "The Willowbank Report," 82.

40. Ibid., 98–99.

41. Ibid., 102.

42. Ibid., 102, 104–5. The Consultation raised questions about how to detect and avoid heresy and syncretism, to which only a short case study of the church in Bali, Indonesia, was given as a response. LCWE, "The Willowbank Report," 104–5.

43. Ibid., 84.

1978 edition to the subject of contextualization.[44] Five leading missiologists (James O. Buswell III, F. Ross Kinsler, Charles H. Kraft, Harvey M. Conn, and Eduardo M. Ramirez) contributed articles, giving a snapshot of the then state of the debate. Other than Buswell,[45] each author regarded contextualization positively and syncretism negatively.[46] Significantly, Kraft, an anthropologist, affirmed contextualization as patterned on the proclamation of the gospel by the apostles evidenced in the New Testament, with Scripture being the starting point and governing principle for contextualization.[47] Nevertheless, he provided minimal evidence from the New Testament to justify his claim.

Building on the International Congress on World Evangelism (Lausanne, 1974) and the Consultation on Gospel and Culture (Willowbank, 1978), the North American Conference on Muslim Evangelization was held 15–21 October 1978, at Glen Eyrie, Colorado Springs. Prior to the conference, forty foundational papers were produced by practitioners and theologians concerned with Muslim evangelization.[48] The reported spirit of the conference was one of sadness and repentance for the failure of the Christian church over its history to adequately evangelize Muslims,[49] and of an openness to explore new approaches to Muslim evangelism.[50]

The Glen Eyrie conference exhibited a number of developments in the contextualization debate. First, contextualization had an established validity as a term and legitimacy as an issue for discussion by the evangelical community.[51] Second, contextualization was now clearly distinguished from in-

44. *EMQ* 14, no. 1 (Jan 1978) 1–64.

45. His article, Buswell III, "Contextualization: Is it Only a New Word for Indigenization?" 13–20, is mostly a summary of his paper delivered at the Trinity Consultation on Theology and Mission, 1976. That being recognized, possibly as an acknowledgment that contextualization was now fairly well established in missiological vocabulary, his article concluded with the hope that contextualization might serve as a "generic concept under which to better organise missiological theory and method." Buswell, "Contextualization," 19.

46. Kinsler, "The Current Debate," 25; Kraft, "The Contextualisation of Theology," 31–36; Conn, "Contextualisation: a new dimension for cross-cultural Hermeneutic," 39–46. Visser't Hooft, *No Other Name: The Choice Between Syncretism and Christian Universalism* is still an excellent treatment of the subject of syncretism.

47. Kraft, "The Contextualization of Theology," 31–36, at 32–33.

48. Lausanne Committee for World Evangelism (LCWE), "1978: The Glen Eyrie Report on Muslim Evangelization," 115–38, at 118–20.

49. Ibid., 122–3.

50. LCWE, "The Glen Eyrie Report," 124–5; McCurry, "A Time for New Beginnings," 13–21, at 17–18.

51. McCurry, "A Time for New Beginnings," 18.

digenization and regarded as a necessary advancement on indigenization.[52] Third, the subject of contextualization had moved on from a generic discussion to one that was now starting to be applied to a specific missiological area—Muslim evangelism. Fourth, the application to a specific missiological issue helped to clarify some of the questions requiring answers concerning the gospel, culture, and contextualization.[53] The fifth development was that these were tentative steps towards changing the praxis of evangelism in the light of contextualization.[54]

In the year following the congress, two of its participants, Bruce Nicholls and Charles Kraft, contributed important publications on contextualization. Kraft, building on the work of Eugene Nida[55] and Daniel von Allman,[56] took the concept of "dynamic equivalence" and applied it to the contextualization of the gospel.[57] Nida had argued that in Bible translation

52. Tabor, "Contextualization: Indigenization and/or Transformation," 107–18, at 107–10.

53. McCurry, "A Time for New Beginnings," 17; Hiebert, "The Gospel and Culture," 22–34. Some of these questions included: How much of their culture can a Muslim Background Believer (MBB) retain? What parts of Muslim culture can be redeemed? Are there cultural customs that are religiously neutral that a MBB can retain? Do MBB's have to join a Western-style church or can they form their own culturally-sensitive church? Would such practices lead to syncretism and theological error?

54. Massih, "The Incarnational Witness to the Muslim Heart," 49–60; Kraft, "Dynamic Equivalence Churches in Muslim Society," 78–92, at 84–87; Tabor, "Contextualization," 113–4, 117–8; Nicholls, "New Theological Approaches in Muslim Evangelism," 119–27.

55. It was Nida who coined the terms 'dynamic equivalence' and 'formal equivalence.' Nida, in his book *Message and Mission,* had highlighted that, in order for a message to be accurately communicated across cultures linguistically, the form of the message must be different if the content was to be equivalent. He stated that what was required was not a "formal equivalence" (such as a literal "word-for-word" translation) but a "dynamic equivalence" (where a different word or phrase is used to convey the same idea). Nida, *Message and Mission: The Communication of the Christian Faith,* 42–61. Nida's earlier volume, *Customs and Cultures: Anthropology for Christian Mission,* articulates his understanding of culture, which *Message and Mission* builds upon.

56. von Allman, "The Birth of Theology," 37–55, at 38. In this highly influential article, von Allman states that there is no single, dogmatic theology but that all theologies, from the Apostle Paul onwards, are contextual theologies.

57. Kraft, *Christianity in Culture: A Study in Dynamic Biblical Theologizing in Cross-Cultural Perspective,* 275–312 (esp. p. 294–300). For his choice of the phrase "dynamic biblical theologizing" rather than contextualization, see Kraft, "The Development," 21. For his earlier work on dynamic equivalence, see Kraft, "Dynamic Equivalence Churches: An Ethnotheological Approach to Indigeneity," 39–57; Kraft, "Dynamic Equivalence Churches in Muslim Society," 78–92. For his development of thought on dynamic equivalence, see Kraft, "Meaning Equivalence Contextualization,"

dynamic equivalence was necessary for effective written communication.[58] Kraft went further in stating that dynamic equivalence was also required for effective communication of that "written witness."[59] Transculturation (which was Kraft's term for contextualization) went beyond translation in that it "attempt[ed] to take both speaker and hearer behind that record into a re-creation of equivalent events in today's cultural context."[60] Kraft argued that if the process of transculturation (contextualization) was done well, it would result in those involved in the cross-cultural communication "equivalently communicating the original message" in the new cultural situation, and eliciting a dynamically equivalent response to that which would have been produced in the original hearers.[61]

Kraft's dynamic equivalence approach to contextualizing Scripture has been highly influential. There are significant dangers, nevertheless, in an uncritical adoption of his approach and underlying epistemology (which includes his view that divine revelation is dynamic rather than static).[62] David Hesselgrave highlights the risks when he argues that Kraft's insistence that the meanings rather than the actual words of the Bible themselves are inspired departs from apostolic Christianity and that "eating . . . [Kraft's] contextualization cheese . . . [risks] getting caught in an epistemic trap."[63]

155–68 (where 'meaning equivalence' is synonymous with 'dynamic equivalence'); Kraft, "Dynamics of Contextualization," 169–82. Kraft's approach in *Christianity in Culture* met with disapproval amongst some in the evangelical community (e.g., Goss, *Is Charles Kraft an Evangelical? A Critique of "Christianity in Culture"*). Donald McGavran was also critical of Kraft's dynamic equivalence approach in McGavran, *The Clash Between Christianity and Culture*.

58. Despite not using the term dynamic equivalence, Jesuit priest to China, Matteo Ricci (1552–1610) approached Bible translation in a similar way. As part of his missionary approach of accommodation, Ricci sought to find Chinese equivalents for Christian words (e.g., the word for God) and rituals (e.g., the rites that related to family and Confucius) so as to reduce the foreignness of Christianity amongst the Chinese as much as possible. Neil, *A History of Christian Mission*, 140.

59. Kraft, *Christianity in Culture*, 280. On p. 275 Kraft states, "[D]ynamic equivalent translations of the Bible cannot do the whole job of communicating the Christian message . . . there must also be frequent explanations of cultural backgrounds, applications to present situations . . . that are not properly a part of translation. These we term 'transculturations.'"

60. Kraft, *Christianity in Culture*, 281.

61. Kraft, *Christianity in Culture*, 280–83.

62. Ibid., 178–192.

63. Hesselgrave, "Contextualization and Revelational Epistemology," 691–738, at 722.

Bruce Nicholls continued his significant contribution to the debate through his 1979 book, *Contextualization: A Theology of Gospel and Culture*. Nicholls begins with anthropological reflections on culture before introducing the concept of supracultural elements of the gospel that are generally not acknowledged by secular anthropologists and sociologists.[64] These supracultural elements are either part of the kingdom of God (God and his heavenly beings) or the kingdom of Satan (Satan and his demonic forces) (e.g., John 12:31; 14:30; 16:11; Rom 8:28–39; 1 Cor 15:24, 26; Eph 1:21; 2:2; 3:10; Col 1:16; 2:10).[65] Nicholl's point is that the supracultural impacts the cultural. While the kingdom of Satan negatively influences culture and impedes the cross-cultural communication of the gospel, the gospel both judges and redeems culture as it is communicated cross-culturally (Rom 8:19–22).[66] Nicholls further explains that these supracultural elements form part of a biblical worldview of culture. God created humankind in his image (Gen 1:26; Rom 5:1), giving them, for example, the gift of creativity to build cities, keep livestock, and engage in creative endeavors that all contribute to the development of culture (Gen 4:17–22).[67] The fall impacted every aspect of culture including "worldview, values, institutions, artifacts and outwards behaviour" (Gen 11:1–9; Rom 1:18–32; 5:12).[68] The gospel liberates culture from the demonic effects that has plagued it since the fall (Gen 3:15), a liberation ultimately realized in the new heavens and new earth (Rev 21:2, 5).[69] As this gospel is communicated cross-culturally through fallen human messengers, God sovereignly draws women and men to himself, creating a redeemed cultural humanity.[70]

Having established biblical foundations for the relationship between gospel and culture, Nicholls traces the history of the contextualization debate, highlighting that the contextualization debate itself is part of a much wider theological debate regarding how the church functions in the world.[71]

---

64. Nicholls, *Contextualization*, 8–15. Nicholls, 13, defines supracultural as "the phenomena of cultural belief and behaviour that have their source outside of human culture."

65. Ibid., 13–15.

66. Ibid., 15.

67. Ibid., 16–17.

68. Ibid., 17–18.

69. Ibid., 18.

70. Ibid., 19.

71. Ibid., 20–23. Hesselgrave and Rommen comment that, since the Uppsala gathering in 1968, the theology in World Council of Churches circles "had become more and more secularized," with universalism the underlying assumption and "conversion downplayed." Hesselgrave and Rommen, *Contextualization*, 52.

Nicholls evaluates different contextual models, the issue of syncretism,[72] the authority of Scripture, and the implications of contextualization of the gospel,[73] applying his findings to the dynamics of cross-cultural communication.[74] Three of Nicholls' contextual principles are worth noting here. First, contextualization can only occur within the context of mission. Second, while upholding the primacy of special revelation, Nicholls advocates the possibility of carefully selected aspects of general revelation being used as a bridge to communicate the gospel effectively. Third, against Kraft's dynamic equivalence of Scripture, Nicholls advocates formal correspondence.[75]

Nicholls' book provided a more substantial biblical basis and more developed framework for understanding the nature of and relationship between gospel, culture, contextualization, and syncretism than most of the publications that had appeared on contextualization up to that point. That being said, the biblical justification for his assertions regarding contextualization is decidedly brief in comparison with the amount of anthropological and practical insights on culture and cross-cultural communication that he presents.

In summary then, while contextualization had been treated with suspicion by evangelicals at the start of the decade due to its ecumenical origins, by the decade's conclusion they had widely embraced it, albeit their understanding and uses of the term differed considerably from ecumenical ones.[76] While some general biblical justification for contextualization had been provided in various gatherings and publications, little detailed or systematic biblical reflection on contextualization had been produced. Throughout the 1970s, the importance of the Bible to contextualization had been more affirmed than demonstrated. The works of the church fathers had not really been offered as a contribution to the debate, despite some acknowledgment that such wisdom should be accessed. The majority of the literature on contextualization had been written from an anthropological or missiological perspective.[77]

---

72. Nicholls, *Contextualization*, 29–30, defines syncretism as "the attempt to reconcile diverse or conflicting beliefs, or religious practices into a unified system," whether this occurs consciously or unconsciously.

73. Ibid., 24–52.

74. Ibid., 53–69.

75. Ibid., 66.

76. Moreau, *Contextualization in World Missions*, 34–35. There was still significant disagreement amongst evangelicals about contextualization at that time.

77. Gilliland, "Introduction," 1–5, at 3.

Positively, during this decade, there was greater clarification and insight around the issues of gospel and culture, and a growing momentum for change in cross-cultural communication practices and theological understanding that both respected culture and upheld biblical fidelity.[78] Some tentative steps had also been made in the implementation of contextualization and communication strategies, with the goal of maintaining faithfulness to Scripture while avoiding syncretism. The bringing together of biblical theologians, missiologists, and anthropologists at some of the consultations was also a recognition that the issue of contextualization required a multidisciplinary approach.

2.3 Stage 2: Expansion of the theory of contextualization (1980–1992)

The theory of contextualization expanded on two fronts during the period 1980–1992. The first front was the continued evangelical acceptance and development of the concept, with the primary aim of that period being to "identify the dimensions and ramifications of contextualization which [still] had not finally been defined."[79] The second front was the proliferation of various contextual models.

2.3.1 The development of the concept

At the 1982 evangelical International Council on Biblical Inerrancy (ICBI) Summit II held in Chicago, November 10–13, David Hesselgrave effectively summarized the status of the contextualization debate when he said:

> Still in its infancy, that word [contextualization] has already been defined and redefined, used and abused, amplified and vilified, coronated and crucified. Not without reason Bruce Fleming concludes that it has already outlived its usefulness and urges evangelicals to lay it to an untimely rest.[80] Now that evangelicals have adopted it into their linguistic family, however, it is more likely that it will get no rest whatsoever.[81]

---

78. René Padilla's article is an excellent example of this. Padilla, "The Contextualization of the Gospel," 286–312.

79. Coleman and Verster, "Contextualisation of the Gospel Among Muslims," 94–115, at 98. The insertion in brackets is my own.

80. Cf. Fleming, *Contextualization of Theology*, 77–78.

81. Hesselgrave, "Contextualization and Revelational Epistemology," 693. The

Despite the lack of consensus on an agreed definition, Hesselgrave was able to delineate the growing scope of missiological contextualization as primarily involving six tasks: the translation of the Scriptures; the interpretation of the Scriptures; the communication of the gospel; the instruction of believers; the incarnation of truth in the individual and corporate lives of believers; and the systematization of the Christian faith (i.e. theologizing).[82]

The following year, Krikor Haleblian, reviewing the literature on contextualization since 1972, listed seven unresolved issues: "1. the definition of contextualization; 2. its differences from indigenization; 3. the legitimate agents for contextualization; 4. syncretism; 5. the limits of contextualization; 6. the gospel core; 7. hermeneutics."[83] His discussion on syncretism and acceptable limits for contextualization highlighted the general rather than specific nature of the contextual limits that had been offered by many evangelicals up to that point in the debate.[84]

As previously noted, the 1978 Lausanne-sponsored "Consultation on Gospel and Culture" sought to bring the disciplines of missiology, anthropology, and theology together to discuss a topic of mutual interest and significance. One of the participants in that consultation, Harvey Conn, continued the dialogue between these three groups in *Eternal World and Changing Worlds: Theology, Anthropology and Mission in Trialogue* (1984). Despite not being an anthropologist himself, he argued strongly for anthropology's seat at the "development of local theologies" table.[85] While his thesis was that the trialogue be engaged for any missiological issue, he singled out contextualization as one issue that would particularly benefit from such a three-way conversation.[86]

Drawing from his own missionary experience in India, anthropologist Paul Hiebert published two influential articles highlighting the challenge of contextualization for the Western missionary. In "The Flaw of the Excluded Middle," Hiebert argues that the Western worldview is two-tiered (due to its dualistic Platonic roots), comprising religion (matters of faith, miracles, the sacred and "other worldly problems") and science (experience, secular

---

insertion in brackets is my own.

82. Hesselgrave, "Contextualization and Revelational Epistemology," 694. His paper proceeds to address each of these issues.

83. Haleblian, "The Problem of Contextualization," 96.

84. Ibid., 99–101.

85. Conn, *Eternal Word and Changing Worlds: Theology, Anthropology, and Mission in Trialogue*, 129–59, 211–60.

86. Ibid., 130.

problems rooted in the natural world).[87] The Eastern worldview, on the other hand, is three-tiered, having a "middle level" between religion and science—the world of ancestors, local gods and goddesses, spirits, demons, souls, magic and the like (what Hiebert calls "the excluded middle").[88] He concludes that missionaries to the East need to understand the middle tier and develop "holistic theologies" in order more ably to contextualize the gospel, answer the questions Eastern converts to Christianity bring, and limit the likelihood of the development of a syncretized form of Christianity.[89]

Hiebert's second influential article was "Critical Contextualization."[90] He begins this article by first describing and then dismissing as deficient two ways missionaries have historically related the gospel to culture ("non-contextualization" and "uncritical contextualization"). Hiebert advocated a middle ground, what he terms "critical contextualization." For Hiebert, critical contextualization seeks to avoid the "ethnocentrism and cultural foreignness" of the non-contextual approach and the "relativism and syncretism" of the uncritical approach.[91] Whereas much of the literature on contextualization previous to Hiebert's article had spoken in general terms about the task of contextualization, Hiebert went a step further by briefly giving specific guidelines, stating that critical contextualization involved three steps: first, the "Exegesis of the culture"—the uncritical gathering and synthesizing of information on an issue primarily by the local church leadership; second, the "Exegesis of Scripture"—where the missionary or pastor leads in relating Scripture to the issue being studied; third, a "Critical response"—whereby the local church people re-examine their local issue in the light of Scripture and make decisions themselves about their response. Hiebert suggests that, as the whole contextualization process is driven by the local church people themselves, it increases the likelihood for compliance and long-lasting change.[92] Hiebert's critical contextualization approach brings together gospel and culture, with both the process and outcome of contextualization governed by Scripture. Nevertheless, Christian thought, and in particular patristic texts, do not feature in his contextualization model.

---

87. Hiebert, "The Flaw of the Excluded Middle," 35–47, at 35–43.

88. Ibid., 43–45. The worldview of John Chrysostom's day included this middle level too. For example, see Chrysostom, *In Col. hom.* 5, PG 62.340, 1–3, 35–37, 45–49.

89. Hiebert, "The Flaw of the Excluded Middle," 45–47.

90. Hiebert, "Critical Contextualization," 104–11.

91. Ibid., 109–10.

92. Hiebert, "Critical Contextualization," 109–10.

Veteran missionary and ecumenical statesman, Lesslie Newbigin, furthered the contextualization debate through two books: *Foolishness to the Greeks* (1986) and *The Gospel in a Pluralistic Society* (1989).[93] While acknowledging the spate of publications on contextualization over almost two decades, he pinpointed a weakness in all of them when he wrote:

> The weakness, however, of this whole mass of missiological writings is that while it has sought to explore the problem of contextualization in all the cultures of humankind from China to Peru, it has largely ignored the culture that is most widespread, powerful, and persuasive among all contemporary cultures—namely . . . Western Culture.[94]

Newbigin rightly understood that contextualization is an issue both for non-Western *and* for Western cultures. The burden of both Newbigin's books is to address this cultural blind spot and answer the question: how can the gospel be contextualized in Western culture, given the reality that there is no such thing as a pure or culture-free gospel?[95] To do so successfully would mean avoiding the problems which sometimes enshrouded previous approaches (inherent in terms like indigenization, adaptation, and accommodation), such as equating the gospel and Western culture, and incorrectly thinking that there is such a thing as a pure, culture-free gospel.[96] Rather, "[contextualization] direct[s] attention to the need to communicate the gospel so that it speaks God's word to the total context in which people are now living and in which they have to make their decisions."[97] Newbigin poignantly highlights the tragic irony whereby the Majority World, having cast aside the colonial yoke of the "synthesis of nationalism and Christianity" inherent in indigenization, adaptation, and accommodation, has now embraced their own synthesis of nationalism and Christianity in the name of "local theologies."[98]

The year 1989 saw two further important publications that impacted upon the contextualization debate, authored by Dean Gilliland, David Hesselgrave, and Edward Rommen.

---

93. Newbigin, *Foolishness to the Greeks: The Gospel and Western Culture*; Newbigin, *The Gospel in a Pluralistic Society*.
94. Newbigin, *Foolishness*, 2–3.
95. Ibid., 4–5; Newbigin, *The Gospel*, 141–5.
96. Newbigin, *The Gospel*, 142.
97. Ibid., 142.
98. Ibid., 143, 148. He cites Liberation Theology, Black Theology, Dalit Theology, and Feminist Theology as examples of local theologies which do not involve the crossing of cross-cultural boundaries.

In *The Word Among Us*, Dean S. Gilliland gathered twelve faculty members of the School of World Mission of Fuller Theological Seminary to contribute to an extensive volume on contextualization, stating that the book's purpose was to demonstrate that properly enacted contextualization was basic to any mission endeavor.[99]

One contributor, Arthur F. Glasser, acknowledged the "broad and somewhat careless" way missiologists had used the word contextualization, the continued lack of agreement amongst missiologists over the change from indigenization to contextualization, and the current desire amongst missiologists to relate the gospel to the material world as much as possible, and pointed to a change in the direction of the debate:[100]

> The concern today is to go beyond the earlier vision of seeking to make sure that the gospel in every place is clothed with appropriate linguistic cultural frames of reference. This is now judged as somewhat superficial. Whereas this urgency remains, the additional task is to ascertain the existential implications of the gospel in any given context. What is important is that the realities of dominant social concerns and ongoing cultural changes are not overlooked, and that the gospel remains free to speak prophetically to a culture from within it. *The stress today is on communication through incarnation* (emphasis his).[101]

The Word Among Us is one of only a few publications up to that point that contained a substantial biblical basis for and reflection on contextualization (three out of fourteen chapters).[102] While the focus of the biblical treatment was to highlight biblical examples of contextualization rather than extract contextual principles that could be applied to mission contexts, at least four contextual principles can be identified. First, the incarnation is the model from which any valid contextualization is derived.[103] Second, in the Old Testament God only had one covenant with his people Israel, but the expression and implications of that covenant varied throughout the ensuing centuries based on the changing nature of their contexts.[104] Third,

---

99. Gilliland, "Contextual Theology as Incarnational Mission," 9–31, at 18.

100. This paragraph is based on Glasser, "Old Testament Contextualization: Revelation and Its Environment," 32–51, at 33.

101. Glasser, "Old Testament Contextualization," 33.

102. Gilliland, *The Word Among Us*, 32–100.

103. Glasser, "Old Testament Contextualization," 49; Gilliland, "New Testament Contextualization: Continuity and Particularity in Paul's Theology," 52–73, at 53.

104. Glasser, "Old Testament Contextualization," 38–49; Van Engen, "The New Covenant: Knowing God in Context," 74–100, at 84–86.

in the contextual process the New Testament authors were prepared to use existing Hellenistic terms (e.g., λόγος, John 1:14) and imbue them with a different meaning in light of the gospel.[105] Fourth, God's self-revelation in a new culture must be consistent with how God revealed himself in Scripture.[106] Compared to Glassen, the other eleven chapters tend to approach contextualization either from an anthropological or from a practical theology perspective, with no consideration of contextualization from the perspective of the church fathers.[107]

The growing emphasis on the contextual communication and application of the gospel is also evident in the 1989 publication by David Hesselgrave and Edward Rommen, *Contextualization: Meanings, Methods, and Models*. It was, and is still, one of the most comprehensive volumes on contextualization from an evangelical perspective. Having reviewed the profoundly different theological orientations of orthodoxy, liberalism, neo-orthodoxy, and neo-liberalism,[108] and surveyed a host of different definitions of contextualization, they offered a suggestion as to why the definitions had been so different:

> One reason is that they are rooted in disparate theological orientations. The more liberal theologies allow for greater concessions to the contemporary context. The more conservative and orthodox theologies are more restrictive in this regard. Some contextualizations, therefore, result in the formation of a "new gospel." Others enhance the communication of the "old gospel."[109]

Hesselgrave and Rommen propose three meanings of contextualization: apostolic, prophetic and syncretistic. In apostolic contextualization (which emphasizes the text), the apostolic faith is carefully adapted and applied to the people of the receiving culture so "as to preserve as much of the original meaning and relevance as possible." In prophetic contextualization (which emphasizes the context), the contextualizer enters a context, seeks

---

105. Gilliland, "New Testament Contextualization," 55–57.

106. Van Engen, "The New Covenant," 90.

107. One further contextual principle from this volume that is pertinent to this thesis comes from Paul Hiebert, who states that cultural objects and symbols are not simply forms but carry meaning, and therefore not every cultural object can be redefined or redeemed in the pursuit of contextualization. Hiebert, "Form and Meaning in the Contextualization of the Gospel," 101–20, at 117.

108. Hesselgrave and Rommen, *Contextualization*, 144–8.

109. Ibid., 148. As one with a more conservative and orthodox theology I advocate for the communication of the "old gospel."

to understand what God is doing and saying in that context, and speaks a prophetic word that seeks to bring about change. In syncretistic contextualization the best insights from "various cultures, religions, and ideologies" are selected and fused into a new sort of faith.[110] Hesselgrave and Rommen favor apostolic contextualization, where Scripture is both the starting point and controlling rubric of contextualization.[111] A second principle that Hesselgrave and Rommen emphasize is that contextualization is both verbal and non-verbal, and its sphere encompasses all missionary activity which legitimately seeks to fulfill the Great Commission.[112]

What is informative about this comprehensive and influential book from two leading evangelical missiologists is not so much what it does contain, but what it does not contain. The book lacks any detailed or systematic biblical demonstration or evaluation of contextualization, and fails to consult the work of the church fathers.[113] In addition, despite the detailed description and analysis of aspects of contextualization, the book fails to provide much in the way of specific evangelical principles to guide the contextual practitioner. Rather, the guiding principles of contextualization are general and not easily applied.

2.3.2 Models of Contextualization

Among a number of helpful publications on contextualization in 1991 was David Bosch's seminal book, *Transforming Mission*.[114] His section on "mission as contextualization" contains a history, explanation, and sympathetic defense of contextual theology.[115] This section takes in what he identifies as

---

110. Ibid., 149–51.

111. Hesselgrave and Rommen, *Contextualization*, 200.

112. Hesselgrave and Rommen, *Contextualization*, 200. They state that this missionary activity includes Bible translation, incarnational living, evangelism, church planting, and liturgical style.

113. The only significant historical references in the book, prior to the twentieth century, are some brief case studies on Bishop Ansgar of Hamburg (831 CE), Constantine of Thessalonica (870 CE), and a few Protestant missionaries of the early eighteenth century. Hesselgrave and Rommen, *Contextualization*, 21–26.

114. Other insightful publications include Hoedemaker, "Contextual Analysis and Unity of Perspective: An Exercise in Missiological Method," 200–9. David Hesselgrave's *Communicating Christ Cross-culturally: An Introduction to Missionary Communication*, 2nd ed., is an extensive revision of the first edition, taking into consideration the proliferation of publications on contextualization since its original publication in 1978.

115. Bosch, *Transforming Mission*, 420–432.

the two major models of contextual theology—the inculturation model and the revolutionary model. The conceptual approach to contextualization, using what have been termed "models," is one of many approaches to contextualization in the literature.[116] Many different proposals for contextualizing the Christian faith had been proposed prior to *Transforming Mission*. Subsequent to its publication a number of scholars grouped contextual examples with similar characteristics into larger groupings—termed models.[117] Approaching a subject such as contextualization using models facilitates the comparison and evaluation of the respective approaches that would prove difficult otherwise.[118]

Broadly speaking, contextual models are artificially developed approaches to contextualization to which "real-life examples" will tend to conform in a general sense.[119] They are constructions or prototypes and, as such, are not meant to be viewed or used as literally accurate but as simplified general categories.[120] Models are "contextual examples grouped together based on a particular set of criteria . . . Central to the task of distinguishing one model from another is the need to identify and choose the criteria . . . use[d] carefully."[121]

Various models have been proposed for contextualization. One of the problems in comparing models is that different authors use their own criteria without necessarily referencing those of other models.[122] Moreau lists some of the more significant models,[123] including those proposed by Dean Gilliland,[124] Charles Van Engen,[125] Bruce Nicholls,[126] and Robert Schreiter,[127] with the most influential and widely used models those of

116. A "models approach" is used to facilitate "an understanding of a complex or difficult theological issue." Bevans, *Models of Contextual Theology*, 28. He cites Avery Dulles and H. Richard Niebuhr as examples of authors who have used a models approach as the basis of their work.

117. Moreau, *Contextualization in World Mission*, 32.

118. Schreiter, *Constructing Local Theologies*, 6.

119. Moreau, "Evangelical Models of Contextualization," 165–93, at 166.

120. Ibid., 166–7.

121. Moreau, *Contextualization in World Mission*, 36–37. For more discussion of the concept of models, see Bevans, *Models of Contextual Theology*, 28–33.

122. Moreau, *Contextualization in World Mission*, 36–37.

123. Ibid., 37.

124. Gilliland, "The Incarnation as Matrix for Appropriate Theologies," 493–519.

125. Van Engen, "Five Perspectives of Contextually Appropriate Missional Theology," 183–202.

126. Nicholls, "Towards a Theology of Gospel and Culture," 49–62.

127. Schreiter, *Constructing Local Theologies*, 1–38.

Catholic theologians Stephen Bevans and Robert Schreiter.[128] Between them, Bevans and Schreiter span the broad spectrum of models used.[129]

In *Models of Contextual Theology*, Bevans posits six different models for contextual theology: translational, anthropological, praxis, synthetic, transcendental and countercultural. After defining contextual theology as "the attempt to understand Christian faith in terms of a particular context" and as something "new," he clearly sides with the argument of the *Ministry in Context* document as to why a contextual approach is a "theological imperative" for both First World and Majority World churches.[130]

Robert Schreiter, in *Constructing Local Theologies*, suggests three broad contextualization models (with a number of subgroups): translation, adaptation, and contextual.[131] While each of the three categories of models is important, he suggests that contextual models are the most important and bases the rest of his book on them.[132]

There are strengths and weaknesses in each of Bevans' and Schreiter's models but what they do highlight is that that there is no single or exclusive way of doing contextual theology. Moreau critiques Bevan's and Schreiter's respective models when he states that, although they describe the different approaches that can be taken to contextualization, they do not show the "relative significance" of each approach to one another, i.e. which of the models are more commonly used or potentially more useful.[133] Neither do they demonstrate that within any of the different models there are numerous expressions and variations.[134] In addition to Moreau's comments, it is notable that both Bevans' and Schreiter's books lack biblical and patristic reflection and critique of the various models they describe. Furthermore, Schreiter's book demonstrates more of an anthropological rather than biblical approach to contextual theology.

In summary, over the period 1980–1992, the contextualization debate developed significantly. First, contextualization became almost universally

128. Moreau, *Contextualization in World Mission*, 37; Bevans, *Models of Contextual Theology*, 28–137.

129. Moreau, *Contextualization in World Mission*, 37.

130. Bevans, *Models of Contextual Theology*, 3, 12–15, 26. Cf. TEF Staff, *Ministry in Context*, 17–20.

131. Schreiter, *Constructing Local Theologies*, 6–16.

132. In Moreau, *Contextualization in World Mission*, 37, Table 1.2 contains Moreau's comparison of the respective models of Bevans and Schreiter, with models that are next to one another in the same row "roughly equivalent to each other" while "shaded boxes indicate a lack of a discernible match."

133. Moreau, *Contextualization in World Mission*, 44–45.

134. Ibid., 44.

accepted by evangelicals not just as an end but as the means for gospel communication and the development of theology. Second, a range of models and approaches to the task of contextualization had developed over the twenty years since the debate began. Third, evangelicals, with a high view of Scripture, tended to favor translation contextual models which emphasized the careful transmission of the apostolic faith to the receiving culture. Fourth, the debate moved from a discussion of the legitimacy of contextualization to a discussion of principles for how to consistently engage in it. Fifth, the contextual principles that had been articulated were, in the main, general rather than specific. The sixth development was that the necessity of an interdisciplinary approach to contextualization was increasingly recognized and adopted. Somewhat paradoxically for evangelicals, the contribution of biblical studies and Christian thought to the debate was relatively small in proportion to the insights drawn from anthropology and practical theology, thus continuing the trend of the 1970s.

2.4 Stage 3: Maturation and splintering of contextualization (1993–2015)

Since 1993 the contextualization debate has splintered into a number of different yet related debates. Reflection on contextualization has gone down many individual channels, with individual reflections in numerous locales around the globe including Asia,[135] Africa,[136] Europe,[137] and Latin America,[138] demonstrating a maturation of the discipline. The most prominent area where the contextualization debate has moved to is the area of Muslim evangelism. Significantly for my research, the Muslim evangelism aspect of the debate has largely been driven by missiologists and practitioners who have drawn predominantly on insights gleaned from cultural anthropology and practical theology.

---

135. For example, Imamura, "A Cambodian Christmas Celebration," 161–3; Huilin, "The Contextualization of Chinese Christian Theology and Its Main Concerns," 197–204; Manhong Lin, "A Chinese Christian's Reading of Two Ethical Themes of Zhuangzi," 355–66.

136. For example, Kallon, *Contextualization of Christianity in Africa: A Case Study of the Kpelle Tribe in Liberia*.

137. For example, Tiplady, "The Pilgrim Church Needs a New Home," 141–7.

138. For example, Hector Pivaral, "Guatemala: A Case Study—The Evangelical Church and the Influential Animistic Mayan Spirituality," 129–39.

2.4.1 Muslim evangelism

Despite the pioneering work amongst Muslims by Majorcan Ramon Llull, little had been written on the area of Muslim evangelism until Samuel Zwemer began his innovative work in the Middle East in 1890.[139] While different models of Muslim evangelism have been tried since Zwemer's time,[140] evangelism amongst Muslims has been characterized as slow, difficult work filled with many disappointments and few converts.[141]

The contextualization debate was taken up by practitioners engaged in Muslim evangelism during the 1970s, with four influential articles helping to move the discussion from merely abstract definitions to one of applied contextualization in the Muslim context.[142] It was Phil Parshall's *New Paths in Muslim Evangelism* (1980), however, that significantly fueled the debate which subsequently exploded in the 1990s.[143] Parshall, with over twenty years' experience in Muslim ministry, had become frustrated with the traditional, ineffective approaches to Muslim evangelism. This led him to propose a more contextualized approach, which included: missionaries looking and dressing like Muslims; adopting Muslim dietary practices; re-

---

139. Cate, "What will it take to win Muslims?", 230-4, at 230. Llull's missionary efforts in North Africa were inspired by the prior missionary endeavors of St Francis amongst Muslims in the Crusades during the early part of the thirteenth century. St Francis had sought to convert the Sultan of Egypt to Christianity in order to end the Crusades.

140. Terry, "Approaches to the Evangelization of Muslims," 168-73, at 170-2. Terry lists five models of Muslim evangelism that have been used since the eighteenth century (although mainly since the time of Zwemer): 1. Confrontational; 2. Traditional evangelical; 3. Institutional; 4. Dialogical; 5. Contextualization. The sheer weight of publications on contextualization in Muslim evangelism since 1993 suggests that contextualization has been the main approach used during this period.

141. Cate, "What will it take?", 230.

142. Arredondo, "An Analysis of Missionary Contextualization in the Muslim Evangelism of Phil Parshall", 6. The four articles are: Anderson, "Missionary Approach to Islam: Christian or Cultic?" , 285-300; Wilder, "Some Reflections on Possibilities for People Movements among Muslims," 301-20; Conn, "The Muslim Convert and His Culture," 61-77; Kraft, "Dynamic Equivalence in Muslim Society," 79-88.

143. Parshall, *New Paths in Muslim Evangelism: Evangelical Approaches to Contextualization*. This was later republished as *Muslim Evangelism: Contemporary Approaches to Contextualization*. Preceding this publication were two articles which warned of the dangers inherent in some aspects of contextualization generally (Yego, "Appreciation for and Warnings about Contextualization," 153-6), and Muslim contextualization specifically (Schlorff, "The Hermeneutical Crisis in Muslim Evangelization," 143-51). An opposing view is found in Dretke, *A Christian Approach to Muslims: Reflections from West Africa*. In this book, Dretke, like Parshall, explores new approaches to evangelizing Muslims.

moving shoes before entering a place of Christian worship; placing Bibles in folding stands as are used for the Qur'an; lifting up hands during prayer and using Muslim tunes in Christian worship.[144] Underlying Parshall's approach were two contextual principles, outlined at the start of the book, based on his interpretation of 1 Cor 8–9. First, "it is meaning which determines the acceptability or unacceptability of cultural forms. If the meaning is intrinsically contrary to Christian truth, no Christian may participate. If, however, the practice is wrong only in the view of some people, then the Christian must abstain only in their presence."[145] Second, Christian freedom breaks all "cultural bondages." Paul was free to adopt any methodology he wished, based on the context, in order to see Jews brought to faith in Christ. By corollary, Christians are free to adopt any number of methodologies in order for Muslims to be brought to faith in Jesus.[146]

Despite being avowedly evangelical, and seeking to distance his approach from the charge of syncretism, Parshall correctly anticipated a negative reaction to his proposals from the evangelical community.[147] A sympathetic and relatively positive review of *New Paths in Muslim Evangelism*[148] was followed by a stinging critique by Richard Heldenbrand. Two of Parshall's proposals, that Heldenbrand both questioned and dismissed, were particularly pertinent. The first was Parshall's preference for Muslim background believers (MBB's) to observe the fast during Ramadan and the Sheep Feast (as it identifies them as Muslims and not Christians). The second was Parshall's proposal of referring to Jesus as "Isa" (as the Isa of the Qur'an has "different attributes from Jesus of the Bible"). Heldenbrand's conclusion was that Parshall's book was a "well-meaning but sub-biblical approach to the Muslim world."[149] While Heldenbrand misrepresents Parshall at points, Parshall's reply that his book was written not as a "dogmatic treatise" but rather to stimulate ongoing discussion and debate on the meth-

---

144. Parshall, *New Paths*, 97–125, 157–80. For a significant treatment of Parshall on Muslim contextualization, see Arredondo, "An Analysis of Missionary Contextualization."

145. Parshall, *Muslim Evangelism*, 39.

146. Ibid., 40. The majority of the book contained no sustained biblical justification for his approach.

147. Parshall, *New Paths*, 16–18, 43–53, 233–9.

148. Hess, "Book Review: New Paths in Muslim Evangelism," 188–9.

149. Heldenbrand, "Mission to Muslims: Cutting the Nerve," 135–9, at 136–7. He also strongly critiqued Charles Kraft, whom he assessed as having a similar viewpoint regarding experimental approaches to Muslim evangelism ("the Christian-Qur'an Hermeneutic," p. 134) leading to Kraft's rebuttal in Kraft, "My Distaste for the Combative Approach," 139–42.

THE CONTEXTUALIZATION DEBATE   63

odology of Muslim evangelism[150] is contradicted by the prescriptive nature of his recommendations.[151]

Further publications on Muslim evangelism ensued, following either a traditional and/or relational methodology,[152] or pursuing a more experimental approach to Muslim evangelism,[153] with critics of these approaches debating where the acceptable limits for evangelical contextualization lay.[154] The overall trajectory was towards increasing degrees of contextualization, some of which surpassed even that advocated by Parshall, most notably the work of John Travis.[155] It was Travis who introduced the ground-breaking scale for categorizing six stages of contextualization in Muslim outreach, known as the "C-Spectrum." The C-Spectrum is a tool which "compares and contrasts [different] types of Christ-centred communities" which already exist in the Muslim world. The C-Spectrum ranges from minimal contextualization (C1) to a high degree of contextualization (C5 and C6).[156]

The C1–C6 scale helped crystallize the debate on Muslim evangelism, becoming known as the C4/C5 debate.[157] Parshall and others consider C4[158] communities legitimate and appropriate expressions of contextualization in a Muslim context, but believe that C5[159] communities have contextualized

150. Parshall, "I am Really only Asking Questions," 142–4.

151. This is seen particularly in Part II of his book, "Application of Contextualization," (chaps. 6–11).

152. See Anderson, "The Lessons of 27 Years Gleaning Among Muslims," 362–6; Cate, "What will it take?", 230–4; Brown, "Is Church Planting in the Muslim World 'Mission Impossible'?" 156–65; Corwin, "Reaching the Resistant," 144–5.

153. Terry, "Approaches," 168–73; Richard, "Is Extraction Evangelism Still the Way to Go?", 170–7; Speers, "Should Missionaries Keep the Muslim Fast?", 356–9.

154. Eenigenburg, "The Pros and Cons of Islamicized Contextualization," 310–15; Racey, "Contextualisation: How Far is too Far?", 304–9.

155. Travis, "The C1 to C6 Spectrum," 407–8.

156. For an outline of Travis' C-Spectrum, see Travis, "The C1 to C6 Spectrum," 407–8.

157. There is little disagreement in the literature regarding the acceptability of C1–C3. C4 is broadly considered acceptable by missiologists, although some still consider C4 as potentially over-contextualized. C5–C6 are considered by some as overcontextualized. Woodberry, "To the Muslim I Became a Muslim?", 23–28, at 24.

158. C4 refers to contextualized Christ-centered communities who use insider language and biblically permissible cultural and Islamic forms. Some of these permissible forms include avoiding pork, raising hands when praying, and using Islamic terms and dress. C4 believers often refer to themselves as "followers of Isa the messiah" and are usually not seen as Muslims by their Muslim communities. At best they are considered a deviant form of Islam. Travis, "The C1 to C6 Spectrum," 407–8.

159. C5 refers to communities of Muslims who follow Jesus yet remain culturally

too much, resulting in syncretistic expressions of Christianity.[160] Travis and others consider C5 communities to be appropriate expressions of Christianity.[161] Over time, somewhat ironically, Parshall, the seemingly radical contextualizer, began being viewed as the new conservative.[162]

The C1–C6 scale, along with the growing openness to experiment with new approaches to contextualization, contributed to the development of the term Insider Movement,[163] which has been defined by proponent Rebecca Lewis in the following way:

> An "insider movement" is any movement to faith in Christ where a) the gospel flows through pre-existing communities and social networks, and where b) believing families, as valid expressions of the Body of Christ, remain inside their socioreligious communities, retaining their identity as members of that community while living under the Lordship of Jesus Christ and the authority of the Bible.[164]

Kevin Higgins seeks to clarify the relationship between C5 communities and the Insider Movement when he states that "Insider movements combine the insights of people movement or mass movement thinking concerning the church with the point of view often referred to as C5."[165] Whereas C5 encourages the establishment of a new, highly contextualized community of believers (even if they call themselves "Muslims"), "Insider

---

and officially Muslim. These communities of believers consider themselves as Muslim followers of Jesus and are viewed as Muslims by the Muslim community. They meet regularly with other C5 believers, evangelize unsaved Muslims, and use many Islamic forms in their C5 meetings. Some C5 believers still attend and participate in Islamic worship at a mosque. Travis, "The C1 to C6 Spectrum," 407–8.

160. Parshall, "DANGER!", 404–10.

161. Travis, "Must all Muslims Leave 'Islam' to Follow Jesus?", 411–5; Travis, "Messianic Muslim Followers of Isa: A Closer Look at C5 Believers and Congregations," 53–9; Gilliland, "Context is Critical in 'Islampur' Case," 415–7.

162. Gilliland, "Context is Critical," 415–6; Parshall, "DANGER!", 405.

163. Higgins, "Inside What? Church, Culture, Religion and Insider Movements in Biblical Perspective," 74–91, at 75; Higgins, "The Key to Insider Movements: The 'Devoted's' of Acts," 155–65.

164. Lewis, "Promoting Movements to Christ Within Natural Communities," 75–6, at 75; Coleman, *A Theological Analysis of the Insider Movement From Four Perspectives: Theology of Religions, Revelation, Soteriology, and Ecclesiology*, 6–7. For more on the Insider Movement, see Wolfe, "Insider Movements: An Assessment of the Viability of Retaining Socio-Religious Insider Identity in High Religious Contexts."

165. Higgins, "Inside What?", 76. He also notes that most "practitioners," including Travis himself, are moving away from the C-scale, or, at the very least, distinguishing between C5 and the Insider Movement.

Movement followers of Jesus remain part of their pre-faith community."[166] Key advocates of the Insider Movement include John Travis,[167] Rebecca Lewis,[168] Rick Brown,[169] Dudley Woodberry,[170] and Kevin Higgins.[171] Those with significant reservations about the Insider Movement include L. D. Waterman,[172] Phil Parshall,[173] Gary Corwin,[174] and Timothy Tennant.[175]

While a variety of theological positions and practices exist among Insider Movement proponents, a number of their contextual principles are largely indicative. First, faith in Jesus Christ does not require a person to leave their pre-faith socio-religious community because God has already pre-determined "the community a person is born into" (Acts 17:26).[176] The term Muslim can be viewed sociologically rather than religiously, because "[f]or many Muslims, being a Muslim is an inseparable part of their self-identity, their background, their family, their community, their cultural heritage, regardless of what they actually believe about God."[177] The second

---

166. Coleman, *A Theological Analysis*, 8.

167. See Travis, "Appropriate Approaches in Muslim Contexts," 397–414.

168. See Lewis, "The Integrity of the Gospel and Insider Movements," 44–48; Lewis, "Insider Movements: Retaining Identity and Preserving Community," 16–19; Lewis, "Insider Movements: Honouring God-Given Identity," 33–36.

169. See Brown, "Biblical Muslims," 65–74; Brown, "Brother Jacob and Master Esau: How One Insider Movement Began," 41–42.

170. See Woodberry, "To the Muslim," 23–28. Cf. Woodberry, "Contextualization among Muslims: Reusing Common Pillars," 171–86.

171. See Higgins, "Acts 15 and Insider Movements among Muslims: Questions, Process and Conclusions," 29–40; Higgins, "Beyond Christianity," 12–13; Higgins, "Speaking the Truth about Insider Movements: Addressing the Criticisms of Bill Nikides and 'Phil' relative to the Article 'Inside What?'" 61–86.

172. See Waterman, "Contextualization: A Few Basic Questions," 166–73; Waterman, "Do the Roots Affect the Fruits?" 57–63.

173. See Parshall, "Lifting the Fatwa," 288–93. Interestingly, Parshall states that he is willing to accept C5 as a starting point but with the view to the community becoming C4 over a period of time. See Travis et al., "Four Responses to Tennant," 124–6, at 125.

174. See Corwin, "Insider Movements," 10–11; Corwin, "A Humble Appeal to C5/Insider Movement Muslim Ministry Advocates to Consider Ten Questions (with responses from Brother Yusef, Rick Brown, Kevin Higgins, Rebecca Lewis and John Travis)," 5–20; Corwin, "A Response to My Respondents," 53–56.

175. See Tennant, "Followers of Jesus," 101–15; Tennant, *Theology in the Context of World Christianity: How the Global Church is Influencing the Way We Think About and Discuss Theology*. See also Tennant, "The Challenge of Churchless Christianity: An Evangelical Assessment," 171–7.

176. Lewis, "Insider Movements," 16–17.

177. Brown, "Biblical Muslims," 65; Higgins, "Identity, Integrity and Insider

principle is related to the first. If the term Muslim can be viewed sociologically, then various Muslim practices such as attending the mosque, saying the Shahāda, and keeping Ramadan may continue to be practiced by MBB.[178] Third, because of many incorrect connotations with the term "Christian," a MBB is not required to self-identify as a Christian.[179] Rather, they are able to describe themselves as a "Bible-believing Muslim who follows Jesus as their Lord and Saviour."[180]

A significant number of publications on contextualization in Muslim evangelism have centered on the related issue of the point at which contextualization efforts go too far and lead to syncretism, but the issue remains unresolved.[181] What is so striking throughout this literature, written mainly by practitioners, has been the data from which they have drawn both to justify their respective positions and to critique the positions of others. Whichever position an author has argued, the primary data source has largely been drawn from practical experience (their own and/or others), or from an anthropological perspective. Considering the prolific publications on Muslim evangelism, there has been proportionately little attention given to the biblical data, while the writings of the church fathers have been almost completely ignored. Where the Bible has been used to support a position the author has often just referred to a few texts but failed to argue extensively from Scripture.[182] This has contributed to the confusion and lack of consensus regarding acceptable evangelical parameters for Muslim contextualization.[183]

Movements: A Brief Paper Inspired by Timothy C. Tennant's Critique of C5 Thinking," 117–23, at 118–21.

178. Brown, "Biblical Muslims," 70–73; Brown, "Contextualization without Syncretism," 127–33, at 132.

179. Lewis, "Insider Movements," 17.

180. Brown, "Biblical Muslims," 69. Cf. Higgins, "Acts 15 and Insider Movements," 34–37.

181. For example, see the publications listed above in chapter 2.

182. For example, see Higgins, "Acts 15 and Insider Movements," 29–40, Higgins, "Identity, Integrity," 117–23; Lewis, "Insider Movements: Honouring God-Given Identity," 16–19; Lewis, "The Integrity of the Gospel," 44–48. Coleman, *A Theological Analysis of the Insider Movement From Four Perspectives*, is a notable exception. In each of his four main chapters on theology of religions, revelation, soteriology, and ecclesiology he provides a detailed biblical analysis and critique of the Insider Movement. Furthermore, Tennant's article, "Followers of Jesus," 101–15, also contains a detailed biblical examination of contextualization in Muslim contexts.

183. This is further evidenced in Hesselgrave and Stetzer, *Missionshift: Global Mission Issues in the Third Millennium*, 82–163.

2.4.2 Evangelical parameters for contextualization

The lack of consensus amongst evangelicals regarding acceptable parameters and principles for contextualization has been a constant throughout the history of the debate. Three substantial volumes released over the past decade have sought to provide a theologically robust approach to establishing and confirming evangelical parameters and principles of contextualization.

Dean Flemming's *Contextualization in the New Testament: Patterns for Theology and Mission* is the first serious monograph on New Testament contextualization from an evangelical perspective. The book's aim is twofold: first, to examine the New Testament for examples of contextualization of the gospel; second, to consider possible implications of these "patterns and precedents" for mission in diverse contexts today.[184] Flemming's thesis is that each New Testament book is a contextualized document which explains and applies the gospel to particular audiences. He also suggests that the Gospels and Acts are accounts by the respective evangelists whereby they arrange their material about Jesus and the early church and are thus illustrations of contextualization of the gospel in various contexts. For Flemming, these examples or "New Testament precedents function for us primarily in an analogous and exemplary sense."[185] Flemming provides many evangelical contextual principles and comes to a number of important conclusions on contextualization in his book, including the following:[186]

1. There is no single formulation for the gospel. It should be explained and applied in a diverse number of ways that make sense to the particular audience;

2. Fresh, innovative images and metaphors need to be discovered so as to communicate the gospel in different contexts. Certain images and metaphors will communicate more clearly in some contexts than others, whether drawn from the biblical text or the everyday world of the audience.

3. The gospel is first and foremost a coherent narrative about the life, death, and resurrection of Jesus Christ. It is this narrative that needs to be contextualized, with people locating their own personal story within the larger metanarrative of the gospel story;

4. It is not always easy to delineate where contextualization ends and where syncretism begins;

---

184. Flemming, *Contextualization*, 15–16.
185. Ibid., 296.
186. Ibid., 296–322.

5. There is no such thing as a "pure" gospel or "culture-free" gospel. Every presentation of the gospel is culturally conditioned. "A supracultural gospel may be a theoretical possibility but we have no access to it. Cultural forms and supracultural content cannot be easily separated like oil and water;"[187]

6. The church is integral to the task of incarnating and proclaiming the gospel.

Flemming suggests four New Testament tests or criteria to assist in the assessment of authentic contextualization of the gospel and in discerning contextual limits:[188]

i. How does it compare with the gospel revealed in Scripture? There is only one apostolic gospel (e.g., 1 Cor 15:3–5, 11; Gal 1:6–9) and all contextual theology needs to be tested against this apostolic gospel.

ii. Is there confirmation by the Holy Spirit for the theologizing that has been done?

iii. How does it compare with the reflections of the wider Christian community (including the reflections of the historic church through the centuries as well as the current global church)?

iv. Does the contextualization result in transformed lives and the spread of Christian mission? Any contextual theology that does not shape the Christian community to be more deeply and sacrificially committed to the Lord Jesus and his kingdom is a distorted application of the gospel.

Dean Flemming has made a significant contribution to the contextualization debate through a well-argued and thought-provoking treatment of contextualization in the New Testament. Flemming's book offers a helpful guide in the task of uncovering a biblical theology of and approach to contextualization, and I will adopt a number of features of his approach in chapter three. That being said, despite the book's title, many parts of the New Testament are not covered in any depth, making any conclusions he draws regarding contextualization in the New Testament incomplete. There is still much of the New Testament, and the Bible as a whole, that needs to be explored to give a comprehensive picture of biblical contextualization.[189]

187. Ibid., 306; C.f. Newbigin, *The Gospel in a Pluralistic Society*, 142, who makes the same point.

188. Flemming, *Contextualization*, 303–5.

189. Flemming acknowledges that due to limitations of space he is not examining all of the New Testament but only representative sections that he considers contain some of the "clearest and most suggestive New Testament examples of doing

In chapter three my thesis will therefore examine two additional texts that Flemming's book doesn't consider, as well as re-examine two texts he covered, in order to evaluate and establish evangelical contextual principles.

Two companion volumes on contextualization have recently been released—one by the World Evangelical Association Theological Commission (WEATC) and the other by the World Evangelical Alliance Mission Commission (WEAMC), giving a snapshot of the current debate from an evangelical perspective. *Local Theology for the Local Church* (2010) focuses on the theology of contextualization, with the goal of providing contextual principles.[190] *Global Mission: Reflections and Case Studies in Contextualization for the Whole Church* (2011) deals with some additional theological and practical issues with contextualization.[191] The main part of *Global Mission* comprises twenty contextual case studies from a range of emerging scholars across the globe, mostly from the Majority World.[192] The book is further evidence that in recent decades, theologians from Africa,[193] Asia,[194] and Latin America[195] have increasingly contributed to and influenced missiological

---

context-orientated evangelism and theology." Flemming, *Contextualization*, 16. My critique underscores the point being made here.

190. Cook et al., *Local Theology for the Global Church*.

191. Dowsett, *Global Mission: Reflections and Case Studies in Contextualization for the Whole Church*.

192. The center of Christianity has shifted dramatically southward in less than a century, so that now the major centers of Christian influence are increasingly Latin America, Sub-Sahara Africa and Asia. Walls, *The Missionary Movement in Christian History: Studies in the Transmission of Faith*, 9. See also Jenkins, *The Next Christendom: The Coming of Global Christianity*; Jenkins, *The New Faces of Christianity: Believing the Bible in the Global South*; Walls, *The Cross-Cultural Process in Christian History*.

193. See Bediako, *Jesus and the Gospel in Africa: History and Experience*; Kwarne Bediako, "Five Theses on the Significance of Modern African Christianity: A Manifesto," 51–67; Bediako, *Christianity in Africa: The Renewal of a Non-Western Religion*; Sanneh, *Translating the Message*.

194. See Ingleby et al., *Contextualisation and Mission Training: Engaging Asias's Religious Worlds*; Kim, *Christian Theology in Asia*; Lee, *The Trinity in Asian Perspective*; Yung, *Mangoes or Bananas? The Quest for an Authentic Asian Christian Theology*; Ariarajah, *Gospel and Culture: An Ongoing Discussion Within the Ecumenical Movement*.

195. See Padilla, *Bases Biblicas de la Mision: Perspectivas Latinoamericanas*; Costas, *Liberating News: A Theology of Contextual Evangelization*; Escobar, *The New Global Mission*.

debate, including the contextualization debate, through publications[196] and conference participation.[197]

The contribution of both WEATC volumes to an evangelical approach is significant. The volumes display a maturation of thought regarding a whole range of contextualization issues that have been discussed throughout the four decades of the debate, highlighting points of agreement and issues where there is still a lack of consensus amongst evangelicals. They also display a healthy balance between theology and application of that theology, what Dowsett calls "informed practice."[198] Nevertheless, both volumes display similar deficiencies. Like many previous publications on contextualization, there is still a tendency towards theological discussion on contextualization which is not translated into more specific contextual principles that could guide the contextual practitioner.[199] A second deficiency is that, while biblical reflection is present in both books, it is largely confined to one or two chapters, and is partial and selective rather than comprehensive. Furthermore, neither book evidences material from the writings of the church fathers.

Conclusion

This chapter has sought to achieve two aims. The first has been to answer the twin questions: how have evangelicals gone about the task of developing an evangelical approach to contextualization and what are some of the contextual principles they have determined? What this chapter has demonstrated is that evangelicals have robustly debated the issue of contextualization, and the understanding and application of contextualization has developed, changed, and matured over time. Evangelical thinking about contextualization has traversed the spectrum from initial rejection, to reformulation of

---

196. See Greenman and Green, *Global Theology in Evangelical Perspective: Exploring the Contextual Nature of Theology and Mission*; Bevans and Tahaafe-Williams, *Contextual Theology for the Twenty-First Century*; Dyrness, *Emerging Voices in Global Christian Theology*; Ott and Netland, *Globalizing Theology: Belief and Practice in an Era of World Christianity*.

197. Tennant's comment is that since "Majority World Christianity is to a large extent morally and theologically conservative" this may well contribute to a more conservative approach to contextualization than has been exhibited over the previous forty years. Tennant, *Theology*, 10.

198. Dowsett, "Rainbow Faith," 3–10, at 9.

199. One chapter that does provide specific evangelical contextual principles is that of Ronaldo Lidório, "A Biblical Theology of Contextualization," 11–23. As helpful as some of his principles may be, there is no detailed biblical justification of them.

its meaning and parameters, to final acceptance as a theological necessity. Issues of gospel and culture have been defined and redefined. Various meanings, methods, and models have been proposed, yet agreement has been far from universal. Evangelicalism still remains divided over many aspects of contextualization, as evidenced by the variety of approaches to Muslim evangelism.[200] There also remains a considerable gap between the theory of contextualization and the application of that theory in missiological contexts. Furthermore, even after more than forty years of debate, evangelical principles and parameters of contextualization continue to be identified and discussed, but consensus remains elusive. A different evangelical approach to contextualization is needed in order to break the deadlock.

Second, this chapter has demonstrated that the development of an evangelical approach to contextualization has been dominated by theorists and practitioners from the disciplines of anthropology and practical theology. There has been a corresponding lack of detailed engagement with Scripture and the writings of the church fathers. While the need for a multidisciplinary approach to contextualization has been recognized, it has rarely been consistently engaged. The result has been the development of evangelical parameters, principles, and approaches to contextualization, many of which have been skewed in favor of anthropology and practical theology, in particular.

In developing an evangelical approach to contextualization, a number of correctives are needed in order to begin to address this imbalance. First, Scripture needs to be studied, analyzed, and applied in a systematic and comprehensive way in terms of contextualization, and contextual principles developed. Second, there is a need for the writings of the church fathers to be analyzed for how the Fathers sought to contextualize the gospel in their respective contexts, and contextual principles developed. Third, the contextual principles derived from the analysis of Scripture and the church fathers are points of comparison to confirm, challenge, critique or add to the contextual principles developed over the history of the contextualization debate.

The following chapters take an initial step towards addressing these deficiencies, drawing from the disciplines of biblical studies and Christian thought. By examining contextualization in the book of Acts (chapter three) and contextualization in the homilies of John Chrysostom (chapters four and five), I will seek to demonstrate the contribution they can respectively make to the contextualization debate. In doing so I will suggest a way to establish clearly and transparently stated evangelical parameters and principles for contextualization.

---

200. As displayed in the recent publication, Hesselgrave and Stetzer, *Missionshift*, 82–163.

Chapter 3

Contextualization in Acts

IN CHAPTER ONE I argued that Scripture should inform missiological debate. Chapter two demonstrated that, despite the prolific publications on contextualization, biblical studies has not featured significantly in the debate, and that this deficiency needs to be addressed. This chapter will begin addressing the deficiency by examining texts in the book of Acts which record examples of the early church engaged in contextualization to both Jewish and Gentile audiences.

The chapter will answer two main questions: 1. How did the early church contextualize the gospel to their respective audiences? 2. What contextual principles did the early church use?

To answer these two questions, a representative selection of the recorded speeches of the early church, delivered to these various audiences, by a variety of early church leaders, will be examined: first, speeches to a Jewish audience (Acts 2:14–31; 7:1–53; 13:13–47); second, a speech to a Gentile audience (17:16–34).[1] Following analyses of these four speeches, contextual principles will be drawn. Before examining these speeches, however, there are four literary, hermeneutical, and contextual issues that need to be considered which both underpin and frame this discussion: i. contextualization in the New Testament; ii. authorship, audience, and purpose of Luke–Acts; iii. rhetoric in the New Testament; iv. the nature of the speeches in Acts.

---

1. The categories used in examining the various speeches in Acts (i. context, audience and setting; ii. contextual approach; iii. contextual message) have been informed by Flemming, *Contextualization*, 57–66.

3.1 Contextualization in the New Testament

Despite contextualization being a relatively new missiological term, the activity of contextualization is not new. Since the time of Pentecost, Christians have sought to present the message of the gospel in terms that are understandable and culturally relevant to their hearers. In other words, they have sought to contextualize the gospel—defined earlier as the message of God's good news centered on the birth, life, death, resurrection, and ascension of Jesus Christ and the implications of that message for daily life. The New Testament documents are themselves contextualized documents, written to explain and apply the gospel to the lives of their respective audiences. The New Testament documents also contain examples of people engaged in the activity of contextualization.[2] In the Gospels, for example, Jesus, the contextualizer par excellence, is presented speaking to Jews in categories that were relevant and understandable to their worldview. He spoke about lilies, clothing, worry, planting and reaping crops, taxes, sheep, the Roman authorities, marriage, Old Testament characters, and Jewish customs (Matt 6:19–34; Mark 4:1–20; 12:13–17; Luke 5:33—6:11; 11:29–32; 19:9; 20:27–47; John 8:31–41; 10:1–18). The recorded responses that Jesus' words elicited from his audiences highlight the level of understanding and impact that Jesus' words and actions achieved (Matt 6:28–29; 8:27; 9:8; 21:45–46; Mark 2:12; 5:18–19; Luke 18:22–25; 10:24; John 6:52, 60, 66–68).[3] The book of Acts is replete with examples of the early church engaged in the task of living and proclaiming a contextualized message, to Jews, Samaritans, and Gentiles (e.g., Acts 2:14–40; 4:8–22; 7:2–60; 10:34–43; 13:16–47; 15:1–30; 17:16–33; 20:18–35; 22:1–21; 24:10–21). The New Testament epistles provide examples of the gospel contextually applied to subjects such as division in the church, marriage, divorce, sexual immorality, Christian freedom, syncretism, food sacrificed to idols, forgiveness, money, false teaching, perseverance, favoritism, and suffering (1 Cor 1:10–17; 3:1–23; 5:1–12; 6:12–20; 7:1–40; 8:1–13; 10:14–31; 2 Cor 2:5–11; 6:14–18; 8:1—9:15; Eph 5:22–33; Phil 4:2–3; Col 2:16–23; 3:18–25; 1 Tim 1:3–11; 4:1–5; 2 Tim 3:1–9; Heb 9:19–39; Jas 2:1–13; 1 Pet 3:1–22; 2 Pet 3:3–9). The book of Revelation is also highly contextualized, written in a form (apocalypse) and with many symbols and imagery that would have been very familiar to its audience (e.g., Rev 2:18–29; 3:14–18; 4:6–8; 7:1–8; 9:1–11; 12:1–17; 17:1–6; 18:15–20; 20:1–15; 21:15—22:5).[4]

---

2. Flemming, *Contextualization*, 15.
3. Lidório, "A Biblical Theology of Contextualization," 11.
4. Flemming, *Contextualization*, 272–273.

Norman Ericson aptly highlights the value of the New Testament for contextualization studies when he states that "the New Testament is a prime example of contextualization . . . there are patterns in the New Testament which give us direction as to the nature of acceptable contextualization, indicating both imperatives as well as implications."[5] Dean Flemming similarly elevates the importance and usefulness of the New Testament in developing a theology and practice of contextualization of the gospel when he asserts that the New Testament documents provide "mentoring in the task of doing theology in different cultural settings" and "show us the process as well as the product of this contextualizing activity."[6] As a window into contextualization in the New Testament, this chapter will focus on the book of Acts, which most ably illustrates the post-resurrection early church engaged in the task of contextualizing the gospel for the first-century world. A detailed examination of all New Testament books would provide a comprehensive picture of contextualization in the New Testament. Flemming, *Contextualization,* more systematically traces the theme of contextualization throughout various sections of the Gospels, Acts, selected epistles and Revelation. My examination of speeches in Acts extends Flemming's work. First, it examines in detail two speeches not covered by Flemming (Acts 2:14–21; 7:1–53). Second, it facilitates a comparison between the contextual method and message of Peter, Stephen, and Paul to Jewish audiences. Third, it re-evaluates two passages previously examined by Flemming, and provides some additional findings. Fourth, it identifies contextual principles in Acts not highlighted by Flemming. Fifth, it examines how these contextual principles compare with principles previously established throughout the course of the contextualization debate.

3.2 Author, audience and purpose of Luke–Acts

Three significant literary issues in Luke–Acts are: the author, audience and purpose of Luke–Acts and will be considered briefly here. First, the author. The common authorship of both the gospel of Luke and Acts is the general scholarly consensus, given that both books mention Theophilus in their introduction (Luke 1:3; Acts 1:1).[7] Tradition has attributed authorship of Luke–Acts to a second generation Christian, educated in Hellenistic

---

5. Ericson, "Implications," 71. By "patterns" I understand Ericson to mean principles, which are not necessarily prescriptive.

6. Flemming, *Contextualization,* 15.

7. Peterson, *The Acts of the Apostles,* 4; Bock, *Acts,* 15; Witherington III, *The Acts of the Apostles: A Socio-Rhetorical Commentary,* 51–56; Bruce, *The Book of Acts,* 7.

Greek called Luke, a likely travel companion of the apostle Paul.[8] Second, in terms of audience, both Luke and Acts are addressed to "Theophilus" (Luke 1:3; Acts 1:1), who was most likely a Gentile Christian or at least a Gentile sympathetic toward the Christian faith.[9] He may have even been Luke's patron.[10] While three main identities for the specific Lukan audience in Luke-Acts have been proposed,[11] Luke's explanation of Jewish customs (e.g., Luke 22:1, 7) and his emphasis on the Gentile mission in Acts suggest that a Gentile Christian audience is most likely.[12] Third, concerning Luke's purpose, if the third gospel and Acts are considered a unity, a two-volume work, then "there are sufficient grounds for considering it one project with a common aim."[13] Many purposes for Luke's gospel have been proposed.[14] Despite the multiplicity of views, there has been a growing number of proponents who have concluded that Luke's main purpose in writing Luke-Acts was to present an apologetic history[15] to persuade his audience of the credibility of the Christian faith they had been taught, therefore providing a defense of and assurance concerning the Christian faith.[16] That is the view I will adopt here.

3.3 Rhetoric in the New Testament

Rhetoric in the New Testament has been a significant field of research in recent decades. Stretching back to the time of Aristotle, rhetoric refers to

8. Witherington, *Acts*, 56; Peterson, *Acts*, 2.
9. Gallagher and Hertig, "Introduction: Background to Acts," 1-17, at 6.
10. Wenham, "The Purpose of Luke-Acts," 79-103, at 95.
11. The proposals are: a. non-Christian (mainly Roman); b. Jewish Christian; c. Gentile Christian. Thompson, *One Lord, One People: The Unity of the Church in Acts in its Literary Setting*, 10-11.
12. Cf. Esler, *Community and Gospel in Luke-Acts: The Social and Political Motivations of Lucan Theology*, 24-26, 30-45; Fitzmyer, *The Gospel According to Luke (I-IX)*, 57-58. For a more detailed argument for a Gentile Christian readership, see Stein, *Luke*, 26-27; Keener, *Acts*, 1:426-28.
13. Peterson, *Acts*, 36. Cf. Maddox, *The Purpose of Luke-Acts*, 4.
14. Darrell Bock lists eleven main proposals that have been put forward. Bock, *Luke 1:1—9:50*, 14. For a more detailed treatment of different proposals for the purpose of Luke-Acts, see Keener, *Acts*, 1:435-58.
15. For example, Peterson, *Acts*, 36; Bruce, *The Book of Acts*, 12-13; Green, *The Gospel of Luke*, 21-25. For different interpretations of the phrase "apologetic purpose," see Peterson, *Acts*, 36-39. On Luke and historical writing, see Green, "Learning Theological Interpretation from Luke," 55-78, at 61-66. Contrast Schnabel, *Acts*, 32-33.
16. Keener, *Acts*, 1:132.

the ability to convince or persuade an audience.[17] Central to ancient rhetoric was shaping the content to be delivered and the style of delivery to suit the audience.[18] Rhetorical speech was classified as judicial, deliberative, or epideictic, with the particular occasion determining which style was used. Judicial speeches, which were also referred to as forensic speeches, were given before a jury or judge, and passed judgment on an action in the past. Deliberative speeches were used in political debate in a council, with the audience determining a future action. Epideictic speeches were used on memorial occasions, where the audience was not called upon to make a decision but rather to listen to praise or blame directed towards someone in the present.[19]

Rhetorical speech would normally have "three emotional phases":[20] i. Ethos: establishing rapport with the audience (usually in the introduction); ii. Logos: presentation of logical arguments (most suited to the body of the argument); iii. Pathos: an appeal to the emotions ("most effective in the conclusion").[21]

After Aristotle, various rhetorical devices that Witherington refers to as "micro-rhetoric" were also employed by rhetoricians:[22] i. *exordium:* an introduction of the speech; ii. *narratio:* an explanation of the issue at hand or relevant facts to the discussion; iii. *propositio:* the "thesis statement"; iv.

---

17. Witherington III, *New Testament Rhetoric: An Introductory Guide to the Art of Persuasion in and of the New Testament*, ix; Aristotle, *The Art of Rhetoric*, 1.2, 245–61. Rhetoric as a term was possibly first used by Socrates in the fifth century and later featured in Plato's dialogue *Gorgias*. Although rhetoric predates Aristotle, his oft-cited *The Art of Rhetoric* was the first treatise on rhetorical theory and has been influential in the study of rhetoric since. Kennedy, *A New History of Classical Rhetoric*, 3, 35–39, 51–63.

18. Quintilian *Inst. Or.*, 11.1.43–56; Gempf, "Public Speaking and Published Accounts," 259–303, at 263.

19. Aristotle, *The Art of Rhetoric*, 1.3; Kennedy, *A New History*, 3–4; Mack, *Rhetoric and the New Testament*, 34; Witherington III, *What's in the Word: Rethinking the Socio-Rhetorical Character of the New Testament*, 13.

20. Edwards Jr., *A History of Preaching*, 12; Witherington, *New Testament Rhetoric*, 15–16.

21. Edwards Jr., *A History of Preaching*, 12; Witherington, *New Testament Rhetoric*, 15–16; Carey, "Rhetorical Means of Persuasion," 26–45, at 26–27 (and see n2).

22. Witherington, *New Testament Rhetoric*, 7; See also: Aristotle, *The Art of Rhetoric*, 3.13–19; Quintilian, *Inst. Or.*, 4.1–5; Mack, *Rhetoric*, 41–42; Witherington III, *Conflict and Community in Corinth: A Socio-Rhetorical Commentary on 1 and 2 Corinthians*, 44. Deliberative speeches had the same features as judicial ones, but had greater flexibility, including not having to include narration. Epideictic speeches simply required an introduction, body and conclusion. Edwards Jr., *A History of Preaching*, 13.

probatio: arguments that support the proposition; v. *refutatio:* refutation of opposing arguments; vi. *peroratio:* summary of the argument and final appeal.[23]

The impact and influence of rhetoric in the New Testament has been a significant area of study in recent years. There is both a recognition of some aspects of Greco-Roman rhetoric employed by various New Testament authors, and an ambivalence towards rhetoric in other respects.[24] While there is general scholarly consensus regarding evidence of micro-rhetoric within the New Testament documents, there is conjecture about the evidence for macro-rhetoric.[25] The speech summaries in Acts, however, are well recognized as evidencing rhetoric at macro level.[26] As both Witherington and Satterthwaite note, the rhetorical nature of the presentation of the material in Acts, and the speeches in particular, do not simply reflect the rhetorical nature of their sources.[27] They also reflect the rhetorical skill of both Luke as the author of Acts and of those who delivered the actual speeches (e.g., Peter, Stephen, and Paul).[28] As evangelists, both Luke and those whose speech summaries he records were not seeking merely to present information but rather to present it in such a way as to persuade their respective audiences, a feature that will be highlighted later in this chapter.[29]

---

23. Figures of sound (alliteration, assonance), figures of speech, as well as figures of thought were all part of the rhetorician's arsenal. Edwards Jr., *A History*, 14.

24. Kennedy, *A New History*, 258–59; Pernot, *Rhetoric in Antiquity*, 203.

25. Witherington, *What's in the Word*, 13. For a critique of the view within rhetorical criticism that applies the categories of Greco-Roman rhetoric to the New Testament documents (particularly as espoused by Ben Witherington), see Porter and Dyer, "Oral Texts? A Reassessment of the Oral and Rhetorical Nature of Paul's Letters in Light of Recent Studies," 323–41.

26. Witherington, *New Testament Rhetoric*, 16, 19, 44; Schnabel, *Acts*, 112. Chapters 4 and 5 will also argue that John Chrysostom's homilies strongly reflect his training in the rhetorical tradition under the rhetorician Libanius.

27. The sources used by Luke include both oral tradition and written sources.

28. Witherington, *New Testament Rhetoric*, 45; Satterthwaite, "Acts Against the Background of Classical Rhetoric," 337–79; Kennedy, *A New History*, 258; Perelman and Olbrechts-Tyteca, *The New Rhetoric: A Treatise on Argumentation*, 7.

29. For further on rhetoric in Acts and the New Testament in general, see Black II, "The Rhetorical Form of the Hellenistic Jewish and Early Christian Sermon: A Response to Lawrence Wills," 1–18; Kinneavy, *Greek Rhetorical Origins of the Christian Faith: An Inquiry*; Kennedy, *New Testament Interpretation through Rhetorical Criticism*; Betz, *Galatians: A Commentary on Paul's Letter to the Churches in Galatia*.

3.4 The speeches in Acts

Speeches played an important role in ancient historical documents, particularly for "educated audiences."[30] While the speeches in Acts do not fit the classical Greek pattern, and may have been significantly influenced by "Jewish rhetorical conventions," the speeches in Acts nevertheless display familiarity with and even some reliance upon Greek rhetorical conventions.[31]

The speeches in Acts make up almost one third of the text in Acts.[32] That Luke devotes such a significant amount of his narrative to speeches is not surprising when one considers the nature and purpose of his work. Scholars offer a number of suggestions regarding the purpose and function of the speeches in Acts. For example: speeches link the various parts of the narrative and help hold it together; they provide clues to Luke's theological interpretation of events; they explain the gospel and provide examples of the gospel being contextually preached to different audiences (Jewish/Gentile); they have an apologetic function, defending the legitimacy of the Christian gospel against both Jewish and Roman antagonists.[33] Keener is surely right to conclude on this point that "Acts must include a significant proportion of material including speeches because proclamation is the focus of his work."[34] In Acts, the historian Luke is not only tracing the historical impact and spread of the Christian gospel in the first century, but also outlining the content of that proclaimed gospel.[35]

There has been considerable debate regarding the historicity of the speeches in Acts.[36] On one side of the debate are those who doubt the historical accuracy of the speeches.[37] These scholars consider Luke to have paid minimal or no attention to an actual event that took place; rather, he constructed the speeches as deemed appropriate to the situation. In this view,

---

30. Keener, *Acts: An Exegetical Commentary*, 1:259. For a detailed treatment of the speeches in Acts, see Soards, *The Speeches in Acts: Their Content, Context and Concerns*.

31. Keener, *Acts*, 1:259–60.

32. Polhill, *Acts*, 43. Pollhill states that approximately 300 of the 1000 verses in Acts are devoted to speeches.

33. Keener, *Acts*, 1:264–7.

34. Keener, *Acts*, 1:261.

35. Keener similarly argues that one of the purposes of Acts was to provide a "model for missions." The speeches then serve not only an apologetic function but also provide various models for mission that could guide Luke's audience in their evangelistic endeavors. Keener, *Acts*, 1:262, 266.

36. Bock, *Acts*, 20; Keener, *Acts*, 1:258.

37. Bock, *Acts*, 21.

the speeches are primarily literary or theological devices, or conventions of ancient historiography used for the purposes of narrative development and unity and a mechanism for presenting the theological argument of the book.[38] Conversely, another group of scholars acknowledge that the speeches in Acts reflect Luke's editorial work on his various sources, yet at the same time are historically accurate speech summaries based on actual events.[39]

Colin Hemer outlines the three key objections to claiming the speeches are faithful summaries and then provides rebuttals to each objection. First, to the objection that the ancient standard of historiography would naturally have led to the invention of speeches when it suited the author's intention, Hemer replies that ancient historians wrote with academic rigor and that recorded speeches sought to remain as true as possible to the actual speech.[40] Second, to the objection that the style and vocabulary between the speeches and that of the whole book of Acts is too similar, showing there was only one composer, Hemer argues that the speech summaries are Lukan summaries and so naturally reflect Luke's style and theology.[41] Third, to the objection that there is a "continuity of content" across the speeches in Acts, irrespective of the nominated speaker, Hemer demonstrates that this view is inaccurate. Citing the Miletus speech (Acts 20:17-38) as one example, Hemer identifies various linguistic, biographical, and theological characteristics that are distinctly Pauline.[42] Hemer concludes that the speeches in

---

38. Dibelius, *Studies in the Acts of the Apostles*, 138-85; Schweitzer, "Concerning the Speeches in Acts," in *Studies in Luke-Acts: Essays Presented in Honour of Paul Schubert*, 208-16; Horsley, "Speeches and Dialogues in Acts," 609-14; Fitzmyer, *The Acts of the Apostles*, 103-8.

39. Dodd, *The Apostolic Preaching*, 7-24; Bruce, *The Book of Acts*, 34-40; Polhill, *Acts*, 43-47; Keener, *Acts*, 1:925-7; Larkin Jr., *Acts*, 55; Witherington, *Acts*, 46-49; Peterson, *Acts*, 19-29. Scholarly consensus regards the recorded speeches in Acts in the same light as other recorded speeches in antiquity—that is, they are summaries, not complete transcripts. Hemer, *The Book of Acts in the Setting of Hellenistic History*, 418. Gempf's view is representative when he writes, "It is a fact that the major historians of the ancient world liberally sprinkled accounts of speeches in their narratives. These accounts, although very often presented in the form of direct speech, are not transcripts of the speeches presented at the occasion." Gempf, "Public Speaking," 263-4. In this article Gempf also argues that any historical speech, including those in Acts, should not be evaluated in terms of whether or not they are accurate transcripts/summaries of the reported speeches but rather whether they are faithful/unfaithful records of the particular historical events (see particularly, pp. 302-3). Cf. Peterson, *Acts*, 384.

40. Hemer, *The Book of Acts*, 420-1.

41. Ibid., 420, 421-4.

42. Ibid., 420, 424-6; Schnabel, *Acts*, 128, similarly argues that the content and theological perspectives across the speeches are sufficiently diverse to counter the suggestion of Luke having invented the content of the speeches.

Acts reflect faithful Lukan summaries rather than Luke's authorial creations designed to further his theological purposes.[43] Ancient historians did not have permission to fabricate speeches, but rather were required to record them accurately, "though in the words of the historian, and always with the reservation that the historian could clarify."[44] Peterson expresses this same thought when he concludes,

> Although we must allow for Luke's own influence in the editorial process, there are sufficient differences between the sermons with respect to style and content to warrant the conclusion that they substantially reflect the standpoint of the preachers to whom they are attributed.[45]

Keener similarly states:

> Virtually no scholars publishing in mainstream academic circles argue that the speeches in Acts are verbatim. Verbatim reproduction of speeches was not possible, expected, or necessarily even desirable in ancient historiography . . . All scholars agree that the speeches in Luke are compositions.[46]

Therefore, however one interprets the speeches in Acts, what is apparent is that Luke has recorded at best summaries of the speeches, something

---

43. Hemer, *The Book of Acts*, 427. Cf. Gempf, "Public Speaking," 263–4.

44. Fornara, *The Nature of History in Ancient Greece and Rome*, 145.

45. Peterson, *Acts*, 384; Hengel, *Acts and the History of Earliest Christianity*, 87–98. Dean Flemming acknowledges that "Paul's" sermons in Acts, for example, are not Paul's record of his own preaching but a Lukan presentation of what was said. Luke's reports of these sermons are not verbatim transcripts but rather summaries of what Paul said at different times, which Luke's readers would expect to be faithful representations of what was said. Flemming states that although throughout his book he will refer to "Paul" as the preacher of a particular sermon it is with the understanding that " . . . what Paul says in Acts . . . also reflects Luke's own literary and rhetorical concerns." By extension, this would also apply to Peter's sermons or anyone else's in Acts. See Flemming, *Contextualization*, 56n1. Here he also references Porter, *The Paul of Acts: Essays in Literary Criticism, Rhetoric and Theology*, which argues strongly for the coherence between Paul as represented in Acts and Paul in his letters. This thesis reflects the same understanding and approach as Flemming, and will refer to "Paul's" sermons or "Peter's"sermons in Acts as a shorthand way of saying "Luke's presentation of Paul/Peter' etc. For further discussion on the authenticity of the speeches in Acts, see Keener, *Acts*, 1:271–84, 309–11.

46. Keener, *Acts*, 1:309; Schnabel, *Acts*, 127, gives two key reasons why scholars do not think the speeches in Acts are recorded verbatim: 1. The recorded speeches are too short to be actual speeches, with Luke sometimes indicating that more was said that he did not record (e.g., Acts 2:40); 2. Peter most likely spoke in Aramaic but Luke wrote in Greek, so at best Luke has provided Greek translations of what Peter said.

that Luke also expected his audience to understand.⁴⁷ Luke sought to preserve "the authentic theological message and traits of the speakers, albeit selectively," adjusting them to fit his larger work of Acts.⁴⁸

The epistemological approach to the speeches in Acts that I adopt in this thesis is critical realism, which views the Lukan narratives having several strata which overlay each other.⁴⁹ The first strata is that of the actual speeches by the original speakers themselves, which were contextualized to their audiences. The second strata is that of the Lukan summaries of these speeches as recorded in the book of Acts, which itself is a contextualized document,⁵⁰ persuasively written to a target audience for the purpose of presenting an apologetic history.⁵¹ When examined from a missiological perspective, this second strata at least can be examined for the presence of objective contextual principles which can then potentially contribute to the current contextualization debate. This investigative method therefore takes into account the co-location of these principles in both the speeches as originally preached and the Lukan summaries of those sermons, as well my own interpretive activity.

3.5 Preaching to the Jewish Diaspora in Jerusalem (Acts 2:1-40)

3.5.1 Context, audience and setting.

Context: This sermon in Jerusalem comes at a critical time in Acts as it launches the early church's mission. Jesus has ascended to heaven leaving the disciples in Jerusalem with both a promise and a task (Acts 1:6-11). The promise was that that they would soon be baptized by the Holy Spirit (1:4-5, 8). The Holy Spirit would empower them for the task of being μάρτυρες to the life, death, and resurrection of Jesus (1:8; cf. 1:22). Their witness was not to be confined to their present locale in Jerusalem but was to extend throughout all of Palestine (ἐν πάσῃ τῇ Ἰουδαίᾳ καὶ Σαμαρείᾳ) and then to the ends of the earth (Acts 1:8). Matthias is chosen as a replacement for Judas, and, along with the other eleven apostles, becomes part of the leadership of a symbolically restored Israel (1:12-26; cf. 1 Kgs 12:16-20; Acts

---

47. Keener, *Acts*, 1:260.
48. Keener, *Acts*, 1:318.
49. Osmer, *Practical Theology: An Introduction*, 74.
50. Flemming, Contextualisation, 26-28.
51. See from 3.1 to 3.4 (inclusive).

1:6).⁵² Despite Peter's previous denial of Jesus, he emerges as the leader and spokesperson for the gathered disciples (Luke 22:54-62; Acts 1:15-).

Audience and setting: In fulfillment of Jesus' promise (ἐν τῷ συμπληροῦσθαι, Acts 2:1; cf. 1:4-5; Luke 9:51), the Holy Spirit descends on the gathered believers in Jerusalem (2:1-5a).⁵³ The Spirit was physically manifested through sound (ἦχος ὥσπερ φερομένης πνοῆς βιαίας), sight (γλῶσσαι ὡσεὶ πυρός) and speech (ἤρξαντο λαλεῖνἑτέραις γλώσσαις, 2:2-4). This event occurred on the day of Pentecost, part of the Jewish festival the Feast of Weeks (2:1; cf. Exod 34:22a; Deut 16:10),⁵⁴ and attracted Jews from παντὸς ἔθνους τῶν ὑπὸ τὸν οὐρανόν who were part of the Jewish Diaspora (Acts 2:5).⁵⁵ The unusual sound brought these Diaspora Jews together with the gathered disciples, but this led to further bewilderment and amazement at hearing Galileans speaking to them in their own languages from right across the Mediterranean world: Parthians, Medes, Elamites; residents of Mesopotamia, Judea, Cappadocia, Pontus, Asia, Phrygia, Pamphylia, Egypt, parts of Libya near Cyrene, Rome, and Cretans (Acts 2:6-11), not to mention resident Jews of Jerusalem itself (2:14). The gathered Diaspora crowd had witnessed the unusual phenomenon but needed the experience interpreted in light of their Jewish background, asking "What does this mean?" (2:12).⁵⁶ Some in the crowd explained the event by charging the disciples with drunkenness (2:13). Peter stood in their midst and preached a contextualized message which addressed the charge and gives a different explanation for the phenomena. His proclamation of the gospel "clarifies who Jesus really is and articulates the nature of the salvation he has made possible for all who repent and are baptized in his name."⁵⁷ In his paradigmatic address, Peter preached the first Christian sermon to Jews as a fellow Jew, interpreting the events the crowd had just witnessed in light of their shared Jewish heritage and history.⁵⁸

---

52. Peterson, *Acts*, 126.
53. Ibid., 131.
54. Bruce, *The Book of Acts*, 49-50.
55. In Acts 2:5, the absence of Ἰουδαῖοι from א and placed in different parts of the verse in two other uncials has raised the question of whether Ἰουδαῖοι was inserted into later texts. It is more likely that Ἰουδαῖοι was in the original text but was either "dropped as seemingly contradictory to ὑπὸ τὸν οὐρανόν or moved to a position considered less objectionable from a stylistic point of view." Metzger, *A Textual Commentary on the Greek New Testament*, 251.
56. Witherington, *Acts*, 137. Cf. Keener, *Acts*, 1:868-9.
57. Peterson, *Acts*, 130.
58. As Witherington states, this sermon is paradigmatic of an articulation of the gospel by a Jew to a Jewish audience, and therefore contains "a fullness of expression

3.5.2 Peter's contextual approach

There are three features of Peter's recorded address in Acts 2:14–40 that reflect his contextual approach:

i. *His informal manner of address to the gathered Diaspora.* Like any good orator, Peter seeks to quickly establish rapport with his audience.[59] He does this by initially addressing his audience formally as ἄνδρες Ἰουδαῖοι ("men of Judea," Acts 2:14) and Ἀνδρες Ἰσραηλῖται ("men of Israel," 2:22), but later in his speech he uses the informal term ἀδελφοί ("brothers," 2:29). This, along with the fact that his audience also use ἀδελφοί to refer to Peter and the other apostles (2:37), is suggestive that Peter not only established early rapport but was progressively winning over his kinsmen.[60]

ii. *His knowledge and use of the shared narrative that shapes community.* Throughout his address Peter drew on the knowledge that he shared with his listeners, both of the Jewish Scriptures and of recent events concerning Jesus of Nazareth in Jerusalem (e.g., Acts 2:22, 23). Peter wished to convince his audience of the divinity of Jesus and the authority Jesus had over their lives, but he didn't start with this point (2:36). Some of those in the crowd had sought to explain away the Pentecost experience with the charge of drunkenness (2:12, 14). Peter countered the charge by offering an alternate explanation, appealing to the source that would have been considered the highest authority to the gathered Jews—their own Scriptures (2:15, 17–19).

In the recorded sermons to a Jewish audience of both Stephen (Acts 7:1–53) and Paul (13:16–41), the route taken to explaining the death and resurrection of Jesus was primarily a selective retelling of Jewish history, focused on the patriarchs and David, demonstrating that Jesus was a continuation and fulfillment of the history. In contrast, Peter's Pentecost sermon recounted little of Jewish history but rather had three distinctive foci. First, Peter quotes from texts familiar to his audience in order to explain the phenomenon the crowd had just

---

about what conversion entails that is not usually the case in the speeches that follow." Witherington, *Acts*, 139. Fernando adds that the large amount of space Luke dedicates to this speech means that Luke intended it to be an exemplar of evangelistic preaching. Fernando, *Acts*, 107.

59. Witherington, *New Testament Rhetoric*, 49.

60. Zehnle, *Peter's Pentecost Discourse: Tradition and Lukan Reinterpretation in Peter's speeches of Acts 2 and 3*, 27. Zehnle also notes Paul adopting the same method to win over his Jewish audience in Acts 13:16, 26, 38. Cf. Witherington, *Acts*, 138–9.

witnessed (e.g., Joel 2:28–32; Ps 16:8–11; 110:1; Acts 2:1–12).[61] Second, he highlights that Jesus is the Messiah and the implications for his hearers (e.g., 2:36–41). Third, Peter offers an alternate interpretation of these texts to what his hearers would have expected. He does this by placing Jesus of Nazareth as the new hermeneutical key for interpreting not just those texts but by implication all biblical texts. Peter's contextual approach of starting with, and also interacting with, texts that were familiar and authoritative to his hearers enabled many of his hearers to be progressively won over to his point of view (2:37, 41).[62]

iii. *His use of rhetoric.* As recorded in Acts 2:14–40, Peter carefully constructed his sermon in order to persuade his Jewish audience, with various elements of rhetorical speech evident.[63] The speech can be divided into two sections:

a. Acts 2:14–21: *Exordium* (2:14, where Peter addresses his audience), *narratio* (Acts 2:15-2, containing a *refutatio* [2:15, these men are not drunk as it is too early in the day]); *propositio* (2:17, their behavior is due to God's Spirit); *probatio* (2:17–21, this was predicted in Joel 2:28–32);

b. Acts 2:22–39: *Exordium* (2:22, Peter appeals again to his audience), *propositio* (2:24, God raised Jesus from the dead); *probatio and refutatio* (2:25–28, David prophesied that God's holy one would not be abandoned to death in Psalm 16:8–11; 2:29–31, and the Psalm wasn't about David because he died. Rather, it was about Jesus, who was raised from the dead and is now seated at the right hand of God as prophesied in Ps 16); *peroratio* (2:36–39, Jesus is both Lord and messiah, so save yourselves).[64]

---

61. It is more than likely that Peter quoted additional texts to the ones Luke records in Acts 2:14–31 (see Acts 2:40, ἑτέροις τε λόγοις πλείοσιν διεμαρτύρατο, καὶ παρεκάλει αὐτούς).

62. Witherington, *New Testament Rhetoric*, 49.

63. Witherington classifies Acts 2:14–36 as an example of forensic rhetoric, with 2:38–40 an example of deliberative rhetoric. Witherington, *Acts*, 138. Similarly, Mack, *Rhetoric*, 117. Keener furthermore finds evidence of Peter's use of rhetoric yet argues that, unlike the later speeches in Acts, Peter's speech is not as heavily influenced by rhetorical devices. He attributes this to Peter's Jewish background which likely meant he had had little exposure to Greco-Roman rhetoric. Keener, *Acts*, 1:862–3.

64. Mack, *Rhetoric*, 89–92. George Kennedy identifies Luke using both judicial and deliberative rhetoric in his presentation of this speech. He also asserts, without any justification, that Acts 2:16–40 is a Lukan insertion which functions simply to highlight and explain the events narrated in Luke 2:1–4. As previously stated, another explanation is that Luke was accurately summarizing an event that actually occurred

The response to Peter's speech suggests significant rhetorical success in persuading his audience (2:37, 41).[65]

3.5.3 Peter's contextual message

Having addressed the accusation that the glossolalia witnessed by the Jewish crowd was not evidence of drunkenness but rather the pouring out of the Holy Spirit as prophesied by Joel (Acts 2:14-21; cf. Joel 2:28-32), Peter takes the opportunity to further explain the salvific work of the Lord that the prophecy referred to (Joel 2:32).[66] Some of the major themes in Peter's contextual gospel message are: the centrality of Jesus Christ;[67] the humanity and divinity of Jesus (Acts 2:22, 36); the unjust crucifixion of Jesus (2:23, 36); the vindication of Jesus through his bodily resurrection from the dead by God (Acts 2:24-35); the fulfillment of Scripture (Acts 2:25-31, 34-35);[68] forgiveness of sins and receiving of the Holy Spirit is now possible, through repentance (Acts 2:38b, 38c, 38a); and, *the necessity of salvation through Jesus Christ* (Acts 2:38-40).

3.5.4 Conclusion to Peter's Pentecost sermon

Peter's Pentecost sermon to the Jewish Diaspora in Jerusalem is a highly contextualized proclamation of the gospel to his audience—both in method and message. The glossolalia of the gathered group of believers brought about through the Holy Spirit's descent upon them provides Peter with the opportunity not only to explain this phenomenon but to explain the

---

rather than fabricating the event for rhetorical purposes. Kennedy, *New Testament Interpretation*, 117.

65. Witherington, *New Testament Rhetoric*, 49; Mack, *Rhetoric*, 118. Witherington helpfully highlights a well-known rhetorical device that Luke makes use of throughout the speeches in Acts—that of "summary." Luke states upfront that he is "deliberately summarizing his material" and selectively presenting material particularly pertinent to the occasion (Acts 2:40a). Witherington, *Acts*, 139.

66. Keener, *Acts*, 1:872-3.

67. Of the seventeen verses in Peter's recorded speech to the Jewish Diaspora, sixteen verses refer to Jesus Christ.

68. The striking note that Peter sounds is that not only was the pouring out of the Holy Spirit and accompanying glossolalia a fulfillment of Scripture, but so was the resurrection of Jesus (Ps 16:8-11, cf. Acts 2:25-31). Importantly for his Jewish hearers, Jesus is not a departure from Judaism so much as the fulfillment of it. Jesus is the one to whom the Scriptures pointed and the hermeneutical key for their interpretation (Acts 2:25a, 30-31, 34-36).

death and resurrection of Jesus. Speaking as a fellow Jew, Peter explains that not only is the witnessed glossolalia a fulfillment of the Jewish Scriptures but so is the life, death, resurrection, ascension and lordship of Jesus. The speech is the first of many in Acts where Jesus' identity and significance are explained.[69] Jesus is the hermeneutical key to understanding the Jewish Scriptures, the long-awaited Jewish messiah, and the ruling Lord of the universe. The proper response to Jesus' lordship is repentance and faith.

Three points that relate to the proclamation of the gospel in Acts can be taken from Peter's Pentecost sermon. First, the kerygma that Peter proclaims is centered on Jesus Christ, climaxing in his death and resurrection. His unjust treatment and crucifixion, and his vindication through being raised from the dead, has resulted in forgiveness of sin and freedom from the weight of the law, available to everyone who believes in Jesus Christ. Second, the sermon before Jews in Jerusalem is an exemplary model of someone contextualizing their message to suit their audience. Using the tools of ancient rhetoric, Peter sought to persuade his audience through drawing on common ground, drawing on their own Scriptures, and interacting with their Jewish worldview. In doing so, Peter is able to communicate the gospel to his audience in ways that would have made sense to them. Third, Jesus is presented as the fulfillment of and interpretive key for understanding the Jewish Scriptures, directly challenging the prevailing Jewish worldview. Not only had the Jews not recognized their own messiah but they had crucified him. Jesus stands as the savior of the world, fulfillment of the Davidic promise and Jewish Scripture. Only through Jesus can people find forgiveness of sin and freedom, unobtainable through the Law of Moses.

3.6 Preaching to the Jewish Council in Jerusalem (Acts 7:1–60)

3.6.1 Context, audience and setting

Context: Stephen is first introduced in Acts 6:5 and a considerable amount of background is given before his speech in 7:1–60 (cf. 6:5–15). Stephen is a recognized leader in the church, one of those chosen to serve alongside the apostles (6:5–6). He is described as a man full of faith, full of the Holy Spirit, full of grace and full of wisdom, doing great signs and wonders among the people (6:5, 8, 10). Stephen's sermon is the third recorded speech of a leader in the early church before the Jewish authorities, with hostility towards the early Christians intensified from warnings (4:17–18), to flogging (5:40–41),

---

69. Schnabel, *Acts*, 109.

to stoning (7:58-60).[70] As Witherington notes, from Luke's perspective the death of Stephen results in a crisis for the early church in Jerusalem, and it is a pivotal juncture in the narrative of Acts with local persecution breaking out. The result is the scattering of the believers across the regions of Judea and Samaria (cf. 8:1-4; 11:19; 22:20).[71] Ironically, the consequence of this persecution is the advancement of the gospel throughout these regions as it is spread by the dispersed believers (8:1—9:43). From this point the focus of the Acts narrative shifts from the spread of the gospel in Jerusalem to its spread throughout Judea, Samaria, and the ends of the earth (cf. 1:8).[72] Saul, briefly introduced at the conclusion of the chapter (7:59), becomes the dominant character of the Acts narrative (from 13:1).[73]

As the longest of the recorded speeches in Acts, the length of Stephen's speech may suggest its importance for Luke.[74] In his description of the unjust trial and persecution of Stephen, Luke portrays Stephen as being in continuity with Jesus and most notably the Old Testament prophets themselves.[75] Stephen's speech is a model sermon of gospel contextualization, to a Jewish Diaspora audience, in the context of persecution.

Audience and setting: Various members of one or more synagogues in Jerusalem disputed what Stephen was teaching but were unable to defeat his arguments due to his Spirit-inspired σοφίᾳ (Acts 6:10; cf. 6:3).[76] The synagogue members were fellow Diaspora Jews, from a variety of locations— Africa (Cyrenians and Alexandrians), Cilicia and Asia (6:9). Paul may well

---

70. Stephens's ministry is described in similar terms to that of the apostles. Cunningham notes the similarity in Acts 3-7 between the negative treatment the apostles received at the hands of the Jewish Council and that which Stephen receives, with Stephen's death the climax to the growing persecution of the believers. Scott Cunningham, "*Through Many Tribulations: The Theology of Persecution in Luke-Acts,*" 204-5. Cf. Schnabel, *Acts*, 340-1.

71. Witherington, *Acts*, 252. He also notes that this is the first occasion where the Jewish people in general and not just the authorities are antagonistic towards the early church.

72. Cunningham, "*Through Many Tribulations,*" 205.

73. Ibid., 205.

74. Witherington, *Acts*, 251.

75. Keener, *Acts*, 2:1311, 1326-7. For a comparison between the passions of Jesus and Stephen, see Witherington, *Acts*, 253.

76. Lack of clarity in the Greek syntax has led to a dispute as to how many synagogues are being referred to in Acts 6:9. Some suggestions include: one (synagogue of freedmen); two (one with Cyrenians and Alexandrians, the other with Cilicians and Asians; and four (one each with Cyrenians, Alexandrians, Cilicians, Asians). There is insufficient evidence to determine the number definitively. Keener, *Acts*, 2:1302-10; Bock, *Acts*, 270.

have grown up in this synagogue and been one of Stephen's opponents (6:9; 7:58; 22:3).[77] Stephen himself may even have been a former member of the synagogue.[78] In any case, Stephen's Hellenist opponents are vigorous defenders of the temple and Jewish Torah (Acts 6:13-14). Stephen's opponents conspire against him and stir up the people, elders and scribes, resulting in false charges of blasphemy being laid against him (6:12-14).[79] Stephen is brought before the Jewish Sanhedrin and asked by the high priest to speak to the charges (6:12; 7:1).[80] In the context of a hostile crowd of Jewish leaders, Diaspora Jews and the rest of the people gathered there (τὸν λαὸν, 6:12), Stephen addresses his fellow Diaspora Jews, tailoring his address to make it understandable for his Jewish audience.

3.6.2 Stephen's contextual approach

Stephen had been charged with speaking blasphemously against God and against Moses (namely, the temple and the Law, Acts 7:11, 13-14). There are three features of Stephen's recorded address that reflect his contextual approach in seeking to convince his audience otherwise, showing both similarities and differences to Peter's approach in Acts 2.

 i. *His manner of address to the gathered Diaspora.* Stephen begins by addressing them as "brothers and fathers" (Ἄνδρες ἀδελφοὶ καὶ πατέρες, Acts 7:1). This appropriate and respectful address assists him in gaining an initial favorable hearing from his audience and immediately connects Stephen with his audience.[81] Stephen refers to "our fathers" (πατέρες ἡμῶν) eight times (7:2, 11, 12, 15, 38, 39, 44, 45) and "our race" (τὸ γένος ἡμῶν) once (7:19). Stephen's use of first person plural pronouns "continually reminds Stephen's (and Luke's) audience that he is a fellow Jew who shares in this story."[82]

---

77. Keener, *Acts*, 2:1309.
78. Williams, *Acts*, 124.
79. Keener, *Acts*, 2:1315-8, 1326.
80. Chance, *Acts*, 108.
81. Parsons, *Acts*, Paideia, 90. Bock further notes that Stephen addressing the Sanhedrin as πατέρες was very respectful. Bock, *Acts*, 281.
82. Parsons, *Acts*, 90; Bock, *Acts*, 282. In Peter's Pentecost sermon he uses familial terms on three occasions only: ἄνδρες Ἰουδαῖοι (Acts 2:14), Ἄνδρες Ἰσραηλῖται (Acts 2:22), and ἀδελφοί (Acts 2:29), in contrast to Stephen's use of ἀδελφοί eight times. However, it is likely that the reason lies in the different contexts in which the two speeches were given. Stephen delivered his speech in the context of significant opposition and threat, which was not the case for Peter, who had a far more neutral audience.

ii. *His use of Jewish history.* Stephen argues his case through narrating selective parts of Jewish history which he shared with his audience, drawing from Old Testament books including Leviticus, Numbers, Joshua, 1 Kings, 1–2 Chronicles, Nehemiah, Psalms, Jeremiah and Hosea (cf. Acts 2:14–40). He also quotes directly from the LXX itself (Genesis, Exodus, Deuteronomy, Amos and Isaiah; cf. Acts 7:42b–43, 49–50).[83] The Scriptures were authoritative for Stephen's audience and therefore added considerable weight to his argument. Furthermore, narrating from his audience's own history would have had the effect of helping him maintain favor with his audience and have them listen to his defense for a longer period than they might have otherwise.

iii. *His use of rhetoric.* Darrell Bock describes the rhetorical structure of Stephen's speech as: *exordium* (call to hear; Acts 7:2a); *narratio* (preparatory discourse; 7:2b–34); *propositio* (proposition; 7:35); *argumentatio* (argument-application; 7:36–50); and *peroratio* (polemical application; 7:51–53).[84] While Keener identifies this as a forensic speech with an offensive rather than defensive emphasis,[85] the seriousness of the charges and the hostility of his audience meant that Stephen chose his rhetorical approach carefully. Witherington calls Stephen's approach *insinuatio*, stating:

> A certain amount of indiscretion is needed if the audience is going to listen to this discourse at all. This speech is long precisely because of the adoption and adaption of this technique. It takes a good deal of building up before Stephen can really broach the real bone of contention. If it is to persuade at all it cannot be just

---

Stephen had to defend himself against the serious charge of blasphemy, which carried the death penalty (cf. Acts 7:58). In an effort to maintain favor with his audience and to encourage them to continue listening to his defense (instead of prematurely interrupting it), he interspersed his defense with familial references to the Jewish heritage he shared with his hearers. That Stephen seems to have been able to complete most of his speech suggests he was quite successful in his endeavor.

83. Schnabel, *Acts*, 362. Cf. Witherington, *New Testament Rhetoric*, 59.

84. Bock, *Acts*, 277. Dupont's rhetorical analysis identifies the elements of: *exordium* (Acts 7:2a), *narratio* (7:2b–34), *propositio* (7:35), *probatio* (7:36–50), *peroratio* (7:51–3). Dupont, "La structure oratoire du discours d'Etienne (Actes 7)," *Biblica* 66 (1985): 153–67, at 155–61. Cf. Witherington, *New Testament Rhetoric*, 59, contra Schnabel, who sees limited value in such analysis for this particular speech due to lack of scholarly agreement on its structure. Schnabel, *Acts*, 355.

85. Keener, *Acts*, 2:1332–3.

pure polemics; it must solicit and garner some approval of the audience along the way.[86]

One of the significant differences between Stephen's speech and any other speech in Acts is that almost the entire speech is devoted to narrating Jewish history (the exceptions being Acts 7:52–53, 56, 60) with Jesus only mentioned briefly at the speech's end (Acts 7:52, 56).[87] Stephen focuses on Abraham (7:2–8a), Isaac and Jacob (7:8b), Joseph (7:9–16), Moses (7:17–43), the tabernacle and temple (7:44–50), before providing a sharp rebuke to his Jewish audience (7:51–53).[88] Stephen positively portrays each of the Old Testament Jewish figures while slowly introducing his opposition to the Jewish council he is addressing.[89] Stephen had been charged with speaking against both Moses (i.e. the Law) and the Jerusalem temple. Stephen skilfully defends himself against both accusations in a contextual address and an offensive approach. The main purpose of his speech is to criticize those throughout Jewish history who have rejected God's prophets and their prophetic message, with whom Stephen's hearers stand in continuity (7:51–53) and of those who hold "naïve assumptions" that God dwells in man-made structures such as the temple.[90]

3.6.3 Stephen's contextual message

Four significant themes dominate Stephen's contextual message.[91] First, throughout Israel's history God repeatedly raised up leaders, whom the Israelites consistently rejected. Second, throughout Israel's history they consistently rejected God and embraced idolatry. Third, throughout Israel's history they also failed to understand God's relationship to the tabernacle

---

86. Witherington, *New Testament Rhetoric*, 58.
87. Bock, *Acts*, 276.
88. Dupont, "La structure oratoire," 153.
89. Kennedy, *New Testament Interpretation*, 121. There is no evidence to support Kennedy's assertion that Stephen thinks there is no possibility of the Council understanding the place and importance of Jesus in Jewish history and for Jewish history.
90. Witherington, *New Testament Rhetoric*, 58.
91. Cf. Schnabel, *Acts*, 355.

and temple.[92] Fourth, Israel and her current leaders continue to make these same mistakes as their forebears.[93]

Stephen's speech enrages his hearers and he is soon dragged out of the city and stoned to death. Ironically, the Jewish leaders have continued the very pattern which Stephen spoke out against—rejecting and killing God's appointed leader.

3.6.4 Conclusion to Stephen's sermon in Jerusalem

Stephen's sermon before his Jewish accusers and the Sanhedrin in Jerusalem is a highly contextualized speech—both in method and message. Having had accusations of speaking against the temple and against the Law brought against him, Stephen is invited by the Sanhedrin to defend the charges. Stephen's counter to the charges through the constraints of forensic rhetoric is in many ways a classic argument of defense. Through use of biblical examples Stephen redefines the charge brought against him and demonstrates the exact opposite—that he (the defendant) is innocent, while his accusers are guilty of precisely the charge they have brought against him.[94] Beginning with Abraham, Stephen selectively traces Israel's history by highlighting key figures such as Jacob, Joseph, and Moses and argues that Israel's history is one of God's people consistently rejecting God's appointed leaders. Stephen further highlights Israel's historical penchant for inappropriate worship—both through the repeated embrace of idolatry along with the false understanding of the relationship between God and the tabernacle and temple. Stephen concludes his address by accusing his hearers of being stiff-necked

---

92. It is important to note that up to this point Stephen has not said anything against the temple, or anything to which his Jewish hearers could really object. Stephen has simply carefully recounted select parts of Israel's history which have demonstrated his respect for Moses, the law and the temple—countering the false charges that had been brought against him (6:13–14). Peterson, *Acts*, 265; Bock, *Acts*, 303–4.

93. As a further indictment, Stephen states that the current Jewish leadership are even more guilty than their forefathers, for while their forefathers persecuted and killed the prophets who predicted the coming of the Righteous One (Jesus), these leaders are guilty of betraying and murdering the very Righteous One that the prophets predicted would come. As Bock insightfully comments, "Regarding charges of violating God's will, the roles are reversed, according to Stephen. It is not he who breaks the law, as the Jews have charged. Rather, it is his accusers who have broken the law and covenant by slaying the Righteous One." Bock, *Acts*, 306.

94. Cf. the discussion about Palladius' use of forensic rhetoric in the *Dialogue on the Life of St John Chrysostom* to acquit Chrysostom and impugn his persecutors in, Demetrios Katos, "Socratic Dialogue or Courtroom Debate? Judicial Rhetoric and Stasis Theory in the *Dialogue on the Life of St John Chrysostom*," 42–69.

and having uncircumcised hearts and ears—just like their forefathers. This indeed is prophetic, as just like their forefathers, his Jewish hearers reject and murder God's appointed leader.

Stephen's answer to the charges brought against him "shows why the church must move beyond the temple and the law."[95] Stephen's speech points away from such Israelite institutions and instead points to the God behind these institutions.[96] Stephen was the first person in the early church to realize that, not just Judaism, but also the early church had to "expand beyond Jewish categories" such as the law and temple, with his speech in effect functioning in Acts as a "farewell speech to Judaism" and setting the course for the early church to embark on mission to the Gentiles.[97]

Three points that relate to the proclamation of the gospel in Acts can be made from Stephen's sermon to the Jewish Sanhedrin. First, there is a significant degree of flexibility evident in the content of Stephen's contextualized message when compared with Peter's Pentecost sermon. While Peter highlights a number of messianic texts and argues for Jesus as the fulfillment of them, Stephen's speech is far more of a selective summary of Israel's history designed to highlight her history of rejecting God and his appointed leaders. Stephen barely mentions Jesus, and only right at the end of his speech, although this may have been because his speech was interrupted by the hostile reception. If Stephen had been able to finish his speech, he may well have spoken more about Jesus, as is evidenced in Peter's speech. Second, Stephen's sermon is an exemplary model of someone contextualizing their message to suit their audience. Using the tools of ancient rhetoric, Stephen drew on common ground and on their knowledge of the Scriptures, while interacting with their Jewish worldview. While the Jewish leaders ultimately rejected Stephen's message, their strong reaction indicates that they understood it. The third point is that both the speeches of Peter and Stephen are examples of contextualization to their own cultural group. Both were Jews, speaking to fellow Jews. Whereas Peter's sermon is focused on highlighting his Jewish audience's ignorance of Jesus the Messiah and their need to respond in repentance and faith, Stephen's speech is different. In essence, Stephen's speech draws a line under Judaism, demonstrating the failure of his audience to faithfully keep their own religion, and opens the door for Gentiles to become believers.[98]

---

95. Keener, *Acts*, 2:1330.
96. Ibid., 2:1331.
97. Keener, *Acts*, 2:1330. Cf. Peterson, *Acts*, 244–5.
98. What is also being evidenced here in Stephen's speech is Luke's own progressive message, which moves from an insider approach to mission directed at Jews, to an

3.7 Preaching in the synagogue in Pisidian Antioch (Acts 13:13–47)

3.7.1 Context, audience and setting

Context: The sermon at the synagogue in Pisidian Antioch comes at an important moment in the church's mission in Acts. Up to this point the church's mission focus had been almost exclusively on the Jews (Acts 2:5, 14; 3:1–26; 4:1–4; 9:20–30; 13:5–6).[99] But with the emergence of Paul's ministry, and following Jewish rejection of the gospel, the emphasis shifts towards mission to the Gentiles (9:1–35; 11:25–30; 12:25; 13:1–12). This sermon is the only detailed record of Paul preaching in a synagogue, although some of its features are reflected in shorter accounts that occur elsewhere in Acts where he addresses Jewish audiences (e.g., 17:2–3; 18:5–6; 19:8; cf. 2:14–40; 3:11–26; 4:8–12; 7:1–53).[100] As well as being a message delivered to a specific audience at a particular time, Luke's presentation of this sermon is a model or exemplar sermon to a synagogue audience of Greek-speaking Diaspora Jews.[101]

Audience and Setting: Pisidian Antioch was a Roman colony and the most important city in the southern region of the province of Galatia, serving as a strategic military and political center.[102] It was a cosmopolitan city of approximately ten thousand people, with a substantial Jewish population.[103] Eckhard Schnabel identifies seven different groups of people in Pisidian Antioch with whom Paul and his companions had contact: i. the officials of the synagogue (Acts 13:5); ii. Jews who attended the synagogue on the Sabbath (13:14); iii. devout proselytes (13:43); iv. God-fearers (13:16); v. devout

---

approach that is directed to Gentile outsiders (cf. Acts 1:8).

99. In Acts 10–11 the gentile mission is introduced. While Stephen's speech is a highly contextualized speech, what we also see in Luke's speech summary of Stephen's sermon is Luke contextualizing the gospel message for his own audience and recording the historical speech in such a way that it acts as a forensic defense against Jewish criticism of Christianity.

100. Williams, *Acts*, 229; Peterson, *Acts*, 384.

101. Flemming, *Contextualization*, 57. Keener further argues that what Luke is doing in this episode in Pisidian Antioch is introducing early on in Paul's ministry a typical (even paradigmatic) mission scenario that Paul faced and then "providing salvation-historical justification for preaching also to the Gentiles and revealing the conflicts attending mission." Keener, *Acts*, 2:2026.

102. Schnabel, *Early Christian Mission Vol. II: Paul and the Early Church*, 1098.

103. Ibid., 1103–4; Bock, *Acts*, 450. Keener notes that while Antioch may have had a large Jewish population, some of the non-Lukan evidence that supports this claim is now questioned. Keener, *Acts*, 2:2043, n660.

Gentile women of prominent standing in the city (Acts 13:50); vi. Gentile inhabitants of Antioch who came to listen to Paul's sermon but who were not God-fearers or devout Gentile women (14:44); vii. the leading men of the city (13:50).[104] Paul's address, at the invitation of the synagogue rulers (13:15), is to both Jewish people (Ἄνδρες Ἰσραηλῖται) and Gentiles who had not yet become proselytes (οἱ φοβούμενοι τὸν θεόν).[105] In the context of the synagogue, the center of Jewish and religious life, Paul tailors his address by speaking as a Jew to fellow Jews, using the common "framework of the Jewish Scriptures and the worship of the God of Israel."[106]

3.7.2 Paul's contextual approach

There are three features of Paul's recorded address that reflect his contextual approach:

i. *Paul's use of ancient rhetoric.* Reflecting ancient rhetorical aims, Paul carefully structured his speech in order to persuade his synagogue audience.[107] The speech's structure is consistent with the traditional forms of rhetorical speech, having a *narratio*, *argumentatio* and *peroratio*.[108] Hence, in Acts 13:16–42: *narratio* (13:16b–25, selective summary of salvation history); *argumentatio* (13:26–37, the significance of Jesus to this salvation history and to the synagogue audience); and *peroratio* (13:38–41, a plea for repentance).[109] According to Witherington, the speech "not only has the form of deliberative rhetoric but it reflects the patterns of early Jewish augmentation."[110] J. W. Bowker

---

104. Schnabel, *Early Christian Mission*, 1103–4. Cf. Bock, *Acts*, 451.

105. Acts 13:16.

106. Flemming, *Contextualization*, 58.

107. Ibid., 58. Cf. Witherington, *Acts*, 408.

108. Schnabel, *Paul the Missionary*, 158. Cf. Fitzmyer, *The Acts of the Apostles*, 506–7; Keener, *Acts*, 2:2054.

109. Schnabel, *Paul the Missionary*, 158; Fitzmyer, *The Acts of the Apostles*, 506–7; Black, "The Rhetorical Form," 8–10; Witherington, *New Testament Rhetoric*, 63. Lawrence Wills similarly argues that Paul's speech in Acts 13:16–41 is based on the basic pattern of: i. *exempla*—quotations from Scripture or other authoritative evidence (13:16b–37); ii. a *conclusion*—drawn from the evidence presented and applied to the lives of those being addressed (13:38–9); iii. an *exhortation* based on that conclusion. Lawrence Wills, "The Form of the Sermon in Hellenistic Judaism and Early Christianity," 277–99. He also argues that this same pattern is found in other λόγος παρακλήσεως ("words of exhortation"), e.g., Heb 2:1; 3:1; 4:1, 14b–16; 1 *Clem.* 7.2; 13.1a; 40.1b. Wills, "The Form of the Sermon," 281–2, 284–5.

110. Witherington, *Acts*, 408.

further argues that the speeches to Jewish audiences as recorded in Acts generally, and Paul's speech in 13:16-41 in particular, reflect the form of a Jewish proem homily, with the seder text being Deut 4:25-46 and the haftarah text 2 Sam 7:6-16.[111]

ii. *His identification with the religious heritage of the synagogue congregation.* Paul begins by respectfully addressing the synagogue rulers (ἄνδρες Ἰσραηλῖται, Acts 13:16).[112] Having established rapport with his largely Jewish audience, he immediately identifies their common ground—their Jewish ancestry. Paul was a fellow Jew (see Phil 3:4b-6) and so could legitimately use phrases such as, "the God of the people of Israel chose *our* fathers" (Acts 13:17)[113] and "what God promised the fathers he has fulfilled for *us*, their children" (13:32b-33a).[114]

iii. *His knowledge and use of the shared narrative that shapes community.* The particular good news that Paul was eager to proclaim (Acts 13:32)[115] was centered on Jesus Christ, particularly the forgiveness of sins that Jesus' death and resurrection made possible (13:26-41). But Paul doesn't begin his message with these points. Rather, just like Peter on the day of Pentecost (2:16-21) and Stephen before his stoning (7:1-47), Paul begins with the common history he shares with his hearers—that of the Jewish nation.[116] He recounts important moments in that history, such as: God's choice of the people of Israel (13:17a); their captivity in Egypt (13:17b); the Exodus (13:17c); the nation's forty years in the wilderness (13:18); their possession of the promised land under Joshua (13:19-20a); the period of the Judges (13:20b); and the kingships of Saul and David (13:21-22). Paul's tracing of Jewish history is selective and compressed, focusing on the Davidic kingship.[117]

---

111. Bowker, "Speeches in Acts: A Study in Proem and Yelammedenu Forms," 96-111. Bowker admits that his conclusions are tentative, particularly due to a lack of direct quotation of the seder and haftarah (either in Acts 13:15 or in Paul's response in Acts 13:16-42). Nevertheless, his argument is persuasive. Witherington outlines a number of other suggestions that have been put forward, particularly about the seder text, in Witherington, *A Socio-Rhetorical Commentary on Acts*, 408-9.

112. Keener, *Acts*, 2:2056.

113. ὁ θεὸς τοῦ λαοῦ τούτου Ἰσραὴλ ἐξελέξατο τοὺς πατέρας ἡμῶν. Emphasis mine.

114. τὴν πρὸς τοὺς πατέρας ἐπαγγελίαν γενομένην. Emphasis mine.

115. εὐαγγελιζόμεθα ("we proclaim the good news").

116. Gaventa, *Acts*, 198.

117. Peterson, "The Motif of Fulfilment and Purpose of Luke-Acts," in *The Book of Acts in its First Century Setting Vol. I: Ancient Literary Setting*, 83-104, at 99.

Through this selective historical account Paul is seeking to demonstrate the continuity between the history of Israel through the line of David and the story of Jesus. If his hearers were to embrace the good news about Jesus, they would not be embracing some new teaching divorced from their Jewish heritage but rather would be embracing the fulfillment of that heritage (13:32–33a).[118]

Having drawn from the Jewish history of many of the synagogue audience (Acts 13:17–22) and having introduced Jesus as a continuation and fulfillment of this history (13:23–32), Paul seeks to clinch his argument and draw out some of its implications through allusions to and direct quotations from the authoritative synagogue text itself—the Jewish Scriptures (13:33–35, 41, 47).[119] Starting with the Jewish texts Psalm 2:7 (13:33), Isaiah 55:3 (13:34), Psalm 16:10 (Acts 13:35), Habakkuk 1:5 (Acts 13:41), and standard Jewish interpretation of those texts,[120] Paul proceeds to offer what he sees as a more developed interpretation.[121] Paul does this by suggesting Jesus' death and resurrection is the fulfillment of these texts.[122] In doing so he introduces Jesus Christ as the hermeneutical key to the interpretation of all Jewish Scripture.

3.7.3 Paul's contextual message

Paul carefully weaves the kerygma, the "good news" (εὐαγγελιζόμεθα, Acts 13:32) that he proclaimed in the synagogue, into his contextual message to the Jewish synagogue. Eight important themes shape this kerygma: the centrality of Jesus Christ (13:23–39); the continuity of Jesus with Jewish history (13:22–23); the divinity of Jesus (Acts 13:33–35, 37b); the unjust crucifixion of Jesus (13:27–29); the vindication of Jesus through his bodily resurrection from the dead (13:30, 35, 37); the fulfillment of Scripture;[123] forgiveness and

---

118. Pelikan, *Acts*, 156.

119. Hansen, "The Preaching and Defence of Paul," in *Witness to the Gospel: The Theology of Acts*, 295–324, at 298–9.

120. Keener, *The IVP Bible Background Commentary: New Testament*, 360.

121. For how Paul was building on traditional Jewish understandings of these texts, Marshall, "Acts," in *Commentary on the New Testament Use of the Old Testament*, 582–7.

122. Hansen develops the idea of the resurrection being the focal point of Paul's sermon by stating that Paul demonstrates the resurrection of Jesus as the climax of salvation-history, the fulfillment of the Old Testament promise, and the basis for forgiveness of sins and justification by God. Hansen, "Preaching and Defence," 300–5.

123. The coming of Jesus as the savior of Israel (Acts 13:23), Jesus' rejection by his

freedom are now possible through Jesus (13:38b-39); and the necessity of salvation through Jesus Christ (13:38-41).

Both Flemming and Keener note significant parallels in the kerygma between Paul's inaugural sermon in the Jewish synagogue of Pisidian Antioch and Peter's inaugural sermon to the Diaspora Jews in Jerusalem.[124] These parallels may well have been Luke's way of communicating to his readers that there was just one apostolic gospel.[125] Yet, even if there was one apostolic core, there are still nuances in how the kerygma was presented, even amongst different Jewish audiences. The kerygma is contextualized to the particular Jewish audiences that are addressed.[126]

3.7.4 Conclusion to Paul's sermon in Pisidian Antioch

Paul's sermon to those gathered in the Jewish synagogue in Pisidian Antioch is a highly contextualized proclamation of the gospel to his audience—both in method and message. At the invitation of the synagogue rulers, Paul addresses his Jewish brethren as well as God-fearing Gentile worshippers of Yahweh. In a similar manner to Stephen, Paul selectively traces Israelite history and presents the life, death, resurrection, ascension and lordship of Jesus as both a continuation of and fulfillment of that history. Like Peter and Stephen before him, Paul presents Jesus as the hermeneutical key to understanding the Jewish Scriptures. The proper response for both Jew and Gentile to Jesus' lordship is repentance and faith. The rejection of the offer of eternal life by some of the Jews at Pisidian Antioch opened the way for the

---

own people (13:27), their subsequent mistreatment of him, including crucifixion and his resurrection from the dead (13:28-29, 33-37), did not happen by accident. God was in control, having predicted these events in Scripture and then sovereignly bringing about their fulfillment. Keener, *Acts*, 2:2069-74.

124. Keener tables six parallel statements: 1. "You killed Jesus" (Acts 2:22-23; 13:27-28); 2. "God raised him up" (2:24; 13:30); 3. David says in Psalm 16 (2:25-28; 13:35); 4. David remains dead (2:29; 13:36); 5. God raised up Christ from David's seed (2:30; 13:23); 6. Jesus did not experience corruption (2:31; 13:37). Keener, *Acts*, 2:2052; Flemming, *Contextualization*, 61.

125. Flemming, *Contextualization*, 61. In a more recent monograph, Zhang draws parallels between the inaugural sermons of Jesus (Luke 4:10-30), Peter (Acts 2:14-40) and Paul (Acts 13:16-41). His main thesis regarding Acts 13:16-41 is that Paul's sermon here is representative of his preaching to Jews throughout the whole book of Acts. Zhang, *Paul Among Jews: A Study of the Meaning and Significance of Paul's Inaugural Sermon in the Synagogue of Antioch in Pisidia (Acts 13:16-41) for his Missionary Work among the Jews*.

126. Flemming, *Contextualization*, 61.

gospel message to go to the Gentiles, heralding a new era in Paul's ministry and the evangelistic emphasis of the early church.

Two important conclusions can be drawn from this incident in Pisidian Antioch. First, the kerygma that Paul proclaimed was centered on Jesus Christ, climaxing in his death and resurrection. Jesus stands in continuity with Jewish history and fulfills Jewish Scripture. His unjust treatment and crucifixion and his vindication through being raised from the dead has resulted in forgiveness of sin and freedom from the weight of the law, available to everyone who believes in Jesus Christ. Second, Jesus is presented as the new hermeneutical key to interpreting Jewish history, directly challenging the prevailing Jewish worldview. Not only had the Jews not recognized their own messiah but had crucified him. Jesus is the savior of the world, fulfillment of the Davidic promise and Jewish Scripture. Only through Jesus can people find forgiveness of sin and freedom, unobtainable through the law of Moses.

3.8 Preaching to sophisticated Gentiles in Athens (Acts 17:16–31)

3.8.1 Context, audience and setting

Context: Paul and Barnabas left Pisidian Antioch due to the opposition they faced and continued their missionary journey throughout Iconium, Lystra and Derbe before eventually returning to Syrian Antioch (Acts 13:50—14:28). After meeting with the Jerusalem Council and officially resolving the issue that the Gentile converts were not required to follow Jewish customs and laws in order to become believers (15:1–35), Paul and Barnabas had a disagreement that caused them to part company (15:36–41). Paul's ongoing mission to the Gentiles continued as he embarked on a second missionary journey with other companions (including Timothy and Silas) throughout the region of Macedonia (16:1–38). Having been forced out of Thessalonica and Berea, Paul was escorted to Athens by some Berean Christians. Paul was left in Athens alone, awaiting the arrival of Silas and Timothy from Berea (Acts 17:1–15).[127]

Audience and setting: Athens had been the intellectual, cultural and philosophical heart of Greece since the fifth century BC.[128] Amongst other things, it was famous for its Hellenistic architecture, its religious temples and

---

127. Schnabel, *Acts*, 715, 719.
128. Bruce, *The Book of the Acts*, 348; Keener, *Acts*, 3:2566.

idols, and its philosophical heritage (the birthplace of Socrates and Plato).[129] Whilst waiting for his companions, Paul toured the city and was greatly distressed (παρωξύνετο, 17:16) because of the many idols he observed.[130] So moved, Paul adopted his usual practice of reasoning (διελέγετο, Acts 17:17) in the synagogue with the Jews and God-fearing Greeks there (see 14:1; 17:2, 10–12).[131] The main public space in the city was the Agora (17:17), "the hub of urban life—a centre for commerce and trade, but also for the sharing of ideas."[132] It was in this strategic location where Paul further reasoned with any of the Athenians who happened to be there.[133]

Philosophical debates characterized Athenian life in the Agora, and it was while Paul preached there that he came to debate with two of the major philosophical schools in Athens—the Epicureans and the Stoics (Acts 17:18).[134] The Epicureans were polytheistic but were indifferent to religious deities, considering them to be too removed from daily life to be concerned about.[135] Keener notes that "[t]he popular stereotype was that the Epicureans denied the gods, denied providence, and rejected theodicy."[136] The Stoics, on the other hand, had a very different philosophical view. They were essentially pantheists, believing that nature and the divine (the logos) were all one, and so rejected the concept of an individual, personal god.[137] While Stoics believed that the gods existed, in contrast to the Epicureans, they believed that the gods were very involved and influential in world affairs and the lives of women and men on earth.[138] Both philosophical schools were confused by Paul's evangelistic teaching about Jesus and the resurrection, thinking Paul was advocating new deities.[139] They brought Paul to the

---

129. Gill, "Achaia," 433–53, at 441–5.

130. BDAG, παροξύνω, 780. BDAG suggests that the distress may have been due to anger, grief or a desire to convert the idolaters. Peterson, *Acts*, 488–9, argues that it was Paul's jealousy for God's name and reputation in the face of rampant rejection of his uniqueness and holiness which prompted such a strong reaction in him.

131. Peterson, *Acts*, 489.

132. Ibid., 489; Gill, "Achaia," 445–6.

133. Peterson, *Acts*, 489.

134. Schnabel, *Paul the Missionary*, 100.

135. Bock, *Acts*, 561.

136. Keener, *Acts*, 3:2589. For further on Epicureanism, see Keener, *Acts*, 3:2584–93.

137. Peterson, *Acts*, 490.

138. Keener, *Acts*, 3:2595. For further on Stoicism, see Keener, *Acts*, 3:2593–5.

139. Richard Gibson argues that Paul's debating in the Athenian marketplace was an "unambiguous" reference to Paul evangelizing the Stoics and Epicureans, with a message centered on Jesus and his resurrection (Acts 17:17–18). Gibson, "Paul and

Areopagus to explain his new ideas (17:18–22).¹⁴⁰ The Areopagus was "Athens' chief legislative and judicial council" and the decision-makers on religious matters.¹⁴¹ Paul addresses an Areopagan audience made up of these two philosophical schools, and quite possibly others as well (e.g., "Men of Athens," 17:22; "Damaris, and some others," 17:34).¹⁴² Where Paul's sermon in the synagogue of Pisidian Antioch had been to a mainly Jewish audience, his sermon in the Areopagus in Athens was to a sophisticated Gentile audience (17:22–31). That Paul addresses some of the cultural and intellectual elite, in one of the leading cities of the empire, is significant for Luke. This sermon is more than simply the word of God being proclaimed in an intellectual Gentile setting (although it is that). Rather, as Flemming aptly states:

---

the Evangelization of the Stoics," in *The Gospel to the Nations: Perspectives on Paul's Mission*, 309–26, at 318.

140. Tannehill, *The Narrative Unity of Luke–Acts: A Literary Interpretation*, 216–7. Cf. Flemming, *Contextualization*, 74; Gill, "Achaia," 447–8. Despite the polytheism of the Hellenistic worldview, there was a general reticence towards the introduction of new religions or religious deities. Such introductions had to be sanctioned by the State. Perhaps the Epicureans and the Stoics thought that Paul was introducing new deities when he talked about Jesus and *anastasis* (resurrection), and so brought Paul before the Areopagan Council for assessment. Paul is at pains to point out that he is not introducing a new cult, nor did he require land, temples or cultic personnel. Rather, he is proclaiming a deity already heralded in Athens through a dedicated altar. Schnabel, *Paul the Missionary*, 100–4, 168. Jipp translates Acts 17:19b (δυνάμεθα γνῶναι τίς ἡ καινὴ αὕτη ἡ ὑπὸ σοῦ λαλουμένη διδαχή) as "We have the right to know what this new teaching is of which you are speaking." Jipp then argues that Paul is not being invited to a "placid discourse" on different worldviews but, like Socrates, is on trial before this significant philosophical council over his understanding of God against the polytheistic Hellenistic view. Jipp, "Paul's Areopagus Speech of Acts 17:16–34 as *Both Critique and Propaganda*," 567–88, at 574. Keener states that the majority of scholars understand the charge of preaching foreign divinities brought against Paul is a Lukan allusion to the charge of "introducing new religion" previously brought against Socrates. Luke's purpose in comparing Paul with Socrates was to enhance Paul's standing amongst his readership who held Socrates in high regard as a philosopher. Keener, *Acts*, 3:2604–7. Jipp similarly frames Paul as Socrates redivivus. Jipp, "Paul's Areopagus Speech," 569–75.

141. Larkin, *Acts*, 253.

142. Peterson, *Acts*, 493; There is significant debate regarding the correlation between Paul's recorded speech in Acts 17 and Rom 1:18–32, with some commentators concluding that the theology of the two passages is so different that in fact the record in Acts 17:16–34 is a Lukan construction rather than an accurate summary of the actual speech. Following Witherington and Bruce, Peterson argues that the seeming differences between the two passages are able to be satisfactorily accounted for. Peterson, *Acts*, 486–7 and n47. Cf. Witherington, *Acts*, 533–5; Bruce, *The Book of Acts*, 379.

Paul's address to the Athenians in Acts 17 is perhaps the outstanding example of intercultural evangelistic witness in the New Testament. This makes it a pivotal text for [studying] . . . New Testament patterns of contextualization . . . Luke does not want his audience to hear this speech simply as a record of Paul's preaching on an isolated occasion. This sermon synopsis offers a paradigmatic case of Paul's approach to an educated pagan audience.[143]

3.8.2 Paul's contextual approach

There are three features of Paul's recorded address in Acts 17:22–31 that reflect his contextual methodology:

i. *Paul's use of ancient rhetoric.* The adaptation of a speech to a particular audience was an essential part of a philosopher's rhetorical arsenal and had already been demonstrated in Paul's sermons to Jews (Acts 13:16–47) and rustic Gentiles (14:15–17).[144] Schnabel identifies the rhetorical structure of Paul's address as: *exordium* (17:22–23, introduction, followed by a commendation[145] of his hearers [*capatatio benevolentiae*]);

---

143. Flemming, *Contextualization*, 72. Keener states that many contemporary authors identify Paul's speech in Athens as a model of contextualization, listing representative authors in Keener, *Acts*, 3:2565, n2659. Gibson, "Paul and the Evangelization of the Stoics," 309–23, argues against Acts 17:22–31 being a paradigmatic evangelistic sermon to a Gentile audience. While acknowledging the sermon contains the elements of God's judgment and a call to repentance, too much of the core content of the gospel is missing for it to qualify as a "definitive evangelistic sermon" (particularly without a direct mention of Jesus, although Jesus was raised in the market place debates in 17:17–18). For Gibson, the evangelistic content would undoubtedly have been delivered to those who returned to discuss things with Paul subsequent to the address. Gibson's view fails to sufficiently take into account Paul's contextual approach whereby Paul is indeed explaining the gospel but in categories that were more likely to be understood by his Athenian audience. For example, while Jesus is not explicitly named in Paul's address, he is indirectly referred to in Acts 17:31 in terms of his humanity (ἐν ἀνδρὶ), his role as divine judge of the world (ᾗ μέλλει κρίνειν τὴν οἰκουμένην), and his divine vindication through his resurrection from the dead (ἀναστήσας αὐτὸν ἐκ νεκρῶν). Paul's contextual message is summarised in 3.8.3. On the purpose of Paul's speech, see Sandnes, "Paul and Socrates: The Aim of Paul's Areopagus Speech," 13–26.

144. Keener, *Acts*, 3:2614.

145. There is debate as to whether δεισιδαιμονεστέρους (Acts 17:22) should be interpreted negatively as a rebuke or positively as a compliment. The word can be translated negatively as meaning superstitious or it could be translated positively as meaning devout or religious. Later in his speech Paul points out that the Athenians'

propositio (17:24, a summary of the subject matter—the identity of the unknown god); *argumentatio* (7:24-29, proofs offered regarding the character of this unknown god as the creator and sustainer of all living things); and *peroratio* (7:30-31, his conclusion that God commands all people to repent).[146] Not only did Paul construct his speech using rhetorical conventions but he also used rhetorical devices such as seeking to establish common ground with his audience.[147]

His identification of common ground with his audience (Acts 17:22-23). Just as Paul had sought favor with the Pisidian Antioch synagogue congregation by addressing them in a respectfully appropriate manner, so does he here (ἄνδρες Ἀθηναῖοι, 17:22). In Pisidian Antioch Paul's entry point into his discussion with the synagogue congregation had been the common ground of their shared Jewish ancestry. In Athens, Paul is able to find common ground with his audience in terms of their religiosity.[148] Having walked through the city, Paul had observed evidence of their desire to worship the divine through objects of worship, most likely statues, idols and altars, including one altar with the inscription, "To the unknown God" (Ἀγνώστῳ θεῷ, 17:23). This unknown god that the Athenians worshipped was not the same God that Paul worshipped and would proclaim to them in his address, but "the altar is a segue into discussing the one true God. What they cannot name and seek to worship he will explain to them."[149] Keener notes that Paul's identification of common ground between Judaism and

---

devoutness has been misplaced and done in ignorance (17:30), leading them to grope for God but not find him (17:27). Having begun his address in a cordial manner, however, Paul must be making at least something of a positive statement here regarding their devoutness. BDAG, "δεισιδαιμονία," 216. Cf. Bock, *Acts*, 564 (against Peterson, *Acts*, 494).

146. Schnabel, *Acts*, 719. Similarly, Witherington, *Acts*, 518 and Keener, *Acts*, 3:2619.

147. Keener, *Acts*, 3:2614. Keener, 2618, summarises the work of rhetorical critics who have identified a number of rhetorical elements in the speech, including: unifying key terms (e.g., πᾶς, in 17:22, 24, 25, 26, 30, 31), alliteration, hyperbaton, and litotes.

148. Keener argues that with Epicureanism Paul could only establish minimal philosophical and religious common ground, but with Stoicism he was able to establish greater common ground with respect to some aspects of ethics, theology, and cosmology. Paul was able to use some of the language of the Stoics while communicating a different understanding of some of the content behind the language. Keener, *Acts*, 3:2614.

149. Bock, *Acts*, 564.

Hellenistic philosophy (particularly Stoic philosophy) is an important element of his contextualized approach to his Hellenistic audience.[150]

ii. *His interaction with their worldviews.* In Pisidian Antioch Paul had interacted with the Jewish worldview of his audience. In Athens, Paul interacts with the Hellenistic worldview through both affirmation and critique. To cite just six examples:

   a. Paul's emphasis on God being the creator of everything was similar to the Epicurean philosophy of the gods being the causative agents of the universe (Acts 17:24, 26).[151]

   b. Paul's description of God as independent of humanity and not needing them for anything was consistent with the Greek ideology of the self-sufficiency of the gods (17:25).[152]

   c. Paul's proclamation of monotheism was a critique of the polytheistic Greek worldview (17:24, 36–27, 30–31).

   d. Paul's declaration that the Lord of heaven and earth cannot be confined to a man-made structure was a critique of the dominant (though not exclusive) Greek worldview that held that temples could house the gods (17:24).[153]

   e. Whereas the Epicureans thought that the gods were too distant to impact the lives of humans, and the Stoics that the divine being was impersonal, Paul proclaimed that God was in fact quite near, that he desired people to find him and relate to him, and would call everyone to account (17:27, 31).

   f. In Pisidian Antioch Paul cited Jewish authors that the synagogue audience themselves agreed with in order to clinch his argument. Paul's contextualization to his Athenian audience saw Paul quote directly from Greek poets to strengthen his case and, once again, to provide a new hermeneutic through which to understand them (17:28). Humanity is not the offspring of a Greek god, but of the one, creator God (17:29).

---

150. Keener, *Acts*, 3:2614. Keener, 2626, further posits that while Paul sought to find common ground where he could with his Athenian audience, "he also ultimately proclaims his message even where it violates their system."

151. Bock, *Acts*, 565; Keener, *Acts*, 3:2614. Nevertheless, a significant difference between the two is that the Epicureans believed that the gods had no ongoing interest or involvement in human affairs, where Paul affirmed the creator God as being intimately involved and in control of human affairs.

152. Bock, *Acts*, 565; Fitzmyer, *Acts*, 608.

153. Bock, *Acts*, 565.

Paul's use of philosophical language, common ground, and interaction with the Hellenistic worldview had a purpose beyond simply providing information or even a personal defense against the accusation that he was preaching about foreign divinities. Rather, Paul garners all of these rhetorical devices in order to bring about a transformation of his audience's worldview.[154]

3.8.3 Paul's contextual message

It was Paul's teaching about Jesus and the resurrection that led to Paul being brought to the Areopagus in the first place (Acts 17:18-20), and there are clearly major points that Paul wishes to communicate in his Areopagus address (17:30-32; cf. 13:33-37). In both the Pisidian Antioch and the Areopagus addresses, Paul delays introducing these major points until near their end. Yet the respective contextualized messages see Paul arrive at these important points through different routes i.e., through different presentations of the Christian gospel.

Following Peterson, we can summarize Paul's contextual message to the Athenians under three categories:[155]

i. *The truth about God* (Acts 17:24-26). Paul's survey of Athens had identified the polytheistic nature of its citizens (17:16, 22-23). Amongst the various idols Paul discovered one titled: to the unknown god (Ἀγνώστῳ θεῷ, 17:23). The fact that such an altar existed pointed to a form of ignorance on the part of the Athenians.[156] Greek culture highly valued knowledge and ignorance was considered a vice, not a virtue. Paul downplayed the ignorance in his speech so as not to cause direct offense (17:23, 30). Paul used this particular idol, however, as a segue into explaining the truth about God.[157] In contrast to Greek polytheism, Paul proclaimed that there was only one true God, the Lord of heaven and earth, who created the world and everything in it, including every person and nation (17:24, 26). This creator God is therefore

---

154. Flemming, *Contextualization*, 79.

155. Peterson, *Acts*, 495-503.

156. Such altars were not unique to Athens and were reported in a number of places, including throughout Attica. They had cultic significance, functioning as a religious safety net for the inhabitants of the city where these altars were built, built to appease any god they might not know about who might cause the city harm. Larkin, *Acts*, 255.

157. Keener, *Acts*, 3:2634-6.

sovereign and supreme, having authority over all humanity.[158] The creator God's transcendence means that he cannot be contained in a building, nor does he even need a temple, nor is he dependant on or need anything from the human beings he created (17:25a). Rather than God being dependent on humanity, humanity is dependent on God—for life, breath and everything (17:25b). Humanity's dependence on God includes the rise and fall of nations. Nations are not in control of their own destiny but are completely dependent on the periods and dwelling places that the creator God has allotted to them (ὁρίσας προστεταγμένους καιροὺς καὶ τὰς ὁροθεσίας τῆς κατοικίας αὐτῶν, 17:26). Therefore, following Keener, what can be concluded is that, while Paul has been culturally respectful towards the Athenians' idolatry and has employed "culturally intelligible" language up to this point, Paul's contextualized approach does not lead him to proclaim a distorted or syncretistic gospel (17:22–23).[159] Rather, Paul's statements in Acts 17:24-26 are both an affirmation and an affront to Athenian religious practice.[160]

The truth about humanity (Acts 17:27–29). Having introduced the idea of humanity's dependence on God, Paul establishes further truths about humanity. Against the Stoic rejection of a personal god, Paul argues that God created humanity to be in relationship with himself (17:27). Humanity is estranged from God and is ignorant of how to find him (17:27). God's desire is for each person to find him, for he is accessible (17:27). The Athenians have been worshipping many deities whilst being ignorant of the Creator God, whose very statue in their city testify to his nearness and accessibility. The Athenians should be seeking their Creator but are, at best, groping after him (ψηλαφήσειαν αὐτὸν, 17:27), hardly a positive description. What Paul is saying is that God's closeness to the Athenians is a reflection of God's kindness rather than the Athenians insight.[161]

ii. In order to further establish his argument about the close relationship between the Creator and his creatures, Paul quotes from work considered authoritative by his audience, Greek poetry. Greek poetry was a staple of Greek education and an essential part of society's "cultural

---

158. Paul's description of a transcendent creator God who was not dependent on humanity intersected with the Epicurean worldview.

159. Keener, *Acts*, 3:2640.

160. Ibid., 3:2640.

161. Ibid., 3:2652-3.

fabric."¹⁶² While some dispute exactly which poet(s) Paul is quoting in Acts 17:28, the way that Paul uses the quotes to build his argument is clear.¹⁶³ Humanity are the direct result of the creative work of God, his offspring (τοῦ γὰρ καὶ γένος ἐσμέν, 17:28), with God in effect living in his offspring (ἐν αὐτῷ γὰρ ζῶμεν καὶ κινούμεθα καὶ ἐσμέν, 17:28).¹⁶⁴ As his offspring, Paul further argues, God should not be thought of as an idol made from things from the material world (gold, silver, stone, 17:29) for, unlike the Athenian idols, the Creator God lives and moves (17:28).¹⁶⁵ He is a relational God, desiring humanity to seek him and be in relationship with him. Failure to enter into such a relationship brings significant consequences, as Paul explains when he concludes with the truth about divine judgment (17:30–31).

iii. *The truth about divine judgment* (Acts 17:30–31). Having previously introduced the idea of the Athenians' ignorance of God (17:23), Paul returns to the theme (17:31). Whereas God has previously overlooked their ignorance of God, demonstrated by their idolatry, that period of grace is coming to an end. God has appointed a day when the world will be called to account and be judged righteously by his appointed person, Jesus Christ, whom he raised from the dead (17:31–32). It is Paul's hearers, to whom he has just declared his message, along with πάντας πανταχοῦ (17:30) who would be without excuse. The coming of God's righteous judge into the world has introduced a new era of accountability and culpability.¹⁶⁶ This same man, whom God raised from the dead, is God's appointed judge who will judge the world in righteousness (17:31). Paul therefore calls on all humanity, including his hearers, to repent (μετανοεῖν, 20:30) before it's too late.

---

162. Ibid., 3:2653.

163. It is unclear exactly whom Paul is quoting with "ἐν αὐτῷ γὰρ ζῶμεν καὶ κινούμεθα καὶ ἐσμέν." Epimenides may be the source but this is far from certain. The phrase, "Τοῦ γὰρ καὶ γένος ἐσμέν" is attributed to Aratas of Cicilia (third century BC), who meant by the phrase that human beings were the offspring of the Greek god Zeus. Peterson, *Acts*, 499–500; Keener, *Acts*, 3:2653–61.

164. This is congruent with the Stoic idea of God pervading everything and of God being father of all human beings. Keener, *Acts*, 3:2659, 2663.

165. At this point Paul is providing a stinging rebuke to Athenian's idolatry.

166. Keener, *Acts*, 3:2670.

3.8.4 Conclusion to Paul's speech in Athens

At the invitation of the Stoic and Epicurean philosophers that he had conversed with in the Agora, Paul is invited to address the Areopagus and explain his ideas, particularly concerning Jesus and the resurrection. Paul's proclamation of the gospel to an educated Gentile audience is similar in method but more flexible in message than the one he proclaimed in the Jewish synagogue in Pisidian Antioch.

Paul's contextual approach to the Athenians is not unlike the contextual approach that Peter, Stephen, and Paul himself used to Jewish audiences, as already examined in this chapter. He adopts a style of address familiar to his audience (ancient rhetoric); he identifies common ground with his audience through a shared religiosity; and he interacts with the Hellenistic worldview of his audience even to the point of quoting from their own poet(s). Paul's contextual message to the Athenians is a radical departure from that adopted by Peter, Stephen, and Paul himself to the Jewish audiences. Rather than selectively tracing key people and events in Jewish history as recorded in Scripture, and arguing for Jesus as the hermeneutical key to interpret the Scriptures, Paul's Athenian address to educated Gentiles argues the case for truth on three main fronts: the truth about God, the truth about humanity, and the truth about divine judgment. From Paul's perspective, the proper response to the truths is repentance to the resurrected one who will judge the world in righteousness.

Three important conclusions can be drawn from this speech before the educated Gentile Areopagan audience. First, the kerygma that Paul proclaimed is centered on Jesus Christ and his resurrection. While this sermon isn't recorded as directly naming Jesus or referencing his crucifixion, it speaks of his humanity, his vindication through bodily resurrection, and the necessity of responding to him through repentance. At the same time, the speech emphasizes other aspects of the gospel, including: God as the transcendent Creator and ruler of the world; a coming day when all people will be judged; and Jesus the resurrected one being God's appointed righteous judge. The speech also presents a contextualized explanation for sin, describing it in terms of ignorance of the Creator God and idolatry rather than in terms of the rejection and crucifixion of God's Son Jesus, as has already been noted in the speeches to a Jewish audience. Second, this sermon is a further model of a speaker contextualizing his address to a particular audience. Third, Jesus is presented as the new hermeneutical key to interpreting religious life, directly challenging the prevailing polytheistic Hellenistic worldview.

3.9 Contextual principles that can be drawn from Peter, Stephen, and Paul's speeches

PRINCIPLE 1: The early establishment of common ground provides a platform for the gospel to be heard. The speeches of Peter, Stephen, and Paul to Jewish audiences examined in this chapter were all occasional addresses delivered to Jewish audiences, people with whom the early church leaders did not have a prior relationship. This is in contrast to John Chrysostom, as will be seen in chapters four and five, who regularly preached to the same group of people in his congregation. Peter, Stephen, and Paul sought to establish rapport with their respective audiences through identifying common ground, particularly the Jewish history they shared with their respective audiences, and through respectfully addressing their audiences. Paul also took this approach in his speech to the Athenians through drawing on their shared religiosity. Reflecting on Paul's cultural sensitivity in Acts 17, Dean Flemming draws the following contextual principle: "The church must always sensitively listen to the culture in which it ministers and draw upon that culture's internal resources if it hopes to proclaim the gospel in a credible and convincing way."[167] My first principle is consistent with that of Flemming. In the activity of contextualization, a person should look to establish rapport with their audience, particularly through addressing their audience in culturally appropriate ways that do not offend, along with identifying and utilising areas of common ground where possible. The goodwill that this generates can provide a platform for people to keep listening to the message rather than rejecting it early in its presentation.

PRINCIPLE 2: For contextualization to be effective, the gospel needs to be explained in ways that engage the worldview of the target audience. Peter, Stephen and Paul were Jewish and therefore familiar with the worldview of the Jewish audiences they were addressing. When seeking to reason with their respective audiences, Peter, Stephen, and Paul argued from the text that their audiences regarded as authoritative—the Jewish Scriptures. Their method involved tracing important historical figures and moments in Israel's history, quoting various Old Testament Scriptures, showing their knowledge of standard interpretations of these Scriptures, and occasionally drawing illustrations or observations from the everyday lives of their audiences (e.g., Acts 2:15). The effect of this approach was to make their speeches comprehensible and cohesive and their arguments persuasive for their audiences. This principle is consistent with that of Flemming who

---

167. Flemming, *Contextualization*, 82.

states that fresh, innovative images and metaphors, whether drawn from the biblical text or the everyday world of the audience, need to be discovered so as to communicate the gospel in different contexts.[168] Flemming's principle, however, can be said to be further extended by this research. Just as Peter, Stephen, and Paul quoted from works authoritative to their respective audiences, some of the fresh metaphors and images for contextualization Flemming refers to may also be drawn from local texts and contexts. There may be great value in engaging with: texts that are authoritative for the particular audience (for example, Qur'an, Hadiths, Vedas, Tipitaka, Tanak), and drawing illustrations from the everyday lives of the audience (such as the works of musicians, writers, and poets known and accepted by the audience), even where the ideas or worldview of the audience is being challenged (e.g., Acts 2:31–36; 7:51–52; 13:36–39).

PRINCIPLE 3: Faith in Jesus Christ does not necessarily mean social dislocation. Chan states that that it is possible for people to become Christians in their own culture, with a minimum of social dislocation, and with a culturally adapted gospel.[169] This principle is affirmed in the speeches of Peter, Stephen and Paul to Jewish audiences. In these speeches Jesus is not presented as the founder of a new religion but as the fulfillment of Old Testament Judaism. For a Jew to embrace faith in Jesus Christ they were not necessarily required to reject their cultural Jewish heritage such as food, manner of address, social customs, and the like.[170] Rather, through the discernment of the Holy Spirit, Jewish Christians were free to live out their Christian faith in their Jewish contexts, albeit with a transformed worldview and new hermeneutic for interpreting the Scriptures. This principle is important in the contextualization debate with new MBB, for example. While the distinctive demands of the gospel are to be proclaimed and embodied, there are many cultural elements that can be retained or adapted that avoid syncretism.[171]

PRINCIPLE 4: There is no fixed presentation of the gospel as contextual sensitivity requires flexibility. The close proximity of Jesus' death and resurrection to Peter's Pentecost sermon, both in time and location, afforded Peter the opportunity to focus on a number of salient messianic texts in order to

168. See end of 2.4.1.

169. See 2.2.

170. Just like Gentiles in Acts 15:1–33, Jews were not required to give up their cultural heritage in order to become Christians, but were able to express their new found faith in culturally relevant ways that were consistent with Christian teaching.

171. See 3.9, Principle 3.

argue for the reality of Jesus' bodily resurrection and to demonstrate Jesus as the fulfillment of those texts. Stephen and Paul travelled a different route in order to be able to speak about Jesus. While their cultural contexts were Jewish, their settings and occasions were such that a different approach was required—tracing the history of Israel in order to show Jesus' continuity with that history. In the activity of contextualization, there is no one single acceptable approach but many acceptable approaches that can be adopted, affirming the principle of Dean Flemming highlighted earlier.[172] The context, audience and setting should all affect the way a person presents, explains, and lives out the gospel.[173]

PRINCIPLE 5: There is a core content to the gospel, applicable to all cultures. While Peter, Stephen and Paul demonstrated flexibility in their contextualized gospel presentations, there were common elements in the content of their gospel presentation. Namely, each of the three sermons communicated a gospel core, centered on the ministry, death, and resurrection of Jesus, the need for repentance, and the availability of forgiveness of sin. The gospel is not whatever people want it to be. There is a core content to the gospel which is not negotiable and applies to all cultures. This principle affirms a key tenet of the Lausanne Covenant, as well as that of Ericson, and Flemming, whereby the gospel is said to be centered on the person and work of Jesus Christ and the implications of this for daily living.[174] The degree to which various elements of the gospel are presented at any one time, and the way they are communicated, should be influenced by the cultural and situational context.[175]

PRINCIPLE 6: Cultural pressure must not lead to a dampening down of the challenging demands of discipleship. Peter, in an environment of confusion and ridicule, challenged his hearers regarding the uniqueness of Christ, their culpability over Jesus' crucifixion, and their need to repent of their sins in order to escape God's judgment (Acts 2:12–13, 36, 38–41). Stephen, in an openly hostile environment, boldly confronted the Jews over their historical

---

172. See end of 2.4.1.

173. For example, as Peter, Stephen and Paul were addressing Jewish audiences their contextualized gospel addresses incorporated Judaist references that do not really feature in Paul's addresses to Gentile audiences (e.g., Acts 14:15–17; 17:22–31; 20:17–35).

174. For Lausanne, see 2.2, n219; for Ericson, see 2.2 and n27–29. Cf. LCWE, "The Willowbank Report," 86; for Flemming, see 2.4.2.

175. This will be further demonstrated in the Chrysostom homilies examined in chapter 5.

rejection of God's messengers, the most recent being Jesus (6:12–14, 51–53). Both Peter and Stephen are exemplars for those who claim allegiance to the God of the gospel. The gospel challenges and critiques aspects of all cultures, and can provoke a negative reaction from those who perceive that challenge and critique. The temptation therefore to dampen down some of the challenging demands of the gospel due to cultural pressure can be high. The pressure, however, as Benjamin Moreas affirmed at Lausanne, is to be resisted.[176] This principle challenges some of the principles advocated by Phil Parshall, along with various proponents of the Insider Movement, such as Rick Brown and Rebecca Lewis, who are open to MBB retaining Muslim practices and customs.[177] The distinctive challenging demands of the gospel are to be both verbally proclaimed and embodied in the life of the believer.[178]

PRINCIPLE 7: Existing cultural terms and forms can be used and imbued with new meaning in light of the gospel. In the Greco-Roman world the word θεός was a general word used to denote a supreme being or deity.[179] As has already been highlighted, the respective Epicurean and Stoic worldviews articulated significantly different understandings of θεός.[180] Dean Gilliland has already emphasized how, in the contextual process, the early church was prepared to use Hellenistic words, such as λόγος, and imbue them with a new meaning in light of the gospel.[181] In Paul's Areopagan speech this same contextual principle can be seen at work, but this time with the word θεός. In his speech Paul highlights his Epicurean and Stoic audiences' ignorance of θεός, while simultaneously explaining the truth about θεός from his biblical worldview. A contextual approach allows Paul both to affirm and critique aspects of his audience's understanding of θεός while ultimately offering a different understanding of the term that is contextually appropriate. The principle of taking an existing cultural term and imbuing it with a new meaning in light of the gospel can significantly impact liturgical thinking and practice. For example, Christian gatherings of Muslim background

---

176. See 2.2.

177. For Parshall, see 2.4.1; for Higgins, Brown, and Lewis see 2.4.1.

178. This will be further demonstrated in the Chrysostom homilies examined in chapter 5, particularly those in the *De statuis* and *Adversus Judaeos* series where Chrysostom consistently emphasizes that the spiritual transformation of a person should be visible in how they daily live out their faith.

179. *BDAG*, "θεός," 450.

180. See 3.81–3.82.

181. See 2.3.1.

believers may well be able to incorporate Muslim terms into their liturgy while imbuing them with different theological understanding, without the contextual practice drifting into the realm of syncretism.

Furthermore, carefully selected objects and aspects of general revelation can be a bridge to communicate the gospel. Paul was able to use an existing form, such as a statue, and the work of local poets as segues to explain the gospel (Acts 17:23, 28). In the same way, carefully selected objects and aspects of general revelation (e.g., musical instruments, music, clothing, festivals, and literature) can be used in the service of the gospel, as Nicholls affirms.[182] This approach supports the principle established by Ericson that meaning usually takes precedence over form, although Christians need to take care that the culturally correct meaning is communicated by the form.[183] This principle partly, but not completely, supports Phil Parshall's thesis.[184] While Parshall overemphasizes the role of meaning over form, there is *potential* at least for some of the cultural forms he suggests (for example, mode of dress, removing shoes upon entering a place of worship, and lifting up hands during prayer) to be used by MBB's.

PRINCIPLE 8: Culture is both positive and flawed and needs redemption through the gospel. The LCWE described culture as both positive and flawed, needing redemption through the gospel. The gospel itself does not belong to any one culture.[185] Paul was able both to affirm and critique aspects of his audience's culture. While affirming their religiosity, he critiques its misdirection (Acts 17:22–23). While affirming the work of their poets, he points to a transformed understanding of their words (17:28–29). While affirming his audience's sincerity, he critiques its ignorance (17:23, 27, 30). While affirming the created order that he shared with his audience, he critiques their view of the end point of that created order (17:24–26, 30–31).

Conclusion

This chapter has considered contextualization of the gospel to the Jews and Gentiles in the book of Acts. The purpose of the chapter has been to examine both how the early church contextualized the gospel and what contextual

---

182. See 2.2. While upholding the primacy of special revelation, Nicholls advocates the possibility of using carefully selected aspects of general revelation as bridges to effectively communicate the gospel.

183. See 2.2.

184. See 2.4.1.

185. See 2.2, n236.

principles it used. To answer these issues a representative selection of the recorded speeches of the early church were examined—given both to Jewish insiders (Acts 2:14-31; 7:1-53; 13:13-47) and Gentile outsiders (17:16-34).

Each of the speeches examined has been shown to be a highly contextualized proclamation of the gospel to their respective audiences—both in method and message. While the homiletical methods of Peter, Stephen, and Paul share some significant similarities (such as use of Greco-Roman rhetoric, establishment of common ground, and interaction with their audiences' worldview), the context, audience and setting of each speech has made for significant differences in the message that each speaker proclaimed.

Following the examination and analysis of these contextualized speeches, eight contextual principles have been identified and compared with those highlighted in chapter two. Each of these principles have confirmed, critiqued, or nuanced contextual principles identified in the literature:

Principle 1: The early establishment of common ground provides a platform for the gospel to be heard;

Principle 2: For contextualization to be effective, the gospel needs to be explained in ways that engage the worldview of the target audience;

Principle 3: Faith in Jesus Christ does not necessarily mean social dislocation;

Principle 4: There is no fixed presentation of the gospel as contextual sensitivity requires flexibility;

Principle 5: There is a core content to the gospel, which is for all cultures;

Principle 6: Cultural pressure must not lead to a dampening down of the challenging demands of discipleship;

Principle 7: Existing cultural terms and forms can be used and imbued with new meaning in light of the gospel;

Principle 8: Culture is both positive and flawed and needs redemption through the gospel.

The outcome of this chapter therefore has been the establishment of contextual principles that are based on a deeper analysis of Scripture than has been the case in much of the contextualization debate. Even where the chapter has affirmed previously stated principles, it has provided a more solid biblical basis for these principles than has been the case in much of the literature on contextualization.

Based on the historical nature of the discipline of missiology, in chapter one I identified two deficiencies in the contextualization debate–the relative paucity of contributions from biblical studies and Christian thought. The examination and analysis of speeches from the book of Acts in chapter three has begun to address the deficiency of biblical studies' contribution to the debate. Chapter five will address the second deficiency—Christian thought's contribution to the contextualization debate—through the examination of homilies of John Chrysostom. First, however, the case needs to be made that the works of the church fathers in general, and John Chrysostom in particular, can indeed be appropriated for the contextualization debate. Chapter four is devoted to that endeavor.

Chapter 4

Bridging the Gap
The case for appropriating the church fathers for contextualization

UNDERPINNING THE EXAMINATION OF the works of John Chrysostom in relation to contextualization is that the works of the church fathers can legitimately be used to inform contemporary issues of Christian witness and practice. There is no doubt that the works of the Fathers have significantly contributed to theological discussion and the formation of Christian doctrine over the centuries.[1] It is still an open question, however, as to what degree the works of the Fathers can legitimately contribute to contemporary missiological debates—like contextualization. This chapter will first address the broader question of the place and relevance of the church fathers in contemporary Christian witness and practice in general, and the contextualization debate specifically. Second, it will establish a set of criteria by which the suitability of a church father to inform the contextualization debate can be measured. Third, it will consider the possibility and legitimacy of the works of one church father, John Chrysostom, to inform the contextualization debate through evaluating his potential contributions against these established criteria and through an evaluation of various historical, hermeneutical, and contextual issues in his homilies.

---

1. For example, David F. Wright, *Infant Baptism in Historical Perspective*.

4.1 The legitimacy of patristics for contemporary ministry and witness

The relevance of patristics for answering twenty-first-century questions about contemporary Christian witness and practice has been debated by scholars in recent years. A recent example is found in the area of Catholic social thought.[2] In 2007, Brian Matz, while working as a researcher with the Centre for Catholic Social Thought at the Catholic University in Leuven, analyzed the impact of patristics on Pope Benedict's encyclical *Deus Caritas Est*. He discovered that of the approximately 13,000 words in this document, 1,030 (8%) were drawn from a patristic source.[3] While this was the highest percentage for any Catholic social teaching document up to that point, it raised the question for Matz as to the degree to which patristic teaching had influenced Catholic social teaching documents more broadly.[4] Subsequently, Matz conducted a study of twenty-one significant Catholic social teaching documents for their use of patristic sources.[5] His conclusion was that patristic sources played little meaningful role in the Catholic social teaching in these documents.[6]

During that same year, as part of an ongoing research project at the Catholic University in Leuven, Matz participated in a gathering of scholars from both patristic and Catholic social thought disciplines, examining the "potential for dialogue" between patristics and Catholic social thought.[7] A selection of papers was published in *Reading Patristic Texts on Social Ethics: Issues and Challenges for Twenty-First-Century Christian Social Thought*, which reflects the divide between scholars on the relevance of patristics for Catholic social thought today.

---

2. Catholic social thought is defined as "the extension of the official teachings of the Catholic Church into the day-to-day lives of Catholic men and women who work on behalf of social justice." Catholic social teaching, as a subset of Catholic social thought, "refers to the official teaching of the Vatican or regional bishops' conferences on socio-ethical topics." Leemans et al., "Introduction," xi–xviii, at xi. See also Harrison, Ashkelony, and De Bruyn, *Patristic Studies in the Twenty-First Century: Proceedings of an International Conference to Mark the 50th Anniversary of the International Association of Patristic Studies*.

3. Matz, "Problematic Uses of Patristic Sources in the Documents of Catholic Social Thought," 459–85, at 459.

4. Ibid., 460.

5. Ibid., 462–76.

6. Ibid., 461, 476, 479.

7. Leemans et al., "Introduction," xi.

Pauline Allen and Wendy Mayer were two of the participants in the Leuven gathering who were cautious about the possible contribution of patristics to Catholic social thought.

Allen, while not dismissing the potential contribution of patristics to Catholic social thought, highlighted some of the risks and challenges associated with seeking to bridge the gap between patristic sources and the twenty-first century, including:[8]

1. the lack of genuine certainty regarding the authorship of many homilies, which can impact the certitude of conclusions drawn from patristic texts;
2. the importance of reading patristic texts in context;
3. the "high mortality rate of ancient letters," which can result in skewed conclusions due to lack of all the relevant data;[9]
4. the need for an appreciation of the biases of the individual patristic authors;
5. the impact that patristic use of rhetoric has on the interpretation of their works;
6. the importance of knowing the background of the patristic audiences.

Wendy Mayer, drawing on the example of John Chrysostom, reinforced some of Allen's concerns as well as raised further issues. Like Allen, Mayer argued for the critical importance of reading patristic texts within their own contexts, by which she meant: understanding the homily author's personal agenda; appreciating the character and constituency of the target audience; and, appreciating the "social concepts prevalent among the audience to which it was directed."[10] In addition, Mayer highlighted the different types of audiences (both intended and unintended) that need to be considered before attempting to appropriate patristic homilies for contemporary Christian audiences.[11]

Of the participants in the Leuven gathering who were more optimistic regarding the role of patristics in Catholic social thought, Brenda Llewellyn

---

8. Allen, "Challenges in Approaching Patristic Texts from the Perspective of Contemporary Catholic Social Teaching," 30–42.

9. Allen, "Challenges," 32.

10. Mayer, "The Audience(s) for Patristic Social Teaching: A Case Study in *Reading Patristic Texts on Social Ethics: Issues and Challenges for Twenty-First-Century Christian Social Thought*, 85–99, at 85–7, 99.

11. Mayer, "The Audience(s)," 88–98.

Ihssen[12] and Thomas Hughson[13] are representative. Ihssen examines the issue of usury in the writings of select Greek Fathers, beginning with a detailed summary of the teaching of various Fathers on the subject of usury,[14] before outlining some conditions or limits in applying patristic thought on usury to Catholic social teaching.[15] Ihssen concludes by suggesting three points of theological connection between the teaching of the Greek Fathers and contemporary Catholic social thinking about usury. First, both believe that wealth does not exist to be accumulated but to be shared.[16] Second, "both believe that there is an intrinsic connection between economic and moral activities,"[17] that is, a person's morality is reflected to some degree in their attitude and behavior towards poverty and the poor. The third connection Ihssen highlights is that both the Greek Fathers and Catholic social thought deal with the emotional state of the person who, impacted by consumerism, desires to acquire more.[18] The brevity and generalized nature of these three points, in contrast to the relative length and specific detail in the rest of the article, somewhat detracts from her argument for the relevance of the Fathers to Catholic social thought.

Thomas Hughson examines the issue of social justice. In contrast to Ihssen, who draws on a variety of texts from different Fathers, Hughson considers just a single text, Lactantius's *Divine Institutes*. Hughson identifies a number of points of continuity between the *Divine Institutes* and social justice in Catholic social thought, including: the belief that all human beings are equal due to being made in the *imago Dei*;[19] that societal structures are rightly critiqued by Scripture, tradition, and human reason;[20] and the

---

12. Ihssen, "That Which has been Wrung," 124–60.

13. Hughson, "Social Justice in Lactantius's *Divine Institutes*: An Exploration," 185–205.

14. Ihssen, "That Which has been Wrung," 124–52.

15. Ihssen, "That Which has been Wrung," 152–4. Ihssen states that three concerns have to be taken into account before applying the reflections of the Fathers on usury to Catholic social thinking today: i. the Fathers had a different understanding of money and economics compared to twenty-first-century notions; ii. many of the Fathers spoke from a monastic background; iii. the new slant they bring to the conversation is that, like wealth, usury is a potential barrier to having a relationship with God and that those who practice usury are "in danger of losing their salvation" (p. 154).

16. Ibid., 155.

17. Ibid., 155.

18. Ibid., 156.

19. Hughson, "Social Justice," 199–200, 205.

20. Ibid., 200–2, 205.

importance of advocacy for social change.[21] In addition to these points, Hughson suggests that the *Divine Institutes* are useful because they raise questions which challenge the thinking of current Catholic social thought practitioners and scholars regarding the dignity of the human person and political theology. Overall, he makes a more substantial case for the potential contribution of patristics to Catholic social thought than Ihssen does.

The editors of *Reading Patristic Texts on Social Ethics* introduce the volume declaring their personal optimism regarding the role of patristics in Catholic social thought, stating, "Our own research has suggested that the Fathers are not superfluous to the debate."[22] From the perspective of these editors, the Fathers do not simply repeat New Testament statements or arguments. Rather, the Fathers express biblical ideas in different ways that can lead to a fresh appreciation and interpretation of the biblical text, as well as lead to new and developed forms of application to everyday life.[23] Even so, the Leuven conference reached no consensus on the legitimacy and value of the patristics in developing Catholic social thought, with Richard Shenk concluding that, "[n]o one direction represented by the papers seemed superfluous or singularly conclusive,"[24] and "[t]he manuscript seems to result in something of a 'split decision.'"[25]

What can at least be concluded here is that both Matz' article and the Leuven conference sound a number of warning bells for those who are positive about using patristic texts to inform current debates on Christian ministry and practice.[26] While the focus of Matz' article and the associated Leuven conference was the potential benefit of discussion between scholars from the fields of patristics and Catholic social thought, many of the issues and concerns raised are also relevant to applying patristic teaching to other current ministry and practice debates (e.g., contextualization). There is a significant historical, contextual, and hermeneutical gap between the patristic world and that of the twenty-first century. Therefore, as Allen succinctly states, seeking to bridge that gap is fraught with "difficulties, pitfalls,

---

21. Hughson, "Social Justice," 205.

22. Leemans et al., "Introduction," xiii.

23. Ibid.

24. Shenk, "The Church Fathers and Catholic Social Thought: Reflections on the Symposium," 209–21, at 221.

25. Shenk, "The Church Fathers," 209.

26. Matz, in *Patristics and Catholic Social Thought: Hermeneutical Models for a Dialogue*, further demonstrates the challenge of bridging the gap between patristics and contemporary thought.

and caveats."²⁷ In examining patristic texts in order to glean some modern relevance, there are barriers that will need to be overcome if genuine insights into current debates are to be gained. In order to draw missiological principles from the homilies of John Chrysostom in chapter five, serious consideration therefore will need to be given to the sorts of issues raised by Allen and Mayer in the Leuven conference including: the authorship of the homily; its provenance; the homiletician's audience; the context of the homily; and the homiletical style and particular bias of the patristic preacher.

The inconclusive outcome of the Leuven conference on the place of patristics in informing current debates on Christian ministry and practice was not shared by participants at the 2007 Wheaton Theology conference, whose proceedings were published in *Ancient Faith for the Church's Future*. The Wheaton conference "sought to demonstrate the vitality and promise of an evangelical engagement with the early church . . . believ[ing] that Christianity cannot meet the challenges of modernity and postmodernity without returning to the tradition of the early church."²⁸ All of the fourteen contributors to the volume were positive about patristic sources making a significant contribution to the theology and practice of the twenty-first-century church, consistent with a Protestant evangelical *ressourcement* theology.²⁹ That being said, Daniel H. William's chapter is to some extent different to the other papers in the volume, providing a tempered assessment of the

---

27. Allen, "Challenges in Approaching Patristic Texts," 30.

28. Husbands, "Introduction," 9–23, at 12.

29. *Ressourcement* theology refers to a movement that began in the mid-twentieth-century through a number of French (e.g., Henri de Lubac, Henri Bouillard, Louis Boyer, Marie-Dominique Chenu) and Swiss (Hans Urs von Balthasar), theologians that advocates going 'back to the sources', i.e., going back to the Scriptures and writings of patristic theologians in particular and using them as sources for the renewal of the contemporary church. Husbands, "Introduction," 10–12. Although *ressourcement* began as a movement in Catholic theology, there was also a corresponding Protestant *ressourcement* movement. The Reformation period sparked something of a similar movement, with the church fathers being somewhat nostalgically appealed to and applied in preaching and teaching. This earlier "pre-ressourcement" movement initiated a scientific study of patristics which resulted in the translation and editing of many of their works. For example, John Calvin's preaching was significantly influenced by Chrysostom's preaching method and his theology of divine adaptation. See Moore, "Gold Without Dross: An Assessment of the Debt to John Chrysostom in John Calvin's Oratory". For an introduction to *ressourcement* theology, see Flynn and Murray, *Ressourcement: A Movement for Renewal in Twentieth-Century Catholic Theology*; Williams, *Retrieving the Tradition and Renewing Evangelicalism: A Primer for Suspicious Protestants*; Williams, *Evangelicals and Tradition: The Formative Influence of the Early Church*. For a recent publication on Catholic ressourcement see Flynn and Murray, *Ressourcement: A Movement for Renewal in Twentieth Century Catholic Theology*.

potential relationship between patristics and issues of contemporary Christian witness and practice, and therefore will be considered in more detail.[30]

While Williams certainly sees a place for patristics informing twenty-first-century evangelical theology, his paper does not advocate a wholesale embrace.[31] Rather, he is somewhat cautious about the recent enthusiasm by evangelicals "who might be tempted to tame the early fathers by making them speak to our current situation in ways alien to the ancients themselves . . . creat[ing] the early Fathers in our own image."[32] Williams critiques evangelical authors who give an idealized and romanticized picture of the writings of the Fathers, as if everything the Fathers wrote is a helpful guide for the modern church.[33]

In his chapter, Williams identifies what he considers some of the main differences between the church fathers and Protestant evangelicalism.[34] Yet it is his argument on how *not* to use the writings of the Fathers that is the most relevant in articulating further issues and principles for evangelical *ressourcement*. In order for evangelicals authentically to engage with the patristics, Williams warns against viewing the Fathers as a panacea for solving all ecclesiastical problems, against assuming that the early church had a universally accepted theology and practice, and against using the writings of the Fathers to justify "proto-Protestant doctrines or practices . . . that support the evangelical point of view."[35]

30. Williams, "Similis et Dissimilis," 69–89.
31. Husbands, "Introduction," 12.
32. Williams, "Similis et Dissimilis," 70.
33. Ibid., 70, 77.
34. Williams cites four differences or challenges that evangelicals will face in reading patristics. Each of his points can be challenged. First, the anti-Jewish stance of many patristic writers (although I disagree with his placement of John Chrysostom in this category. I will argue from Chrysostom's *Adversus Judaeos* that Chrysostom was not anti-Jewish but rather against Judaising Christians who syncretistically blended Christianity and Judaism). Second, patristic acceptance of slavery. To make that claim, Williams would also have to add that the New Testament writers accepted slavery as well. Slavery was an integral part of society for both the New Testament writers and Chrysostom, not something they promoted. Third, the elevation of asceticism and virginity over marriage. This point does not reflect an accurate reading of Chrysostom. For while Chrysostom does see the value of asceticism and virginity for gospel ministry, he also notes that this way of life is not for all. Chrysostom also positively endorses marriage and the sexual side of marriage. Fourth, the general lack of documented overt evangelism after the apostolic period. Williams lists a few notable exceptions (Ulfilas, Patrick), but fails to mention John Chrysostom, whose significant missionary activity will be documented later in this chapter. Williams, "Similis et Dissimilis," 73–6.
35. Williams, "Similis et Dissimilis," 77–80.

The first section of *Ancient Faith for the Church's Future* is titled, "Evangelical Ressourcement: Retrieving the Past with Integrity." William's chapter, as part of this section, seeks to highlight some of the dangers and challenges in the development of an evangelical *ressourcement* theology. Other authors take up the challenge as they examine topics as diverse as hospitality, wealth and poverty, evangelism, worship, and prayer in the Fathers, and apply these reflections to the twenty-first-century church.

This conference further highlights something of a resurgent interest in evangelical ressourcement over the past two decades. Daniel H. Williams again writes,

> A nerve within contemporary evangelicalism has been hit, and its effects are ushering in enormous potential change . . . The last half decade or so has seen a readiness amongst evangelicals and many mainline Protestants to open the door that has been closed to tradition, finding in it potential resources for understanding their own Christian heritage. Likewise, a literature is beginning to develop around the notion of Christian tradition, especially as it concerns the relevance of the legacy of the early church for today's church.[36]

Robert E. Webber has been a significant contributor to this growing body of evangelical protestant ressourcement literature. His work has drawn from authors spanning from the first through to the twenty-first century while addressing diverse issues in practical theology—including worship,[37] evangelism,[38] faith,[39] and spirituality.[40] The *Ancient Christian Commentary on Scripture* series[41] has been a substantial undertaking to make the writings of selected patristic authors over a seven-hundred-year period (from Clement of Rome to John of Damascus) more accessible to a broad ecclesiastical

---

36. Williams, *Evangelicals and Tradition*, 15. Williams applies his ressourcement methodology to the issue of the nature and authority of Scripture in Williams, *Tradition, Scripture, and Interpretation: A Sourcebook of the Ancient Church*.

37. Webber, *Worship Old and New*.

38. Webber, *Ancient-Future Evangelism: Making Your Church a Faith-Forming Community*.

39. Webber, *Ancient-Future Faith: Rethinking Evangelicalism for a Postmodern World*.

40. Webber, *The Divine Embrace: Recovering the Passionate Spiritual Life*; Webber, *Ancient-Future Time: Forming Spirituality through the Christian Year*.

41. Oden, *Ancient Christian Commentary on Scripture*.

readership "who study the Bible regularly and who earnestly wish to have classical Christian observation on the text readily available to them."[42]

While the scholarship of Oden, Williams, Webber and the like already cited may support the view of a growing fascination for ressourcement among evangelicals in the past thirty years, Kenneth J. Stewart advocates that the evangelical neglect of patristic ressourcement is more of a historical phenomenon. His argument is that "the period 1500–1900 was characterized by a much deeper familiarity with the Early Church and a much freer appropriation of its teaching and practices."[43] Since 1900, however, there has been almost wholesale neglect of appropriating the writings of the early church to current issues such as in ministry and mission, until the resurgent interest over the past few decades.[44]

So far this chapter has highlighted, at the very least, that there are evangelical scholars who not only believe but who also have demonstrated that patristic writers can inform twenty-first-century questions of Christian witness and practice. The particular issue of Christian witness and practice this thesis addresses is contextualization. While a case has been made for Protestant ressourcement, that does not mean that every patristic author can be drawn upon to inform the topic. What needs to be established now is a set of principles against which any patristic writer can be assessed in order to evaluate the legitimacy of their work being used to inform the contextualization debate.

4.2 Principles for appropriating the church fathers for the contextualization debate

As established in chapter one, evangelical contextualization involves the gospel, as outlined in Scripture, being brought to culture in the context of mission.[45] Therefore, in order for a responsible engagement with the church fathers that might legitimately inform the contextualization debate, there are at least four criteria that any church father must meet:

i. The Father has a theology of Scripture consistent with that of evangelicalism;

---

42. Weinrich, *Revelation*, xi.

43. Stewart, "Evangelical and Patristic Christianity: 15717 to the Present," 307–21, at 321.

44. Ibid., 321.

45. For gospel, see 1.1.3.

ii. The Father's understanding of the gospel is clearly established and does not differ significantly from an evangelical understanding;

iii. The Father's cultural milieu and worldview corresponds in some way to mission contexts in the twenty-first century;

iv. The Father demonstrates a significant interest in mission.

I will now evaluate John Chrysostom against these four criteria to see whether he represents a potentially valid test case of a church father whose works can inform the contextualization debate.

4.3 John Chrysostom as a potentially valid test case

i. *The Father has a theology of Scripture consistent with that of evangelicalism.*[46] Chrysostom views Scripture as divinely inspired, God's word spoken through human authors, and normative for the Christian life–consistent with the evangelical view.[47]

ii. *The Father's understanding of the gospel is clearly established and does not differ significantly from an evangelical understanding.*[48] In order to understand the place the gospel played in Chrysostom's teaching and how he sought to communicate the gospel in ways that were understandable and relevant, it is necessary to distil Chrysostom's understanding of the gospel.

Chrysostom's love for God gave him a love for Scripture, to which his many exegetical homilies attest. But of all the biblical authors, the one who most drew him, for whom he had the greatest affection, was the apostle Paul.[49] The apostle's writings both captivated and invigorated Chrysostom.[50] Chrysostom's understanding of the gospel is amply reflected in his expositions on the Pauline epistles (including

---

46. See 1.1.1.

47. *In John* 2; PG 59.29–32; *In Gen* 7.7; PG 53.64. Cf. Rylaarsdam, *John Chrysostom on Divine Pedagogy: The Coherence of his Theology and Preaching*, 111–5.

48. See 1.1.3.

49. Chrysostom's regard for the Apostle Paul is reflected in his statement, "I love all the saints, but I love most the blessed Paul, the chosen vessel, the heavenly trumpet." *In 2 Cor hom.* 11; PG 51.301. Translation in Mitchell, *The Heavenly Trumpet: John Chrysostom and the Art of Pauline Interpretation*, 1.

50. Mitchell, *The Heavenly Trumpet*, 1; Rylaarsdam, *John Chrysostom*, 157–8.

Romans, 1 & 2 Corinthians, Ephesians, and Philippians) and so will be basis for this study, starting with Rom 1:1–7.[51]

Chrysostom states that the gospel of God is the unveiling of the Father and Son to the entire world.[52] It is not a new message but an old one, predating Greco-Roman culture.[53] It was promised beforehand in the writings of the Hebrew prophets, counterpointing the prophets' "accusations" and "charges" with "glad tidings" and "countless blessings."[54] The gospel is not Paul's own message but has its origin in God, proclaimed both by word and deed.[55] The gospel concerns God's Son, Jesus, who was God incarnate—both God and man.[56] As to his human nature, Jesus was of Davidic descent, but his resurrection from the dead powerfully displayed his divinity.[57] Through the incarnation, the divine Son, Jesus Christ, humbly came to earth in human form in order to rescue humanity from their alienation from God brought about by sin.[58] Humanity, therefore, is under God's rightful judgment and in need of redemption by and reconciliation to God.[59] Jesus Christ "died for our sins" and was raised to life on the third day, as predicted in the Scriptures.[60] For Chrysostom, "the Cross is for our sakes, being the work of unspeakable love towards man, the sign of his great concern for us."[61] Jesus' sacrificial death on the cross has opened the way of salvation, for those who believe.[62] Responding by faith to the gospel is a gift of grace from God, not a reward for a person's "toilings and labours."[63] All people who receive this gift of salvation

---

51. For a summary of Chrysostom's soteriology and Christology that undergirds his understanding of the gospel, see Rylaarsdam, *John Chrysostom*, 132–140, 144–5.

52. *In Rom hom*. 1; PG 60.396, 35 (NPNF 01.11, 339).

53. *In Rom hom*. 1; PG 60.396, 52–60 (NPNF 01.11, 339).

54. *In Rom hom*. 1; PG 60.396, 37–43 (NPNF 01.11, 339).

55. *In Rom hom*. 1; PG 60.396, 39, 49–50 (NPNF 01.11, 339–40).

56. *In Rom. hom*. 1; PG 60.397, 38 (NPNF 01.11, 340).

57. *In Rom. hom*. 1; PG 60.397, 44–51 (NPNF 01.11, 340).

58. *In Phil. hom*. 7; PG 62.231, 14–232, 15 (NPNF 01.13, 214–5).

59. *In Rom. hom*. 7; PG 60.442–3, 60–3, 1–15 (NPNF 01.11, 377); *In Eph. hom*. 4; PG 62.32, 24–37 (NPNF 01.13, 65–6).

60. *In 1 Cor. hom*. 38; PG 61.324, 10–20 (NPNF 01.12, 227–8); *In 1 Cor. hom*. 38; PG 61.324, 52–326, 13 (NPNF 01.12, 228–9).

61. *In Rom. hom*. 2; PG 60.408, 35–37 (NPNF 01.11, 348).

62. *In Rom. hom*. 2; PG 60.408, 35–39 (NPNF 01.11, 348).

63. *In Rom. hom*. 2; PG 60.409, 29–31 (NPNF 01.11, 349); *In Eph. hom*. 4; 63.33, 47–34, 1.

are freed from the eternal punishment that awaits them, are justified before God, and are clothed with the righteousness of Christ.⁶⁴ Having been "born again by the Spirit" the believer is now a new person in Christ.⁶⁵ Chrysostom further elaborates that, because of this new birth, the believer is no longer to gratify the desires of their human nature but to live lives of "good works" which reflect their new Spirit nature.⁶⁶ These good works are to be evidenced in the day-to-day life of the believer.⁶⁷ Believers are to present their lives as living sacrifices, which Chrysostom elaborates as follows:

> Let the eye look upon no evil thing, and it has become a sacrifice; let the tongue speak nothing filthy, and it has become an offering; let your hand do no lawless deed, and it has become a burnt offering. Or rather, this is not enough, but we must have good works also: let the hand do alms, the mouth bless them that cross one, and the hearing find leisure evermore for lections of Scripture. For sacrifice allows no unclean thing: sacrifice is a first-fruit of other actions. Let us then from our hands, and feet, and mouth, and all other members, yield a firstfruit unto God.⁶⁸

For Chrysostom, the gospel was more than simply facts to be learnt: it was a message to be proclaimed and lived. As the majority of Chrysostom's audiences in Antioch and Constantinople would have considered themselves Christians, the burden of Chrysostom's preaching lay not in the annunciation of the gospel kerygma but rather in how the gospel translated into sanctified living. As Maxwell remarks, Chrysostom's preaching focused on carefully explaining "what was

---

64. *In Rom. hom.* 2; PG 60.409, 32–36 (NPNF 01.11, 349); *In Rom. hom.*7; PG 60.443, 19–21 (NPNF 01.11, 377); *In Rom. hom.*7; PG 60.444, 15–26 (NPNF 01.11; 377).

65. *In 2 Cor. hom.* 11; PG 61.475, 34–44 (NPNF 01.12, 332).

66. *In 2 Cor. hom.* 11; PG 61.475, 34–50 (NPNF 01.12, 332); *In Rom. hom.* 14; PG 60.523, 33–51 (NPNF 01.11, 439).

67. *In Eph. hom.* 4; PG 62.34, 7–28 (NPNF 01.13, 68).

68. *In Rom. hom.* 20; PG 60.595, 55–596, 18 (NPNF 01.11, 496): "Μηδὲν ὀφθαλμὸς πονηρὸν βλεπέτω, καὶ γέγονε θυσία· μηδὲ ἡ γλῶσσα λαλείτω αἰσχρόν, καὶ γέγονε προσφορά· μηδὲν ἡ χεὶρ πραττέτω παράνομον, καὶ γέγονεν ὁλοκαύτωμα. Μᾶλλον δὲ οὐκ ἀρκεῖ ταῦτα, ἀλλὰ καὶ τῆς τῶν ἀγαθῶν ἡμῖν ἐργασίας δεῖ, ἵνα ἡ μὲν χεὶρ ἐλεημοσύνην ποιῇ, τὸ δὲ στόμα εὐλογῇ τοὺς ἐπηρεάζοντας, ἡ δὲ ἀκοὴ θείαις σχολάζῃ διηνεκῶς ἀκροάσεσιν. Ἡ γὰρ θυσία οὐδὲν ἔχει ἀκάθαρτον, ἡ θυσία ἀπαρχὴ τῶν ἄλλων ἐστί. Καὶ ἡμεῖς τοίνυν καὶ χειρῶν καὶ ποδῶν καὶ στόματος καὶ τῶν ἄλλων ἁπάντων ἀπαρχώμεθα τῷ Θεῷ."

and what was not proper Christian belief and behaviour" and sought to persuade or cajole his audience to agree with him.[69] He did this in different ways, depending on the audience and the context in which the homilies were delivered. In other words, Chrysostom contextualized the gospel, something he observed the Apostle Paul also did.[70]

Chrysostom compares the Apostle Paul's willingness to contextualize the gospel to his different audiences to that of a doctor treating different patients and a teacher teaching different children:

> Thus both the physician and the teacher are used to [i.e. also] do. For neither does the physician treat alike his patients in the first stage of their disorder, and when they have come to the point of having health thence-forth, nor the teacher those children who are beginning to learn and those who want more advanced subjects of instruction.[71]

Paul was a master contextualizer and Chrysostom drank deep from his well, both in content and in method. Chrysostom's homilies, like Paul's epistles (and his recorded speeches in Acts), are examples of the gospel being contextually explained and applied to particular audiences.

iii. *The Father's cultural milieu and worldview corresponds in some way to mission contexts in the twenty-first century.*[72] The loci of much of twenty-first century mission is Asia, Africa, and Latin America—places where the world of ancestors, local gods and goddesses, spirits, demons, souls, magic, and the like are integral to the worldview of the people (what Hiebert calls "the excluded middle").[73] This was largely the cultural milieu during the period of the church fathers, including John Chrysostom, in contrast to the dualistic mindset of western society.[74] Potentially, the writings of Chrysostom can communicate

---

69. Maxwell, *Christianization and Communication in Late Antiquity: John Chrysostom and his Congregation in Antioch*, 4, 7.

70. As Maxwell elaborates, "[Chrysostom] crafted his homilies with his audience in mind in order to try and teach as much as possible to as many as possible." Maxwell, *Christianization*, 91, 111.

71. *In Rom., The Preface*; PG 60.2,393, 55–394, 2 (NPNF 01.11, 337): Οὕτω καὶ ἰατρὸς καὶ διδάσκαλος ποιεῖν εἰώθασιν· οὔτε γὰρ τοῖς ἐξ ἀρχῆς νοσοῦσιν ὁ ἰατρός, καὶ τοῖς πρὸς τὸ τέλος λοιπὸν τῆς ὑγείας ἐλθοῦσιν, οὔτε τοῖς ἐξ ἀρχῆς μανθάνουσι παιδίοις ὁ διδάσκαλος, καὶ τοῖς τῶν τελεωτέρων δεομένοις διδαγμάτων, ὁμοίως χρήσονται.

72. See 1.1.5.

73. Cf. 2.3.1.

74. Florence Heintz, for example, identifies the residents of Antioch during

directly to those in the twenty-first century with this eastern mind-set and challenge mission in the west for those whose worldview does not readily embrace a three-tiered worldview.

iv. *The Father demonstrates a significant interest in mission.*[75] The significance of mission in the life of Chrysostom and his missiological approach is important to establish, as it not only affirms the rationale for examining Chrysostom's works for missiological principles for contextualization, but also provides a theological context for the examination of *Homilia habita postquam presbyter Gothus concionatus fuerat*[76] that will be examined in chapter five.

Chrysostom's promotion of mission amongst the Goths while he was bishop of Constantinople has been recognized by several authors, but presented as if that work was the extent of his missionary activity.[77] The focus of such authors is on Chrysostom's support of Gothic ministry outside of Constantinople in particular, with Liebeschuetz representative when he states, "[Chrysostom] found objects for his missionary zeal elsewhere" i.e., outside of Constantinople, through supporting ministry to the Goths.[78] Chrysostom's missionary activity as bishop was much broader than this, and included addressing issues such as paganism in Constantinople and its impact on his congregants.

---

the third and fourth centuries CE living in fear of magic spells. Professional orators, teachers of rhetoric, business people, athletes, competitive horse riders, and even high ranking officials were just some of the people afraid of, injured by, and users of magic—despite its practice being illegal in the empire. She further notes, "The zealous Christian orator, John Chrysostom himself, only a child at the time, narrowly escaped execution after fishing out of the Orontes a magic book that someone had discarded in fear. Heintz, "Magic Tablets and the Games at Antioch," 163–7, at 163. For an excellent treatment on the fourth century worldview of the supernatural see Trzcionka, *Magic and the Supernatural in the Fourth Century Syria*.

75. See 1.1.2.

76. *Goth. concin.*; PG 63.499–510. This homily is examined in detail in chapter 5.

77. de Wet, "John Chrysostom and the mission to the Goths: Rhetorical and ethical perspectives," 1–10; Kelly, *Golden Mouth: The Story of John Chrysostom: Ascetic, Preacher, Bishop*, 142–4; Chitulescu, "Activitatea misionara a Sf. Ioan Gura de Aur," 97–105. Chitulescu largely covers the same territory on Chrysostom and Gothic mission as Kelly does. Chitulescu, however, does draw an interesting link between Chrysostom's zeal in reforming his clergy in Constantinople and his zeal in promoting mission amongst the Syrians and Goths, seeing both activities as practical extensions of Chrysostom's love for God and his desire for righteous living and orthodox faith amongst all people.

78. Liebeschuetz, *Barbarians and Bishops: Army, Church, and State in the Age of Arcadius and Chrysostom*, 168.

Liebeschuetz states that, "[t]here is little in Chrysostom's sermons to suggest that he was worried about paganism at Constantinople."[79] This statement is nevertheless incorrect and reflects a common misreading of Chrysostom's homilies. During Chrysostom's years as bishop of Constantinople, Christianity was the official religion of the Roman Empire. Emperor Arcadius, himself a Nicene Christian, was also based at Constantinople. These two facts would have given Chrysostom a measure of confidence that the city was unlikely to return to Greco-Roman paganism at that time. Nevertheless, Chrysostom's sermons show that he was still acutely aware of the reality that most of the citizens of Constantinople were pagan rather than Christian.[80] Chrysostom's sermons show his intense desire for his congregation to live in ways that reflect God's holiness,[81] demonstrated in his appeals for his hearers to reject pagan practices and embrace a life of godliness in thought, speech, and act.[82] For those in the congregation imbued with paganism, the starting point was repentance and availing themselves of God's mercy in Christ.[83] It can therefore be concluded that Chrysostom's preaching was missionary preaching and his sphere of missionary activity was first and foremost the congregations where he preached regularly, both in Antioch and Constantinople.

Nevertheless, Liebeschuetz is correct in identifying Chrysostom's missionary heart for the Goths during his bishopric in Constantinople, even if Chrysostom's focus was Nicene orthodoxy.[84] Despite refusing the request from one of the imperial generals, Gaïnas, for a church in Constantinople where he and his Arian Gothic troops could hold church services, Chrysostom did assign one church to the Goths

79. Ibid., 168.

80. Despite the growing influence of Christianity in the empire during the fourth century, Krupp states that Chrysostom's preaching against the pagan lifestyle and its societal impact shows that Chrysostom never really believed he was living in a Christian society or that paganism would not dominate the empire again in the future. Krupp, *Shepherding the Flock of God: The Pastoral Theology of John Chrysostom*, 7. Cf. Costanzo, *Harbor for the Poor: A Missiological Analysis of Almsgiving in the View and Practice of John Chrysostom*, 28.

81. Maxwell, *Christianization and Communication*, 111, 144–68.

82. *In Acta hom* 4; PG 60.50, 8–22 (NPNF 01.11, 31); *In Acta hom* 6; PG 60.60, 5–36 (NPNF 01.11, 43); *In Acta hom* 51; PG 60.357, 55–358, 60 (NPNF 01.11, 43).

83. *In Eph. hom* 4; PG 62.33, 47–34, 7 (NPNF 01.13, 67–8).

84. Liebeschuetz, *Barbarians and Bishops*, 110, 168–71. For an extensive treatment of Chrysostom's ministry to the Goths, see Stanfil, "Embracing the Barbarian: John Chrysostom's Pastoral Care of the Goths."

where orthodox church services were held.[85] His accommodation to the Goths included "appointing Gothic-speaking priests, deacons, and readers to preach to them."[86] On one occasion, at least, he preached in the Gothic church. Following the sermon by a Gothic priest, Chrysostom then stood and preached a sermon which, among other things, reflected his missionary theology which was that the gospel was for all people, whether Greek or barbarian.[87] He also organized missionary work amongst Goths outside Constantinople, including the nomadic Goths along the Danube and the Goths in the Crimea, and established a Gothic monastery.[88]

Chrysostom's missionary zeal amongst the Goths was unusual amongst priests and bishops, something which Liebeschuetz attributes to Chrysostom's fierce determination not to embrace the attitudes of the cultural elite of his day who scorned barbarians.[89] De Wet speculates that Chrysostom's motives for missionary activity amongst the Goths may not have been pastoral and evangelistic but instead a "political or a religious strategy . . . [due to the] growing influence and strength of the barbarian presence inside and outside the empire."[90] He goes on to add:

> Mission can therefore be seen in this instance as an apparatus of security and technology of governmentality. It was also supposed to help late ancient Romans with population issues. Other

---

85. Stanfil, "John Chrysostom's Gothic Parish and the Politics of Space," 345–9, at 345.

86. Liebeschuetz, *Barbarians and Bishops*, 169.

87. *Goth. concin*; PG 63.499–510; Liebeschuetz, *Barbarians and Bishops*, 169.

88. Theodoret, *Hist. Eccl.* 5: par. 30–31; de Wet, "John Chrysostom," 3–10; Liebeschuetz, *Barbarians and Bishops*, 170; *The Funerary Speech of John Chrysostom*, by Barnes and Bevan, 52–54. Chrysostom's support of missionary work in general continued even during the years he was in exile, as is reflected in his letter to the presbyter Rufinus. What is interesting about this letter is that John offers to send Rufinus some relics, and that Chrysostom considers the use of relics a natural part of the evangelistic process. *Epistulae* 126; PG 52.685–7 (trans. Mayer: *St John Chrysostom: The Cult of the Saints*, 261–3).

89. Liebeschuetz, *Barbarians and Bishops*, 170; de Wet, "John Chrysostom," 259; Stanfil, "John Chrysostom's Gothic Parish," 346. Chrysostom maintained this missionary zeal even during his second exile. Kelly, *Golden Mouth*, 264–5; Stanfil, "John Chrysostom's Gothic Parish," 349. Stanfil notes that there is no evidence of any Nicene bishop prior to Chrysostom seeking to convert the Goths. Stanfil, "Embracing the Barbarian," 30.

90. de Wet, "John Chrysostom," 6.

similar apparatuses were barbarian recruitment into the army, trade relations with barbarians, and intermarriage with Roman citizens.[91]

De Wet's reinterpretation of Chrysostom's missionary motives, activity, and sphere of influence amongst the Goths can be challenged on the grounds that it fails to take into account the broader picture of Chrysostom's preaching. As has already been argued, all of Chrysostom's preaching was missionary preaching. Chrysostom's missionary emphasis amongst the Goths was simply an extension of the evangelistic thrust demonstrated in his pastoral preaching and ministry amongst his congregations in Antioch and Constantinople.[92] Stanfil persuasively argues for three coalescing factors to explain Chrysostom's mission emphasis: first, the discipleship of two bishops while he was in Antioch who themselves had a focus on the "Christianization of the surrounding Syrian countryside;" second, his understanding of the Bible in general, and of the ministry of the apostle Paul in particular, that led him to view mission as a biblical imperative; third, as Bishop of Constantinople, he had opportunity, power, and resources at his disposal to minister to the sizable Gothic population in that city.[93]

Chrysostom's commitment to mission to the Goths was attested in a funeral oration by ps-Martyrius spoken soon after Chrysostom's death, where he said: "As if the whole of our civilized world was not sufficient to occupy his pastoral care, he went into the land of the barbarians: he planted churches . . . now in the lands of the Goths, using for this purpose whatever ministers the grace of the Spirit suggested to him."[94]

---

91. Ibid., 7.

92. Stanfil, "Embracing the Barbarian," 8. For an insightful analysis of how the second and third-century Christians sought to express their Christian faith within their culture, see Rhee, *Early Christian Literature: Christ and Culture in the Second and Third Centuries*. Rhee examines literature from the Apologies, Apocryphal Acts, and Martyr Acts to show how they present the superiority of Christian monotheism, sexual morality, and loyalty to the empire to a culture largely hostile to Christianity. By the time of Constantine in the fourth century, Christianity was becoming the dominant culture, with an estimated six million Christians, representing ten percent of the empire's population. Kreider, "'They Alone Know the Right Way to Live:' The Early Church and Evangelism," 169–86, at 169. Rodney Stark suggests that a growth rate of forty percent per decade would be a "plausible estimate" for Christianity in its first few centuries. Stark, *The Rise of Christianity*, 6.

93. Stanfil, "Embracing the Barbarian," 282–3.

94. Ps-Martyrius, *Orat. Funeb.* 25. Cf. Stanfil, "Embracing the Barbarian," 3–4.

The point that ps-Martyrius makes is crucial for the next chapter, as part of a justification of how Chrysostom's homilies can contribute to an evangelical approach to contextualization. As previously stated, contextualization as a missiological term has only been used since 1972. In chapter three, I nevertheless established that the practice of explaining and applying the gospel in ways understandable and relevant to the receiving culture can be traced back at least to the period of the early church. The book of Acts demonstrates Peter, Stephen, Paul, and Christians in general, motivated by missionary zeal, engaged in contextualizing the gospel through their words and deeds, to Jews, Gentiles, and fellow Christians. In other words, they engaged in contextualization. More than three centuries later, John Chrysostom, motivated by missionary zeal, adopted the same contextual approach, even if contextualization was not part of his vocabulary (although see below). Throughout his ministry in Antioch and Constantinople, Chrysostom explained, applied, and lived out the gospel to Christians and pagan Gentiles alike. It is Chrysostom's missionary zeal, combined with his consistent practice of contextualization of the gospel to his hearers, which makes him an excellent case study of contextualization.

Therefore, Chrysostom fulfills the four criteria for a church father whose work can potentially contribute to the contextualization debate established above. There are also two additional points about Chrysostom that highlight him as a particularly valid test case for the contribution of the Fathers to the contextualization debate.

v. *Chrysostom foregrounds adaptation (synkatabasis) as his key principle in teaching the gospel (a principle that aligns closely with the modern concept of contextualization).* David Rylaarsdam has demonstrated that the rhetorical principle of adaptation (συγκατάβασις) is integral to Chrysostom's whole theology and teaching,[95] and is an example "of a Christian leader's attempt to form a Christian culture using methods which he assumes are imitating the pedagogy of God himself."[96] Chrysostom defines divine adaptation this way:

> What is this συγκατάβασις? It is when God appears and makes himself known not as he is, but in the way one incapable of beholding him is able to look upon him. In this way God reveals

---

95. Rylaarsdam, *John Chrysostom*, 4.
96. Ibid., 5.

himself proportionally to the weakness of vision of those who behold him.[97]

For Chrysostom, God is incomprehensible, and cannot be known as he truly is but only as he chooses to reveal himself.[98] God, the divine teacher, uses adaptation in order that he might be known "to those with whom he is communicating."[99] Rylaarsdam adds, "In his adaptation, God remains what he is and yet becomes knowable by revealing himself in a human fashion."[100] In other words, "God adapts his revelation to the capacity of humans."[101] For Chrysostom, God accommodates his revelation for the intended human audience. In other words, God contextualizes his speech in order for it to be understood by humanity.

Chrysostom taught that divine adaptation is something that should be "emulated" and adopted by all people—particularly preachers.[102] Chrysostom observed that in the writings of the Apostle Paul he imitated divine adaptability as a pedagogical technique, and Chrysostom sought to imitate that in his own preaching, for imitation of Paul meant imitation of Christ.[103] Therefore, many of the concepts inherent in contextualization are integral to Chrysostom's theology and practice of συγκατάβασις.

vi. *Chrysostom engages with issues inherent in the contextualization debate.* In addition to his foundational theology of divine adaptation, Chrysostom's sermons engage with issues inherent in the contextualization debate such as syncretism (e.g., *Adversus Judaeos*) and gospel proclamation across cultures (e.g., *Homila Habita*).

Finally, the benefit of using Chrysostom in the contextualization debate is strengthened even further by two recent monographs (examples of evangelical Protestant *ressourcement*), which seek to apply the work of Chrysostom to a twenty-first-century mission context. Won Sang Lee's *Pastoral Leadership: A Case Study, including Reference to John Chrysostom,* identifies the pastoral principles of John Chrysostom and how these principles can legitimately be applied today in

97. *De Incomp.* 3.15. Translation is from Rylaarsdam, *John Chrysostom*, 17.
98. Rylaarsdam, *John Chrysostom*, 13, 16.
99. Ibid., 17.
100. Ibid., 17.
101. Ibid., 18.
102. Ibid., 158.
103. Ibid., 158, 173.

order for the church to fulfill the Great Commission.[104] Eric Costanzo's book, *Harbor for the Poor: A Missiological Analysis of Almsgiving in the View and Practice of John Chrysostom*, seeks to appropriate Chrysostom's teaching on almsgiving to the problem of urban poverty in the developed world.[105] Costanzo acknowledges that his approach of seeking to uncover principles in Chrysostom's homilies which can inform the practice of almsgiving today "undoubtedly bears the challenges of historical, temporal, and cultural distances."[106] However, Costanzo contends that these challenges can be overcome through a careful missiological analysis of Chrysostom's homilies.[107]

In conclusion, an examination of Chrysostom against the four criteria established for a church father to be responsibly considered to be able to contribute to the contextualization debate, along with Chrysostom's foundation theology of divine adaptation, the intersection of his sermons with some of the issues inherent in the contextualization debate, and recent monographs demonstrating how Chrysostom's work can contribute to current missiological issues has shown Chrysostom to be an excellent choice. As previously highlighted in the work of Mayer and Allen,[108] in order to legitimately draw missiological principles from the homilies of John Chrysostom in chapter five and bridge the hermeneutical gap between the fourth century and the twenty-first century, consideration also needs to be given to such issues as the delivery of the sermons in the context of Chrysostom's own life (his life and times), Chrysostom's audience, and his homiletical style and method. The chapter will conclude with an examination of these issues.

4.4 Chrysostom's Life and Times

A history of Chrysostom's life and the times in which he lived provides context for his various homilies, letters, and sermons, as well as insight into

---

104. Lee, *Pastoral Leadership: A Case Study, including Reference to John Chrysostom*.

105. Costanzo explains his methodology: "Serious questions have surfaced . . . as to how effective the average believer and church can be in meeting the deepest needs of the poor in any culture. This study takes a unique approach to addressing such deficiencies by applying what I consider to be sound principles from a patristic source which are to be applied to a twenty-first century, developed, and urban setting." Costanzo, *Harbor for the Poor*, 2.

106. Costanzo, *Harbor for the Poor*, 2.

107. Ibid.

108. See 4.1.

Chrysostom's personal context (such as his personality, and his personal and theological biases).

John of Antioch, later known as *Chrysostomos* (Golden Mouth), was born in or around 349,[109] in Antioch of Syria, into a well-to-do family.[110] His father died while he was young, so he was raised by his widowed Christian mother, Anthusa.[111] He likely trained under the famous rhetorician Libanius, and received theological training under Diodore of Tarsus.[112] For six years he served under the Antiochene Nicene orthodox bishop, Meletius, before adopting a strict ascetic lifestyle in the Antiochene mountains.[113] There he lived for a further six years. Historians maintain that for two of these years he had little sleep and minimal food while he committed himself to memorising the entire Old Testament and New Testament.[114] The strictness of his regime resulted in a deterioration of his health, causing him to return to Antioch in 378.[115] For the remainder of his life, as much as he was able, Chrysostom continued to practice the "monastic austerities" he had employed in the mountains, and at heart never ceased thinking of himself as a monk.[116]

109. Dates given for his birth range from 344–54. For arguments supporting this date of 349, see Appendix B in Kelly, *Golden Mouth*, 296–8. Kelly's biography forms the basis for this summary of the life and times of Chrysostom, unless otherwise referenced. See also Palladius, *Dialogue on the Life of St. John Chrysostom* (SC 341 and 342) and Baur, *John Chrysostom and his Time*, for ancient and classic biographies.

110. Kelly, *Golden Mouth*, 4.

111. *De sacerdotio hom.* 1; PG 48.624 (NPNF 01.09, 34, 5); Neander, *The Life of St. Chrysostom*, 4; Kelly, *Golden Mouth*, 5. For more on Chrysostom's upbringing, see Jones, "St John Chrysostom's Parentage and Education," 171–3.

112. Kannengiesser, *Handbook of Patristic Exegesis*, 783; Quasten, *Patrology*, 424–5; Sozomen, *Hist. eccl.* 8.2 (NPNF 02.02, 399); Rousseau, *The Early Christian Centuries*, 252; Maxwell, *Christianization and Communication*, 2; Costanzo, *Harbor for the Poor*, 31.

113. There is some debate as to what degree Meletius held to Nicene orthodoxy. Geoffrey Dunn records that at the time of his appointment as bishop, Meletius apparently held a *homoousios* position regarding the relationship between the Father and the Son. However, soon after becoming bishop, he espoused a Nicene *homoiousios* position. Dunn further specifies that some scholars regard Meletius as having changed his theological position over time. Dunn, "The Roman Response to the Ecclesiastical Crisis in the Antiochene Church in the Late-Fourth and Early-Fifth Centuries," 112–28, at 114–6.

114. Mayer and Allen, *John Chrysostom*, 6; Kelly, *Golden Mouth*, 32.

115. Kelly, *Golden Mouth*, 32–4. The return or likely return of Bishop Meletius may well have been another contributing factor in his return to Antioch. Brändle, *John Chrysostom: Bishop, Reformer, Martyr*, 16; Mayer and Allen, *John Chrysostom*, 6.

116. Kelly, *Golden Mouth*, 35. Kelly, 35, further notes that, "Consistently with

The timing of Chrysostom's return is significant in that it coincided with a significant theological shift in the Eastern Empire, which became increasingly Nicene from 378. This theological shift was the result of a combination of factors which included the death of the pro-Arian emperor, Emperor Valens (9 August 378), the subsequent "edict of toleration" by the pro-Nicene emperor, Emperor Gratian, which allowed freedom of worship, the promotion of a strict Nicene, general Theodosius, to the role of Augustus of the East (January 379), and further edicts by Emperor Gratian which outlawed all forms of heresy (3 August 379) and defined orthodoxy in terms of Nicene theology (28 February 380).[117] Gratian's edict of toleration allowed the exiled Meletius to return to Antioch and resume his role as bishop. Chrysostom's return to Antioch saw him once again serve under Bishop Meletius, who ordained him as a deacon in 381.[118] While Chrysostom was not licensed to preach in this role he had freedom to write, which he did with great alacrity, producing various apologetic works[119] and treatises.[120]

---

this, he never hesitated as bishop, when the needs of the church seemed to warrant it, to call monks from their seclusion and either ordain them and associate them with his ministry or employ them as missionaries." For more on Chrysostom's attitude to monks, asceticism, and his personal appropriation of ascetic practices, even while he was bishop at Constantinople, see Sterk, *Renouncing the World yet Leading the Church*, 141–60. Mayer, however, questions the inherent reliability of the sources that have led to this general consensus of Chrysostom returning to Antioch solely due to health reasons and also never ceasing to think of himself as a monk. She suggests that Chrysostom's return to Antioch may have been more of a personal choice rather than something that was forced upon him, and that he may even have thought the city a more strategic place to live than in the mountains. To support her view, Mayer cites a number of Chrysostom's letters from exile that reflect his negativity concerning his living conditions and life in general. She argues that, since in exile he probably would have shared many of the same austerities as he experienced as a monk in the Antiochene mountains ("physical and social isolation and deprivation"), this period should not have proven a great hardship for him. Mayer, "What Does It Mean to Say that John Chrysostom was a Monk?", 451–5. See also Mayer, "John Chrysostom as Crisis Manager: The Years in Constantinople," 129–43, at 133–4.

117. Kelly, *Golden Mouth*, 35.

118. Brändle, *John Chrysostom*, 18.

119. For example, see *De s. Babyla c. Iulianum et Gentiles*; PG 50.533–72; *Adv. Iudaeos et Gentiles demonstratio quod Christus sit dues*; PG. 48.813–38.

120. For example, see *De compunction*; PG 47.393–432; *Ad Stag.*; PG 47.423–94; *De virginitate*; PG 48.533–96. More than one thousand of Chrysostom's works are extant. Mayer highlights a number of relevant problems surrounding these works. First, it is still an unverifiable assumption that the texts we have today are exactly (or close to) what Chrysostom actually preached. Second, it is still an assumption that Chrysostom customized his preaching to the occasion and audience (this may or may not have been the case). Third, the presentation of his material in rhetorical form further clouds

Upon the death of Meletius, the new bishop of Antioch, Flavian, who was strongly Nicene, ordained Chrysostom as priest in 386.[121] For the next eleven years Chrysostom pastored a large church in Antioch (most likely the Golden Church) and developed a reputation as a strong exegetical and somewhat controversial preacher.[122] Through his instructor Diodore, of the Antiochene school, Chrysostom had learnt the grammatical and historical method of biblical interpretation, which he generally adopted in his exegesis, rather than the allegorical interpretation of the Alexandrian school.[123]

interpretation. Fourth, the quality of some of the texts or parts of texts is poor, leaving lacunae in the Chrysostom literature. Fifth, the works that can definitely be attributed to Chrysostom are not absolute. And sixth, the "provenance and chronology" of John's homilies is not as certain as once thought. Mayer, "John Chrysostom: Extraordinary Preacher, Ordinary Audience," 105–37, at 107–9; Cunningham and Allen, "Introduction," 1–20, at 3–4. That being said, the current textual material is all that we have to work from. Therefore, I will follow the consensus of current scholarly opinion (Mayer, Baur, Kelly) in assuming that the texts attributed to Chrysostom listed in Geerard, *Clavis Patrum Graecorum. II. Ab Athanasio ad Chrysostomum* (Corpus Christianorum) [= CPG], are in fact his work and that they represent largely or completely what he said and/or wrote. Mayer, *The Homilies of St John Chrysostom—Provenance: Reshaping the Foundations*, 27–9; Baur, *John Chrysostom and his Time*, vol. 1, xix; Kelly, *Golden Mouth*, 92–4. For further discussion on Chrysostom's letters, see Mayer, "The Ins and Outs of the Chrysostom Letter Collection: New Ways of Looking at a Limited Corpus," 129–53.

121. Brändle, *John Chrysostom*, 23; Kelly, *Golden Mouth*, 55.

122. Kelly, *Golden Mouth*, 57. While serving as a priest in Antioch, Chrysostom also wrote many sermon commentaries and a number of treatises, most notably *De Sac. libri* 1–6; PG 48.623–92. As Mayer and Allen note, little information about this period in John's life (386–397) currently exists, with many accounts of his activities during these years speculative. Palladius and church historians Socrates and Sozomen focus more on his subsequent years upon becoming bishop of Constantinople. Mayer and Allen, *John Chrysostom*, 6. On why Chrysostom's challenging preaching did not get Chrysostom into "serious trouble" in Antioch, whereas it did in Constantinople see Mayer, "John Chrysostom as Bishop: The View from Antioch," 455–66, at 463–5. Mayer suggests that the fact that Chrysostom was only assisting the bishop in Antioch rather than actually being the bishop, his distance from the imperial court in Constantinople, and his reduced influence in Antioch due to the ecclesiastical schism there were all mitigating factors.

123. Mayer and Allen, *John Chrysostom*, 26–7; Kelly, *Golden Mouth*, 17, 40–4; Neander, *The Life of St. Chrysostom*, 17; Pelikan, *Divine Rhetoric: The Sermon on the Mount as Message and as Model in Augustine, Chrysostom, and Luther*, 72–6. Chrysostom would, however, occasionally adopt an allegorical interpretation of Scripture when it suited him. For example, he took an allegorical interpretation of Jesus' words about eunuchs in Matthew 19:12, interpreting becoming a eunuch as a call to a celibate lifestyle, saying, "But when He [Jesus] says that they made themselves eunuchs, he means not the excision of the members, far from it, but the putting away of wicked thoughts" and that the physical castration was in fact "the beginning of a work of

During this period in Antioch, Chrysostom preached different types of homilies,[124] including: exegetical homilies on biblical books;[125] doctrinal homilies, such as *On the Incomprehensible Nature of God* (targeted at the extreme Arian sect known as the Anomoeans),[126] and *Against Judaizing Christians* (targeted at Christians who were attracted to Jewish rituals and the Jewish faith);[127] homilies which eulogized martyrs or hallowed saints;[128] homilies on special feast days, such as Pentecost Sunday[129] or Christmas;[130] and occasional homilies in light of incidents that occurred in the city or beyond, his most famous being his Lenten *On the Statues* homilies (preached following the Antiochene riots of 387).[131]

---

demoniacal agency, and satanic device." *In Matt hom.* 62; PG 58.599 (NPNF 1.10, 664–5). Elizabeth Clarke comments that this is a further demonstration that what had been regarded as an "allegorical" interpretation in previous centuries could now be considered a "literal" interpretation. Clarke, *Reading Renunciation: Asceticism and Scripture in Early Christianity*, 160n33. On different patristic interpretations regarding what constituted a "literal interpretation" view, see Blowers, "Interpreting Scripture," 618–36, esp. 630–2. For more on the exegetical difference between the Alexandrian and Antiochene schools, see Neil, "Towards Defining a Christian Culture: The Christian Transformation of Classical Literature," 317–42, at 318–21. For a more nuanced view of what constituted Alexandrian and Antiochene exegesis, see Young, "The rhetorical schools and their influence on patristic exegesis," 182–99.

124. Following Cunningham and Allen, I adopt a broad definition of homily to include "works prepared beforehand or delivered impromptu at ceremonies which had some kind of liturgical content, but which were not always held in a church building." Cunningham and Allen, "Introduction," 1. Cf. Neil, "Towards defining a Christian Culture," 329. John's sermons varied in length from ten minutes to one and a half hours. He preached without notes, with the sermons recorded by a stenographer. The sermons were then published, usually after a quick editing by Chrysostom himself. Brändle, *John Chrysostom*, 31. More than 1000 of his works are extant. Mayer, "John Chrysostom," 141–54, at 141.

125. For example, *In Gen. hom.* 1–67; PG 53.21–54.580; *In Matt. hom.* 1–90; PG 57.13–58.794; *In Joan. hom.* 1–88; PG 59.23–482; *In Rom. hom.* 1–32; PG 60.391–682; *In 1 Cor. hom.* 1–44; PG 61.9–382; *In 2 Cor. hom* 1–30; PG 61.381–610; *In Eph. hom.* 1–24; PG 62.9–176; *In 1 Tim. hom.* 1–18; PG 62.501–600; *In 2 Tim. hom.* 1–10; PG 62.599–662; *In Titum hom.* 1–6; PG 62.663–700; Kelly, *Golden Mouth*, 89–94.

126. *De Incomp.* 1–5; PG 48.701–48.

127. *Adv. Jud.*; PG 48.843–942.

128. For example, *De s. Pelagia;* PG 50.579–84; *De beato Philogonio;* PG 48.747–56; *In s. Meletium;* PG 50.519–526. For an introduction to the rise of cult of the saints, its place in the thinking of Chrysostom and a translation of selected homilies on various saints and martyrs, see Mayer, *St John Chrysostom: The Cult of the Saints*.

129. For example, see *De s. Pent. Hom;* PG 50.453–64.

130. For example, see *In diem nat.;* PG 49.352–62.

131. *De Statuis;* PG 49.15–222; Brändle, *John Chrysostom*, 28–30.

In October or November 397 Emperor Arkadios appointed Chrysostom to the prestigious post of bishop of Constantinople, a role he fulfilled until his first exile in 403.[132] Constantinople was the official residence of the Eastern emperor, and Chrysostom lived close to the emperor's court and the cathedral, the Great Church, where John would regularly preach.[133] Emperor Arkadios and Empress Eudoxia would attend the Great Church on important occasions.[134] Upon installation as bishop, Chrysostom quickly set out to reform the See.[135] He began by redressing areas of wasteful extravagance, both in the church and in his own palace, and redirecting the money to places where he felt it was better used, such as hospitals.[136] He also conducted a spiritual audit of his clergy and imposed his own high ethical, moral and financial standards on them. This quickly led to resentment from the clergy and monks of Constantinople.[137] In contrast, he was enormously popular with his congregation at the Great Church, who flocked to hear his preaching.[138]

As he did in Antioch, in Constantinople Chrysostom preached many expository sermons on biblical books,[139] including fifty-five homilies on the book of Acts.[140] A number of homilies centered on veneration of saints and martyrs, and the reception of holy relics led John to preach encomia, such as *Homily Delivered after the Remains of Martyrs*.[141] Occasional sermons would also address issues of the day. For example, in *Against the Games and Theatres,* Chrysostom railed against and lamented over the population's

132. Mayer and Allen, *John Chrysostom*, 7–8; Costanzo, *Harbor for the Poor*, 28.

133. Kelly, *Golden Mouth*, 107, 130.

134. Ibid., 109.

135. For a helpful description of the life and role of a bishop in society, see Gwynn, "Episcopal Leadership," in *The Oxford Handbook of Late Antiquity*, 876–915; van Dam, "Bishops and Society," 343–66.

136. Mayer, "Welcoming the Stranger in the Mediterranean East: Syria and Constantinople," 89–106, at 95.

137. Brändle, *John Chrysostom*, 64–66.

138. Kelly, *Golden Mouth*, 130; Liebeschuetz, *Barbarians and Bishops*, 172.

139. For example, see *In Phil. hom.* 1–15; PG 62.177-298; *In Col. hom.*1–12; PG 62.299-392; *In 1 Thes. hom.* 1–11; PG 62.391-468; *In 2 Thes. hom* 1—5; PG 62.467-500; *In Philem. hom.* 1–3; PG 62.701-20; *In Heb. hom.* 1–34; PG 63.9-236. There is some dispute as to which of Chrysostom's homilies can definitely be attributed to him in Constantinople. For a detailed analysis, see Mayer, *The Homilies of St John Chrysostom*. Mayer argues that CPG 4305–4472 are the only ones that can with certainty be attributed to Chrysostom at Constantinople.

140. *In Acta* 1–55 (PG 60.13-384); Liebeschuetz, *Barbarians and Bishops*, 172.

141. *Hom. dicta post.*; PG 63.467-72.

attachment to attending chariot racing and the theater instead of church.[142] Other recurrent sermon themes included marriage and sexuality, condemnation of the rich, and upholding the plight of the poor.[143]

While he initially enjoyed the support of the emperor and empress, their support waned over time. Chrysostom's harsh dismissal and the subsequent recall of Syrian Bishop Severian, at the demand of Empress Eudoxia,[144] his involvement in a dispute between the Bishop of Alexandria and a group of Nitrian monks (the "Affair of the Tall Brothers"),[145] false charges brought against Chrysostom by his adversaries, and preaching which allegedly insulted Empress Eudoxia all came to a head in 403.[146] Chrysostom was tried *in absentia* at the Synod of the Oak, deposed, and exiled.[147] Public outcry and a personal tragedy for Eudoxia (most likely a miscarriage, which she superstitiously interpreted as a sign of God's displeasure) resulted in Chrysostom's almost immediate recall to Constantinople.[148] In 404 he was deposed and exiled a second time, to Cucusus in eastern Turkey.[149] Despite the difficult conditions he experienced in Cucusus, due to lack of amenities, harsh weather, frequent bouts of ill-health, and the persistent threat of Isaurian invaders, John penned many letters, some 240 still extant.[150] In 407 Chrysostom was further banished to Pityus on the Black Sea, but died en route, on 14 September of the same year.[151]

Largely due to public pressure, Chrysostom's dignity and honor were restored over the next thirty years.[152] Chrysostom was formally exoner-

---

142. *C. Lud. et theat.*; PG 56.263–70.

143. For example, see *In Act. hom.* 7; PG 60.252; *In Act. hom.* 35; PG 60.252; *Golden Mouth*, 136.

144. This incident would have been personally humiliating for Chrysostom.

145. See Brändle, *John Chrysostom*, 95–104.

146. Mayer and Allen, *John Chrysostom*, 9–10; Bowes, *Private Worship, Public Values, and Religious Change in Late Antiquity*, 118–9. Palladius states that Chrysostom was removed from office because he called the empress "Jezebel," although this is disputed by some scholars. Palladius, *Dialogue*, 57. Mayer, "Media Manipulation as a Tool in Religious Conflict," 151–166. For further discussion on the relationship between Chrysostom and Eudoxia, see Barnes and Bevan, *The Funerary Speech for John Chrysostom*, 28–32.

147. Brändle, *John Chrysostom*, 104–14.

148. Brändle, *John Chrysostom*, 115; Quasten, *Patrology*, 426.

149. Barnes and Bevan, *The Funerary Speech*, 3; Brändle, *John Chrysostom*, 120–4.

150. Kelly, *Golden Mouth*, 260.

151. Mayer and Allen, *John Chrysostom*, 11; Barnes and Bevan, *The Funerary Speech*, 4.

152. Barnes and Bevan, *The Funerary Speech*, 4–5.

ated of the charges that had been laid against him, and his remains were fetched from Comana and personally received by the emperor, Theodosios II, who begged forgiveness for the injustices his parents had done to John. Chrysostom's body was then ceremonially buried at the Church of the Holy Apostles—"the traditional burial place for bishops and emperors."[153] In 451 the Council of Chalcedon honored Chrysostom with the title of doctor of the church.[154]

4.5 Chrysostom's audience

A consideration of the social, religious, and economic background, and changing nature of Chrysostom's audiences in Antioch and Constantinople provides a general picture of the identity and worldview of those to whom Chrysostom was preaching.

The issue of Chrysostom's audience is a complex and, until recently, largely neglected area of study.[155] The difficulty in precisely identifying the composition of Chrysostom's audiences in Antioch and Constantinople is reflected in three quite different conclusions drawn from the same data. Ramsay MacMullen argues that Chrysostom's audiences were predominantly male, wealthy, and from the elite class of society, with women, landowners, and the poor a minority of the attendees.[156] Philip Rousseau takes a broader view. He notes that, while the preacher would have often been part of the elite, and spoke in a way customary for the elite, his preaching would have appealed to a broader audience than just that social class. Rousseau concludes that a wider audience, therefore, cannot be ruled out.[157] Wolf Liebeschuetz, Jaclyn Maxwell, and Wendy Mayer take a third view, arguing that Chrysostom's audiences were a mix of all social classes.[158] Men, women,

153. Kelly, *Golden Mouth*, 286–90; Quasten, *Patrology*, 427; Rousseau, *The Early Christian Centuries*, 253.

154. Costanzo, *Harbor for the Poor*, 13.

155. For a more detailed review of past scholarship on Chrysostom's audience and an introduction to some its complexities, see Mayer, "John Chrysostom: Extraordinary Preacher," 105–37. For a detailed and well researched re-evaluation of the provenance of Chrysostom's homilies, see Mayer, *The Homilies of St John Chrysostom*.

156. MacMullen, "The Preacher's Audience (AD 350–400)," 503–11; MacMullen, *Christianity and Paganism in the Fourth to Eighth Centuries*, 10. MacMullen also suggests that in country towns and on feast days the audience for a preacher's homily may have been a broader representation of the community. MacMullen, *Christianity and Paganism*, 10.

157. Rousseau, "'The Preacher's Audience': A More Optimistic View," 391–400.

158. Liebeschuetz, *Barbarians and Bishops*, 173; Maxwell, *Christianization and*

wealthy people, slaves, visiting monks, visiting bishops, the emperor, and the empress are all mentioned in various homilies and so must have comprised part of his audience.[159] Following Cunningham and Allen, therefore, what we can at least conclude about the general makeup of Chrysostom's congregations in Antioch and Constantinople is that the audiences were mostly orthodox Christians from a variety of backgrounds—both rich and poor.[160]

Wendy Mayer is more precise about the identity of Chrysostom's audience, and highlights something of the complexity of the debate when she states,

> In almost every study John's audience is treated as a homogenous entity, as often as not without distinction between the two different cities in which he preached. Even in those studies which are careful to distinguish the two, the audience within each city is more often discussed collectively than separated into the individual groups that attended the different churches. The views derived from these approaches tend to obscure the complex network of audiences, preaching places and preacher-audience interaction that can be found embedded within the evidence—networks that in turn form an integral part of the social fabric peculiar to each city.[161]

For Mayer, a close reading of individual homilies reveals that in both Antioch and Constantinople, "John's audience is neither static nor

---

Communication, 67–87; Mayer and Allen, *John Chrysostom*, 34–46; Mayer, "Who Came to Hear John Chrysostom Preach? Recovering a Late Fourth Century Preacher's Audience," 73–87, at 73–80, 87. Mayer points out that the homily that Liebeschuetz uses as the basis of his conclusion regarding audience may not actually be by Chrysostom.

159. MacMullen, "The Preacher's Audience," 503–11; Mayer, "John Chrysostom: Extraordinary Preacher," 117–33. Mayer also states that, since the poor are referred to in various homilies, it is at least suggestive they could have been in his audience at different times as well. Taft, "Women at Church in Byzantium: Where, When, and Why?" 27–87, argues in detailed and convincing fashion that women comprised part of Chrysostom's audiences.

160. Cunningham and Allen, "Introduction," 13.

161. Mayer, "John Chrysostom: Extraordinary Preacher," 113. Mayer highlights a notable exception to this lack of detailed analysis of Chrysostom's audiences in two excurses found in Frans van de Paverd's book on the *Homilies of the Statues*. One excursus is devoted to the weekday times of Chrysostom's preaching of these homilies and the likely impact on civilian life in Antioch, and another excursus on the identity of part of John's audience. van de Paverd, *St John Chrysostom, The Homilies of the Statues. An Introduction*, 110–11.

homogenous but a constantly changing entity."[162] Mayer posits that factors including the city the homily was preached in, the occasion of the address (e.g., a feast day, receiving of relics), the location (e.g., church, shrine, Gothic church), in which of the churches in the city the homily was preached, which other events were occurring in the city on the day that the homily was preached (e.g., chariot races, theater), and even the presence of dignitaries (e.g., emperor, empress) all influenced the make up of the audience for a particular homily.[163]

These factors raised by Mayer will be taken into account when three Chrysostom homilies are examined in chapter five. As Mayer has also highlighted, individual homilies (even if part of a larger series of homilies) need to be examined in their own right, while simultaneously keeping political, social, and religious contexts in mind, so as to accurately determine the composition of the audience of the homily. Furthermore, a series of homilies (e.g., *In Matt. hom.* 1–90, *In Gen. hom.* 1–67 etc.) was not necessarily preached sequentially or in a single location. Care will need to be taken in determining the degree to which general comments about the provenance and audience for a series of homilies apply to individual homilies.[164]

4.6 Chrysostom's homiletical style and method

An appreciation of how and why Chrysostom preached as he did is a necessity if we are to competently interpret the particular words and phrases Chrysostom used. The impact of Chrysostom's rhetorical background and training on his preaching, the motivation behind his preaching, Chrysostom's treatment of Scripture, and the subject matter of his sermons will be considered in this section.

The large quantity of surviving homiletical material and commentaries by early Christian preachers provides the observant reader with significant insights into how preachers pastored their congregations and sought to contextualize the unchangeable word of God to their respective audiences.[165] This is never more the case than for John Chrysostom, the most prolific of the Greek Fathers,[166] whose literal interpretation of Scripture and

162. Mayer, "John Chrysostom: Extraordinary Preacher," 122.

163. Mayer, "John Chrysostom: Extraordinary Preacher," 114–122.

164. Mayer, *The Homilies of St John Chrysostom*, 512–3.

165. Olivar, "Reflections on Problems Raised by Early Christian Preaching," 21–32, at 23.

166. Kennedy, *Greek Rhetoric Under Christian Emperors: A History of Rhetoric*, 242–3. The sermon texts that exist for Chrysostom are largely those prepared by a

direct application to daily life gripped his congregations at Antioch and Constantinople.

Christian homilies during the fourth and fifth centuries were not classical rhetorical speeches, but rather Christian modifications of preexisting Greco-Roman models.[167] As a skilled rhetorician, Chrysostom's mastery of his craft allowed him to modify the rhetorical techniques he had previously learnt and employ them to powerful effect in his preaching.[168] Not only did Chrysostom possess a comprehensive knowledge of the Bible, his own culture, and human nature but he also had impeccable rhetorical skill.[169] The combined effect of all these attributes was an ability to communicate profound truths simply.[170] Of his use of rhetoric George A. Kennedy states that Chrysostom made,

> abundant, even excessive, use of the stylistic devices of the sophists, especially tropes and figures involving pleonasm, such as

---

stenographer rather than by Chrysostom himself. Chrysostom edited some texts before they were published, but others he did not. There are many occasions where two editions of a homily exist—one with smooth language and the other with relatively rough language (this is particularly so with his homilies on Acts). The former is considered a "deliberate later revision of the latter," leaving the rough text the authoritative version. Quasten, *Patrology*, 433, 441. Cf. Allen et al., *Preaching Poverty in Late Antiquity: Perceptions and Realities*, 37.

167. Allen et al., *Preaching Poverty in Late Antiquity*, 35; Maxwell, *Christianization and Communication*, 89. Mayer notes that earlier scholarship on Chrysostom sought to locate his homilies within the "classical rhetorical tradition" but recent scholarship posits Chrysostom's homilies as Christian exploitation of this rhetorical tradition. Mayer, "John Chrysostom: Extraordinary Preacher," 112. For more on the early Christian homily, see Mayer, "Homiletics," in *Oxford Handbook of Early Christian Studies*, 565–83; Olivar, *La Predicación Cristiana Antigua. Sección de Teología y Filosofía*; Maxwell, *Christianization and Communication*, 11–41.

168. Liebeschuetz, *Barbarians and Bishops*, 166, 182; Rylaarsdam, *John Chrysostom*, 18; Mitchell, *The Heavenly Trumpet*, 24–28; Young, "The Rhetorical Schools," 189; Wilken, *John Chrysostom and the Jews: Rhetoric and Reality in the Late Fourth Century*, 6, 106–12; Rylaarsdam, *John Chrysostom*, 18. Alberto Quiroga adds that Chrysostom's use of rhetoric was not a replication of the Second Sophistic but part of a Christianised adaption of rhetoric, known as the Third Sophistic. Quiroga, "From Sophistopolis to Episcopolis: The Case for a Third Sophistic," 31–41, at 37–38, 41.

169. The pagan philosopher Libanius so esteemed Chrysostom's rhetoric ability that one Christian historian, Sozomen, reports a story from Socrates who claimed that Libanius, on his deathbed, told friends that Chrysostom would have become his successor "had not the Christians taken him from us." Sozomen, *Hist. eccl.* 8.2 (NPNF 02.02, 399).

170. Laird, *Mindset, Moral Choice and Sin in the Anthropology of John Chrysostom*, xi; Cunningham, "Preaching and Community," 29–46, at 34.

anaphora, or sound, such as paronomasia, or vivacity, such as rhetorical question or question and answer.[171]

David Rylaarsdam identifies six characteristics of classical rhetorical oratory that are also representative of Chrysostom's homiletical style:[172]

i. *Harsh and gentle speech.* Hellenistic philosophers developed a method of teaching, referred to by scholars today as psychagogy, which sought to guide the souls and develop the personal growth of their students— intellectually, spiritually, and morally.[173] This would involve carefully adapting and nuancing the tone of speech appropriate to the needs of the particular student on that occasion—whether harsh or gentle. A wise psychagogue, such as Chrysostom, knew "when to afflict the comfortable and when to comfort the afflicted."[174]

ii. *Corporeal images.* Classical orators often built their arguments by describing objects or "human experiences" in order to create mental pictures which could change the hearers' perception of reality.[175] Chrysostom himself adopted this approach.[176] Rylaarsdam states that Chrysostom regularly crafted and managed a plethora of visual images in the minds of his listeners, so that they "reconceive[d] reality through the lens of Scripture and [were] persuaded towards a wise way of life."[177] Chrysostom's goal in creating such images was to lead his listeners into a deeper Christian faith."[178]

iii. *Models for imitation.* Greek education saw children learn by imitating models—particularly famous orators from history.[179] Chrysostom

171. Kennedy, *Greek Rhetoric*, 248.

172. Each of these six characteristics will be demonstrated in Chrysostom homilies in chapter 5.

173. Rylaarsdam, *John Chrysostom*, 32–33.

174. Rylaarsdam, *John Chrysostom*, 77, 230–1. Cf. 279–81. For examples of gentle speech, see *De Stat.* 2; PG 49.34, 41–44; *De Stat.* 6; *De Stat.* 6; PG 49.81, 14–17; PG 49.83, 54; *Goth. concin*; PG 63.500, 55–56, 501, 12–13; *Goth. concin.*; PG 63.501, 28–30; *Goth. concin.*; PG 63.501, 51–55. For examples of harsh speech, see *Adv. Jud.* 1; PG 48.846, 65–847, 3; 12–19; *Adv. Jud.* 1; PG 48.853, 26; *Adv. Jud.* 1; PG 48.853, 35–40.

175. Rylaarsdam, *John Chrysostom*, 68.

176. For example: *De Stat.* 2; PG 49.35, 5–7; *De Stat.* 6; PG 49.85, 39–40, 44; *De Stat.* 17; PG 49.172, 25; *Adv. Jud.* 1; PG 48.845, 3; *Adv. Jud.* 1; PG 48.846, 65–847, 3; 12–19; *Adv. Jud.* 1; PG 48.847, 35–38; 848, 59–849, 3; 851, 58–852 1; *Goth. concin.*; PG 63. 501, 12–18.

177. Rylaarsdam, *John Chrysostom*, 228–9.

178. Ibid., 239.

179. Ibid., 73.

finds many examples in Scripture of divine adaptation where God presents biblical examples as models or exemplars which are to be emulated (e.g., Abraham).[180] As part of adapting his own preaching to reflect this divine pedagogy, some of the corporeal images that Chrysostom uses are also drawn from Scripture and are presented as models for imitation.[181]

iv. *Lofty and lowly teachings.* Chrysostom was fascinated by the pedagogical methods of the Apostle Paul. He was convinced that Paul's methods were modeled on divine pedagogy and were a model for all church leaders (including Chrysostom himself) to follow.[182] Chrysostom identified in Paul's writings the way he regularly alternated between lofty and lowly teaching. He described Paul's approach as like a man gently leading people up to a lofty place, inviting them to look down, but when they feel giddy and confused he takes hold of their hands and leads them to a lower place so that they can take a breather. And then, when they have recovered, he leads them up again, and then brings them back down again etc. They do not stay on the heights for too long but the eventual result is that the people are gradually brought to a higher plane "of vision and insight."[183] Chrysostom himself modeled this method, mixing brief descriptions of lofty theology with extended, lowly teaching directed at the level of the average listener.[184]

v. *Progressive education in the gospel and correction of error.* Like that of the apostle Paul, Chrysostom's adaptation was progressive. He did not try and address everything at once. Rather, he would seek to have his listeners understand and secure a gospel truth or accept a correction of erroneous thinking or behavior, before building on it. Over a period of time he would have led his audiences further and further towards gospel truth and away from error.[185]

---

180. *In Gen.* 42; PG 54.391–2.

181. Rylaarsdam, *John Chrysostom*, 73–74. For example: *De Stat.* 3; PG 49.49, 43–45; PG 63.502, 34–37; PG 63. 503, 27–32; *Goth. concin.*; PG 63. 502, 37–39, 46–49; 503, 21–26; 507, 24–29.

182. Rylaarsdam, *John Chrysostom*, 192–3.

183. Ibid., 190.

184. Ibid., 270–1. For example, see *De Stat.* 6; PG 49.2, 25–31; *De Stat.* 6; PG 49.85, 20–31; *Goth. concin.*; PG 63. 501, 12–18, 28–34.

185. Cf. Rylaarsdam, *John Chrysostom*, 191. For example, see *De Stat.* 6; PG 49.82, 31–44; *De Stat* 17; PG 49.180, 22–33; *Adv. Jud.* 1; PG 48.846, 65–847, 3; 12–19; *Adv. Jud.* 1; PG 48.851, 18–19, 38–40; *Adv. Jud.* 1; PG 48.851, 18–19, 21–26.

vi. *Ethical concessions.* Chrysostom varied his presentations of ethical standards to suit the particular context and issue he was dealing with. Rylaarsdam illustrates this when he says, "Chrysostom appropriates his listener's pursuit of wealth, honor, and pleasure, but argues that these are but shadows, excrement, chaff, and dreams compared with their heavenly counterparts . . . Chrysostom temporarily employs the values of his audience in order to transform them."[186] Chrysostom recognized that his ethical approach was subject to the charge of inconsistency, but for him it was simply applying the principle of divine adaptation to achieve a higher goal—that of removing ungodly vices in his audience and replacing them with virtues of godliness.[187] On that measure he therefore considered himself to be acting responsibly and consistently in his ethical teaching.[188]

Liebeschuetz describes Chrysostom's homiletical style as offering "lively comparisons, vivid descriptions, the whole range of figures of speech, passionate denunciations, enthusiastic praise, and every trick that will move an audience to enjoyable emotion."[189] That being said, not everyone would have experienced enjoyable emotions while listening to Chrysostom. For example, the rich,[190] those who attended the hippodromes and theaters,[191] and those who attended Jewish festivals[192] all experienced Chrysostom's stinging rebukes. According to the Christian historian Sozomen:

> By the same eloquence, John attracted the admiration of the people while he strenuously convicted sinners even in the churches, and antagonized with boldness all acts of injustice, as if they had been perpetrated against himself. This boldness pleased the people, but grieved the wealthy and the powerful, who were guilty of most of the vices which he denounced.[193]

The directness in Chrysostom's preaching is a reflection of his primary homiletical motivation. Whether Chrysostom was delivering

---

186. Rylaarsdam, *John Chrysostom*, 255.

187. Ibid., 230–1. For example, see *Adv. Jud.* 1; PG 48.851, 18–19, 38–40.

188. Rylaarsdam, *John Chrysostom*, 271–3.

189. Liebeschuetz, *Barbarians and Bishops*, 182; Maxwell, "Pedagogical Methods in John Chrysostom's Preaching," 445–50, at 445–6; Brändle, *John Chrysostom*, 33.

190. For example, see *In Matt. hom.* 35; PG 57.409, 4–410, 55 (NPNF 1.10, 235–236); *In Matt. hom.* 50; PG 58.509, 4–24 (NPNF 01.10, 313).

191. *Contra ludos et theatra*; PG 56.263–70.

192. *Adversus Judaeos*; PG 48.843–942.

193. Sozomen, *Hist eccl.* 8.2 (NPNF 02.02.400).

encouragement or rebuke, his goal was not praise or self-aggrandisement. Rather, it was the salvation of the souls of his hearers, and their progress in Christian maturity, reflected by godliness in their daily living.[194] As Rylaarsdam aptly summarizes, "Through his preaching, Chrysostom hopes to provide a philosophical discourse which heals the eye of the soul so that the world is perceived correctly and values are aligned."[195]

Chrysostom's preaching style reflected the conventions of earlier Christian preaching. Many of his sermons begin with a short summary of what was said in the previous sermon.[196] This would be followed by a long section of verse-by-verse exegesis of a biblical passage and finally by a shorter section of ethical application of some part of the passage.[197] A feature of Chrysostom's preaching was his many biblical citations.[198] In his introduction to Chrysostom's Genesis homilies, Robert C. Hill comments on Chrysostom's homiletic style:

> Normally, there was the opening reading of the day's verse(s). Chrysostom would then link the day's sermon with the previous day's, often through some figure as the laying of a table; this [linking] could occasionally develop into a lengthy moral/dogmatic/

---

194. Laird, *Mindset*, 18. Chrysostom's motivation is eloquently captured when he addresses the pointlessness of regular church attendance while living a life untouched by the gospel: "Think how sick at heart it must make me, to see it all like [so much water] poured into a cask with holes in it . . . Why else do I weary myself in vain and talk uselessly, if you are to remain in the same state, if the Church services work no good in you? . . . Many a time have I determined to hold my peace, seeing no benefit accruing to you from my words . . . because I ardently desire your salvation, until I see you to have made good progress, I think nothing done, because of my exceeding eager desire that you should arrive at the very summit." *In Acts hom.* 29; PG 60.218 (NPNF 01.11, 186). See also Rylaarsdam, "Painful Preaching: John Chrysostom and the Philosophical Tradition of Guiding Souls," 463–8, at 467. In Laird, "John Chrysostom and the Anomoeans: Shaping an Antiochene Perspective on Christology," 129–49, at 130–1, Laird states that Chrysostom's focus as a preacher was to be a shepherd of the souls committed to his care rather than a defender of religious orthodoxy. For more on Chrysostom's psychagogy and its relation to Pauline psychagogy, see Rylaarsdam, *John Chrysostom*, 183–8.

195. Rylaarsdam, *John Chrysostom*, 254.

196. Maxwell, *Christianization and Communication*, 92; Rylaarsdam, *John Chrysostom*, 214.

197. Cunningham and Allen, "Introduction," 10; Liebeschuetz, *Barbarians and Bishops*, 178.

198. In a review of both Chrysostom's treatises and about six hundred Chrysostom sermons, C. Baur noted 18,000 Scripture citations (7,000 from Old Testament, 11,000 from New Testament), with Matthew and Psalms the most often cited. Kannengiesser, *Handbook*, 786.

polemical excursus unrelated to the *Gn* text and supported from other Scriptural loci. Then –sometimes with abruptness and difficulty after such a lengthy digression . . . he would take up the day's text for exegesis/commentary. Finally, after a substantial time on the text, he would move to a parenetic conclusion, quite perfunctorily done by way of "supplying you with the customary *paraklēsis*," and not always arising naturally from the exegetical material.[199]

This summary of Chrysostom's homiletic on Genesis is indicative of many of Chrysostom's exegetical homilies.[200] Chrysostom was not the only Antiochene preacher to take an exegetical approach but his focus on clear, practical, and moral applications of the text to his hearers (a good balance of "orthodoxy" and "orthopraxy") differentiates Chrysostom's preaching from others of the Antiochene tradition.[201] Johannes Quasten encapsulates Chrysostom's propensity to apply Scripture practically, when he writes:

> Always anxious to ascertain the literal sense and opposed to allegory, he [Chrysostom] combines great facility in discerning the spiritual meaning of the scriptural text with an equal ability for immediate, practical application to the guidance of those committed to his care . . . He is equally at home in the books of the Old and the New Testament and has the skill to use even the former for the conditions of the present and the problems of daily life.[202]

Effective preachers aimed their sermons at "the social level and cultural background" of their audience, drawing on topics and images that were familiar and easily understood by their audience.[203] A survey of Chrysostom's

---

199. Hill, *The Homilies on Genesis of St. John Chrysostom*, 77.

200. Edwards, *A History of Preaching*, 77.

201. Costanzo, *Harbor for the Poor*, 11; Rylaarsdam, *John Chrysostom*, 157. For further discussion on Antiochene exegesis, see Gorday, *Principles of Patristic Exegesis: Romans 9–11 in Origen, John Chrysostom, and Augustine*, 104–7. In addition to literal interpretation of the text, Gorday identifies a salvation-historical reading of the Old and New Testaments (progressive revelation) as another feature of Antiochene exegesis.

202. Quasten, *Patrology*, 433. Cf. Neander, *The Life of St. Chrysostom*, 17. Robert Hill notes that, like previous Greek-speaking Antiochene preachers before him, Chrysostom was unfamiliar with the Hebrew text and so had to rely on the LXX rather than the original Hebrew text for his exegesis, which was a "significant handicap" for his preaching from the Old Testament. Hill, *Reading the Old Testament in Antioch*, 50–54.

203. Allen and Mayer, "Computer and Homily: Accessing the Everyday Life of

homilies reveals that he spoke on a wide variety of subjects that touched the lives of his hearers, including: marriage, family life, almsgiving to the poor, wealth and materialism, lack of church attendance, virginity, sexuality, marriage, various saints and martyrs, the imperial couple, Anomeans, Christian attendance at Jewish festivals, the priesthood, the devil, repentance, the life of faith, and godly living.[204] Chrysostom also used simile, metaphor and vivid imagery, which brought the sermon to life. Combined with his plain manner of speaking, illustrations drawn from the daily lives of his hearers (e.g., athletic, military, maritime, medical, agricultural images) and his eloquence, it is not surprising that he quickly established a rapport with his audiences.[205]

Conclusion

This chapter has tested the hypothesis that it is possible to appropriate the works of the church fathers in general, and John Chrysostom in particular, to inform the contextualization debate. The starting point for this discussion was the ambivalence and lack of consensus amongst evangelical Protestants that the works of the church fathers can inform current missiological debates. Even amongst those who are somewhat positive towards the endeavor they are quick to point out the historical, hermeneutical, and cultural gap that needs to be bridged in order for an informed and responsible engagement with the church fathers to take place, with any attempt to bridge that gap fraught with challenges. Some of the pitfalls in reading and appropriating the church fathers include uncritically reading and embracing the teaching of the Fathers, seeking to use the Fathers to justify personal or denominational theology, and adopting the view that the early church possessed a monochrome theology and practice.

Early Christians," 260–80, at 264; Brändle, *John Chrysostom*, 31–32. For how Chrysostom, in his adaption of speech in order to connect with specific audiences, was simply applying a concept inherent in classical rhetoric, see Rylaarsdam, *John Chrysostom*, 18–22.

204. Cf. Lim, *Public Disputation, Power and Social Order in Late Antiquity*, 178; Allen and Mayer, "Computer and Homily," 264–6; Neil, "Towards defining a Christian Culture," 330; Kalantzis, "Crumbs from the Table: Lazarus, the Eucharist and the Banquet of the Poor in the Homilies of John Chrysostom," 156–168.

205. Edwards Jr, *A History of Preaching*, 80; Kelly, *Golden Mouth*, 134; Allen and Mayer, "Computer and Homily," 260–4; Liebeschuetz, *Barbarians and Bishops*, 170. On Christian homilies as a window into the everyday life and thought of the early Christians, see Allen, "John Chrysostom's Homilies on I and II Thessalonians: The Preacher and His Audience," 3–21, at 3–11.

Four criteria for facilitating a responsible engagement with the church fathers on the subject of contextualization were proposed and subsequently applied to a representative church father, John Chrysostom, with Chrysostom demonstrated to fulfill each of these criteria. Furthermore, Chrysostom's theology of divine adaptation, the intersection of his sermons with some current issues in the contextualization debate, and recent monographs demonstrating that Chrysostom's homilies were appropriated for current missiological issues lead to the conclusion that Chrysostom is a suitable church father to examine regarding contextualization.

This conclusion is significant for my thesis as I seek to examine the homilies of John Chrysostom for principles that can be brought to bear on the current contextualization of the gospel debate in chapter five. In chapter one, I argued for the place of Christian thought (and patristics in particular) in missiological debate. This chapter has further nuanced the argument. Not only has it confirmed that the church fathers can contribute to missiological debate, but it has also qualified the nature and limits of that contribution. The teachings of the Fathers cannot simply be removed from their original context and inserted as proof-texts or exemplars into current missiological debates. Rather, in order for patristic teaching to make authentic and meaningful contributions to missiological discussions from an evangelical perspective, they must pass through two filters. The first filter, established in chapter one, is the filter of Scripture.[206] The second filter, established in this chapter, is a critical reading of patristic works and a consideration of various historical, hermeneutical, and contextual issues.

This chapter has established that it is possible to appropriate the works of the church fathers in general, and John Chrysostom in particular, to inform contemporary missiological and ministry issues. The next chapter will conduct a missiological analysis of contextualization of the gospel in a selection of homilies of John Chrysostom. The selected homilies are considered representative of the whole and are like a series of case studies in

---

206. See chapter 1, p. 3 where this "filter of Scripture" refers to the sixty-six books regarded as canonical by Protestantism. Therefore, the application of this principle to patristic literature is that any patristic writing has to be first evaluated against this norm of Scripture. It is acknowledged that Chrysostom felt free in his homilies to quote from other texts considered sacred at that period (whether included in the Protestant canon of Scripture of its sixty-six books but not considered canonical by him, or whether outside of the sixty-six canonical books such as Tobit, Judith, Wisdom, Sirach, Baruch, Maccabees. In terms of evaluating the homilies of Chrysostom for potential contribution to an evangelical approach to contextualization, any sources he uses outside of current sixty-six book canon of Scripture would need to be evaluated against this canon. For a helpful article on the church fathers' understanding and use of Scripture see Bromiley, "The Church Fathers and Holy Scripture," 199–220.

contextualization of the gospel. In these selected homilies, Chrysostom contextualizes the gospel as he deals with issues which include: the relationship between Christians and the State; poverty and wealth; syncretism; carnality; and mission. Like a master physician, Chrysostom carefully applies the salve of the gospel to these different spiritual wounds which were afflicting his respective audiences. Chrysostom's approach is a reflection of the contextual principles from which he operated. What will be demonstrated is that Chrysostom's contextual principles are instructive for current theology and the practice of contextualization.

Chapter 5

Contextualization in John Chrysostom

THIS CHAPTER SEEKS TO answer three questions. First, how did John Chrysostom contextualize the gospel to his particular audiences? Second, what contextual principles did Chrysostom use? Third, how do these principles compare with those already outlined in this thesis? To answer these three questions a representative selection of homilies that Chrysostom preached in both Antioch and Constantinople will be examined:[1]

i. *De statuis* (*On the Statues*).[2] These twenty-two homilies were preached in Antioch following the riots of 387. *Hom.* II, III, VI and XVII will be considered in this chapter. They address issues concerning God's sovereignty, Church and State, and godly living.

ii. *Adversus Judaeos* 1 (*Against Judaising Christians Oration* 1).[3] This homily is the first of a series of eight that were preached in Antioch against Christians who were frequenting Jewish festivals.

---

1. As already highlighted, the provenance of the bulk of Chrysostom's homilies is difficult to establish. These six homilies have been chosen precisely because not only are they representative of Chrysostom's preaching, and offer examples of contextualization in a variety of settings, but are all able to be attributed to Antioch or Constantinople with absolute certainty, thus satisfying the requirement from chapter 4 that audience and context be clearly established.

2. *De Stat.* (PG 49.15–222).

3. *Adv. Jud.* 1 (PG 48.843–56). There has been debate surrounding whether the *Adversus Judaeous* sermons were directed against "Judaising Christians" or whether they were directed against Jewish people themselves (and were therefore anti-Semitic). For my argument on why I think these sermons were directed against Judaising Christians see chapter 5, pp. 189–193.

iii. *Homilia habita postquam presbyter Gothus concionatus fuerat* (*Homily preached after the Gothic priest*).[4] This homily was preached in the church of the Goths in Constantinople and addressed the issue of the place of barbarian Christians in God's kingdom.

Luke's account in Acts of the sermons of Stephen, Peter, and Paul (examined in chapter three) are examples of sermons preached to different audiences, in different contexts, dealing with different contextual issues. They are a representative sample of contextual preaching and practice in Acts. In the same way, the selection of Chrysostom homilies above were homilies preached to different audiences, in different contexts, dealing with different contextual issues, and so provide a representative sample of contextual preaching and practice from Chrysostom's homiletic oeuvre.

The same analytical and evaluative approach that was applied to the sermons of Peter, Stephen, and Paul in chapter three will be used in the analysis of the selected Chrysostom sermons. First, the context, audience, and setting of each homily will be considered. Second, Chrysostom's contextual methodology will be evaluated. Third, Chrysostom's contextual message will be analyzed. Throughout the evaluation of these three aspects of Chrysostom's sermons, not only will Chrysostom's expertise in contextualization be demonstrated but his principles of contextualization will be highlighted and compared with those previously outlined in this thesis, with conclusions drawn regarding their relevance to the current contextualization debate.

5.1 On the Statues homilies II, III, IV, XVII

5.1.1 Context, audience and setting

Context. Chrysostom's twenty-two homilies *On the Statues* were preached following the Antiochene riots of February 387.[5] The riots were triggered by

---

4. *Goth. concin.* (PG 63.499–510).

5. Brändle, *John Chrysostom*, 28–30. The first of these sermons (*Ad illuminandos cat.* 2) was actually preached the week prior to the riots, but has been traditionally included in this series in many manuscripts. Kelly, *Golden Mouth*, 76. Frans van de Paverd argues both for including *Ad illuminandos cat.* 2 in the *De Statuis* series and for homily 2 being the first sermon in the series preached after the riots. van de Paverd, *St John Chrysostom, The Homilies of the Statues: An Introduction*, 205–33, 293–6. David Hunter suggests that the *De statuis* sermons were fueled by an ongoing debate between Chrysostom and his former rhetorical instructor Libanius. He argues that the Chrysostom's sermons were not only a means for consoling and encouraging the congregation but also polemical religious propaganda, advocating the triumph of Christianity over paganism. Hunter, "Preaching and Propaganda in Fourth Century Antioch: John

an unexpected government decree of an "exorbitant" new tax which would affect the entire populace.[6] When the city councillors and other prominent citizens were unable to convince the provincial governor who was present at the announcement to reverse the decision, the news of the new tax soon spread throughout the city.[7] A crowd rushed to Bishop Flavian's residence seeking his support in having the decision overturned. Not finding him at home, a mob began damaging property such as the governor's residence, public baths, and paintings and statues of the emperor.[8] Archers and police quickly moved in to quell the violence and bring the situation under control. As many rioters as could be found were soon rounded up, tried, and brutally executed.[9]

The riots left the Antiochene population fearful of further imperial retribution.[10] This fear caused many Antiochene citizens to flee the city, fearing total destruction of the city by fire and military might.[11] Approximately a fortnight after the riots, the commissioners appointed by emperor Theodosius conducted their investigations of the riots and passed judgment. The city councillors were held predominantly responsible and were subsequently arrested and tried,[12] while the city itself was largely spared, to the enormous relief of its citizens.[13] Antioch's main punishment was being stripped of its status as a metropolis and having its theaters, racecourse, and public baths shut down.[14] Chrysostom preached this series of homilies, *De Statuis* (*On the Statues*), during these turbulent few weeks, from prior to Lent through to Easter 387.[15]

Chrysostom's *Homilies on the Statues*," 119–38.

6. Kelly, *Golden Mouth*, 73; van de Paverd, *St John Chrysostom*, 19–20.

7. van de Paverd, *St John Chrysostom*, 21.

8. Ibid., 21–23; Kelly, *Golden Mouth*, 73.

9. Brändle, *John Chrysostom*, 29; van de Paverd, *St John Chrysostom*, 33–34; Kelly, *Golden Mouth*, 73–74.

10. *De Stat.* 2; PG 49.172, 34–38 (NPNF: 01.09, 453).

11. *De Stat.* 2; PG 49.34, 58–35, 5 (NPNF: 01.09, 345); van de Paverd, *St John Chrysostom*, 39, 42.

12. On the division amongst scholars on the degree of culpability for the riots that can be attributed to the city councillors, see van de Paverd, *St John Chrysostom*, 82–86.

13. Brändle, *John Chrysostom*, 30; *De Stat.* 17; PG 49.171, 21–27 (NPNF: 01.09, 452). Cf. van de Paverd, *St John Chrysostom*, 122.

14. *De Stat.* 17; PG 49.176, 1–8 (NPNF: 01.09, 452); Kelly, *Golden Mouth*, 74–75.

15. Mayer and Allen, *John Chrysostom*, 7. Frans van de Paverd convincingly argues that *De Stat. hom.* 2 was preached on 27 February, which was the Saturday before Lent. Van de Paverd, *St John Chrysostom*, 25.296, 316–317. While this could have been up to a week after the riots, van de Paverd surmises that it may well have been only

Audience and setting. Chrysostom's Antiochene homilies, at different times, refer to men, women, the elite, wealthy people, poor people, artisans and workers, farmers, children, catechumens, other clergy and monks, and so these people may well have been the main composition of his congregation, in a general sense.[16] In *De Statuis* 2, 3, 6, 17 there are only two direct references to the make-up of the audience. The first indicates the presence of both men and women.[17] The second reference suggests that people wealthy enough to have servants were in attendance, at least on the day that *De Statuis* 2 was preached.[18] In *De Statuis* 4 Chrysostom may well provide an important clue to his audience constituency for the series when he said to his congregation,

> I see you are attending to us with much good will, and with an intense earnestness . . . The forum is indeed empty, but the church is filled . . . [T]he tempest of the city drives together every one from all sides into the church, and by the bond of love knits the members close to one another.[19]

Chrysostom's phrase, πάντας εἰς τὴν ἐκκλησίαν συνελαύνει πάντοθεν, could be understood to mean that people from all parts of the city, i.e. all its different constituents, have been brought together in the church by the

---

one or two days subsequent to the riots. Van de Paverd, *St John Chrysostom*, 25–27, 37. *De Stat. hom.* 3 was preached 1–3 days later, possibly the Sunday before Lent, following the departure of Bishop Flavian to beseech Emperor Theodosius on behalf of the citizens of Antioch. van de Paverd, *St John Chrysostom*, 297; *De Stat.* 3; PG 49.47, 9–13 (NPNF: 01.09, 354). *De Stat. hom.* 6 was preached on the Tuesday of the first week of Lent, while the city was still fearfully awaiting the emperor's judgment. Van de Paverd, *St John Chrysostom*, 299. *De Stat. hom.* 17 was preached on Saturday 27 March, during the fourth week of Lent, subsequent to the announcement that the city would be spared major retribution from the emperor. Van de Paverd, *St John Chrysostom*, 352–7; *De Stat.* 17; PG 49.171, 21–27 (NPNF: 01.09, 452).

16. Maxwell, *Christianization and Communication*, 65–87; Mayer and Allen, *John Chrysostom*, 34–40.

17. *De Stat.* 3; PG 49.49, 48–51 (NPNF: 01.09, 356): "Let every man and woman among us, whether meeting together or at church, or remaining at home, call upon God with much earnestness, and He will doubtless accede to these petitions."

18. *De Stat.* 2; PG 49.40, 3–6 (NPNF: 01.09, 348): "Tell me, indeed, for what reason do you lead around so many servants, parasites, and flatterers, and all the other forms of pomp? Not for necessity, but only for pride."

19. *De Stat.* 4; PG 49.59, 21–22, 33–34, 46–49 (NPNF: 01.09, 364): ὑμᾶς δὲ ὁρῶ μετὰ πολλῆς τῆς εὐνοίας καὶ σφοδρᾶς τῆς σπουδῆς ἡμῖν προσέχοντας . . . Κεκένωται μὲν ἡ ἀγορά, ἡ δὲ ἐκκλησία πεπλήρωται . . . ὁ τῆς πόλεως χειμὼν, πάντας εἰς τὴν ἐκκλησίαν συνελαύνει πάντοθεν, καὶ τῷ συνδέσμῳ τῆς ἀγάπης σφίγγει μετ' ἀλλήλων τὰ μέλη.

current crisis. It is therefore reasonable to suggest that, for the duration of the crisis, the congregation listening to the *De Statuis* series broadly reflected the constituency of the Antiochene population.

Antioch was a diverse and cosmopolitan city, with Greek the main language of use. The majority of its citizens were Christians,[20] but there was also a substantial Jewish population and a number of synagogues,[21] along with Eustathians,[22] Anomeans,[23] and pagans.[24] Antiochene citizens were generally wealthy, with a smaller percentage of abjectly poor people in comparison with other similar sized cities.[25] Kelly describes the citizens of Antioch as having "had a reputation for pleasure-seeking, worldliness, fickleness and cynicism," as well as a passion for theater and horse racing.[26] By the time of Chrysostom's ministry in Antioch, Christianity was the official religion of the empire but adherence to Christianity was not yet compulsory.[27] Approximately only ten percent of the empire were Christians, representing some five or six million people.[28] Therefore, like other preachers of his day,

---

20. Chrysostom once stated that the city of Antioch had one hundred thousand Christians. *In Matt hom.* 85; PG 58.763, 1–2 (NPNF 01.10, 510).

21. Downey, *A History of Antioch in Syria from Seleucus to the Arab Conquest*, 447–9.

22. Eustathians were a group who tenaciously held to Nicene orthodoxy.

23. Anomeans were extreme Arians who not only denied that the Son had a similar nature to the Father (the standard Arian position), but denied there was any similarity in the natures of the Father and the Son. Brändle, *John Chrysostom*, 150. For Chrysostom's sustained critique of Anomean theology, see *De Incomp.* 1–4; PG 48.701–748.

24. Kelly, *Golden Mouth*, 2–3. Daphne, a suburb of Antioch which hosted the Olympic Games, also housed a number of pagan temples, as did Antioch itself. Downey, *A History of Antioch*, 643, 649–50. It is unclear how many of these temples were still functional during Chrysostom's time. For further discussion, see Saliou, "Les lieux du polythéisme dans l'espace urbain et le paysage mémoriel d'Antioche-sur-l'Oronte, de Libanios à Malalas (IVe–VIe s.)," 38–70.

25. John describes the Antiochene population as, "a tenth part is of rich, and a tenth of the poor who have nothing at all, and the rest of the middle sort." *In Matt. hom.* 66; PG 58.630, 5–9 (NPNF 1.10, 706). Allen et al., *Preaching Poverty*, 71–74.

26. Kelly, *Golden Mouth*, 3; Wilken, *John Chrysostom*, 4. For more on the theaters, hippodromes, and festivals see Costanzo, *Harbor for the Poor*, 54–58.

27. Costanzo, *Harbor for the Poor*, 27.

28. Keith Hopkins, "Early Christian Number and its Implications," 185–226, at 195. This represents a dramatic difference from approx. 7,000 Christians (0.01% of the population in the empire) in 100 CE and 200,000 (0.35 %) in 200 CE. Cf. Costanzo, *Harbor for the Poor*, 28.

Chrysostom would have to convince people of the truth of Christianity rather than simply assume their acceptance of the religion.[29]

Chrysostom likely preached the *De Statuis* series at the main church in Antioch, known as the Great Church. This would be in keeping with the fact that these sermons were preached during Lent, a major event on the liturgical calendar, which would almost certainly have occasioned his using the main church in the city. That being said, Mayer suggests that there may well have been more than one church in Antioch where regular synaxes could occur (e.g., the Old Church), so it cannot be ruled out that these homilies were preached at a venue other than the Great Church.[30]

5.1.2 Chrysostom's contextualized approach in De Statuis homilia 2, 3, 6, 17

Chrysostom's contextual approach in these four *De Statuis* homilies is demonstrated in two different ways. The first is the way he is able through his preaching to establish and maintain a personal relationship with his congregation. The second way is Chrysostom's ability to interact with the worldview of his congregation.

> i. *His personal connection with his audience.* In chapter three it was demonstrated how Peter, Stephen, and Paul sought to establish rapport with their respective audiences early on in their homilies. Like every good rhetor, Chrysostom followed suit. As presbyter and regular preacher at the church in Antioch (following his installation as presbyter the previous year) Chrysostom would already have enjoyed a level of rapport with the regular congregation. In *De Statuis* 2 he extends this rapport in his opening lament that displays something of the grief that he and his congregation share when he says: "What shall I say, or what shall I speak of? The present season is one for tears, and not one for words . . . Who, beloved, has bewitched us? Who has envied us?"[31] What Chrysostom wants to communicate is that the distress,

---

29. Wilken, *John Chrysostom*, 17.

30. Mayer, "John Chrysostom and His Audiences: Distinguishing Different Congregations at Antioch and Constantinople," 70–75, at 72. The titles of both *De statuis hom.* 1 and 2 state that these homilies were delivered in the *palaia* (old) church. The location at which the rest were delivered is less certain, although in *hom.* 3 Chrysostom explicitly refers to the vacant *thronos*, usually occupied by Flavian, which might indicate that he was preaching in the Great Church on that occasion. This is a rare example of explicit provenance. (W. Mayer, 2015, pers. comm., 9 July).

31. *De Stat.* 2; PG 49.34, 38–39, 34, 41–42 (NPNF 01.09, 344). This is an example

pain, and sense of bereavement that the congregation feels, he equally feels. He and his congregation are knit together in sorrow. This immediate identification with his audience allows Chrysostom to adopt the posture of a loving father with a distressed child, rather than that of the distanced, expert orator in the pulpit. Out of their shared sorrow Chrysostom is able to apply "the medicine of consolation" to his fellow Antiochenes.[32]

Chrysostom maintains the personal connection with his congregation during the *De Statuis* series through at least two rhetorical devices. The first device is one identified in chapter three that was adopted by Peter, Stephen, and Paul when addressing fellow Jews—the regular use of the first person plural pronoun. One of many examples can be found in *De Statuis Homilia* 2, where Chrysostom laments,

> Who, beloved, hath bewitched *us*? Who hath envied *us*? Whence hath all this change come over *us*? Nothing was more dignified than *our* city! Now, never was anything more pitiable.[33] (emphasis mine)

Another example is in a section of *De Statuis* 6, where Chrysostom has been seeking to relieve the distress of his congregation by giving reasons for his confidence that the emperor will not destroy the city of Antioch. Here, as well as using the first person plural pronoun, Chrysostom uses the additional word ἀλλήλους ("each other") which further serves to emphasize the reciprocal nature of the relationship Chrysostom and his congregation share:

> For our very meeting together daily as we do, and having the benefit of hearing the divine Scriptures; and beholding *each other*; and weeping with *each other*; and praying, and receiving Benedictions, and so departing home, takes off the chief part of our distress.[34] (emphasis mine)

---

of Chrysostom choosing a form of speech (gentle speech) in order to meet what he perceived to be the emotional needs of his audience (see 4.6).

32. *De Stat.* 6; PG 49.81, 17 (NPNF 01.09, 381).

33. *De Stat.* 2; PG 49.34, 41–44 (NPNF 01.09, 344): Τίς ἡμῖν ἐβάσκηνεν, ἀγαπητοί; τίς ἡμῖν ἐφθόνησε; πόθεν ἡ τοσαύτη γέγονε μεταβολή; Οὐδὲν τῆς πόλεως τῆς ἡμετέρας σεμνότερον ἦν· οὐδὲ γέγονε ἐλεεινότερον νῦν.

34. *De Stat.* 6; PG 49.85, 5–9 (NPNF 01.09, 384). Αὐτὸ γὰρ τὸ καθ' ἑκάστην ἡμέραν συλλέγεσθαι, καὶ τῆς τῶν θείων Γραφῶν ἀκροάσεως ἀπολαύειν, καὶ ἀλλήλους βλέπειν, καὶ πρὸς ἀλλήλους ὀδύρεσθαι, καὶ εὐχομένους καὶ εὐλογίας δεχομένους, οὕτως οἴκαδε ἀπιέναι, τὸ πλέον ἡμῖν ὑποτέμνεται τῆς ὀδύνης.

The warm bond between preacher and audience is further demonstrated in *De Statuis* 17, where the shared distress of the previous few weeks turns to shared elation, following the good news that Antioch will be spared, with Chrysostom saying:

> *Let's* give thanks, therefore . . . not only because he's saved *us* from shipwreck, but because he also allowed *us* to fall into such great anguish and allowed the extreme danger to hang over *us*.[35] (emphasis mine)

What we can therefore conclude to this point is that part of Chrysostom's contextual approach in *De Statuis* was to quickly establish rapport with his audience and then to consistently reinforce their shared relationship throughout his homily. This contextual approach would have had the effect of not only reducing the emotional distance between the preacher and the congregation but also of assisting Chrysostom to persuade the congregation of his point of view. The persuasion was further enhanced by Chrysostom's ability to engage with the text that was authoritative for his hearers (the Scriptures), and to speak in a way that interacted with the day-to-day life of his audience.

ii. *His interaction with and challenge of his audience's worldview.* For contextualization to be effective, the gospel needs to be explained in ways that engage the worldview of the target audience—a principle already outlined in the speeches of Peter, Stephen, and Paul.[36] Chrysostom demonstrated this principle in a number of ways. First was through his use of corporeal images.[37] He spoke of bees and hives,[38] pugilists (boxers) in the stadium and wrestlers in the theater, harbors and shipwrecks,[39] doctors and tumors,[40] and pedagogues,[41] images very familiar to his audience. Second was through his use of shared narrative. The homilies are replete with references to the ri-

---

35. PG 49.171, 27–29 (trans. Mayer and Allen, 105; NPNF 01.09,452): Εὐχαριστήσωμεν τοίνυν . . . μὴ μόνον ὅτι τῆς ναυαγίας ἡμᾶς ἀπήλλαξεν, ἀλλ' ὅτι καὶ πρὸς τοσαύτην ἀγωνίαν κατα ἀπήλλαξεν, ἀλλ' ὅτι καὶ πρὸς τοσαύτην ἀγωνίαν καταπεσεῖν ἀφῆκε.

36. Principle 2. See 3.9.

37. See 4.6.

38. *De Stat.* 2; PG 49.5, 5–7 (NPNF 01.09, 345).

39. *De Stat.* 6; PG 49.85, 39–40, 44 (NPNF 01.09, 384).

40. *De Stat.* 6; PG 49.81, 17, 22 (NPNF 01.09, 381).

41. *De Stat.* 17; PG 49.172, 25 (Mayer and Allen, 106; NPNF 01.09, 453).

ots and subsequent events. This approach reinforced for his audience that Chrysostom knew and understood their historical and cultural context, and it would have given the audience confidence in what he as their presbyter and spiritual guide said. A third way was through Chrysostom's expert use of various Greco-Roman rhetorical devices, a style of speaking familiar to his audience. He readily employed, for example, repetition,[42] emotion,[43] contrast,[44] hyperbole,[45] rhetorical questions,[46] and personification.[47]

The cumulative effect of Chrysostom's contextual approach, using words, phrases, and illustrations drawn from his congregation's daily experience, Greco-Roman rhetoric and the authoritative Scriptures, was profound. Not only did Chrysostom's words powerfully connect with and move his regular congregation, but they also drew many "pagans" to come and listen to him as well, and established him as "Antioch's leading preacher."[48] Eric Costanzo argues that his particular contextual approach is not limited to the *De Statuis* homilies but is a feature of Chrysostom's preaching in general. Costanzo states, "Chrysostom understood the importance of rhetoric, contextualization, and clear communication. He went to great lengths to communicate the gospel in ways that were relevant, memorable, and applicable."[49] Chrysostom's approach aligns with those missiologists who argue that communicating the gospel in ways that are relevant, memorable and applicable to the receiving culture should be a guiding principle for all evangelical contextualization.[50]

---

42. *De Stat.* 3; PG 49.49, 30–51 (NPNF 01.09, 356).

43. *De Stat.* 2; PG 49.34, 38–46 (NPNF 01.09, 344); *De Stat.* 2; PG 49.36, 42–56 (NPNF 01.09, 346).

44. *De Stat.* 6; PG 49.81, 30–52 (NPNF 01.09, 381).

45. *De Stat.* 3; PG 49.48, 38–49, 11 (NPNF 01.09, 355); *De Stat.* 3; PG 49.49, 30–51 (NPNF 01.09, 356).

46. *De Stat.* 3; PG 49.49, 36, 52 (NPNF 01.09, 356).

47. *De Stat.* 2; PG 49.34, 49–50 (NPNF 01.09, 344).

48. Kelly, *Golden Mouth*, 82.

49. Costanzo, *Harbor for the Poor*, 98.

50. Cf. Principle 2. See 3.9

5.1.3 Chrysostom's contextualized message

In the four homilies from *On the Statues*, three major themes frame Chrysostom's contextual message to a city plunged into crisis. The first is that God is sovereign and will bring good from this situation. The second is that the emperor and his rulers are to be respected and obeyed, being God's chosen means of maintaining order in society. The third major theme is that the populace need to live in light of their eternal citizenship rather than their present circumstances.[51]

5.1.3.1 God is sovereign and will bring good from this situation

The levels of taxation on the Antiochene population had been steadily increasing in the lead-up to the imposition of the new tax that triggered the riots.[52] Nevertheless, the riots themselves were unexpected, and surprised both the Antiochene government officials and the general populace.[53] The reaction of the *comes Orientis*, government officials, and the emperor himself subsequent to the riots left the Antiochene citizens grief-stricken, fearful, and uncertain of their personal and collective futures.[54] The riots raised a number of personal and theological questions for the crisis-stricken Antiochenes: Why did God permit the riots to occur? Were the riots a random event or was there some divine purpose behind them? Was God in control of the situation? What would the immediate and long-term future of the city be? Many people had forsaken the city: had God forsaken her as well?[55]

---

51. Alberto Puertas provides an important hermeneutic for reading Chrysostom's *De statuis* homilies. He argues that, while Chrysostom was legitimately addressing the situation of the riots through his preaching, he had a further agenda. In Chrysostom's time there were two bishops in Antioch (as had been the case for much of the fourth century). Chrysostom's consistent praise of Bishop Flavian in these homilies was part of Chrysostom's attempt to convince his audience that Flavian (rather than Paulinus) was the true Antiochene bishop, and therefore that Flavian's faction was the one that his audience should support. Quiroga Puertas, "Deflecting attention and shaping reality with rhetoric: the case of the riot of the statues of A.D. 387 in Antioch," 137–53.

52. van de Paverd, *St John Chrysostom*, 20.

53. One may have expected armed guards present at *dikasterion* when the emperor's letter was read, for example, if the riots had been anticipated by the government.

54. Chrysostom compares the impact of the recent riots to that of a recent earthquake which had afflicted Antioch. "Lately our city was shaken; but now the very souls of the inhabitants totter! Then the foundations of the houses shook, but now the very foundations of every heart quiver." *De Stat.* 2; PG 49.34, 38–41 (NPNF 01.09, 345).

55. *De Stat.* 2; PG 49.35, 14–16 (NPNF 01.09, 345): "For the help from above

Chrysostom's approach to such questions is instructive. Having acknowledged the congregation's devastation regarding the events that had just unfolded,[56] he begins to answer such questions by focusing his congregation's attention on God's sovereignty in the current situation. With rhetorical flair, in *De Statuis* 2 Chrysostom compares Antioch's present situation with the calamitous circumstances that befell Job. The biblical author clearly portrays Job's loss of children, livestock, property, and his own health as having been orchestrated by Satan, but sovereignly permitted by God (Job 1:6–12; 2:1–10). In like manner, Chrysostom vividly attributes the riots and subsequent events as having been orchestrated by Satan, but also sovereignly permitted by God, stating:

> For even as the devil then leapt violently [upon] the flocks, and herds, and all the substance of the just man [Job], so now has he raged against this whole city. But then, as well as now, God permitted (συνεχώρησε) it; then, indeed, that he might make the just man more illustrious by the greatness of his trials; and now, that he might make us more soberminded by the extremity of this tribulation.[57]

Chrysostom continues his theme of God's sovereign permission (συνεχώρησε) in *De Statuis* 3. In a section where Chrysostom contrasts the

---

having forsaken her, she stands desolate stripped of almost all her inhabitants." Mayer notes that these are precisely the same questions that Chrysostom's followers were asking themselves when Chrysostom was exiled, and that Chrysostom sought to address from exile. Chrysostom's use of Scripture and the framing of his message about God's sovereignty in the situation, within psychagogic terms from traditional Hellenistic culture, are equally prominent there. Mayer, "The Persistence in Late Antiquity of Medico-Philosophical Psychic Therapy."

56. *De Stat.* 2; PG 49.34, 38–42 (NPNF 1.09, 344).

57. *De Stat.* 2; PG 49.33, 50–54 (NPNF 1.09, 344): Καθάπερ γὰρ τότε ὁ διάβολος εἰς τὰ ποίμνια καὶ τὰ βουκόλια, καὶ πᾶσαν ὠρχήσατο τοῦ δικαίου τὴν οὐσίαν· οὕτω νῦν εἰς τὴν πόλιν ἅπασαν ἐβάκχευσεν. Ἀλλ' ὁ Θεὸς καὶ τότε καὶ νῦν συνεχώρησε· τότε μὲν, ἵνα τὸν δίκαιον λαμπρότερον ποιήσῃ τῷ μεγέθει τῶν πειρασμῶν, νῦν δὲ, ἵνα ἡμᾶς σωφρονεστέρους ἐργάσηται τῇ τῆς θλίψεως ταύτης περβολῇ. BDAG states that συγχωρέω can have two different meanings. First, it can refer to displaying a willingness to cooperate, giving some ground to someone in the sense of a concession. Second, it can also refer to granting or permitting something as a privilege. The first meaning better fits the context of Chrysostom's statement. God gave ground to Satan in a sense, permitting him to afflict Job in order that Job would be even greater (more illustrious) because of the trial. God's sovereign permission of Satan's actions was in order for a positive benefit to accrue to Job. In like manner, Chrysostom states that God's sovereign permission of the events that befell the citizens of Antioch in Chrysostom's day was in order for a positive benefit to accrue to the Antiochenes—that of greater sober-mindedness. BDAG, "συγχωρέω," 954.

riots (which he describes as a singular insult against the emperor) with the ongoing, hourly insults directed against God through "evil speaking . . . foul language [and] blasphemy,"[58] he tells his congregation:

> He [God] has permitted [συνεχώρησεν] our fellow servant [the emperor] to be insulted, in order that from the danger which has happened through this insult, you may learn the generosity of the Lord.[59]

Chrysostom had already suggested in *De Statuis* 2 a possible reason for God's permission of all the riot events—that God was wanting to teach the Antiochenes sober-mindedness, that is, to be humble and unassuming before him.[60] Presuming a positive resolution to the current dire circumstances, Chrysostom adds a second purpose—that his congregation would learn something of the nature of God's generosity or kindness. As part of his progressive education of his audience,[61] later in *De Statuis* 3 he suggests a third purpose for God's sovereign permission of these events—that the congregation would gain greater diligence in their pursuit of the Christian faith and that their faith would be refined, becoming more virtuous and modest.[62]

Chrysostom's assertion of God's sovereignty in the opening two homilies of *De Statuis* would have given hope and comfort to a congregation whose collective spirits neared despair. Chrysostom continued his theme of God's sovereign permission of events in *De Statuis* 6. He recounts how on the very day that the riots occurred, some couriers immediately set off to carry the "evil tidings" to the emperor, maybe with the hope of having the emperor make a decision to act severely against the city before he was presented with all the facts of the matter.[63] The fact that that these couriers had set off so quickly following the riots had frightened the whole Antiochene

---

58. *De Stat.* 3; PG 49.56, 2–4 (NPNF 1.09, 361).

59. *De Stat.* 3; PG 49.56, 15–18 (NPNF 1.09, 361): "Διὰ τοῦτο συνεχώρησεν ὑβρισθῆναι τὸν ὁμόδουλον, ἵνα ἀπὸ τοῦ κινδύνου τοῦ διὰ τὴν ὕβριν γενομένου ταύτην τοῦ Δεσπότου τὴν φιλανθρωπίαν μάθῃς."

60. *De Stat.* 2; PG 49.34, 55–56 (NPNF 1.09, 344): [God permitted these events so] "that he may make us more sober-minded by the extremity of this tribulation."

61. See 4.6.

62. *De Stat.* 6; PG 49.82, 41–44 (NPNF 01.09, 382): "Let us not then be grieved, beloved, by the fear of our rulers, but let us give thanks to God that He hath removed our listlessness, and rendered us more diligent . . . and that the city is now in all respects, like the pattern of a modest and virtuous woman."

63. *De Stat.* 6; PG 49.83, 18 (NPNF 01.09, 382).

populace, but not their priest.⁶⁴ Chrysostom had a different perspective, viewing it through the lens of God's sovereign permission. In *De Statuis* 6 Chrysostom states that God had allowed/permitted (ἀφίημι) these couriers to set off quickly, but was still working behind the scenes for the good of the citizens of Antioch.⁶⁵ Two or three days later, Bishop Flavian set out on an embassy to ask the emperor to be merciful towards the city of Antioch. It was thought that the bishop's mission would be futile because he had left such a long time after the couriers, but this proved not to be the case.⁶⁶ The couriers' journey was hindered, which allowed Bishop Flavian to make up time on them, something Chrysostom attributed directly to God: "For that this hindrance [of the couriers] on the road was not without God's interposition is evident."⁶⁷

While Chrysostom told his congregation that God had been sovereignly at work throughout the events both during and subsequent to the riots, the degree to which he actually believed it himself needs to be assessed. Chrysostom faced a despondent and grieving congregation, to whom he wished to provide comforting words.⁶⁸ An appeal to God's sovereignty could have largely been a rhetorical device to raise the collective spirits of his audience and ease some of their anxiety. For example, that some rhetorical license is being used in *De Statuis* 3 is almost certain, whereby Chrysostom (positively) anticipates what Bishop Flavian will say to the emperor when the bishop reaches Constantinople in order to defend the city of Antioch.⁶⁹ It is instructive to note, nonetheless, that divine sovereignty permitting seeming evil or difficult events to happen, for the purpose of bringing some ultimate good, is a theme to which Chrysostom regularly returns in his preaching. For example, in *In Acta apostolorum* 6, Chrysostom reflects on the divine sovereignty and human responsibility at work in Jesus' betrayal and crucifixion described in Acts 2:23: "τοῦτον τῇ ὡρισμένῃ βουλῇ καὶ προγνώσει τοῦ θεοῦ ἔκδοτον διὰ χειρὸς ἀνόμων προσπήξαντες ἀνείλατε."⁷⁰ Chrysostom's conclusion is that none of those events would have occurred,

---

64. *De Stat.* 6; PG 49.83, 56–57 (NPNF 01.09, 383).
65. *De Stat.* 6; PG 49.83, 54 (NPNF 1.09, 383).
66. *De Stat.* 6; PG 49.83, 58–59 (NPNF 1.09, 383).
67. *De Stat.* 6; PG 49.83, 29–30 (NPNF 1.09, 382).
68. *De Stat.* 6; PG 49.81, 14–17 (NPNF 1.09, 381).
69. *De Stat.* 6; PG 49.81, 14–83, 14 (NPNF 1.09, 354–6).
70. Acts 2:23 "This [Jesus], delivered up by the predetermined purpose and foreknowledge of God, you [Jews] killed by the hand of the lawless who crucified him." (my translation)

if God had not permitted [συνεχώρησε] them; it was God who delivered Him [Jesus] up.[71]

Chrysostom expresses the same idea, but from a different perspective, in *In epistulam ad Romanos* 15. Commenting on Rom 8:28, that God sovereignly works even painful events for the benefit of those who love him, Chrysostom cites the example of the three Israelites cast into the fiery furnace (Dan 3:8–30). On this occasion, rather than saying that God permitted the three men to be cast into the furnace, Chrysostom expresses it in the negative: God did not "prevent" [ἐκώλυσεν] them from falling into the furnace, nor did he "extinguish the flame[s]" once they were cast into them.[72]

The consistency in Chrysostom's theology of divine sovereignty in the homilies on Acts, Romans and *De Statuis* (just considered) is significant. It suggests that while Chrysostom uses some rhetorical license at points in *De Statuis*, fundamentally Chrysostom believes that as the all-powerful Creator, God is sovereignly in control of the events in Antioch.[73] For this reason Chrysostom urges his congregation to pray to God and entreat him on behalf of the city.[74] Deliverance is to be found in God alone. Wealth, money and houses had proven no refuge or source of deliverance during the current crisis.[75] All hope, from a human perspective, hinges on imperial clemency. Nonetheless, while the emperor may be God's ruler on earth, the emperor is not the ultimate ruler and source of power. That honour belongs to God himself, leading Chrysostom to conclude: "On this account then let us take refuge in the King that is above. Let us call Him in to our aid. If we may not obtain the favor of heaven, there is no consolation left for what has befallen us!"[76]

---

71. *In Acta hom.* 6; PG 60.57, 1–12 (NPNF 01.11, 38): ὅτι οὐ τῆς αὐτῶν ἰσχύος ἦν, εἰ μὴ καὶ αὐτὸς συνεχώρησε καὶ ἐξέδωκεν ὁ Θεὸς αὐτόν.

72. *In Rom. hom* 15; PG 60.540, 61–62 (NPNF 01.11, 453): Οὔτε γὰρ ἐκώλυσεν ἐμπεσεῖν εἰς αὐτήν, οὔτε ἐμπεσόντων τῶν ἁγίων ἐκείνων, τὴν φλόγα ἔσβεσεν.

73. To what extent Chrysostom is correct in his theological interpretation of events surrounding the riots, in light of God's sovereignty, is another question.

74. *De Stat.* 2; PG 49.35, 33–38 (NPNF 1.09, 345): "Let all men learn the sufferings of the city, that, sympathizing with their mother, they may lift up their united voice to God from the whole earth; and with one consent entreat the King of heaven for their universal nurse and parent."

75. *De Stat.* 2; PG 49.40, 12–17 (NPNF 1.09, 349): "Behold now this great danger has overtaken us! Let your houses stand by you! Let them deliver you from the threatened peril! but they cannot! And you yourselves are witnesses, who are leaving them solitary, and hurrying forth to the wilderness; fearing them as you would do snares and nets! Let riches now lend assistance! But it is no time for them to do so!"

76. *De Stat.* 2; PG 49.36, 51–56 (NPNF 1.09, 346).

Chrysostom's confidence that God would sovereignly work things out so that Antioch would be spared severe imperial retribution appears well-placed. In *De Statuis* 17, preached some weeks after the riots, Chrysostom recounts the salvation of the city, which he again attributes to the sovereign permission (συνεχώρησε) of God rather than the clemency of the emperor, saying: "Let us give thanks, then, not only that God has calmed the storm, but that he allowed [συνεχώρησε] it to take place."[77]

There have been significant disagreements amongst Christians regarding the sovereignty of God and the nature of the relationship between divine sovereignty and human responsibility.[78] This has been particularly evident in debates about what is commonly known as the "problem of evil."[79] Whatever view a Christian may take on these issues, the very fact that they pray to God shows an acceptance of God's sovereignty, at least at a basic level. According to J. I. Packer in his opening statement in *Evangelism and the Sovereignty of God*:

> I do not intend to spend any time at all proving to you the general truth that God is sovereign in this world . . . [b]ecause I know that, if you are a Christian, you pray; and the recognition of God's sovereignty is the basis of your prayers . . . When we are on our knees, we know that it is not we who control the world; it is not in our power, therefore, to supply our needs by our own independent efforts; every good thing we desire for ourselves and for others must be sought from God, and will come, if it comes at all, as a gift from his hands . . . In effect therefore, what we do every time we pray is confess our own impotence and God's sovereignty.[80]

---

77. *De Stat.* 17; PG 49.171, 27–29 (trans. Mayer and Allen, 105): "Εὐχαριστήσωμεν τοίνυν, μὴ μόνον, ὅτι τὸν χειμῶνα ἔλυσεν, ἀλλ' ὅτι καὶ γενέσθαι αὐτὸν συνεχώρησε."

78. For example, see Geisler, *Chosen But Free: A Balanced View of God's Sovereignty and Free Will*; Beilby and Eddy, *Divine Foreknowledge: Four Views* (Downers Grove: IVP, 2001); Craig, *The Only Wise God: The Compatibility of Divine Foreknowledge and Human Freedom*; Sproul, *Willing to Believe: The Controversy over Free Will*; Carson, *Divine Sovereignty and Human Responsibility: Biblical Perspectives in Tension*; Clark Pinnock, *The Grace of God, the Will of Man: A Case for Arminianism*; Basinger and Basinger, *Predestination and Free Will: Four Views of Divine Sovereignty and Human Freedom*.

79. For example, see Kushner, *When Bad Things Happen to Good People*; Carson, *How Long, O Lord? Reflections on Suffering and Evil*; John Hick, *Evil and the God of Love*; Plantinga, *God, Freedom, and Evil*.

80. Packer, *Evangelism and the Sovereignty of God*, 17–18.

In *De Statuis* 17 Chrysostom reflects a similar understanding of the relationship between God's sovereignty and prayer, arguing that a reflection on God's sovereignty in events should naturally lead his congregation to pray.[81]

First, Chrysostom instructs his congregation to offer to God prayers of dependency, casting all their cares upon their heavenly Lord.[82] He enjoins them to:

> [B]eseech Him continually; let us be earnest in prayers and supplications; and let us with all strictness give our attention to every other virtue; that so we may escape the danger that now threatens, and obtain the good things to come; which God grant we may all be worthy of, through the grace and loving-kindness of our Lord Jesus Christ.[83]

Second, they are to offer prayers of thankfulness. This thankfulness to God on the congregation's part should not merely be for the fact that the city was not destroyed by the emperor, but also for the fact also that God allowed the city to suffer the distress of the riots in the first place.[84] His reasoning is that, through these distressing circumstances, God had brought about a necessary refinement of the citizens of Antioch.

Chrysostom also makes the point that prayer is not something that should simply be reserved for times of crisis. In *De Statuis* 17, Chrysostom refers back to his earlier emphasis on prayer in *De Statuis* 2:

> When the sad conflagration of these calamities was first kindled, I said, that it was a season not for doctrine, but for prayer. The very same thing I now repeat, when the fire has been extinguished—that it is now especially, and more than before, a time for prayer; that now is the season especially for tears and compunction, for an anxious soul, for much diligence, and for much caution.[85]

---

81. *De Stat.* 17; PG 49.171, 36–39.

82. *De Stat.* 2; PG 49.37, 26–31 (NPNF 1.09, 346).

83. *De Stat.* 2; PG 49.47, 2–8 (NPNF 1.09, 354): παρακαλῶμεν αὐτὸν διηνεκῶς, καὶ εὐχαῖς καὶ ἱκετηρίαις προσανέχωμεν, καὶ τῆς λοιπῆς ἀρετῆς ἐπιμελώμεθα μετὰ ἀκριβείας ἁπάσης, ἵνα καὶ τὸν ἐπικείμενον διαφύγωμεν κίνδυνον, καὶ τῶν μελλόν των ἐπιτύχωμεν ἀγαθῶν· ὧν γένοιτο πάντας ἡμᾶς ἀξιωθῆναι, χάριτι καὶ φιλανθρωπίᾳ τοῦ Κυρίου ἡμῶν Ἰησοῦ Χριστοῦ.

84. *De Stat.* 17; PG 49, 171, 27–32 (trans., Mayer & Allen, 105; NPNF 1.09, 452).

85. *De Stat.* 17; PG 49, 171, 39–45 (trans., Mayer & Allen, 105; NPNF 1.09, 452): Ὅτε παρὰ τὴν ἀρχὴν ἡ χαλεπὴ τῶν κακῶν τούτων ἀνήφθη πυρά, ἔλεγον, ὅτι οὐκ ἔστι καιρὸς διδασκαλίας, ἀλλὰ καιρὸς εὐχῶν· τοῦτο δὴ καὶ νῦν, ἐπειδὴ ἐσβέσθη, λέγω, ὅτι

In other words, prayer is something that Christians should avail themselves of in all situations—whether crisis or calm.

For Chrysostom, the right response to situations of crisis begins with a right understanding of God. Orthodoxy precedes orthopraxy. Trust in the gospel begins with trusting the God of the gospel. To an anxious and fearful congregation in the midst of crisis, who had witnessed events seemingly spiral out of control, Chrysostom points them to the one who is in control. God is the one to whom the congregation must turn with both petition and praise. Deliverance from the present crisis will not be found in any human agency or through financial privilege but solely through trusting the one who rules sovereignly over heaven and earth. Chrysostom's theological approach to this crisis, evidenced both by his direct references to and allusions to Scripture and his interpretation of current events in the light of Scripture, further highlight that for Chrysostom, Scripture is the controlling rubric for contextualization. Scripture is the hermeneutical key to interpret the congregation's current crisis.

5.1.3.2 The emperor and his rulers are to be respected and obeyed, being God's ordained means of maintaining order in society

A second major theme in the four homilies from *De Statuis*, which frames Chrysostom's contextual message to a city in crisis, refers not so much to the congregation's thinking about God as to their thinking about the emperor and other governing authorities. The suddenness of the riots and the swiftness of the response by the authorities had led to widespread fear and panic. In his *De Statuis* series, Chrysostom anticipates and answers various questions his congregation may have had about how they should act towards the Roman State (of whom the emperor is the head) and the relationship between church and state.

In *De Statuis* 2, Chrysostom begins by acknowledging the emperor as the earthly ruler of the world, unequalled in dignity, God's representative here on earth.[86] Therefore, Chrysostom goes on to argue, the riots were not just an insult directed at the emperor but one also directed at God himself.[87]

νῦν μάλιστα καιρὸς εὐχῶν ἢ πρότερον, νῦν μάλιστα καιρὸς δακρύων καὶ κατανύξεως καὶ ψυχῆς πεπονημένης καὶ πολλῆς σπουδῆς καὶ πολλῆς ἀσφαλείας.

86. *De Stat.* 2; PG 49.36, 48–50 (NPNF 1.09, 346).

87. *De Stat.* 2; PG 49.38, 22–26 (NPNF 1.09, 347): "You overlooked the insult that was done unto God!—Behold, he [God] has permitted the Emperor to be insulted, and peril to the utmost to hang over all, in order that we might pay by this fear the penalty

The emperor has the power and authority to punish disobedient subjects,[88] and this is to be respected.[89] The emperor may be "the summit and head of all here below," but he is not the ultimate authority.[90] God, the creator, is ruler of the universe, "the king that is above" is the one who has authority over all things.[91] God has ordained the roles of the emperor and those rulers under him (such as the magistrates) as an act of divine benevolence, and the state leaders are to work symbiotically with the church leaders.[92] Magistrates have been issued power and authority from God, for the good order of society. The power that the magistrates possess should elicit fear amongst those who engage in unlawful behavior but respect amongst those who uphold the law.[93] The magistrates facilitate law and order. Without them, anarchy would have taken hold of Antioch following the recent riots, as Chrysostom (somewhat rhetorically) outlines:

> To what lengths would they [the rioters] not have gone in their madness? Would they not have overthrown the city from its foundations, turning all things upside down, and have taken our very lives? If you were to abolish the public tribunals, you would abolish all order from our life . . . so if you deprive the city of its rulers, we must lead a life less rational than that of the brutes.[94]

The congregation therefore is to respect the emperor and the magistrates, and not so much fear these rulers as be thankful to God that he has used them to purify the city.[95]

In these *De Statuis* homilies Chrysostom is very positive about the emperor and the governing officials and the need (in fact, biblical requirement) for the citizens of Antioch to submit to the governing authorities. This could, of course, simply be a rhetorical device on Chrysostom's part. In

---

of that listlessness."

88. *De Stat.* 2; PG 49.38, 48 (NPNF 1.09, 347).

89. *De Stat.* 3; PG 49.56, 15–18 (NPNF 1.09, 361).

90. *De Stat.* 2; PG 49.36, 52–53 (NPNF 1.09, 346).

91. *De Stat.* 2; PG 49.36, 54 (NPNF 1.09, 346).

92. *De Stat.* 6; PG 49.81, 30–32, 50–52 (NPNF 1.09, 381).

93. *De Stat.* 6; PG 49.82, 25–31 (NPNF 1.09, 382).

94. *De Stat.* 6; PG 49.81, 56–82, 16; 20–23 (NPNF 1.09, 381); *De Stat.* 6; PG 49.19–21 (NPNF 1.09, 381): ποῦ οὐκ ἂν ἦλθον οὗτοι μανίας; ἆρα οὐκ ἂν ἐκ βάθρων ἡμῖν τὴν πόλιν ἀνέτρεψαν, καὶ πάντα ἄνω καὶ κάτω ποιήσαντες, αὐτὰς ἂν ἡμῶν ἀφείλοντο τὰς ψυχάς; Ἐὰν γὰρ τὰ δικαστήρια ἀνέλῃς, πᾶσαν τῆς ζωῆς ἡμῶν ἀνεῖλες τὴν εὐταξίαν . . . οὕτω τῶν πόλεων τοὺς ἄρχοντας ἂν ἀνέλῃς, θηρίων ἀλόγων ἀλογώτερον βιωσόμεθα βίον.

95. *De Stat.* 6; PG 49.82, 41–43 (NPNF 1.09, 382).

light of an offended emperor who had the power of life and death over his citizens, Chrysostom would be unlikely to criticize or oppose the emperor's decisions. Neither would he be likely to challenge the legitimate right of the magistrates to punish those responsible for the riots. The sermons following the riots could therefore be viewed as Chrysostom seeking to protect himself (and the city) from further harm, as a form of insincere flattery designed to garner political capital.

While some of Chrysostom's expressions may well have been rhetorical devices (e.g., referring to the emperor as "a friend of God"),[96] his overall thesis is most likely genuine. This is supported by the fact that his teaching in *De Statuis* about the place of the state in God's economy is consistent with his teaching on Rom 13:1 found in *In Romans* 23. In this homily Chrysostom argues that citizens are to submit to the ruling authorities for God has so ordained "that there should be rulers, and some rule and others be ruled, and that all things should not just be carried on in one confusion . . . this I say is the work of God's wisdom."[97] Chrysostom understands that submission to government authority is a display of obedience to God.[98] Consistent with his comments in *De Statuis,* he argues that those citizens who engage in lawful behavior have nothing to fear from state rulers, but citizens who do evil have everything to fear.[99] Rulers, Chrysostom concludes, are God's means for ensuing an ordered and stable society:

> For there are countless blessings to states through these authorities; and if you were to remove them, all things would go to ruin, and neither city nor country, nor private nor public buildings, nor anything else would stand, but all the world will be turned upside down, while the more powerful devour the weaker.[100]

96. *De Stat.* 17; PG 49.179, 5 (trans., Mayer & Allen, 115; NPNF 1.09, 457).

97. *In Rom.* 23; PG 60.615, 21–24 (NPNF 01.11, 511).

98. *In Rom.* 23; PG 60.615, 65–616, 2 (NPNF 01.11, 512). He is quoting Paul at this point.

99. *In Rom.* 23; PG 60.616, 44–47, 55 (NPNF 01.11, 512). "For he [the governmental ruler] makes virtue easier for you in other ways also, by chastising the wicked, by benefiting and honouring the good [citizens], and by working together with the will of God . . . But if you do that which is evil, be afraid." Cf. *De Stat.* 6; PG 49.82, 31–40 (NPNF 1.09, 381–2). Statements like these are examples of Chrysostom's progressive education of his congregation in the gospel and correction of error (see chapter 4, p. 152). Again and again throughout *De Stat.* 6, Chrysostom returns to the theme of the government being God's instrument for the good of society.

100. *In Rom.* 23; PG 60.617, 20–25 (NPNF 01.11, 513): Καὶ γὰρ μυρία ἀγαθὰ διὰ τῶν ἀρχῶν τούτων ταῖς πόλεσι γίνεται· κἂν ἀνέλῃς αὐτὰς, πάντα οἰχήσεται, καὶ οὐ πόλεις, οὐ χωρία, οὐκ οἰκία, οὐκ ἀγορὰ, οὐκ ἄλλο οὐδὲν στήσεται, ἀλλὰ πάντα ἀνατραπήσεται, τῶν δυνατωτέρων τοὺς ἀσθενεστέρους καταπινόντων.

At one level, Chrysostom's teaching here is consistent with a number of biblical passages on the relationship between church and state. God has appointed governing authorities for the promotion of order within the societies in which they govern (Rom 13:1). The authorities are to be humbly submitted to and to be obeyed (Rom 13:1; Titus 3:1; 1 Pet 2:13). Submission is not only due to the emperor, who is God's supreme representative on earth, but also due to those who govern under the emperor's authority (1 Pet 2:13). Part of the role of these human rulers is to promote lawful behavior and punish wrong behavior (Rom 13:3–4; 1 Pet 2:14). Rulers who do this show themselves to be servants of God (Rom 13:4). But that being said, the homilies also need to be read through the hermeneutical lenses provided by Stephens and Quiroga Puertas.[101] Chrysostom was not simply aligning his teaching with Scripture but also using the occasion to promote the Flavian faction, as well as reinforcing the notion that the bishop, as God's representative, had more authority than the emperor.

5.1.3.3 People need to keep their eyes fixed on the future rather than on the present.

While the *De Statuis* homilies have a strong focus on the present circumstances of the Antiochene populace, they also demonstrate Chrysostom's focus on the future. Chrysostom's third major theme is that his congregation needs to live in light of their eternal citizenship rather than their present circumstances. The way that they are to do this is by living godly lives.

To a congregation beset by despair, Chrysostom offers an antidote by pointing them to their eternal hope. The congregation's comprehensive focus on their present circumstances had left them paralyzed with fear and rendered largely inactive since the riots.[102] Chrysostom seeks to reverse this paralysis by turning their attention away from themselves and their present circumstances, instead highlighting the reality of their heavenly citizenship. To embrace this vision they are to live a life of prayer and godliness. The starting point is prayer, highlighted earlier.[103] Genuine prayer is an acknowledgment by the Antiochenes of their complete reliance on God

---

101. See 5.1.3.1, n843.

102. *De Stat.* 2; PG 49.35, 43–53 (NPNF 1.09, 345).

103. *De Stat.* 2; PG 49.46, 56–47, 2 (NPNF 1.09, 354): "Let us not lament, nor fear the difficulty of the times, for He who did not refuse to pour out His blood for all, and has suffered us to partake of His flesh and of His blood again, what will He refuse to do for our safety? Confident then in these hopes, let us beseech Him continually; let us be earnest in prayers and supplications."

to act in the situation, something that Chrysostom was confident of right from his opening homily.[104] In the turbulence and uncertainty of their present circumstances, prayer would draw the congregation to God who was the foundation of their faith.[105] In *De Statuis* 17, Chrysostom continues to emphasize prayer, reminding his congregation that prayer was not only for a time of crisis but an ongoing part of the believer's life, even after the crisis had ended, accompanied by a life of godliness.[106]

Chrysostom critiques both himself and his congregation for living what he labels as "dissolute and indolent" lives through their preoccupation with present pleasures instead of their eternal futures, saying:

> We do not live with the austerity that is becoming of Christians. On the contrary, we love to follow this voluptuous and dissolute and indolent life; therefore also it is but natural that we cleave to *present things;* since if we spent this life in fastings, vigils, and poverty of diet, cutting off all our extravagant desires; setting a restraint upon our pleasures; undergoing the toils of virtue; keeping the body under [restraint] like Paul, and bringing it into subjection; not "making provision for the lusts of the flesh"; and pursuing the straight and narrow way, *we should soon be earnestly desirous of future things,* and eager to be delivered from our present labours.[107] (emphasis mine)

---

104. *De Stat.* 2; PG 49.37, 25–31 (NPNF 1.09, 346): "But afford me your attention! Lend me your ears awhile! Shake off this despondency! Let us return to our former custom; and as we have been used always to meet here with gladness, so let us also do now, casting all upon God. And *this will contribute towards our actual deliverance from calamity.*" (emphasis mine)

105. *De Stat.* 2; PG 49.37, 35–43 (NPNF 1.09, 346–7).

106. *De Stat* 17; PG 49.171, 39–45 (trans., Mayer & Allen, 106; NPNF 01.09, 452).

107. *De Stat.* 6; PG 49.85, 20–31 (NPNF 01.09, 384): Οὐ ζῶμεν μετὰ τῆς προσηκούσης τοῖς Χριστιανοῖς σκληραγωγίας, ἀλλὰ τὸν ὑγρὸν τοῦτον καὶ διαλελυμένον καὶ χαῦνον ἐζηλώσαμεν βίον· διὸ καὶ εἰκότως τοῖς παροῦσιν ἐμφιλοχωροῦμεν πράγμασιν. Ὡς εἴ γε ἐν νηστείαις καὶ παννυχίσι καὶ εὐτελείᾳ διαίτης τὴν ζωὴν διηνύομεν ταύτην, τὰς ἐπιθυμίας ἡμῶν ἐκκόπτοντες τὰς ἀτόπους, τὰς ἡδονὰς κωλύοντες, τοὺς ἱδρῶτας τῆς ἀρετῆς ὑπομένοντες, κατὰ τὸν Παύλου λόγον ὑποπιέζοντες τὸ σῶμα καὶ δουλαγωγοῦντες, τῆς σαρκὸς πρόνοιαν μὴ ποιούμενοι εἰς ἐπιθυμίας, τὴν στενὴν καὶ τεθλιμμένην ὁδὸν ὁδεύοντες, ταχέως ἂν τῶν μελλόντων ἐπεθυμήσαμεν, τῶν παρόντων πόνων ἀπαλλαγῆναι σπεύδοντες. Chrysostom's call to godly living, as reflected in this quote, has an ascetic bias. (On Chrysostom's ascetic background see chapter 4, p. 141–142). While godly living here is closely tied to sobriety of lifestyle, personal restraint, moderation, and voluntary poverty, Chrysostom has a much greater vision of sanctification. As part of his progressive education of the congregation in the gospel (see 4.6), Chrysostom here is explaining what godliness might look like in this particular crisis situation. In different contexts he gives different

The recent events had had a pruning, sobering, and restraining effect on such behavior, leading his congregation to adopt a life of restraint and seriousness of living.[108] Chrysostom urges his congregation to continue in their earnestness and godly behavior, as befitting children of God.[109] Chrysostom fittingly brings together the threads of God's sovereignty, the importance of prayer, and godly living as he concludes *De Statuis* 17:

> Let's appeal together to him, then, both for present and future events, so that he may snatch us from that [eternal] punishment. Whatever the nature of present events, they can be tolerated and they come to an end. But the torments in the future life are eternal and inescapable. With this consolation let's make an effort not to fall into these kinds of sins any more, since we know that hereafter we shall be able to enjoy pardon. Together, then, let's fall down before God, and both when we're here and when we're at home let's say: '*You are just, Lord, in all your dealings with us, because whatever you brought upon us you've brought upon us with a just judgment* (Neh. 9:33).[110]

5.1.4 Contextual principles that can be drawn from De statuis homilies

Four contextual principles from the *De statuis* can be identified as guiding Chrysostom's method and message. One has previously been highlighted in Acts—Principle 2: For contextualization to be effective, the gospel needs to be explained in ways that engage the worldview of the target audience.[111]

The three contextual principles that are particular to *De statuis* are as follows:

---

applications of what godliness should look like (e.g., see 5.2.3.2–5.2.3.3).

108. *De Stat.* 17; PG 49.171, 39–47 (trans., Mayer & Allen, 106; NPNF 01.09, 452).

109. *De Stat.* 17; PG 49.172, 11–14 (trans., Mayer & Allen, 106; NPNF 01.09, 452).

110. *De Stat* 17; PG 49.180, 22–33 (trans., Mayer & Allen, 116; NPNF 01.09, 458): Παρακαλῶμεν τοίνυν αὐτὸν κοινῇ καὶ ὑπὲρ τῶν παρόντων καὶ ὑπὲρ τῶν μελλόντων, ὥστε κἀκείνης ἡμᾶς ἐξαρπάσαι τῆς κολάσεως. Τὰ μὲν γὰρ παρόντα οἷα ἂν ᾖ, φορητά τέ ἐστι καὶ τέλος ἔχει· τὰ δὲ ἐκεῖ βασανιστήρια ἀθάνατά τε καὶ ἄφυκτα. Μετὰ δὲ τῆς παρακλήσεως καὶ αὐτοὶ σπουδάζωμεν, μηκέτι τοιούτοις περιπίπτειν ἁμαρτήμασιν, εἰδότες ὅτι λοιπὸν οὐδὲ συγγνώμης ἀπολαῦσαι δυνησόμεθα. Κοινῇ τοίνυν τῷ Θεῷ προσπίπτωμεν ἅπαντες, καὶ ἐνταῦθα ὄντες, καὶ κατὰ τοὺς οἴκους γινόμενοι, λέγωμεν· Δίκαιος εἶ, Κύριε, ἐπὶ πᾶσιν οἷς ἐποίησας ἡμῖν, ὅτι ἐν ἀληθινῇ κρίσει ἐπήγαγες, ὅσα ἐπήγαγες.

111. Principles 1–8 were previously established in 3.9.

PRINCIPLE 9: Contextualization is best achieved in the context of relationship. While Chrysostom, as recently installed presbyter to Antioch, would have already had some measure of rapport and relationship with the congregants, he doesn't take it for granted. Throughout the *De statuis* homilies he develops that rapport and relationship through self-identifying with the congregation's grief and troubles and regularly reinforcing their shared relationship. This relationship would have continued to build as each successive *De statuis* sermon was preached, undoubtedly further aiding Chrysostom to contextualize his sermons. The sermons of Peter, Stephen, and Paul examined in chapter three were all occasional addresses, to audiences unfamiliar to the speaker, with each of the speakers trying to quickly establish rapport with their audience in order to build some relational connection. The situation for Chrysostom as he preached the *De statuis* series was, however, somewhat different. Even taking into account what has been already concluded in this chapter regarding the likely audience and setting of the *De statuis* sermons, and how the congregation and even the venue wasn't necessarily identical from sermon to sermon, Chrysostom is very likely to have enjoyed a relational continuity with his audience, not available to Peter, Stephen, and Paul.

The principle that contextualization is best achieved in the context of relationship is one that is consistent with and develops that advocated by Charles Kraft. For Kraft, the personal nature of the relationship between the speaker and hearer significantly affects the communication process, and "the dynamics of the relationship between the communicators and receptors provide them with crucial information concerning how to interpret what is really meant by what each says and does."[112] For Chrysostom, developing a relationship with his audiences was vital, not simply for the sake of facilitating better communication (Kraft), but also for helping him achieve his greater goal of tending to the souls of his hearers—like a master physician with a patient. Contextual preaching in the context of relationship is a hallmark of Chrysostom's preaching, and is a technique which is not only part of his own philosophical psychagogy (normative and cultural) but modeled on divine and Pauline pedagogy.[113]

PRINCIPLE 10: Scripture is both the starting point and controlling rubric of contextualization. Both the ICWE[114] and Hesselgrave and Rommen argue

---

112. Kraft, "Meaning Equivalence Contextualization," 164.
113. Rylaarsdam, *John Chrysostom*, 190–3, 274–7.
114. See 2.2.

for this principle,[115] which is consistent with the basic evangelical tenet of the authority of Scripture,[116] but the principle is one that was already evidenced in Chrysostom's *De statuis* sermons. Like Peter, Stephen, and Paul before him, Chrysostom was not afraid to challenge his audience's worldview on the basis of the Scriptures. Many people had only come into regular contact with Christianity since the conversion of Constantine, so a lot of Christians in the empire were first-or-second-generation Christians, and their churches approximately fifty years old. Therefore, one might surmise that the average level of Bible knowledge in Chrysostom's congregation (at this early point in his ministry at least) was not that high. Chrysostom's approach in *De statuis* was to show how the Bible could be interpreted in light of, and then applied to, the particular situation his audience faced. The Bible then was his means for bringing both comfort and challenge to his audience.[117]

For example, Chrysostom drew an analogy between the current suffering the citizens of Antioch were experiencing and the suffering which befell the inhabitants of Jerusalem and the northern kingdom when their cities were attacked and destroyed (Isa 1:30; Amos 8:9).[118] A second example is where he used the story of Esther saving her fellow Jews through petitioning the king of Persia as a stimulus for the Antiochene congregation to pray for Bishop Flavian's embassy to the emperor.[119] A third example is found where he used the story of God's providential restraint of Jonah, when he sought to flee to Tarshish, as an analogy of how the Antiochene messengers, who, immediately following the riots, tried to take a bad report about the events to the emperor, had been providentially restrained from doing so.[120] While the legitimacy of some of the connections Chrysostom drew between Scripture and the events in Antioch may be open to question, that Chrysostom was using the Bible in order to challenge (and, ideally change) the hearts and minds of his hearers is beyond dispute.

---

115. See end of 2.3.1.

116. See 1.1.1.

117. Chrysostom's use of Scripture included not only exegesis but highlighting the lives of biblical figures as models for imitation (see chapter 4, pp. 146–147).

118. *De Stat.* 2; PG 49.34, 57–35,16 (NPNF 01.09, 345); *De Stat.* 2; PG 49.36, 25–31 (NPNF 01.09, 346).

119. *De Stat.* 3; PG 49.49, 43–45 (NPNF 01.09, 356). Chrysostom is using Esther as a model to imitate.

120. *De Stat.* 6; PG 49.83, 34–84, 5 (NPNF 01.09, 382–3).

PRINCIPLE 11: Every facet of life and witness needs to be contextualized, not just selected facets. To a congregation living in fear of the state authorities, Chrysostom reminds them of the rightful and necessary place of these rulers. The state authorities are God-ordained vehicles for maintaining order in society, which includes promoting good and punishing unlawful behavior. Living out the gospel requires submission to these authorities. In doing so they are obeying God. Chrysostom is doing something very interesting here in regards to contextualization. Not only is Chrysostom's message of submission to authorities a contextual one, it is also an example of Chrysostom explaining what contextual Christian witness should look like for his congregants. Chrysostom's missiological outlook views all of life as an opportunity for Christian witness. Even in the midst of this crisis, Chrysostom still has an eye on how his congregation's behavior can fulfill the Great Commission through exercising godly behavior, simultaneously bearing witness to the Antiochene community and ruling authorities as well as bringing glory to God. Hesselgrave and Rommen emphasize not only the verbal but also the non-verbal aspects of contextualized witness—including incarnational living.[121] Chrysostom does likewise. For Chrysostom, Christian witness involves not only words, but action. Contextualization is both verbal and non-verbal, and it encompasses all missionary activity which legitimately seeks to fulfill the Great Commission.

Conclusion to the De Statuis homilies

In chapter four I argued that the burden of Chrysostom's preaching lies not in the annunciation of the gospel kerygma but rather in how the gospel translates into sanctified living. This has been very much the case in the four *De Statuis* homilies considered in this chapter so far. As Chrysostom is addressing a congregation who would be identified largely as Christian, his presentation of the gospel is not an explanation of the events surrounding the life of Jesus Christ. Rather, Chrysostom's message is a practical application of the gospel truths to his Antiochene congregation. Contextualization is the intersection of gospel and culture. Through practical application, Chrysostom both affirms and critiques culture. His affirmation of culture is reflected in both his support of the Roman government and state offices, and his employment of rhetorical devices and conventions of his day in communicating his message. His critique of culture lies in his condemnation

---

121. See end of 2.3.1.

of licentious practices that characterize a "voluptuous and dissolute and indolent life" and of rebellion against the God-ordained state authorities.[122]

Chrysostom's *De Statuis* homilies offer a highly contextualized theological response to the situation of Christians in crisis, struggling to live in a society dominated by the Roman Empire. The Antiochene congregation, like the rest of their fellow citizens, were fearful about what their future held. Imperial retribution for the riots could mean destruction of the city—something that threatened the homes, livelihoods, and even lives of the congregation members. While Chrysostom ministered in a period when Christianity was an accepted religion of the empire, with a Christian emperor and no direct threat of persecution, Christianity in Antioch was still a minority religion. The dire circumstances in which Chrysostom's congregation found themselves due to the riots called for a fresh translation and application of the gospel message that addressed the situation at hand. Chrysostom's contextual sermons in the weeks subsequent to the riots were crafted in masterly fashion for Christians who needed words of encouragement and hope as well as a fresh vision of how to interpret their current circumstances and live out the gospel in light of them. Chrysostom tailored his new translation of the gospel by drawing on three central themes: God's sovereignty, church and state, and righteous living. The sovereignty of God in current events was paramount in Chrysostom's thinking and was important not only for giving the congregation hope for the future, but also for enabling them to pray confidently in their present crisis. For Chrysostom, God's sovereignty also extended to the leadership structures of the empire which exercized authority over Antioch and which were the God-ordained means of maintaining order in the society. The Christians in Antioch were exhorted to respect the government and its leaders and to live lives characterized by godly behavior. Chrysostom's approach is both theological and pastoral. While Chrysostom clearly and forthrightly addressed three important theological issues, he did not do so insensitively or impersonally. Rather, speaking as a passionate yet grieving pastor to a diverse congregation united by anxiety, grief, and fear, Chrysostom carefully and gently applied the salve of the gospel to the emotional wounds of his flock. Through reminding the congregation of their heavenly citizenship and the necessary implications for daily living, he lifted their eyes away from their present situation to the face of their heavenly Father which was still turned towards them in love.

---

122. *De Stat.* 6; PG 49.85, 21–22 (NPNF 01.09, 384).

5.2 Adversus Judaeos 1
(Against Judaizing Christians Oration 1)[123]

5.2.1 Context, audience and setting

This homily is the first of a series of eight that Chrysostom preached in Antioch against Christians who were frequenting Jewish festivals.[124] The sermons were preached over the 386–387 liturgical year and were later collated into what is known as the *Adversus Judaeos* homilies.[125] *Adversus Judaeos* 1 was preached during Chrysostom's first year as presbyter, just before the three Jewish feast days of the New Year (*Rosh hashanah*), Day of Atonement (*Yom Kippur*), and the Feast of Tabernacles (*Sukkot*), all of which were celebrated in the September–October period.[126] A week after beginning a series of five homilies directed against the Anomean faction of the church,[127] *De incomprehensibili natura dei*,[128] the looming Jewish festivals caused Chrysostom to interrupt urgently that series in order to begin preaching against the Judaizing behavior of some in his congregation.[129] Louis H. Feldman states:

> Chrysostom's sermons against the "Judaizers" come at precisely the time when he is engaged in a bitter controversy with the heretical group known as the Anomeans, who, he [Chrysostom]

123. *Adv. Jud.* 1; PG 48.843–56. The English translation of *Adversus Judaeos* 1 is from Mayer and Allen, *John Chrysostom*, 149–176, unless otherwise indicated.

124. *Adv. Jud.* 1; PG 48.844, 30–36.

125. Fonrobert, "Jewish Christians, Judaizers, and Christian Anti-Judaism," 234–54, at 236; Shepardson, *Controlling Contested Spaces: Late Antique Antioch and the Spatial Politics of Religious Controversy*, 92–93; van der Horst, "Jews and Christians in Antioch at the End of the Fourth Century," 228–38, at 228.

126. *Adv. Jud.* 1; PG 48.844, 30–36. Recent scholarship, based on a newly published manuscript of Discourse 2, has led to the conclusion that Discourse 1 is the only homily of the series preached in 386 CE (just before Rosh Hashanah). In the autumn Jewish holidays of 387 CE Chrysostom preached (in the following order) Discourses 4, 2, 5, 6, 7, 8. Discourse 3 was preached in January 387 CE as a stand-alone homily. Pradels et al., "The Sequence of Dating the Series of John Chrysostom's Eight Discourses *Adversus Iudaeos*," 90–116. Cf. Shepardson, *Controlling Contested Spaces*, 93n2.

127. *Adv. Jud.* 1; PG 48.843, 7–13; 844, 37–845, 3. Raymond Laird notes that Chrysostom's mentoring by Bishop Melitius, along with Chrysostom's knowledge of the Antiochene schism and the ongoing Christological controversy that had occurred since Nicea, gave Chrysostom "ample first-hand experience and knowledge on which to formulate his own understanding of and attitude towards the Anomeans." Laird, "John Chrysostom and the Anomoeans," 130.

128. PG 48.701–812; Wilken, *John Chrysostom*, 15.

129. *Adv. Jud.* 1; PG 48.844, 23–29; Shepardson, *Controlling Contested Spaces*, 94, 99.

says, agree with the Jews in denying the divinity of Jesus (1.1.845). Indeed, we may surmise that it is precisely because Christianity was so busy fighting such heresies at this time that Judaism felt free to embark again upon reaching out.[130]

While only recently installed as presbyter, Chrysostom quickly identified the threat that the Judaizing behavior of some in his congregation posed to the whole church, and acted quickly to address the issue.[131]

In Chrysostom's day, as noted above, Antioch was a diverse and cosmopolitan, Greek-speaking city. While many of its citizens identified as Christians,[132] there was also a substantial Jewish population, with at least two synagogues.[133] One synagogue was located in Antioch itself while the other was in the suburb of Daphne.[134] It was in Antioch, around 40 CE, that the followers of Christ were first called Christians (Acts 11:26), almost three hundred years before Christianity started to gain a significant religious foothold in the empire under the Christian emperor Constantine (324–37).[135] While this Christian ascendancy was a significant threat for Judaism in the empire, the Jewish cause was assisted by two subsequent fourth-century emperors. Julian the Apostate (361–363) sought to restore paganism to the empire, suppressing Christianity while simultaneously showing a measure of

---

130. Feldman, "Proselytism by Jews in the Third, Fourth, and Fifth Centuries," 1–58, at 38; Shephardson's book focuses on the interconnectedness of the *De incomprehensibili natura dei* and the *Adversus Judaeos* homilies. She states: "Both [series of homilies] explicitly addressed the question of how to be correctly Christian; both were concerned with the orthodoxy of people in his church audience and those who should have been there but were not; and both used places to identify correct Christianity, although in interestingly different ways." Shepardson, *Controlling Contested Spaces*, 94. Cf. *Adv. Jud.* 1; PG 48.845, 14–22 where Chrysostom himself links his arguments against the Anomeans with his arguments against Judaizing Christians, in that both groups deny that Jesus was equal with God the Father.

131. Ritter, "John Chrysostom and the Jews—A Reconsideration," 141–54, at 143–4.

132. Kinzig states that the majority of Antioch's population were Christians (at least nominally) and that of a city of at least 150,000 people, 100,000 would have identified as Christian. The Jewish population was much smaller (approx. 22,000) but played a significant role in the life of the city. Kinzig, "'Non-Separation': Closeness and Co-operation Between Jews and Christians in the Fourth Century," 27–53, at 36.

133. Downey, *A History of Antioch*, 447–9; van der Horst, "Jews and Christians," 228. Van der Horst, 230, further adds that in the early centuries of the common era, Antioch was known for its large and vibrant Jewish community. Kinzig, "'Non-Separation,'" 27.

134. *Adv. Jud.* 1; PG 48.852, 1–3; Kinzig, "'Non-Separation,'" 36.

135. Harkins, "Introduction," xxiv–xxv.

favor towards Judaism.[136] The Arian Emperor Valens (364–378) went even further, "persecut[ing] . . . orthodox Christians, permit[ting] public pagan worship, and protect[ing] the Jews."[137] Emperor Theodosius I (379–395) established Nicene Christianity as the official religion of the empire through his decree *Cunctos populos* in 380. While this decree outlawed Arianism it did not outlaw Judaism. Rather, Judaism was protected under his rule.[138]

The *Cunctos populos* did not make everyone in the empire committed Christians.[139] Kinzig argues that the decree *Cunctos populos* was one of the main factors that led to the increase of Judaizing behavior in the church, for it caused "a strong influx of people into the church who were not really committed Christians, people who had previously lived on the fringes of Christianity, Judaism, and pagan religions, who did not really want to commit themselves, and were not willing to give up their old practices."[140] While politically it may have been expedient to identify as Christian, there were many people who were what Chrysostom describes as "half-Christians,"[141] that is, people who were "Christian on the surface" but in reality held a syncretistic mixture of beliefs (such as Christianity and paganism, or Christianity and Judaism).[142] While assenting to Christianity, these half-Christians still had an attachment to the beliefs and practices they had before Christianity, including Judaism, and were represented in Chrysostom's Antiochene congregation.[143]

Chrysostom also faced a strong Jewish community in Antioch, whose rites and practices proved very attractive to many Christians, to the point where some of them actually joined in some Jewish customs and attended the synagogue.[144] It appears that those in Chrysostom's congregation en-

136. Ibid., xxv.
137. Ibid., xxv, xxix.
138. Ibid., xxix–xxx.
139. Kinzig, "Non-Separation," 38; Shepardson, *Controlling Contested Spaces*, 93.
140. Kinzig, "Non-Separation," 38–39.
141. Ibid., 38. Paul Harkins' translation is "demi-Christians." Harkins: "Introduction," xxx, xxxiv. Two articles that argue strongly for the concept of demi/half-Christians are: i. Brottier, "Jean Chrysostome. Un pasteur face à des *demi-chrétiens*," 439–57; ii. Guignebert, "Les demi-chrétiens et leur place dans l'Eglise antique," 65–102. Markus, *The End of Ancient Christianity*, 33, alternatively argues that the idea of "semi-Christians" is really an interpretation by modern day scholars rather than a category used in the works of fourth to sixth century CE authors.
142. Harkins, "Introduction," xxxi.
143. Ibid., xxxiv.
144. Wilken, *John Chrysostom*, 67; Stephen Mitchell, *A History of the Later Roman Empire AD 284–641*, 236; Shephardson, *Controlling Contested Spaces*, 102.

gaging in this behavior were not occasional attendees but regular church members,[145] particularly women and uneducated people.[146] Not only that, but according to A.M. Bibliowicz, these people did not see a dichotomy between participating in both the church and the synagogue.[147] Chrysostom's statement towards the end of the final homily in the series, however, would appear to cast doubt on the veracity of Bibliowicz's statement:

> The way you act when you get to the synagogue makes it clear that you consider it a very serious sin to go to that wicked place. You are anxious that no one notice your arrival there; you urge your household, friends, and neighbours not to report you to the priests. If someone does report you, you fly into a rage. Would it not be the height of folly to try to hide from men your bold and shameless sin when God, who is present everywhere, sees it?[148]

Chrysostom suggests awareness rather than ignorance of the incompatibility of Christianity and Judaism amongst these Judaizing Christians. Chrysostom's *Adversus Judaeos* sermons target the Gentile Judaizing believers rather than directly attacking Judaism itself.[149] Harkins notes, "[t]he fact

145. *Adv. Jud.* 1; PG 48.844, 23–29; *Adv. Jud.* 4; PG 48.875, 2–7. Cf. Wilken, *John Chrysostom*, 75–76; van der Horst, "Jews and Christians," 230.

146. *Adv. Jud.* 2; PG 48.860, 49–861, 3. Kinzig, "'Non-Separation,'" 38. Meeks and Wilkin, *Jews and Christians in Antioch in the First Four Centuries of the Common Era*, 35, question Chrysostom's claim that women and the uneducated were the main offenders in Judaizing behavior. They give no evidence, simply concluding that Chrysostom was engaging in a standard attack on religious deviance. Kinzig, "'Non-Separation,'" 38, argues against Meeks and Wilkin, stating that Chrysostom's comments should be taken at face value.

147. Bibliowicz, *Jews and Gentiles in the Early Jesus Movement*, 188.

148. *Adv. Jud.* 8; PG 48.940, 53–59 (trans. Harkins, *Discourses Against Judaizing Christians*, 237–8):Ὅτι γὰρ καὶ αὐτὸς σὺ μεγίστην ἁμαρτίαν εἶναι νομίζεις τὸ δραμεῖν εἰς τὸ πονηρὸν ἐκεῖνο χωρίον, δῆλον ἀπὸ τοῦ τρόπου τῆς ἀφίξεως. Καὶ γὰρ λαθεῖν σπουδάζεις ἀφικνούμενος ἐκεῖσε, καὶ οἰκέταις καὶ φίλοις καὶ γείτοσι παρακελεύῃ, μὴ κατειπεῖν σου πρὸς τοὺς ἱερέας, κἂν διαβάλῃ τις, ἀγανακτεῖς. Πόσης οὖν οὐκ ἂν εἴη ἀνοίας, ἀνθρώπους πειρᾶσθαι λανθάνειν, τοῦ δὲ Θεοῦ ὁρῶντος.

149. Bibliowicz, *Jews and Gentiles*, 190. The Judaizing behavior by Christians was a problem that stretched back over three hundred years to the time of the early New Testament church. A number of Christian writers had vehemently written against the practice in the intervening period; see Wilde, *The Treatment of the Jews in the Greek Writers of the First Three Centuries*. Both Bibliowicz and Harkins argue that *Adversus Judaeos* belongs in the same polemical tradition as that of the *Epistle of Barnabas*, Justin Martyr's *Dialogue with Trypho*, Tertullian's *Adversus Judaeos*, and Cyprian's *Ad Quirinum testimonia*. Harkins does nonetheless acknowledge that Chrysostom's rhetorical attacks go beyond anything his predecessors wrote. Where Chrysostom's predecessors attacked Judaism, Chrysostom also attacked Antiochene demi-Christians

that all eight *Discourses* end with an exhortation to fraternal correction and a plea to bring back the sheep who have strayed from the church makes it quite clear that not the Jews but the Judaizing Christians are Chrysostom's primary targets."[150]

who were participating in Jewish practices. Harkins, "Introduction," xxxi, xxx–xxxvii. Bibliowicz, *Jews and Gentiles*, 190. Some have argued that the sermons are anti-semitic. For example, Simon, *Verus Israel: A Study of the Relations Between Christians and Jews in the Roman Empire (135–435)*, 217, describes Chrysostom as "the master of anti-Jewish invective," with Chrysostom's *Adversus Judaeos* referred to regularly in studies on Christian anti-Judaism for much of the past century. German scholar, Adolf Ritter, who grew up during the Nazism of WWII, does not view Chrysostom's *Adversus Judaeos* as anti-semitic. Rather, he explains Chrysostom's tone in the homilies this way: "The orator [Chrysostom] apparently regarded the [Judaizing] situation [in his Antiochene congregation] as so dangerous and the attraction, spread by the feasts and customs of the synagogue, as so overwhelming, that it seemed to him not to be sufficient simply to appeal to the judgment of his auditory. It seemed to him to be necessary to engage also the emotions. In any case, he worked himself into a rage, that he could not be excelled, even by the great anti-Semites and murderers of Jews in our [twentieth] century, 'only' in deed, not in word." Ritter, "John Chrysostom and the Jews," 144. For a recent summary of Chrysostom and anti-semitism, see Van Veller, "Paul's Therapy of the Soul: A New Approach to John Chrysostom and Anti-Judaism," 3–8. Van Veller, 94–132, states that Chrysostom's anti-Jewish rhetoric is more vitriolic than that of the apostle Paul. She argues that, since almost four centuries had elapsed between Chrysostom and the apostle Paul, and that since the problem of Judaizing behavior amongst Christians had persisted for this length of time, greater harshness was required in Chrysostom's approach compared to that of Paul.

150. Ritter, "John Chrysostom and the Jews," 144–8; Bibliowicz, *Jews and Gentiles*, 185–6. Bibliowicz states, "[m]any modern scholars have gravitated towards Gentile sympathizers with Judaism as the focus of John's ire. There is a wide consensus that supports the identification of the target audience as Gentiles." Bibliowicz, *Jews and Gentiles*, 188. Bibliowicz, 190, further argues that the images and metaphors Chrysostom used in his arguments against Judaizing Christians are similar to the ones he used in other sermons against "paganizers" in his congregation, which strengthens the argument that Chrysostom was arguing against Judaistic practices, not Judaism. Boin, "Hellenistic 'Judaism' and the Social Origins of the 'Pagan-Christian' Debate," 167–96, examines the way the terms *paganus* and *Hellene* were used by Christians in the fourth century. His conclusion is that the terms were an ideological construct used as a boundary marker or as a way of differentiating between the 'in-group' (Christianity) and 'the out-group' (the 'other'). The purpose was to try to prevent Christians assimilating and accommodating to their surrounding culture. The construct of the 'other' is in effect the same strategy that Chrysostom used with his concept of Judaizers. By effectively labelling and demonising Judaizers, Chrysostom was drawing a clear line in the sand between what was acceptable Christian behavior and what was not. The same labelling of in/out groups is also seen in much of the *Adversus Judaeos* literature of the first three centuries. Cf. Van Veller, "Paul's Therapy of the Soul," 13. Shephardson suggests that the sorts of rhetorical arguments Chrysostom used against the Judaizing Christians in *Adversus Judaeos* are similar to those he used against the

Scholars have reflected on what factors led to people (particularly Christians) being attracted to Judaism.[151] Feldman is representative when he suggests:

> The canons of the Church councils and the pronouncements of the church Fathers, together with the statements of the rabbis and of the inscriptions, shed light on the factors that attracted Christians in particular to Judaism, notably the antiquity of the Jewish people, their respect for law and order, their loyalty to the state, their reputation for wisdom and ethical behavior, their philanthropy and lack of materialism, their contacts with Jewish businessmen throughout the known world, the physical and spiritual features of the Sabbath and the holidays (especially the date of Passover and its special food), the awe of the Torah scrolls and oaths taken before them, admiration for the fairness of Jewish courts, admiration for Jewish martyrs, the solemnity of Jewish ritual baths, admiration for Jewish astronomers and astrologers, the alleged Jewish skill in magic, alchemy, and the occult, and the reputed effectiveness of Jewish physicians.[152]

Anomeans in *De incomprehensibili natura dei*, and built on earlier arguments he used in *De sancto Babyla* against Christians who attended the places that he deemed would corrupt Christians, such as the theater and sporting arenas—further examples of Chrysostom delineating what were acceptable places for Christians to visit and what were not. Seen in this light, Chrysostom's *Adversus Judaeos* sermons are highly polemical. Shephardson, *Controlling Contested Spaces*, 95–98. Shephardson thus reinforces Wilken's statement that Chrysostom's angst in the *Adversus Judaeos* homilies was directed at the Judaistic religious practices that members of his flock had adopted rather than the theology that lay behind those practices. The effect of the congregation members' syncretism was to divide (and therefore "weaken") the church. Wilken, *John Chrysostom*, 77, 78. The *Adversus Judaeos* homilies demonstrate Chrysostom's use of harsh speech in order to turn his audience away from error.

151. Kinzig, "'Non-Separation,'" 37. Scholarship has more traditionally considered that Christianity and Judaism were two clearly separate identities by the end of the first century and remained so in the ensuing centuries. Fonrobert's paper, reflecting current scholarly consensus, is a corrective to that view. Fonrobert instead proposes that the separation between Christianity and Judaism was a "gradual and varied process" that took place much later than many have proposed. If this was the case, it could provide a partial explanation for the ongoing relationship between Christianity and Judaism in the religious practices of some in Chrysostom's congregation. Fonrobert, "Jewish Christians," 241. Koltun-Fromm, "Defining Sacred Boundaries: Jewish–Christian Relations," 556–71, at 559–60, suggests that Jews, pagans, and Christians in Antioch mixed freely and involved themselves in each other's religious activities, to the chagrin of religious leaders like Chrysostom.

152. Feldman, "Proselytism by Jews," 57. For more on the attractiveness of Judaism for Christians, see Wilken, *John Chrysostom*, 66–94; van der Horst, "Jews and

Furthermore, Christianity in Antioch was marked by deep divisions.[153] In 386 CE there were two different Nicene groups and one Arian group.[154] This was in significant contrast to the seemingly strong and united Jewish Antiochene community. Therefore, the combined effect of a divided church, 'half-Christians' in the Antiochene congregation, and an attractive, proselytizing, accommodating, and accessible religion in Judaism—was a significant challenge for Chrysostom. While it appears that the possibility of widespread conversion of Christians to Judaism was low, the "credibility" of Christianity was at stake.[155] The fundamental issue Chrysostom felt compelled to address was that of competing "religious loyalties."[156] In the Old Testament, to an Israelite nation syncretistically engaging with both Judaism and Baal worship, Elijah asked, "How long will you go limping between two different opinions? If the Lord is God, follow him; but if Baal is God, follow him" (1 Kgs 18:21, ESV). Judaism and Baal worship were two distinct and contradictory religions. Elijah called the Israelites to reject their syncretistic lifestyle and embrace worship of Yahweh alone. In a similar vein, Chrysostom confronted his congregation with the idea that Judaism and Christianity were two distinct and largely contradictory religions.[157] Chrysostom called on his Judaizing congregation members to reject their syncretistic lifestyle and embrace the Christian faith alone. Wilken's summary of the situation that faced Chrysostom is apt:

> The Roman Empire in the fourth century was not the world of Byzantium or medieval Europe. The institutions of traditional Hellenistic culture and society were still very much alive in John Chrysostom's day. The Jews were a vital and visible presence in Antioch and elsewhere in the Roman Empire and they continued to be a rival to the Christians. Judaizing Christians were widespread. Christianity was still in the process of establishing

---

Christians," 232–4. Louis Feldman argues that there was more than a simple passive attraction of Christians to Judaism going on. Rather, following the earlier work of Marcel Simon (1948), Feldman contends that Judaism engaged in active proselytization during the period of the third to fifth centuries. Feldman, "Proselytism by Jews," 1–58; Simon, *Verus Israel*, 271–305. Chrysostom himself admitted that "many people respect the Jews and think that their present way of life is honourable." *Adv. Jud.* 1; PG 48.847, 9–10.

153. Kinzig, "'Non-Separation,'" 39; Wilken, *John Chrysostom*, 13.
154. Kinzig, "'Non-Separation,'" 36; Wilken, *John Chrysostom*, 10–15.
155. Feldman, "Proselytism by Jews," 38; Wilken, *John Chrysostom*, 162.
156. Kinzig, "'Non-Separation,'" 41.
157. "[T]o John Christians had to choose between the Church and the synagogue." Wilken, *John Chrysostom*, 78.

its place within the society and was undermined by internal strife and apathetic adherents. Without an appreciation of this setting, we cannot understand why John preached the homilies and why he responds to the Judaizers with such passion and fervor.[158]

Chrysostom's passion and fervor ooze from each of the *Adversus Judaeos* through the rhetorical technique of the *psogos* (invective). The *psogos* was designed to denigrate a subject, focusing on negative aspects and passing over positive ones.[159] Wilken explains:

> [O]ne should not expect a fair presentation in a *psogos*, for that is not its purpose. The *psogos* is designed to attack someone, says Socrates, and is taught by sophists in the schools as one of the rudiments of their skills. It accomplishes its purpose not by sound reasoning, but by recourse to "sneer and contemptuous jests" and by "holding up to derision" someone's good qualities. "For anyone who enters into controversy with another, sometimes trying to pervert the truth, and at others attempting to conceal it, falsifies in every possible way the position of his opponent" (*Hist. eccl.* 3.23).[160]

Christian rhetoricians would at times use *psogos* against religious enemies such as Jews, heretics, and pagans.[161] As presbyter of the Antiochene congregation, Chrysostom was particularly concerned to stop the flow of his members to Jewish festivals and participation in other Jewish rites and activities.[162] In his *Adversus Judaeos* sermons, Chrysostom employed the *psogos* in order to intimidate and place pressure both on those in his congregation who were engaging in Judaizing behavior as well as those congregation members who were reluctant to address the Judaizing behavior of their fellow congregants.[163] Having congregation members involved in Jewish rites and festivals also posed a theological challenge as to whether

---

158. Wilken, *John Chrysostom*, 162.

159. Ibid., 113.

160. Wilken, *John Chrysostom*, 113.

161. Wilken, *John Chrysostom*, 115.

162. *Adv. Jud.* 1; PG 48.851, 38–40: Φεύγετε τοίνυν καὶ τοὺς συλλόγους, καὶ τοὺς τόπους αὐτῶν, καὶ μηδεὶς αἰδείσθω τὴν συναγωγὴν διὰ τὰ βιβλία ("Therefore avoid their gatherings and their places, and let nobody venerate the synagogue because of its books"). Wilken notes that Chrysostom's arguments in the *Adversus Judaeos* are not so much theological as practical. He simply wishes his congregants to avoid participating in Jewish rites. Wilken, *Chrysostom and the Jews*, 75, 77.

163. Wilken, *John Chrysostom*, 149.

Judaism or Christianity was the more legitimate religion, as well as the place of Christian rites.[164] As the first sermon in this series, *Adversus Judaeos* 1 is a highly contextualized sermon by Chrysostom to his Antiochene congregation that addressed the issue of Christian syncretism.

5.2.2 *Chrysostom's contextualized approach in Adversus Judaeos 1*

Two of Chrysostom's guiding contextual principles are evident in his approach. The first is the same as principle 1: the early establishment of common ground provides a platform for the gospel to be heard.[165] The second is the same as principle 9: contextualization is best acheived in the context of relationship.[166] Since he had been a regular preacher at the Antiochene church since his installation as presbyter earlier that year, one could surmise that Chrysostom would already have enjoyed some level of rapport with his congregation.[167] Chrysostom enhances this rapport early in his *Adversus Judaeos* 1 sermon, through praising his congregation for their conduct. Having mentioned the applause his previous sermon had received, with rhetorical flourish he says:

> As for myself, I was delighted, not because I was the one being praised, but because my Master was being glorified: that applause and the praise showed the love that you have in your hearts for God ... by your lavish applause you demonstrated your considerable goodwill towards your Master.[168]

While this encomium may have been standard rhetorical fare, it no doubt would have generated considerable goodwill towards Chrysostom and enhanced his personal connection with his congregation. Chrysostom maintained his affinity with his congregation through at least two rhetorical devices. The first was already identified in the *De statuis* sermons considered

164. Wilken, *John Chrysostom*, 149.
165. See 3.9.
166. See 5.1.4.
167. This is further suggested by Chrysostom's comment that his sermon the previous week had been warmly received by the congregation and generated applause. *Adv. Jud.* 1; PG 48.844, 8–10. καὶ πολὺς ὁ κρότος ἐγίνετο, καὶ διεθερμαίνετο τὸ θέατρον, καὶ ἐπυροῦτο ὁ σύλλογος ("great applause ensued, the theatre became fervent, the assembly was inflamed").
168. *Adv. Jud.* 1; PG 48.844, 10–13, 17–18: Ἐγὼ δὲ ἔχαιρον, οὐχ ὅτι αὐτὸς ἐπῃνούμην, ἀλλ᾿ ὅτι ὁ Δεσπότης ὁ ἐμὸς ἐδοξάζετο. Ὁ γὰρ κρότος ἐκεῖνος καὶ ὁ ἔπαινος τὸ φιλόθεον τῆς ὑμετέρας ψυχῆς ἐνεδείκνυτο ... τῇ τῶν κρότων ὑπερβολῇ τὴν πολλὴν περὶ τὸν Δεσπότην ἐπεδείκνυσθε εὔνοιαν.

earlier in this chapter—his regular use of the first person plural pronoun. One of many examples is where Chrysostom explained the purpose of his sermon directed against Judaizing Christians:

> Another very serious illness bids me to speak in order to cure it, an illness which has sprung up in the body of the church. First, *we* must root it out, then take thought for matters outside. First *we* must cure *our* own people, and then concern *ourselves* with those who aren't *our* people.[169] (emphasis mine)

What Chrysostom wanted to communicate through using the first person plural pronoun was that he and the congregation had a common task, a common mission—to "cure those suffering the Jewish illness"—an illness that would become more manifest with the approaching Jewish feasts.[170] There had been reluctance on the part of the congregation members to address the issue of attendance at Jewish festivals with fellow members who were engaging in such activity.[171] Chrysostom's pre-existing relationship with the congregation, his establishment and maintenance of rapport, along with his inclusive language, were part of his rhetorical repertoire designed to move his audience emotionally to change their thinking and behavior on the issue.

5.2.3 Chrysostom's contextual message in Adversus Judaeos 1

5.2.3.1 A CRITIQUE OF JUDAISM IN GENERAL

Before critiquing individual aspects of the Judaizing behavior (the Jewish "disease"/"illness")[172] of some of his congregation, Chrysostom begins with a general critique of Judaism as a whole. Five times Chrysostom describes Jews as "wretched" (ἀθλίος)[173] because historically the Jews had "spurned"

---

169. Adv. Jud. 1; PG 48.844, 23–29:Ἕτερον νόσημα χαλεπώτατον τὴν ἡμετέραν γλῶσσαν πρὸς ἰατρείαν καλεῖ, νόσημα ἐν τῷ σώματι τῆς Ἐκκλησίας πεφυτευμένον. Δεῖ δὲ πρότερον τοῦτο ἀνασπάσαντας, τότε φροντίσαι τῶν ἔξωθεν· πρότερον τοὺς οἰκείους θεραπεῦσαι, καὶ τότε τῶν ἀλλοτρίων ἐπιμελήσασθαι. See also Adv. Jud. 1; PG 48.845, 2.

170. Adv. Jud. 1; PG 48.845, 3.

171. Adv. Jud. 1; PG 48.848, 14–33; 849, 17–19.

172. Adv. Jud. 1; PG 48.844, 30; 845, 3. On Judaism as a type of disease that can lead to contagion for Christians who come into contact with it, see Van Veller, "Paul's Therapy of the Soul," 134–5, 145–9.

173. Adv. Jud. 1; PG 48.844, 30; 845, 23, 24, 37, 56.

(ἀπώσαντο)¹⁷⁴ the blessings of their inheritance as God's chosen people. While Jesus the Messiah had been a Jew, the Jewish nation had rejected the very one that their prophets had foretold, while Gentile outsiders had warmly received Jesus.¹⁷⁵ The result was a great reversal of fortunes, with the privileges of being God's people transferred from the Jews to believing Gentiles¹⁷⁶—leaving the Jews in a pitiful and wretched state.¹⁷⁷ Garnering the words of Acts 7:51 as evidence,¹⁷⁸ Chrysostom describes the Jews as stiff-necked (Σκληροτράχηλοι.)¹⁷⁹ because they refused to relinquish the yoke of the law for the yoke of Christ.¹⁸⁰ By continuing to live under the burden of the law, the Jews "cast [themselves] out of the kingdom of heaven."¹⁸¹

5.2.3.2 A CRITIQUE OF PARTICULAR JEWISH OBJECTS AND PRACTICES

I. THE SYNAGOGUE. In the eyes of the ancient world, newer religions did not command the respect nor contain the power that older, more established religions carried.¹⁸² At the time Chrysostom delivered *Adversus Judaeos* 1, Christianity had been established in Antioch less than three hundred and fifty years compared to Judaism's much longer history there. The locus of Judaism's religious superior prestige and power was the synagogue and the Jewish holy books contained in it.¹⁸³ The synagogue attracted some members of Chrysostom's congregation who viewed it as a holy place, a place of awe.¹⁸⁴ Part of that awe was due to Hebraic copies of the Law and the

---

174. *Adv. Jud.* 1; PG 48.845, 28. These are further examples of harsh speech, which are an adaptive technique employed in order to turn his hearers away from erroneous behavior (see 4.6).

175. *Adv. Jud.* 1; PG 48.845, 37–39.

176. *Adv. Jud.* 1; PG 48.845, 47–49: Ἀλλ' ὅρα πῶς ἀντεστράφη μετὰ ταῦτα ἡ τάξις, κἀκεῖνοι μὲν ἐγένοντο κύνες, τέκνα δὲ ἡμεῖς ("But see how after that the order was reversed; the Jews became dogs and we [Gentiles] became children").

177. *Adv. Jud.* 1; PG 48.845, 56.

178. *Adv. Jud.* 1; PG 48.845, 62–846, 1: Διὰ τοῦτό φησι, Σκληροτράχηλοι καὶ ἀπερίτμητοι τῇ καρδίᾳ, ὑμεῖς ἀεὶ τῷ Πνεύματι τῷ ἁγίῳ ἀντιπίπτετε ("That is why it says: '*You stiff-necked people, uncircumcised in heart, you always resist the Holy Spirit*'").

179. *Adv. Jud.* 1; PG 48.846, 4, 10; cf. PG 48.846, 22.

180. *Adv. Jud.* 1; PG 48.846, 7–17.

181. *Adv. Jud.* 1; PG 48.846, 18–20.

182. Wilken, *John Chrysostom*, 79.

183. Wilken, *John Chrysostom*, 79.

184. *Adv. Jud.* 1; PG 48.847, 37–38; 848, 6–8; 850, 29–30.

prophets being held there.[185] The magical and mysterious powers attributed to the Jewish holy books also led people to take oaths in the presence of these books in the belief that such oaths were more binding.[186]

Chrysostom forcefully addressed these different issues related to the synagogue by first seeking to discredit the synagogue in general. In order to dissuade his congregants from visiting it at all, he equated the synagogue with known places of iniquity—the theater, the brothel, and the robbers' cave:

> [T]he Jews gather bands of effeminate men and a great mob of female prostitutes; they drag the whole theatre and the actors into the synagogue . . . I said that the synagogue is not better than the theatre and I adduce my evidence from the prophet—the Jews aren't more worthy of belief than the prophets. What, then, does the prophet say? *"You had a prostitute's face; you became shameless before all"* (Jer. 3:3 LXX). Where a prostitute has established herself, that place is a brothel. I should say that the synagogue isn't only a brothel and theatre, but also a cave of robbers and a resting-place for wild beasts.[187]

Furthermore, Chrysostom described the synagogue as a place of idols and demons.[188] While Chrysostom is not to be interpreted as literally saying that there were demons or idols in the synagogue, his point was that just as God is not worshipped in idolatrous temples, or in the company of demons, neither can he be worshipped in the synagogue. The synagogue was not a holy or hallowed place. Rather, the only places that were truly holy, awe-inspiring and powerful were churches:

> Our (churches) aren't [frightening in the way that synagogues are] and [are] filled with awe. For the place where God is present, possessing power over life and death, is a frightening

---

185. *Adv. Jud.* 1; PG 48.850, 29–34.

186. *Adv. Jud.* 1; PG 48.848, 7–8; Wilken, *John Chrysostom*, 80.

187. *Adv. Jud.* 1; PG 48.846, 65–847, 3; 12–19: Οὗτοι δὲ χοροὺς μαλακῶν συναγαγόντες, καὶ πολὺν πεπορνευ μένων γυναικῶν συρφετόν, τὸ θέατρον ἅπαν καὶ τοὺς ἀπὸ τῆς σκηνῆς εἰς τὴν συναγωγὴν ἐπισύρουσι... Εἶπον ὅτι θεάτρου ἡ συναγωγὴ οὐδὲν ἄμεινον διάκειται, καὶ ἀπὸ προφήτου παράγω τὴν μαρτυρίαν· οὐκ εἰσὶν Ἰουδαῖοι τῶν προφητῶν ἀξιοπιστότεροι. Τί οὖν ὁ προφήτης φησίν; Ὄψις πόρνης ἐγένετό σοι· ὁ προφήτης φησίν; Ὄψις πόρνης ἐγένετό σοι· ἀπηναισχύντησας πρὸς πάντας. Ἔνθα δὲ πόρνη ἔστηκεν, πορνεῖόν ἐστιν ὁ τόπος· μᾶλλον δὲ οὐχὶ πορνεῖον καὶ θέατρον μόνον ἐστὶν ἡ συναγωγή, ἀλλὰ καὶ σπήλαιον λῃστῶν, καὶ καταγώγιον θηρίων. This is an illustration of harsh speech, use of corporeal images, and progressive education in the gospel (see 4.6).

188. *Adv. Jud.* 1; PG 48.847, 35–38; 848, 59–849, 3; 851, 58–852, 1.

place—where homilies are delivered on everlasting punishments, on rivers of fire, the poisonous worm, chains that can't be broken, eternal darkness.[189]

Similarly, Chrysostom also dismissed the claim that the presence of the Jewish holy books (the Law and the prophets) made the synagogue a holy place. For, while acknowledging the Jews might keep and read out such books in their synagogue, the benefit of their presence was nullified by the reality that the Jews did not believe the words recorded in them nor accept their evidence.[190] By failing to see how the prophets and the law of Moses point to Christ, they end up dishonoring Moses and the prophets,[191] leaving the Jews under greater divine judgment than if they had not been exposed to the books at all.[192]

Chrysostom draws two points of application for his congregation. The first stems from his stark imagery and his comparison of the church and the synagogue. If the church is the only holy and awe-inspiring place, while the synagogue a powerless, evil and God-dishonoring place, then the synagogue is to be avoided at all costs.[193] It is simply inconsistent for a person who calls him or herself a Christian to associate with such a place. For Chrysostom, such actions were syncretistic.

---

189. *Adv. Jud.* 1; PG 48.848, 44–50: Ἀλλ' οὐ τὰ ἡμέτερα τοιαῦτα, ἀλλ' ὄντως φοβερὰ καὶ φρίκης ἀνάμεστα. Ἔνθα γὰρ Θεός ἐστι ζωῆς καὶ θανάτου ἐξουσίαν ἔχων, οὗτος φοβερὸς ὁ τόπος· ἔνθα μυρίοι περὶ κολάσεων ἀθανάτων λόγοι, περὶ τῶν πυρίνων ποταμῶν, περὶ τοῦ σκώληκος τοῦ ἰοβόλου, περὶ τῶν δεσμῶν τῶν ἀρρήκτων, περὶ τοῦ σκότους. τοῦ ἐξωτέρου. Mayer and Allen, *John Chrysostom*, 155.

190. *Adv. Jud.* 1; PG 48.850, 38–40.

191. *Adv. Jud.* 1; PG 48.850, 49–56: Τοὺς γὰρ προφήτας καὶ τὸν Μωϋσέα μετ'αὐτῶν εἰσήγαγον ἐκεῖ, οὐχ ἵνα τιμήσωσιν, ἀλλ' ἵνα ὑβρίσωσι καὶ ἀτιμάσωσιν. Ὅταν γὰρ λέγωσι μὴ εἰδέναι αὐτοὺς τὸν Χριστὸν, μηδὲ εἰρηκέναι τι περὶ τῆς ἐκείνου παρουσίας, ποία μείζων ταύτης γένοιτ' ἂν εἰς τοὺς ἁγίους ἐκείνους ὕβρις, ἀλλ' ὅταν αὐτῶν κατηγορήσωσιν ὡς τὸν αὐτῶν ἀγνοούντων Δεσπότην, καὶ κοινωνοὺς τῆς ἰδίας ἀσεβείας λέγωσιν εἶναι; ("They [i.e., the Jews] brought the prophets and Moses in with them there, not to honour them but to outrage and dishonour them. For when they say that the prophets and Moses didn't know Christ or said nothing about his coming, what greater outrage could they inflict on these holy men than when they accuse them of not recognising their Master, and call them partners in their own impiety?").

192. *Adv. Jud.* 1; PG 48.851, 1–17.

193. *Adv. Jud.* 1; PG 48.851, 18–19, 38–40: Διὸ παρακαλῶ φεύγειν καὶ ἀποπηδᾶν αὐτῶν τοὺς συλλόγους . . . Φεύγετε τοίνυν καὶ τοὺς συλλόγους, καὶ τοὺς τόπους αὐτῶν, καὶ μηδεὶς αἰδείσθω τὴν συναγωγὴν διὰ τὰ βιβλία, ("So, please avoid and leap away from their gatherings . . . avoid both their gatherings and their places and let nobody venerate the synagogue because of its books").

The second implication was the issue of Christians making oaths in the synagogue. If the synagogue is not a place of holiness, awe or power then, by implication, the oaths made there have no more power or binding force than if made anywhere else. Chrysostom makes this point by giving a personal illustration he claims occurred three days earlier when he intervened in a situation whereby a man confessing to be a Christian forced a Christian woman to accompany him to the synagogue in order to make an oath regarding some business dispute.[194] Some scholars have questioned whether this event actually took place or whether Chrysostom fabricated the story to suit his argument. Either way it allowed Chrysostom to communicate that, for the Christian, "swearing oaths was absolutely forbidden, and so was forcing someone to swear them."[195] Again, becoming involved in such an activity rendered one guilty of religious syncretism.

II. JEWISH FESTIVALS. Some of Chrysostom's congregation attended not only the synagogue but also various Jewish festivals as well, and posed a further theological problem for Chrysostom. Wilkins encapsulates the essence of the issue when he states: "The legitimacy of the rites was measured not by theological arguments, but by participating in the ritual. If one participated in the Jewish festivals, the very act of doing so established the legitimacy of the rite."[196] It was the approaching Jewish festivals and the concern that members of his congregation would attend these festivals that prompted Chrysostom to preach *Adversus Judaeos* 1 in the first place. So, having addressed various Jewish rites attached to the synagogue, Chrysostom soon turned his focus to Christian attendance at Jewish festivals, asking: "Do their [Jewish] festivals have something solemn and great about them?"[197] Chrysostom proceeded to answer his own question by quoting Amos 5:21 ("I've found your festivals, I have thrust them away")[198] before pronouncing his verdict on the matter: "God hates [these Jewish festivals]."[199] Chrysostom moved to justify his claim biblically by linking together various Old Testament verses that express not only God's displeasure but also his re-

---

194. *Adv. Jud.* 1; PG 48.847, 39–848, 8.

195. *Adv. Jud.* 1; PG 48.847, 60–62: καὶ μακρὸν κατέτεινα πρὸς αὐτὸν λόγον, ὅτι οὐ θέμις ὅλως ὀμνύναι, οὐδὲ ἀνάγκην ἐπάγειν ὅρκῳ.

196. Wilken, *John Chrysostom*, 93.

197. *Adv. Jud.* 1; PG 48.853, 20–21: Ἀλλ' αἱ ἑορταὶ αὐτῶν σεμνὸν ἔχουσί τι καὶ μέγα;

198. *Adv. Jud.* 1; PG 48.853, 24–25: αὐτὰς ἀποστρέφεται τῆς ὑπερβολῆς· Μεμίσηκα, ἀπῶσμαι τὰς ἑορτὰς ὑμῶν.

199. *Adv. Jud.* 1; PG 48.853, 26: Ὁ Θεὸς μισεῖ.

jection of festivals and sacrifices connected to the Jewish nation (Isa 1:13; Gen 4:5; 8:21; Jer 7:4).[200] God hated the Jews' practice of these festivals in the Old Testament, so how much more has he hated them since the Jews' crucifixion of Jesus?[201] If Christians attended these festivals, they were effectively joining themselves to a religion in which Jewish ancestors had been abandoned by God and found guilty of provoking their Master—behavior that Chrysostom called "silly" and "deranged".[202]

III. Seeking healing from Jewish magicians and physicians. A third issue facing Chrysostom in relation to Judaism was the practice of some of his congregants seeking out Jewish magicians and physicians for healing.[203] In a later sermon John admits that people were being healed by the Jews[204] which would at the very least give the appearance that Jewish magic was stronger than anything Christianity could offer.[205] Chrysostom took a strong stand on the practice, claiming that seeking a cure from Jewish sources was akin to seeking healing from demons.[206] While the Jewish healers might bring about an effective cure, a cure for their body could cost them their soul.[207] Chrysostom's solution, maybe unpopular with the sick amongst his congregation, was for them not to accept Jewish cures.[208] Rather, they

200. *Adv. Jud.* 1; PG 48.853, 29–854, 7.

201. *Adv. Jud.* 1; PG 48.853, 35–40: "Aren't these sacrifices and offerings [that the Jews in the Old Testament had brought to the temple] abominable? *Incense is an abomination*; isn't the place also an abomination? Before they [i.e., the Jews] committed the worst of crimes, before they killed their Master, before the cross, before the slaying of Christ, it was an abomination. Isn't it much more an abomination now?"

202. *Adv. Jud.* 1; PG 48.854, 7–10.

203. *Adv. Jud.* 1; PG 48.854, 25–26.

204. *Adv. Jud.* 8; PG 48.937, 9–15.

205. Wilken, *John Chrysostom*, 84. For more on Jewish magic and healing, see Trzcionka, *Magic and the Supernatural*, esp. 124–5, 128–9, 139.

206. *Adv. Jud.* 1; PG 48.854, 24.

207. *Adv. Jud.* 1; PG 48.854, 38–42: Εἰ δὲ καὶ ἠδύναντο θεραπεύειν, καὶ ἐβούλοντο, ὅπερ ἀδύνατον, ἀλλὰ δεῖ σε μὴ κέρδους μικροῦ καὶ φθειάδύνατον, ἀλλὰ δεῖ σε μὴ κέρδους μικροῦ καὶ φθειρομένου ζημίαν ἄφθαρτον καὶ αἰώνιον ἀνταλλάξασθαι. ("Even if they [Jewish physicians] *could* cure, and were willing to do so—which is an impossibility—you shouldn't exchange a small, ephemeral benefit for a punishment that is eternal and never-ending. Are you going to cure your body in order to lose your soul? That's bad business on your part: are you going to anger God, who made your body, and call on the demon who plots against you, to cure you?")

208. Chrysostom equates being healed by Jewish healers to being healed by demons. *Adv. Jud.* 1; PG 48.854, 23.

were to turn their back on them.²⁰⁹ It was better to remain ill than fall into transgression.²¹⁰

Attendance at Jewish synagogues, swearing oaths before Jewish holy books, attendance at Jewish festivals, and seeking healing from Jewish magicians were all examples of activities that Chrysostom insisted his congregation avoid. His reason was based on a further underlying principle—principle 12: that practicing the rites and activities of both Christianity and another religion was syncretistic, a denial of the freedom which the death of Christ wrought, and a denial of the gospel itself.

5.2.3.3 Action that Chrysostom wants his Antiochene congregation to take

1. Avoid Jewish gatherings. From Chrysostom's perspective, Christian attendance at the synagogue and Jewish festivals made Jewish gatherings seem superior to Christian gatherings:

> Please avoid and leap away from their gatherings ... For when they see that you, who worship the Christ they crucified, are reverently following their ritual, why wouldn't they believe that all the rituals they perform are the best and that ours are worthless, when after worshipping and paying honour at our mysteries you run to the people who destroy them.²¹¹

Furthermore, a congregant's attendance at a Jewish gathering might also encourage another congregant with a weak conscience to admire Jewish rituals.²¹² If a person admired Jewish rituals, then it communicated

---

209. *Adv. Jud.* 1; PG 48.855, 10–11.

210. *Adv. Jud.* 1; PG 48.855, 24–31: κἂν νοσήσωμεν, βέλτιον ἐν ταῖς ἀρρωστίαις μεῖναι, ἢ διὰ τὴν ἀπαλλαγὴν τῆς ἀσθενείας εἰς ἀσέβειαν καταπεσεῖν· κἂν γὰρ θεραπεύσῃ δαίμων, μεῖζον κατέβλαψεν ἢ ὠφέλησεν. Ὠφέλησε μὲν γὰρ τὸ σῶμα, τὸ πάντως ἀποθανούμενον μικρὸν ὕστερον καὶ σήπεσθαι μέλλον, κατέβλαψε δὲ τὴν ψυχὴν τὴν ἀθάνατον. ("Even if we're sick, it's better to remain in a state of infirmity than to fall into impiety through being freed from weakness. Even if a demon cures you, it's harmed you more than helped you; it's helped your body, which a short time later is going to die and rot away; it's harmed your soul, which is immortal.")

211. *Adv. Jud.* 1; PG 48.851, 18–19, 21–26: Διὸ παρακαλῶ φεύγειν καὶ ἀποπηδᾶν αὐτῶν τοὺς συλλόγους ... Ὅταν γὰρ ἴδωσιν ὑμᾶς τοὺς προσκυνοῦντας τὸν ὑπ' αὐτῶν σταυρωθέντα Χριστόν, τὰ ἐκείνων διώκοντας καὶ σεμνοποιοῦντας, πῶς οὐχ ἡγήσονται ἄριστα αὐτοῖς ἅπαντα πεπρᾶχθαι, καὶ οὐδενὸς ἄξια εἶναι τὰ ἡμέτερα, ὅταν οἱ πρεσβεύοντες αὐτὰ καὶ θεραπεύοντες ὑμεῖς, πρὸς τοὺς καθαιροῦντας αὐτὰ τρέχητε.

212. *Adv. Jud.* 1; PG 48.851, 30–34.

that Jewish rituals were great but Christian ones were false.[213] Furthermore, presence and/or participation rendered the participants guilty before God.[214] The congregants therefore were to "avoid both their [i.e., Jewish] gatherings and their places."[215]

II. ADDRESS THE ISSUE OF JUDAIZING BEHAVIOR WITH THEIR OFFENDING CONGREGANTS. Principle 11, previously identified in *De Statuis*, that every facet of life and witness needs to be contextualized (both verbal and nonverbal elements), not just selected facets, can again be evidenced here.[216] The actions of Christians both individually and corporately as the body of Christ either positively proclaim the gospel or alternatively distort the gospel. Earlier in his sermon Chrysostom had rebuked those in his congregation who were not personally challenging erring fellow congregants who were engaging in Judaizing practices, labelling their inaction as "inhuman and hard-hearted."[217] His enjoinder for them not to be remiss in winning back their erring brothers and sisters[218] was repeated at the end of the sermon:

> Heaven forbid that anyone who hears this advice should ever commit such a sin as to betray a brother or sister on whose behalf Christ died . . . Don't neglect my words. Let the women chase after women, and the men after men, and the slaves after slaves, and the free after freemen, and the children after children, and in general let everyone be very scrupulous in chasing after people who are suffering from this kind of illness.[219]

---

213. *Adv. Jud.* 1; PG 48.852, 28–31: Ὅλως δὲ εἰ θαυμάζεις τὰ ἐκείνων, τίς σοι κοινὸς πρὸς ἡμᾶς ἐστι λόγος; Εἰ γὰρ σεμνὰ καὶ μεγάλα τὰ Ἰουδαίων, ψευδῆ τὰ ἡμέτερα· εἰ δὲ ταῦτα ἀληθῆ, ὥσπερ οὖν καὶ ἀληθῆ, ἐκεῖνα ἀπάτης γέμει ("If you admire their rituals, what have you got in common with us? The point is that, if these rituals are venerable and great, ours are false. But if ours are true, as indeed they are true, theirs are full of deceit").

214. *Adv. Jud.* 1; PG 48.855, 59–67.

215. *Adv. Jud.* 1; PG 48.851, 38–39.

216. See 5.1.4.

217. *Adv. Jud.* 1; PG 48.848, 16–17. Chrysostom surmises that two key reasons for the congregant's failure to act were that they thought it was someone else's responsibility to speak to these people, and that they were afraid of the Jews or Jewish synagogue in some way. *Adv. Jud.* 1; PG 48.848, 17–40.

218. *Adv. Jud.* 1; PG 48.849, 15–19, 8–20, 28–34.

219. *Adv. Jud.* 1; PG 48.856, 37–40, 53–58: Ἀλλὰ μὴ γένοιτο μηδένα τῶν ταύτης ἀκουόντων τῆς συμβουλῆς, τοιαύτην ἁμαρτίαν ποτὲ ἁμαρτεῖν, ὥστε προδοῦναι ἀδελφόν, ὑπὲρ οὗ Χριστὸς ἀπέθανεν . . . Μὴ τοίνυν ὀλιγωρήσητε, ἀλλὰ καὶ γυναῖκες

Chrysostom warns that failure to draw back their erring brethren will render those congregants guilty before God.²²⁰ Conversely, if the congregation does follow Chrysostom's injunction to address the issue with their Judaizing brothers and sisters, then they will be rewarded by God.²²¹

5.2.4 Contextual principles that can be drawn from Adversus Judaeos 1

In *Adversus Judaeos* 1, three contextual principles identified earlier—both from Acts and Chrysostom's *De statuis* sermons—are also evident in *Adversus Judaeos* 1:

> Principle 1: The early establishment of common ground provides a platform for the gospel to be heard;
>
> Principle 9: Contextualization is best acheived in the context of relationship;
>
> Principle 11: Every facet of life and witness needs to be contextualized, not just selected facets. Contextualization is both verbal and nonverbal, whose sphere encompasses all missionary activity which legitimately seeks to fulfill the Great Commission.

In addition to these, one further contextual principle can be drawn:

PRINCIPLE 12: Practicing the rites and activities of both Christianity and another religion is syncretistic, a denial of the freedom which the death of Christ wrought, and a denial of the gospel itself. Having painted such a stark contrast of Judaism and Christianity, the intended implication for Chrysostom's hearers was not only that Christianity and Judaism were incompatible religions but that Judaism was the inferior religion and therefore not one to be embraced by the congregants. Chrysostom developed his theme throughout his sermon by systematically critiquing particular aspects of the Jewish religion that were proving attractive to some of his flock: the synagogue (attending, swearing oaths, venerating the holy books contained in them), attendance and participation in Jewish festivals, and seeking healing from Jewish magicians and physicians. For Chrysostom, it

---

γυναῖκας, καὶ ἄνδρες ἄνδρας, καὶ δοῦλοι δούλους, καὶ ἐλεύθεροι ἐλευθέρους, καὶ παῖδες παῖδας, καὶ πάντες ἁπλῶς μετὰ ἀκριβείας ἁπάσης τοὺς τὰ τοιαῦτα νοσοῦντας θηρεύσαντες.

220. *Adv. Jud.* 1; PG 48.850, 7-9.
221. *Adv. Jud.* 1; PG 48.856, 58-66.

was incompatible for a person who claimed to be a Christian to engage with practices of another religion. Such action amounted to syncretism and was to be avoided by the Christian.[222]

Chrysostom's principle challenges two of the principles identified with respect to contextualization in a Muslim context. The first is the one advocated by Phil Parshall, who argues that meaning takes precedence over form.[223] For Parshall, while some forms are clearly to be avoided by Christians, if a particular practice is deemed unacceptable by some people (but not all) then a person is free to participate in that particular practice whenever those people who are opposed to it are not present. Chrysostom would strongly disagree. There were members in his congregation who considered it acceptable for Christians to attend and participate in activities of both Judaism and Christianity. By Parshall's reckoning, congregation members who held such a view were free to continue the practice while apart from those who held an opposing view. For Chrysostom, however, form is inseparable from meaning. Engaging with the form (Jewish activities and rites) conveys meaning (e.g., that Judaism is at least equal with Christianity, that there are deficiencies in Christianity that Judaism doesn't have, that such practices are acceptable for the Christian).

The second contextual principle that Chrysostom challenges is that advocated by Rick Brown. As an advocate for the insider movement and writing from the perspective of how MBB are to relate to their previous Muslim faith, Brown argues that, if the term Muslim can be viewed sociologically, then various Muslim practices such as attending the mosque, saying the Shahāda, and keeping Ramadan may continue to be practiced by MBB.[224] Admittedly, in *Adversus Judaeos* 1 Chrysostom is not directly dealing with the situation of people from a Jewish background coming to faith in Christ and then seeking to work out how to relate to their former faith—which would be analogous to the situation Brown addresses. But that being said, Chrysostom's principle still speaks to and challenges that of Brown. Because form does convey meaning, and because syncretism is a denial of the gospel, Muslim forms/practices such as those listed by Brown (above) are practices that are incompatible with biblical Christianity—even contextual biblical Christianity.

---

222. See 1.1.6.

223. See 2.4.1.

224. Brown, "Biblical Muslims," 70–73; Brown, "Contextualization without Syncretism," 132.

Conclusion to Adversus Judaeos 1 homily

The historical strength of Judaism in Antioch and the attractiveness of the Jewish lifestyle, synagogue, rituals and festivals presented Chrysostom with significant practical and theological challenges early in his Antiochene ministry. Practically, some of his congregation had been attending and even participating in various Jewish activities, and with the looming Jewish festivals of *Rosh ha-Shana*, *Yom Kippur*, and *Sukkot* there was a real risk that the newly installed presbyter would see increasing numbers of his congregation attending those events. Theologically, Christian participation in Jewish rites raised the issue of which of the two religions was superior—Christianity or Judaism. The seriousness of the threat caused Chrysostom to interrupt his sermon series from the previous week and preach the *Adversus Judaeos* 1 homily. In contrast to the pastoral sensitivity displayed in the *De statuis* homilies considered earlier in this chapter, Chrysostom's new theological context necessitated a different approach. Invoking the rhetorical device of *psogos*, Chrysostom delivered a highly contextualized sermon which vigorously attacked Christian participation in Jewish rites and practices while simultaneously defending the authenticity and legitimacy of Christianity.

Chrysostom's contextualized approach in *Adversus Judaeos* 1 is more practical and theological than pastoral. The pastoral element in Chrysostom's response is evidenced in Chrysostom's genuine concern for the souls of his congregants and his desire for them to avoid being deceived by the wiles of Judaism, or being caught in the trap of syncretism and so finding themselves under God's judgment. Nevertheless, the degree of invective used and the complete demonization of Judaism overwhelmingly suggest that Chrysostom's main concerns were practical and theological. Christian participation in Jewish rites and festivals would suggest to the citizens of Antioch that Judaism was a more powerful and significant religion than Christianity. The newly installed presbyter therefore engages in an all-out attack on the Judaizing practices displayed by some in his congregation as a mechanism to deal with the syncretistic threat. Only by abandoning all participation in Jewish rites and festivals and calling on their fellow congregants to do the same could the congregation retain the favor of God.

5.3 Homilia habita postquam presbyter Gothus

5.3.1 Context, audience and setting

Context: Homilia habita was a sermon that Chrysostom preached to the Gothic congregation of the Church of St. Paul, somewhere "between the inaugural Gothic liturgy (ca. 398–399) and when fire destroyed the church after Gaïnas fled Constantinople (July 12, 400)."[225] Anomean Gothic church services were not permitted to be held in a church building within Constantinople, and therefore were held either in people's homes within the city, or in churches located outside of the city walls.[226] However, as previously mentioned, Chrysostom had appointed one church within Constantinople, the Church of St. Paul, where Nicene Gothic-speaking church services could be held.

The Gothic context of the sermon makes it unique amongst all of Chrysostom's extant homilies—particularly when one takes into account the prevailing societal attitude at that time towards barbarians (of whom the Goths were a sub-group).[227] The concept of 'barbarian' was a Greco-Roman invention, originating in the fifth century BCE, but founded on ideas already inherent in Greek culture and in a context of Greek militarism against the Persians.[228] Edith Hall argues that "Greek writing about barbarians is usually an exercise in self-definition, for the barbarian is often portrayed

---

225. Stanfil, "Embracing the Barbarian," 234, 238. Despite *Homilia habita* being regularly mentioned in discussions regarding Chrysostom and the Goths, it has had minimal treatment from scholars (see Stanfil, "Embracing the Barbarian," 233n1, where he lists examples of this minimal treatment in scholarship). Stanfil's 2015 thesis is a notable exception.

226. Two previous emperors, Constantius and Valens, were supportive of the Nicene church but continued to allow Arianism. This changed from ca. 380 under Theodosius I who enforced Nicene orthodoxy, outlawing both heresy (381) and paganism (391–2). Long et al., *Barbarians*, 2–3.

227. On the anti-Gothic sentiment that confronted Chrysostom in Constantinople, see Stanfil, "Embracing the Barbarian," 252–4. This is the one extant sermon of Chrysostom preaching to a Gothic audience.

228. Geary, "Barbarians and Ethnicity," in *Late Antiquity: A Guide to the Postclassical World*, 107–29, at 107; Hall, *Inventing the Barbarian: Greek Self Definition Through Tragedy*, 1–2. Hyun Jim Kim further suggests that the Greek notion of foreigner (i.e., barbarian) reflected both the Greek fear of being invaded by the Persians and also pride that, unlike the rest of the nations in the Near East who had been invaded by the Persians, the Grecian army had not succumbed. Kim, *Ethnicity and Foreigners in Ancient Greece and China*, 2. In addition, Hall comments that having an "image of an enemy extraneous to Hellas helped to foster a sense of community between the allied states." Hall, *Inventing the Barbarian*, 2.

as the opposite of the ideal Greek. To be barbarian was to be non-Greek, to be other."[229] The Roman Empire incorporated some strands of "Hellenistic thought" about barbarianism, with "rational behaviour and subjection to government . . . central to the difference between being civilised and barbarian."[230] The Roman concept of barbarianism is multifaceted and complex.[231] Barbarians were not a monolithic group, but consisted of a spectrum of relationships between Rome and the various cultural groups. Barbarians were also increasingly incorporated into the Roman army in the latter part of the fourth century, the period leading into Chrysostom's ministry in Constantinople. The Roman attitude towards barbarians and barbarian culture, while carefully managed, was nevertheless one of superiority,[232] making Chrysostom's positive view of the Goths even more remarkable.[233]

The Goths were of Scandinavian and Germanic origin.[234] In the third century CE they settled in the region west of the Black Sea and divided into the Visigoths and the Ostrogoths.[235] The Goths were considered to have a "warlike" temperament, and from ca. 230–272 they enjoyed a number of successful military victories, including some against Roman forces.[236]

---

229. Hall, *Inventing the Barbarian*, 1. Cf. Champion, *Cultural Politics in Polybius's Histories*, 34; Andrew Gillett, "The Mirror of Jordanes: Concepts of the Barbarian, Then and Now," 392–408, at 397.

230. Halsall, *Barbarian Migrations and the Roman West 376–568*, 47.

231. For a helpful introduction to some of these complexities, see Halsall, *Barbarian Migrations*, 35–57; Gillett, "The Mirror of Jordanes," 392–408.

232. Gillett, "The Mirror of Jordanes," 401.

233. Isaac, *The Invention of Racism in Classical Antiquity* is representative of many scholars who share this traditional view regarding Roman superiority in military, intellectual, and cultural endeavors. Cf. Halsall, *Barbarian Migrations*, 45–48; Wilken, *John Chrysostom*, 20. The Goths were not a monolithic group, a point not lost on Chrysostom, who recognised "that there were subgroups within the larger ethnic group . . . Ultimately, it would appear that John's conception of Gothic ethnicity included some kind of association with a specific territory (i.e., they were either in Gothia or presumably from there), a shared cultural or perceived biological traits (i.e., a shared γένος), and a common native language." Stanfil, "Embracing the Barbarian," 17.

234. Heather and Matthews, *The Goths in the Fourth Century*, vii; Bang, "Expansion of the Teutons (to A.D. 378)," 183–217, at 202.

235. Wolfram, *History of the Goths*, 24–26; Heather and Matthews, *The Goths*, 2; Bang, "Expansion of the Teutons," 203. For a description of the effect of Gothic raids in some of the Roman areas of Asia Minor, see Heather and Matthews' translation of Gregory Thaumaturgus' *Canonical Epistle* (PG 10.1020–48) in Heather and Matthews, *The Goths*, 5–11.

236. Mitchell, *A History*, 192; Heather and Matthews, *The Goths*, 2–4; Gerard Friell and Stephen Williams, "Friends, Romans or Countrymen? Barbarians in the Empire," 34–40, at 34. For more on the Gothic invasions during the third century, see

From ca. 272–322 a period of peace between the Goths and Rome ensued, before hostilities resumed during the reign of Constantine.[237] Following a number of battles between the Goths and the Roman forces, the Goths were largely subdued under Roman rule until 378, at which time the Visigoths had a decisive victory against Emperor Valens and his forces.[238] Subsequent to this, Emperor Theodosius I signed a treaty with the Visigoths that made some important concessions, including allowing the Visigoths to live in Roman territory but be self-governing.[239] The Goths were also allowed to join the Roman army on an individual basis and became an increasing part of the Roman fighting force over the next two decades.[240] Under the Scythian general Gaïnas, commander of the Roman army, increasing numbers of Goths populated Constantinople, leading to tension with the local Roman citizens.[241] In 400, fear that the Goths were about to sack Constantinople led panicked Roman citizens to attack the Goths who resided within the city walls, "burning alive many thousands of Goths in a church where they had fled to for asylum."[242] In 410, under the Visigoth leader Alaric, the Visigoths sacked Rome.[243]

The gospel was brought to the Goths in the fourth century, most notably through the missionary Ulfilas.[244] Ulfilas (311–388) was from a Gothic Christian family. He was educated in Constantinople, and in 341 he was appointed as bishop to the Goths north of the Danube by Eusebius of Nicomedia at the Council of Antioch. Ulfilas was effective as a missionary,

---

Wolfram, *History of the Goths*, 43–57.

237. Heather and Matthews, *The Goths*, 19–21; Bang, "Expansion of the Teutons," 210–1.

238. Baynes,"The Dynasty of Valentinian and Thedosius the Great," 218–49, at 233–5; Heather and Matthews, *The Goths*, 21–25; Bang, "Expansion of the Teutons," 216.

239. Cameron et al., *Barbarians and the Politics of the Court*, 1; Friell and Williams, "Friends," 34.

240. Long and Lee, *Barbarians*, 2; Friell and Williams, "Friends" 34. On the recruitment of barbarians (non-Greeks) into the Roman army in the fourth century and the increasing dependence of the empire on these barbarian recruits, see Liebeschuetz, *Barbarians and Bishops*, 1–25.

241. Cameron et al., *Barbarians*, 8.

242. Sozomen, *Hist. eccl.* 6.37 See Heather and Matthews' translation in Heather and Matthews, *The Goths*, 103–109 at 108. Cameron et al., *Barbarians*, 8; Liebeschuetz, *Barbarians and Bishops*, 118.

243. Max Manitius, "The Teutonic Migrations, 378–412," 250–76, at 273; Liebeschuetz, *Barbarians and Bishops*, 72.

244. Cameron, *The Later Roman Empire*, 136.

winning many converts to his Arian[245] brand of Christianity from amongst his fellow countrymen.[246] Ulfilas' legacy was his translation of the Scriptures into the Gothic language.[247] Martin Bang concludes that Ulfilas' translation of the Bible, along with his missionary activity, were the "seeds" which led to "the conversion of the whole Gothic race to Arian Christianity."[248] It was this Arian form of Christianity which Chrysostom faced in his ministry to the Goths both in Constantinople and beyond.[249]

Audience and setting. Based on Stanfil's reconstruction of the Gothic population in Constantinople at this time, the Gothic congregation probably included "Gothic slaves, freemen, soldiers (including veterans and their families) . . . [and] possibly a few elites."[250] On the occasion of Chrysostom's sermon at the Church of St Paul there would also have been some bilingual Goths (who could function as translators of Chrysostom's sermon) and probably a small number of Greek-speaking people who accompanied the bishop on his visit.[251] As Nicene orthodoxy rather than Arian Christianity was taught at this church, the Goths that attended would probably have sub-

---

245. The "Arian controversy" doctrinal debate began ca. 321, was primarily concerned with the nature of the Trinity and significantly shaped Gothic Christianity. Arianism, attributed to the Alexandrian presbyter Arius (254–336), is the theological belief that the Son of God, Jesus Christ, was not eternal but rather created by, and subordinate to, God the Father. Against this, the Council of Nicea (325) affirmed that the Father and Son were of the same substance (ὁμοούσιος), against the Arian doctrine that the Son was of like substance (ὅμοιούσιος). Nevertheless, Arianism continued to influence the empire, and it was not until the Second Ecumenical Council of Constantinople (381) that it was finally defeated. See Hanson, *The Search for the Christian Doctrine of God*, 181–202. For more on the Arian controversy, Arianism and Nicene theology, see Ayres, *Nicea and its Legacy: An Approach to Fourth-Century Trinitarian Theology*; Barnes and Williams, *Arianism After Arius: Essays on the Development of the Fourth Century Trinitarian Conflicts*.

246. Sozomen, *Hist. eccl.* 6.37 views Ulfilas' adoption of Arianism as pragmatic rather than theological. Ulfilas, while in Constantinople on an embassy to the emperor, was promised support for his embassy by some Arian leaders in exchange for Ulfilas adopting Arianism. See *Hist eccl.* 6.37 in Heather and Matthews, *The Goths*, 106–7. For further discussion on the theology of Ulfilas, see Heather and Matthews, *The Goths*, 135–9.

247. Cameron, *The Later Roman Empire*, 136. For more on the life and ministry of Ulfilas, see Wolfram, *History of the Goths*, 75–85.

248. Bang, "Expansion of the Teutons," 212–3.

249. Gwatkin, "Arianism," 118–42, at 118–9. For more on the origin and nature of Gothic Christianity, see Wiles, *Archetypal Heresy: Arianism Through the Centuries*, 40–51.

250. Stanfil, "Embracing the Barbarian," 239.

251. Ibid.

scribed to Nicene theology themselves, or at the very least been positively disposed to it.[252]

As the sermon title *Homilia habita postquam presbyter Gothus concionatus fuerat* states, it was during one of these Gothic-speaking Nicene services, after the reading of the Scriptures and a sermon by a Gothic priest, that Chrysostom stood and preached this sermon in Greek, which was then translated into Gothic.[253] While scholars have traditionally considered the sermon to have been delivered almost impromptu due to Chrysostom unexpectedly having a gathering of Goths at his disposal, Stanfil has recently suggested an alternate view. Based on Chrysostom's recorded frequent involvement in and preaching at the Gothic parish,[254] and the fact that there probably was a stenographer present to record Chrysostom's sermon to the Goths, Stanfil argues that it is probable that this sermon was planned well ahead of time in order to coincide with a particular occasion—such as the inauguration of the Gothic liturgy. Another possibility is that, due to mounting criticism of his mission to the Goths and the legitimacy of the Gothic Nicene church, Chrysostom took the opportunity to defend those accusations.[255] Either way, the sermon is both a celebration and endorsement of Nicene Gothic Christianity and a defense of the legitimacy of Chrysostom's Gothic mission.[256]

5.3.2 Chrysostom's contextual approach

Chrysostom's contextual approach in *Homilia habita* reflects what has been already observed in the *De statuis* and *Adversus Judaeos* 1 homilies. First,

---

252. Goths who wanted a more Arian expression of Christianity may have attended one of the Arian gatherings that were held in various homes in Constantinople. Sozomen, *Hist. eccl.* 7.5 (GCS NF 4.306); Socrates, *HE* 5.20 (GCS NF 1.294). Laird, "John Chrysostom and the Anomeans," 144–5, n86, n87.

253. *Goth. concin.*; PG 63.499, 500; Mayer, *The Homilies*, 472. The English translation of *Homilia habita* in this chapter is by Dr. Bronwen Neil (unpublished) and was reviewed by Mr Kosta Simic.

254. Theodoret, *Hist. eccl.* 5.30; cf. Stanfil, "Embracing the Barbarian," 240n26.

255. Stanfil, "Embracing the Barbarian," 239–41.

256. This concurs with Stanfil's evaluation of the sermon's purpose. Cf. Stanfil, "Embracing the Barbarian," 241. Stanfil persuasively argues that Roman Greek-speakers who were critical of Chrysostom's mission to the Goths, although not present to hear the sermon, were an intended secondary audience, accessing Chrysostom's sermon both through word of mouth and through it being published and distributed. Cf. Stanfil, "Embracing the Barbarian," 247–51.

he seeks to establish and maintain rapport with his Gothic congregation. Second, he interacts with the worldview of his congregation.

i. *His establishment and maintenance of rapport with his audience.* In contrast with the congregational rapport Chrysostom already enjoyed with his own congregations, when he delivered his *De statuis* and *Adversus Judaeos* homilies, Chrysostom's *Homilia habita* was delivered to a cross-cultural audience with whom he had significantly less relationship (not preaching there on a weekly basis).[257] The different context provided Chrysostom with some unique cultural challenges to overcome. A significant point of difference between Chrysostom and the Gothic congregation he addressed was that of their spoken languages. As previously mentioned, the Roman attitude towards barbarians and barbarian culture was one of superiority, which was a potential barrier between Chrysostom and the Gothic congregation. In an effort to reduce (even overcome) that barrier, Chrysostom began his address by distancing himself from pagan Greek-speakers and self-identifying with the Gothic congregation:

> I wish that the pagans could be present today, so that they could hear what has been read, and learn how great is the power of the crucified One, how noble the church, how strong the faith, how vile is error, and how great the mocking of demons. And indeed the words of philosophers were refuted even by those who shared the same tongue, but our Christian teaching has great power even amongst foreigners.[258]

In order to further establish rapport, Chrysostom used first person plural pronouns ("our" and "us") early in his sermon, signifying Chrysostom and his Gothic congregation were not just fellow Christians but had equal standing as Christians.[259] There is no hierarchy in God's kingdom but all are one in Christ Jesus.

---

257. Theodoret, *Hist. eccl.* 5.30.

258. *Goth. concin.*; PG 63.499, 56–500, 56: Ἐβουλόμην παρεῖναι Ἕλληνας τήμερον, ὥστε τῶν ἀνεγνωσμένων ἀκοῦσαι καὶ μαθεῖν πόση τοῦ σταυρωθέντος ἡ ἰσχὺς, πόση τοῦ σταυροῦ ἡ δύναμις, πόση τῆς Ἐκκλησίας ἡ εὐγένεια, πόση τῆς πίστεως ἡ εὐτονία, πόση τῆς πλάνης ἡ αἰσχύνη, πόσος τῶν δαιμόνων ὁ γέλως. Τὰ μὲν γὰρ τῶν φιλοσόφων καὶ παρὰ τοῖς ὁμοφώνοις καταλέλυται, τὰ δὲ ἡμέτερα καὶ παρὰ ἑτερογλώσσοις πολλὴν ἔχει δύναμιν·

259. For example: "but *our* words are have great power even among foreigners . . . but *our* words are different." ("μὲν ἀράχνης εὐκολώτερον διεσπάσθη, τὰ δὲ ἀδάμαντος στερρότερον πέπηγε . . . Ἀλλ' οὐ τὰ ἡμέτερα τοιαῦτα.") *Goth. concin.*; PG 63.500, 55–56, 501, 12–13. (emphasis mine)

Chrysostom maintained rapport through a number of rhetorical techniques. First, he continued self-identifying with the Goths through use of the first person plural pronoun throughout the sermon.[260] A second technique Chrysostom employed was one where, at various times, he spoke very positively about barbarians and, in contrast, somewhat disparagingly about Greek-speakers. For example, Chrysostom rated the Scriptures which had been translated into the Gothic language as of greater validity and value than the words of significant Greek philosophers:

> Where now are those teachings of Plato, of Pythagoras and those who were in Athens? They are extinguished. Where now are those of the fishermen and tent makers? Not in Judea alone, but they shine more splendid than the sun, even in the barbarian tongue, which you heard today. Scythians and Thracians and Sarmatians and Moors and Indians, even those who live in the furthest reaches of the world philosophise over those words, having been translated into their own languages.[261]

A second example finds Chrysostom advocating for the validity and the glory of the presence of barbarian Christians when he said:

> Therefore, let no one think that this is shameful for the church, that barbarians rise up in our midst and we have prepared them to speak: for this is the ornament and beauty of the church, this is the proof of the power which is located in faith.[262]

On a further occasion, when speaking of the question the (barbarian) magi posed to King Herod, 'Where is he who was born king of the Jews?' (Matt 2:2), Chrysostom exclaimed:

---

260. For example: *Goth. concin.*; PG 63.501, 28-30: οἱ δὲ παρ' ἡμῖν οὐχ οὕτως, ἀλλὰ πάντα ταῦτα διακρουσάμενοι; καὶ τὴν ἔξωθεν φαντασίαν ῥίψαντες, φυσικὸν τὸ κάλλος ἐπιδείκνυνται ("but among *us* it is not so; instead, *our* people, by rejecting all these and scorning external pride, reveal their natural beauty") [emphasis mine].

261. *Goth. concin.*; PG 63.501, 1-8: Ποῦ τὰ Πλάτωνος καὶ Πυθαγόρου καὶ τῶν ἐν Ἀθήναις; ἐσβέσθη. Ποῦ τὰ τῶν ἁλιέων καὶ σκηνοποιῶν; οὐκ ἐν Ἰουδαίᾳ μόνον, ἀλλὰ καὶ ἐν τῇ τῶν βαρβάρων γλώττῃ, καθὼς ἠκούσατε σήμερον, ἡλίου φανότερον διαλάμπει· καὶ Σκύθαι καὶ Θρᾷκες καὶ Σαυρομάται καὶ Μαῦροι καὶ Ἰνδοὶ καὶ οἱ πρὸς αὐτὰς ἀπῳκισμένοι τὰς ἐσχατιὰς τῆς οἰκουμένης, πρὸς τὴν οἰκείαν ἕκαστος μεταβαλόντες γλῶτταν, τὰ εἰρημένα φιλοσοφοῦσι ταῦτα·

262. *Goth. concin.*; PG 63.501, 51-55: Μὴ τοίνυν αἰσχύνην τις ἡγείσθω τῆς Ἐκκλησίας, ὅτι βαρβάρους εἰς μέσον ἀναστῆναι καὶ εἰπεῖν παρεσκευάσαμεν· τοῦτο γὰρ τῆς Ἐκκλησίας κόσμος, τοῦτο καλλώπισμα, τοῦτο τῆς ἐν τῇ πίστει δυνάμεως ἀπόδειξις. This is an example of 'gentle' speech (see 4.6).

> O marvellous and unexpected circumstances! Through the voice of a barbarian, the only one born son of God is first preached in Judea, where the prophets, patriarchs and the righteous, and the law, the Ark, the covenant, the temple, the sacrifice and the cult [reside].[263]

The rapport that such an approach would have engendered would have been further strengthened by the theological approach Chrysostom took. In contrast to his *Against the Statues* sermons, in *Homilia habita* Chrysostom does not seek to directly challenge the worldview of his audience. Rather, in *Homilia habita* Chrysostom positively affirms Gothic Christianity and the place of barbarians in God's plan and as well, he provides an apologetic to those Greek-speakers in Constantinople who were disparaging of Gothic Christianity. It is worth noting too that there are two contextual principles previously outlined in Acts and Chrysostom himself that are again evident in *Homilia habita*—principle 1: the early establishment of common ground provides a platform for the gospel to be heard; and, principle 9: contextualization is best achieved in the context of relationship. While Chrysostom did not begin the homily with a significant established relationship with the congregation, he sought to quickly develop one through both his manner of delivery and chosen content.

ii. *His interaction with his audience's worldview.* A second element in Chrysostom's contextual approach is the way that he demonstrates both an awareness of and subsequent interaction with the worldview of his Gothic audience.

This congregation was largely (if not completely) made up of Gothic Christians, whose church services would have included regular reading of the Gothic scriptures. In his sermon Chrysostom regularly drew on his audience's knowledge of the Christian Scriptures, authoritative to his hearers, including references to the crucifixion,[264] Pentecost,[265] Abraham,[266] Moses,[267] and the incarnation of Christ.[268]

---

263. *Goth. concin.*; PG 63.507, 7–14: θαυμαστῶν καὶ παραδόξων πραγμάτων· παρὰ βαρβαρικῆς πρώτης φωνῆς ὁ μονογενὴς Υἱὸς τοῦ Θεοῦ ἐν Ἰουδαίᾳ κηρύττεται, ἔνθα προφῆται καὶ πατριάρχαι καὶ δίκαιοι καὶ νόμος καὶ κιβωτὸς καὶ διαθήκη καὶ ναὸς καὶ θυσίαι καὶ λατρεῖαι·

264. *Goth. concin.*; PG 63.499, 58.

265. *Goth. concin.*; PG 63.501, 34–42.

266. *Goth. concin.*; PG 63.502, 30; 503, 1–13.

267. *Goth. concin.*; PG 63.502, 32; 503, 13–23.

268. *Goth. concin.*; PG 63.505, 15–31.

Chrysostom also contextualized his use of Scripture, with his most prominent sermon illustrations being various barbarians mentioned in Scripture such as Abraham, Moses, and the magi. This had the effect of legitimising barbarian Christians, Chrysostom's ongoing mission to the Goths, and emphasizing the important place of non-Greek speakers in God's plans and purposes for the world.[269]

Chrysostom also drew illustrations from the everyday life of his audience. For example, he spoke of prostitutes,[270] poverty,[271] fishermen,[272] kings,[273] doctors,[274] and astrology.[275] Such illustrations demonstrated that Chrysostom was familiar with the daily life of his audience.[276]

The combined effect of Chrysostom's self-identification with his Gothic audience, distancing himself somewhat from the Greek-speaking populace, his positive stance towards the Goths, and his interaction with his audience's worldview would have assisted him both to gain and maintain rapport with the Gothic congregation. Once again Chrysostom has applied his contextual principle of understanding the audience's worldview and drawing illustrations from their everyday life (principle 2). Chrysostom's approach built a contextual bridge between Greek and Gothic-speakers over which the gospel message could travel.

5.3.3 Chrysostom's contextual message

In *Homilia habita* two related themes shaped Chrysostom's contextual message to his Gothic audience. First, the Gothic church service was a legitimate church service and an authentic expression of Christianity.[277] The second theme was that there was no shame for the church in having barbar-

---

269. Chrysostom also directly quoted Scripture at a number of points, including Ps 19:4-5, Isa 65:25, Rom 1:13-15, 2 Cor 4:17-18. Chrysostom also used biblical figures as models for imitation (see chapter 4, pp. 151-152).

270. *Goth. concin.*; PG 63.501, 13-14.

271. *Goth. concin.*; PG 63.503, 32, 39; 504, 1-11.

272. *Goth. concin.*; PG 63.501, 45.

273. *Goth. concin.*; PG 63.503, 32, 38-39.

274. *Goth. concin.*; PG 63.504, 59-505, 2.

275. *Goth. concin.*; PG 63.504, 12.

276. Reflecting his use of corporeal images (see 4.6).

277. This further justifies Chrysostom's mission to the Goths (see 4.3).

ian Christians in their midst, because barbarians had been proclaimers of the gospel and forerunners of the church since the time of Abraham. In addition to these two themes, Chrysostom also presented a contextualized explanation of the gospel.

5.3.3.1 The Gothic Nicene Church Service is a Legitimate Church Service and Authentic Expression of Christianity

Having argued that the words of Scripture (no matter in what language they were translated) were more powerful than the words of Greek philosophy, Chrysostom further argued that they have also had greater innate beauty. Chrysostom compared the oratory of pagan Greek-speakers with the plain but superior words of Christians who preached Scripture. He likened pagan Greek philosophers to a prostitute who, lacking natural beauty, has to dress herself with jewellery in order to look attractive.[278] In contrast, Christians, armed with the words of Scripture, do not need to add anything in order to make them attractive to other people. Rather, through their righteous words and actions, Christians display the beauty of the gospel.[279]

Chrysostom's main point was that the Greek language was not synonymous with ultimate wisdom. Non-Greek speakers, such as his Gothic audience, could equally espouse wisdom (even greater wisdom) than Greek-speakers. Chrysostom cited the day of Pentecost as further evidence of this truth (Acts 2:1–13). On the day of Pentecost, the Christians who had gathered in Jerusalem were all filled with the Holy Spirit and began to speak in other tongues (ἑτέραις γλώσσαις, 2:4). The result was that devout men from every nation under heaven (ἀπὸ παντὸς ἔθνους τῶν ὑπὸ τὸν οὐρανόν, 2:5) who were residing in Jerusalem heard the Christians speaking in the native, non-Greek languages of those devout men (Acts 2:6–11). Following

---

278. *Goth. concin.;* PG 63.501, 12–18.

279. *Goth. concin.;* PG 63.501, 28–34: οἱ δὲ παρ' ἡμῖν οὐχ οὕτως, ἀλλὰ πάντα ταῦτα διακρουσάμενοι; καὶ τὴν ἔξωθεν φαντασίαν ῥίψαντες, φυσικὸν τὸ κάλλος ἐπιδείκνυνται, οὐ γλῶτταν ἀκονῶντες, οὐδὲ εὐφημίαν διώκοντες, ἀλλ' ἐν δυνάμει νοημάτων φιλοσοφοῦντες, καὶ ἔργων ἐπιδείξει καὶ πολιτείας ἀκριβείᾳ τὴν ἐνοικοῦσαν αὐτοῖς τοῦ Θεοῦ χάριν διὰ πάντων ἀνακηρύττοντες. ("[But] among us [i.e., Gothic Christians] they are not so; instead, by rejecting all these [examples of philosophical rhetorical devices] and scorning external pride, they reveal their natural beauty; and not by sharpening their language, nor by chasing elegant conversation, but doing philosophy in the virtue of their thoughts, and by the example of their works, and by the exact foundations of their life they preach among all that they dwell in the grace of God.")

Peter's recorded Pentecost sermon (2:14–40), about three thousand people became Christians (2:41). Pointing to the Pentecost event, Chrysostom explained that people of all ages, from all parts of the world (both Greek and barbarian), became "caught up" in the Christian "net" through the gospel being proclaimed in many languages.[280] Since Pentecost Christianity had now spread to all parts of the world.[281] Once again he demonstrated the Christian message, whether declared by Greek speakers or barbarians, to be superior to that of Greek philosophy.[282]

Chrysostom immediately applied this truth to his Gothic context, stating that the Gothic Christians who were part of the Gothic-speaking church of St. Paul were legitimate Christians in their own right and a demonstration of the "beauty of the church."[283]

Chrysostom went further, stating that a barbarian-speaking church is actually a fulfillment of Scripture. Chrysostom cited two Scriptural examples, although in both cases he took the verses out of context. First, he quoted Psalm 19:3–4:

> [T]his is even what the Prophet foretold, saying: They are not utterances or speeches whose words are not heard: to the whole earth their sound went out, and their words to the ends of the earth.[284]

---

280. *Goth. concin.;* PG 63.501, 34–41: Διὰ δὴ τοῦτο οὐ τὴν οἰκουμένην μόνον· οὐ τὴν γῆν μόνον, ἀλλὰ καὶ τὴν θάλατταν· οὐ τὰς πόλεις μόνον, ἀλλὰ καὶ τὰ ὄρη καὶ τοὺς βουνοὺς καὶ τὰς νάπας· οὐ τὴν Ἑλλάδα μόνον, ἀλλὰ καὶ τὴν βάρβαρον· οὐ τοὺς ἐν ἀξιώμασι μόνον, ἀλλὰ καὶ τοὺς ἐν ἐσχάτῃ πενίᾳ· οὐκ ἄνδρας μόνον, ἀλλὰ καὶ γυναῖκας· οὐ γεγηρακότας μόνον, ἀλλὰ καὶ νέους ἐσαγήνευσαν. ("For that reason they have caught so to speak in their net not only the inhabited parts of the earth but even the uninhabited parts; not only the earth but also the sea; not only Greece but also the barbarian tribes; not only those who are of noble birth but also those who are in extreme poverty; not only men but even women; not only old men but even youths.")

281. *Goth. concin.;* PG 63.50, 46.

282. *Goth. concin.;* PG 63.501, 45–51: καὶ ὅπουπερ ἂν ἀφίκῃ λοιπὸν, τῶν ἁλιέων ὄψει τὰ ὀνόματα ἐν τοῖς ἁπάντων στόμασι περιφερόμενα, οὐ διὰ τὴν τῶν ἁλιέων δύναμιν, ἀλλὰ τὴν τοῦ σταυρωθέντος ἰσχὺν τὴν πανταχοῦ προοδοποιοῦσαν αὐτοῖς, καὶ τοὺς ἰδιώτας τῶν φιλοσόφων σοφωτέρους, καὶ τοὺς ἀγραμμάτους καὶ ἰχθύων ἀφωνοτέρους ῥητόρων καὶ λογογράφων καὶ σοφιστῶν εὐτονωτέρους ἀποφαίνουσαν. ("[A]nd wherever you go now, you will see the names of the fishermen on the lips of everyone, not on account of the virtue of the fishermen, but because of the power of the Crucified One, which revealed the way to them in every place, and revealed uncultivated people to be wiser than philosophers, and rendered the illiterate and those more mute than fish, more complete than rhetors, orators and sophists.")

283. *Goth. concin.;* PG 63.501, 51–55.

284. *Goth. concin.;* PG 63.501, 55–59: τοῦτο καὶ ὁ προφήτης ἄνωθεν προαναφωνῶν ἔλεγεν· *Οὐκ εἰσὶ λαλιαὶ οὐδὲ λόγοι, ὧν οὐχὶ ἀκούονται αἱ φωναὶ αὐτῶν·*

Chrysostom's point was that that there would be no languages ("utterances and speeches"), including the Gothic language, which would not be heard across the whole world (which would include the churches across the world).[285]

Chrysostom subsequently referred to Isa 65:25:

> And another prophet again showed this, saying the same thing but in different words: Wolves and lambs will lie down together, and the leopard will lie down with the kid, and the lion will eat grass like the cow.[286]

Chrysostom's explanation of Isa 65:25 was that the verse was not about wolves and lambs lying down together but rather prophetic of the day when the wild beasts (barbarians) would join Greek-speaking Christians as part of God's kingdom:

> He was not speaking about lions, lambs, leopards and kids, but foretelling for us and giving a sign of what would happen, that the wild beasts among them would come into that state of meekness, made mild by the philosophy of preaching, so that it would join together with our mildest of men.[287]

εἰς πᾶσαν τὴν γῆν ἐξῆλθεν ὁ φθόγγος αὐτῶν, καὶ εἰς τὰ πέρατα τῆς οἰκουμένης τὰ ῥήματα αὐτῶν.

285. Psalm 19 addresses Yahweh's self-revelation. Yahweh reveals himself through his created works (vv. 1–6) and through his revealed Word (vv. 7–12). God's created order (the heavens/sky above, v. 1; the sun, vv. 4–6) continually (day and night, v. 2) communicate Yahweh's glory (v. 1). While this communication is visual, the psalmist poetically describes creation using terms of speech ["declaring" (v. 1), "proclaims" (v. 1), "speech" (vv. 2–3), "voice" (v. 3, v. 4), "words" (v. 4)]. Verse 4 is making the point that the 'voice' of creation goes out to the ends of the earth. This is in contrast to Chrysostom's interpretation of verse 4 being that all languages (and not just Greek) will be heard throughout the world. Cf. Peter C. Craigie, *Psalms 1–50*, WBC 19, 180–1.

286. *Goth. concin.*; PG 63.501, 59–502, 4: Τοῦτο καὶ ἕτερος παραδηλῶν πάλιν, ἑτέροις ῥήμασιν ᾐνίττετο λέγων· Λύκοι καὶ ἄρνες ἅμα βοσκηθήσονται, καὶ πάρδαλις συναναπαύσεται ἐρίφῳ, καὶ λέων ὡς βοῦς φάγεται ἄχυρα.

287. *Goth. concin.*; PG 63.502, 4–9: οὐ περὶ λεόντων καὶ ἀρνῶν καὶ παρδάλεων καὶ ἐρίφων διηγούμενος, ἀλλὰ προαναφωνῶν ἡμῖν καὶ δεικνὺς, ὅτι δὴ τὸ θηριῶδες τῶν ἀνθρώπων εἰς τοσαύτην ἥξει ἡμερότητα τῇ φιλοσοφίᾳ τοῦ κηρύγματος κερασθὲν, ὥστε μετὰ τῶν ἡμέρων καὶ πραοτάτων ἀνδρῶν συναγελάζεσθαι. Isa 65:17–25 is a prophetic description of the new heavens and new earth, which will be ushered in after the second coming of Jesus. At that time, creation will be restored to its original state (Gen 1–2) before sin entered the world (Gen 3:1–24). A consequence of this new state is that all fear, animosity, and death will be removed (pictured by wolves and lambs/lions and oxen harmoniously residing together—v. 25). This is in contrast to Chrysostom's interpretation of verse 25 referring to Greeks and barbarians together being part

It was at this point that Chrysostom applied the following to his Gothic audience, to which his whole argument had been building:

> And you see this today, namely that those who were more barbaric than any other people, stand with the flock of the church, and use the same pasture and the same sheepfold, and the same table is appropriate for all.[288]

For Chrysostom, it was not just that both barbarian Christians and Greek-speaking Christians were all part of the kingdom of God, but that they were equally so. The Gothic Christians gathered that day in the Church of St Paul, listening to Chrysostom, were equal participants with (μετά) Greek-speaking Christians in the flock of the church, using the *same/common* (κοινήν) pasture and the *same/one* (ἕνα) sheepfold, and the *same/one* (μίαν) table.[289] There was nothing embarrassing or shameful about it (see below). Rather, it was part of God's beautiful plan for the church. Therefore, the Gothic church and its Nicene church services in the Gothic language were legitimate and authentic expressions of Christianity.

5.3.3.2 There is no shame for the church in having barbarian Christians in their midst

In the context of the anti-barbarian sentiment of Chrysostom's day, his advocacy of barbarian Christianity would have been startling, controversial, and potentially embarrassing for the church. Having already stated that the preaching of God's word, and Christianity as a whole, was not restricted to Greek speakers and that there was no shame in having a church of Gothic-speaking Christians, Chrysostom provided added evidence to support his contentious claim and further justify his Gothic mission.[290] He did so by drawing on biblical examples from both the Old and New Testaments of barbarians who proclaimed the gospel, qualifying them as forerunners of the New Testament church.

---

of God's church. Cf. John N. Oswalt, *The Book of Isaiah: Chapters 40-66*, 654-6, 662.

288. *Goth. concin.*; PG 63.502, 9–12: Καὶ τοῦτο σήμερον ἑωράκατε, τοὺς πάντων ἀνθρώπων βαρβαρικωτέρους μετὰ τῶν τῆς Ἐκκλησίας προβάτων ἑστῶτας, καὶ κοινὴν οὖσαν τὴν νομὴν καὶ τὸν σηκὸν ἕνα, καὶ μίαν ἅπασι τράπεζαν προκειμένην.

289. By 'table' Chrysostom means the Lord's Supper—a symbol of Christian fellowship.

290. Chrysostom mentions shame (αἰσχύνη) associated with barbarian Christianity three times in the middle section of his sermon, suggesting that it was an issue of some importance for his audience (*Goth. concin.*; PG 63. 501, 52; 503, 26; 507, 1).

First, quoting Rom 1:13-15, Chrysostom highlighted the apostle Paul's eagerness for the gospel to be proclaimed not only to Greeks but non-Greeks. From New Testament times through to Chrysostom's day, the gospel had been universally and even indiscriminately proclaimed to people of many cultures and languages.[291] Chrysostom further argued that the phenomenon of the gospel being proclaimed to barbarians, and even by barbarians in their native tongue, was not only found in the New Testament but in the Old Testament as well.[292] His evidence consisted of two notable biblical examples of Gentiles/barbarians who, through their actions, proclaimed the gospel. From Chrysostom's standpoint, the actions of the two Gentiles qualified them not only as forerunners of the New Testament church but also as models for Christians (both Greek and barbarian alike) to imitate.[293]

Chrysostom's first example was the patriarch Abraham, a barbarian from the middle of Persia.[294] Abraham did not have prior knowledge of Greek philosophy, or history, or the writings of Moses, or the other Old Testament and New Testament writings, nor did he have anyone to teach him about any of these matters.[295] Despite this, "having been born and raised in

---

291. *Goth. concin.*; PG 63.502, 18–25: Ὥσπερ γὰρ ἥλιος κοινὸς καὶ γῆ κοινὴ καὶ θάλαττα καὶ ἀήρ, οὕτως πολλῷ μᾶλλον ὁ τοῦ κηρύγματος λόγος ἐγένετο κοινός· διὸ καὶ Παῦλος ἔλεγεν·Ἵνα τινὰ καρπὸν σχῶ καὶ ἐν ὑμῖν, καθὼς καὶ ἐν τοῖς λοιποῖς ἔθνεσιν. Ἕλλησί τε καὶ βαρβάροις, σοφοῖς τε καὶ ἀνοήτοις ὀφειλέτης εἰμί· οὕτω τὸ κατ' ἐμὲ πρόθυμον καὶ ὑμῖν τοῖς ἐν Ῥώμῃ εὐαγγελίσασθαι. ("For as the sun is universal and the earth, and the sea and the air, so even preaching of the word has become much more universal: and for that reason Paul said: *"in order that I might have a harvest among you, just as I have had among the other Gentiles.14 I am obligated both to Greeks and non-Greeks, both to the wise and the foolish. 15 That is why I am so eager to preach the gospel also to you who are in Rome."*)

292. *Goth. concin.*; PG 63.502, 25–26: Καὶ τί θαυμάζεις εἰ ἐν τῇ Καινῇ, ὅπου καὶ ἐν τῇ Παλαιᾷ τὸ αὐτὸ τοῦτο γίνεται. ("Why do you marvel that it happened in the New [Testament], since the same thing happened even in the Old?")

293. On models of imitation, see 4.6.

294. *Goth. concin.*; PG 63.502, 26–30: Ὁ γὰρ πρῶτος καὶ τῆς Ἐκκλησίας καὶ τῆς Συναγωγῆς πρόγονος γενόμενος, ἐκείνων μὲν κατὰ σάρκα, ἡμῶν δὲ κατὰ πνεῦμα, βάρβαρος ἦν καὶ ἐκ μέσης Περσίδος ἤγετο, ὁ πατριάρχης λέγω Ἀβραάμ, ("For the first ancestor of both the Church and the Synagogue—of them according to the flesh, but of us according to the spirit—was led by a barbarian and was led from the middle of Persia, namely, the patriarch Abraham").

295. *Goth. concin.*; PG 63.502, 30–34: καὶ οὔτε γραμμάτων ἀκούσας, οὔτε προφητείας μετασχών, οὐ τὸν διδάσκοντα ἔχων, οὐχ ἱστορίαν δεξάμενος· οὔπω γὰρ ἦν Μωϋσῆς γενόμενος· οὐ τῶν πρὸ αὐτοῦ τι μαθών, οὐ τὰ μετ' αὐτὸν ἐσόμενα διδαχθείς, ("And he [Abraham] had never heard of letters [literature], nor was he a sharer of prophecy, nor did he have anyone to teach him, nor had he heard of history. For Moses had not yet come, nor had he learnt anything from his forebears, nor had he been taught what was about to happen after him").

the middle of Persia, so suddenly came he [Abraham] to philosophy, that even many of the commandments of the New Testament he pre-empted and carried out in his works."[296] The main "work" that Abraham carried out was obeying God's command "to leave his homeland, and to abandon his home and his friends and relatives, and to come to a foreign land."[297] Abraham's actions of faith, "leaving [the] certainty and clarity" (φανερὰ καὶ δῆλα ἀφείς) of his homeland in Mesopotamia for "uncertainty and obscurity" (ἀφανῆ καὶ ἄδηλα) in Canaan made Abraham "the forefather of the church" (Ἐκκλησίας πρόγονος) in respect of faith.[298] In other words, through faith Abraham lived out many of the New Testament commands (e.g., Matt 10:8; Rom 8:24; 2 Cor 4:17–18) centuries before they were even penned, and effectively functioned as a proclamation of the gospel to barbarians. Furthermore, his actions as a barbarian set an example for all Christians to follow.[299]

Chrysostom's second Old Testament example of a barbarian who through their actions proclaimed the gospel was Moses. While Moses was an Israelite, like Abraham before him:

> Moses also was raised and grew up in a barbarian's home; but in a similar way he received no blame for this, but he too was brought to philosophy, no less than the patriarch, scorning the table of the Sybarites, being carried higher than their luxury, spurning riches and the rule and sceptre of Egypt. But he willingly transferred himself to working in mud making bricks.[300]

In Chrysostom's mind, Moses' upbringing in the courts of Egypt, with its associated education, language, luxury and sensual pleasures ("the table

---

296. *Goth. concin.*; PG 63.502, 34–37.

297. *Goth. concin.*; PG 63.502, 37–39. Later in the sermon Chrysostom argues that Abraham's refusal to accept financial reward after rescuing his nephew Lot (Gen 14:22–23) is an illustration and fulfillment of Jesus' command in Matt 10:8, "Freely you have received; freely give." PG 63.503, 13.

298. *Goth. concin.*; PG 63.502, 41, 45.

299. *Goth. concin.*; PG 63.502, 46–49: Καὶ γὰρ καὶ ἡμεῖς κελευόμεθα τῶν μὲν βιωτικῶν ὑπερορᾶν πραγμάτων καὶ τῶν φαινομένων, πρὸς δὲ τὰ ἄδηλα τὴν ἐλπίδα τείνειν, καὶ τὴν πίστιν κρατεῖν, τὴν ἄγκυραν τῆς ἡμετέρας σωτηρίας, καὶ ἐκεῖνα ζητεῖν ("For we also are ordered to scorn temporal and external things and to look towards the mysteries of hope, and to keep faith, the anchor of our salvation, and to seek those things").

300. *Goth. concin.*; PG 63.503, 13–20: Καὶ Μωϋσῆς δὲ καὶ ἐν βαρβαρικῇ οἰκίᾳ ἐτράφη τε καὶ ηὐξήθη· ἀλλ᾽ ὅμως οὐδὲν ἐντεῦθεν παρεβλάπτετο, ἀλλὰ καὶ αὐτὸς ἐφιλοσόφει τοῦ πατριάρχου οὐκ ἔλαττον, τῆς μὲν Συβαριτικῆς καταγελῶν τραπέζης, καὶ ὑψηλότερος τῆς ἐκείνων τρυφῆς γινόμενος, καὶ πλοῦτον ἀτιμάζων καὶ βασιλείαν καὶ τὰ σκῆπτρα Αἰγύπτου, πρὸς δὲ τὸν πηλὸν καὶ τὴν πλινθουργίαν αὐτομολῶν.

of the Sybarites ... their delights ... [the] riches and the rule and sceptre of Egypt") qualified Moses to be considered a "barbarian." As a "barbarian," Moses' actions of identifying with his countrymen the Israelites were a demonstration of faith and an identification with the grace of Christ as reflected in Heb 11:26.[301]

Chrysostom reiterated the place and value of barbarians in God's plan for the salvation of the world through a New Testament example, that of the wise men from Persia who came to pay homage to Jesus after he was born (Matt 2:1–12). For Chrysostom it was of great significance that it was barbarians rather than Greek-speakers who sought out and worshipped Jesus Christ following his birth, demonstrated by a threefold repetition:

> [E]ven our Lord Jesus Christ himself, when he came to earth, called barbarians first. For after he was born and placed in the manger, wise men came from Persia, and they paid homage to him. O new and unexpected event![302]

> Therefore, having entered [the world, i.e., having been born], he [Jesus] called the barbarians, nor simply barbarians but magicians, the worst kind of impiety.[303]

> [A]nd when he [Jesus] had come [i.e., been born], he first called the barbarians.[304]

Returning to his earlier theme of shame, Chrysostom stated that a reversal of sorts had occurred between the Jews and barbarians. The result of the magi's acceptance of Jesus in the face of the Jewish rejection of him resulted in the Jews being shamed and the barbarians honored:

> Besides, this even put the Jews to shame: while they hesitated to approach, these [barbarians] had undertaken a long journey

---

301. *Goth. concin.*; PG 63.503, 21–26.

302. *Goth. concin.*; PG 63.503, 27–32: καὶ γὰρ καὶ αὐτὸς ὁ Κύριος ἡμῶν Ἰησοῦς ὁ Χριστὸς παραγενόμενος εἰς τὴν οἰκουμένην, βαρβάρους πρώτους ἐκάλεσεν. Ἐπειδὴ γὰρ ἐτέχθη καὶ ἐπὶ τῆς φάτνης ἐτέθη, καὶ μάγοι ἐλθόντες ἀπὸ Περσίδος αὐτὸν προσεκύνουν· ὦ καινῶν καὶ παραδόξων πραγμάτων!

303. *Goth. concin.*; PG 63.504, 12–13: Εἰσελθὼν τοίνυν, βαρβάρους ἐκάλεσε, καὶ βαρβάρους οὐχ ἁπλῶς βαρβάρους, ἀλλὰ καὶ μάγους, τὸ ἐπιτεταμένον τῆς ἀσεβείας εἶδος.

304. *Goth. concin.*; PG 63.506, 55–56: καὶ παραγενόμενος, πρῶτον βαρβάρους καλεῖ.

to see him and worship him: and standing around him they say, "Where is he who was born the king of the Jews?" (Matt 2:2).[305]

The context of the wise men's question to Herod, "Where is he who is born king of the Jews?" was one of Jewish rejection of the messiah (Matt 2:2-6). Chrysostom identified the wise men's question as nothing less than a barbarian declaration of the Christian gospel which showed the barbarians to be wiser than their Jewish counterparts.[306] Not only had those taught now become the teachers but through their gospel proclamation, they entered the realm of Christian philosophers and were examples for Christians to follow.[307]

A previously identified contextual principle of Chrysostom, principle 10, is again seen in this homily: Scripture is both the starting point and controlling rubric of contextualization—informing, affirming, challenging, and rejecting aspects of culture rather than relativized by culture. As previously noted, in the context of the anti-barbarianism sentiment in Chrysostom's society, his promotion of Gothic Christianity was startling. While Chrysostom used various rhetorical devices in his argument, it is important to note the key arsenal that Chrysostom used in his defense—Christian Scripture. In *Homilia Habita* he both quoted directly from Scripture as well as drew on various biblical examples (Abraham, Moses, magi) in order to challenge the prevailing societal anti-barbarian attitude. In the *De statuis* and *Adversus Judaeos* 1 homilies examined in this chapter, we have seen that Chrysostom used Scripture to inform, affirm, and challenge various aspects and attitudes of his hearers. While the relative place of Scripture has been a point of contention throughout the gospel and culture debate, for Chrysostom the point was settled: Scripture was authoritative over culture. And while some aspects of Chrysostom's exegesis or the legitimacy of his application of Scripture in these homilies has sometimes been questioned, they do not

---

305. *Goth. concin.*; PG 63.507, 1-6: Ἄλλως δὲ καὶ εἰς αἰσχύνην Ἰουδαίων τοῦτο γίνεται, ὅτι ἐκεῖνοι μὲν ἐστασίαζον [ἐδίσταζον] προσελθεῖν, οὗτοι δὲ καὶ μακρὰν ἀποδημίαν ἐστείλαντο, ὥστε αὐτὸν ἰδεῖν καὶ προσκυνῆσαι, καὶ περιιόντες λέγουσι· Ποῦ ἐστιν ὁ τεχθεὶς βασιλεὺς τῶν Ἰουδαίων.

306. *Goth. concin.*; PG 63.507, 7-14.

307. *Goth. concin.*; PG 63.507, 24-29: Ἐπειδὴ γὰρ ἐδέξαντο τὸ κήρυγμα, καὶ φιλόσοφοι καὶ μάρτυρες ζῶντες ἀθρόον γίνονται, κατατολμῶντες θανάτου, καταφρονοῦντες κινδύνων, ὑπερορῶντες τῆς παρούσης ζωῆς, ἐν παρρησίᾳ ἀνακηρύττοντες ὅπερ ἔμαθον, ἐν μέσῳ δήμῳ καὶ μέσῃ πόλει τὸν τεχθέντα ἀναγορεύοντες ("Because they had undertaken to preach, they at once became philosophers and living martyrs, not fearing death, despising danger, scorning the present life, preaching what they had learnt with confidence, in the middle of the city, telling his birth among the people").

negate his underlying principle of Scripture taking precedence over culture (principle 10).

5.3.3.3 A CONTEXTUALIZED EXPLANATION OF THE GOSPEL

Chrysostom's discussion of the visit of the wise men subsequent to the incarnational birth of Jesus served an additional purpose to that of helping him establish the importance of Christian barbarians and their legitimate place in the church. It also afforded Chrysostom the opportunity to explore the nature of the incarnation and contextually explain the gospel to his Gothic audience by linking the barbarian wise men to God's salvific plan for the world. There are four elements in Chrysostom's gospel explanation: Jesus is King and ruler of the world; the sinful state of the Jewish people and all humanity; humanity's subsequent predicament—being under God's judgment and unable to save themselves; and God's solution to humanity's predicament through sending his Son Jesus to earth through the incarnation. These four elements are further explained below, and they highlight two contextual principles previously identified: that is, while there is a basic content and shape to the gospel (principle 5), there is also flexibility in how that message is presented (principle 4). The communicator has freedom to emphasize different aspects of the gospel to the audience, depending on the context.[308]

Chrysostom's description of Jesus as "the king of heaven" (τοῦ βασιλέως τῶν οὐρανῶν)[309] and "creator of all things" (δημιουργὸν τοῦ παντός)[310] establishes Jesus as the Creator, King and ruler of the world. While Jesus chose to enter the world in poverty and a lowly state, rather than demonstrating his divinity through earthquakes, bolts of lightning, splendor and festivity, his humble arrival did not abrogate his supreme position over all the universe.[311]

Jesus' kingly authority had been both challenged and rejected through the disobedience of Adam "who was deceived by the hope [of becoming like God, Gen 3:5], and reached out his hand to the tree, trampled on the law and broke the [i.e., God's] commandment."[312] From that moment on, until the time of the incarnation, Jesus' kingly rule over the Jewish race and the

---

308. See 3.9.
309. *Goth. concin.*; PG 63.503, 38.
310. *Goth. concin.*; PG 63.504, 41–42.
311. *Goth. concin.*; PG 63.503, 38–46.
312. *Goth. concin.*; PG 63.505, 13–15: τῇ ἐλπίδι ταύτῃ ἀπατηθείς, ἥψατο τοῦ δένδρου, καὶ τὸν νόμον ἐπάτησε, καὶ τὴν ἐντολὴν παρέβη.

rest of humanity was rejected. God's chosen people, the Jews, had largely rejected and even killed the prophets that God had sent, ignored God's temporal punishment of the nation, sacrificed their children to foreign gods and through their behavior caused God's name to be blasphemed among the Gentile nations.[313] The rest of humanity also rejected Jesus' kingly rule. Humanity's sinful behavior was progressively worsening, with evil "growing more daring and more confident, but the things that pertain to virtue being driven away".[314] Humanity's spiritual state was like that of a sick and despairing person lying prostrate on their bed, unable to help themselves.[315]

At that point, God intervened to provide a solution to humanity's rebellious state and pitiful plight. That solution came in the form of the incarnation:

> Look at what he does from the beginning [of his incarnation]; he is invested with our nature, which was weak and defeated, in order through [our nature] itself to fight and retrieve it in the contest. And immediately, from the very gates and preludes [of incarnate life] he plucks up the nature of foolishness by its roots, for it has become the cause of every evil.[316]

---

313. *Goth. concin.*; PG 63.504, 16–26.

314. *Goth. concin.*; PG 63.504, 33–34: καὶ ἐν παρρησίᾳ τὰ τῆς πονηρίας, καὶ τὰ τῆς ἀρετῆς ἐκποδών.

315. *Goth. concin.*; PG 63.504, 52–56: Ἐλθὼν τοίνυν καὶ ἰδὼν τὸν κάμνοντα ἐπὶ κλίνης κείμενον καὶ ἀπεγνωσμένον (κάμνοντα δὲ ὅταν εἴπω, τὸ γένος φημὶ τὸ ἀνθρώπινον, οὐκ ἐπὶ κλίνης τοιαύτης, ἀλλ' ἐπὶ κλίνης τῆς πονηρίας) "Therefore, since he had come and seen the sick and despairing lying on his bed (when I say 'the sick', I am speaking about the human race, not lying on a normal bed, but on a bed of wickedness").

316. *Goth. concin.*; PG 63.504, 41–43; 505, 3–9: ὅρα ἐκ προοιμίων τί ποιεῖ· τὴν φύσιν περιβάλλεται τὴν ἡμετέραν, τὴν ἠσθενηκυῖαν, τὴν ἡττηθεῖσαν, ὥστε μαχέσασθαι καὶ ἀναπαλαῖσαι δι' αὐτῆς· καὶ ἐκ τῶν προπυλαίων εὐθέως αὐτῶν καὶ τῶν προοιμίων πρόρριζον ἀνασπᾷ τῆς ἀπονοίας τὴν φύσιν· καὶ γὰρ πάντων αἴτιον τῶν κακῶν τοῦτο γέγονε. The faculty of human reason was corrupted through the act of independence of Adam and Eve (Gen 3:6). Through the incarnation, as well as through the Cross and the work of the Holy Spirit, the foolishness, arrogance, and pride of humanity that wishes to act independently of God is "plucked up by the roots." Jesus is the fully dependent, obedient man who always submitted his will to that of his heavenly Father. Through the incarnation Jesus tossed out independence and foolishness and began reshaping human nature to its original created intention by reshaping the mindset (γνώμη). For a discussion on the relationship between γνώμη and reason in Chrysostom see: Laird, *Mindset, Moral Choice*, 247–51.

Through the incarnation Christ defeated the tyranny of original sin, dealing a death-blow to what was at its very center—pride.[317] And having come into the world, God first called barbarians (wise men) rather than the Jewish hierarchy.[318] That it was barbarians rather than Jews who first sought out the Christ was shame for the Jews but glory for barbarians.[319]

5.4 Contextual principles that can be drawn from Homilia Habita

Four contextual principles previously outlined in Acts, *De statuis* and *Adversus Judaeos* have also been found in *Homilia Habita*:

> Principle 1: The early establishment of common ground provides a platform for the gospel to be heard;
>
> Principle 2: For contextualization to be effective, the gospel needs to be explained in ways that engage the worldview of the target audience;
>
> Principle 4: There is no fixed presentation of the gospel, as contextual sensitivity requires flexibility;
>
> Principle 5: There is a core content to the gospel, which is for all cultures.

Three further contextual principles can also be established from *Homilia Habita*:

PRINCIPLE 13: Contextualization of the gospel leads to transformation in the hearer's self-perception of their identity. In the context of the anti-barbarianism of Chrysostom's day, Chrysostom's contextual message would likely have resulted in a transformation of his audience's self-perception of their identity. Where previously the Goths were cultural outsiders and viewed somewhat negatively by the society at large, Chrysostom elevated their status to that of leaders of the church. While it is the gospel which ultimately gives people a new identity in Christ, it is only as that gospel is explained and applied in a way that makes sense to the hearers in their

---

317. *Goth. concin.*; PG 63.505, 20-24. As Laird helpfully notes, in Chrysostom's theology of original sin, the impact of the fall was not on human nature (which remained unaffected) but on the soul which required complete renovation. Laird, *Mindset, Moral Choice*, 252.

318. *Goth. concin.*; PG 63.506, 56.

319. *Goth. concin.*; PG 63.507, 1-6.

context that, through the agency of the Spirit, transformation occurs in the audience's self-perception of their identity.

PRINCIPLE 14: Access to the word of God in one's native language facilitates the contextual communication of the gospel. Chrysostom's commitment to mission to the Constantinopolitan Goths went beyond simply facilitating their ongoing "Nicene Christianisation." Rather, it extended to valuing and promoting the Gothic language (as well as other barbarian ones) who had had the Bible "translated into their own languages."[320] The fact that the Bible and the liturgy could be communicated in the Gothic language, as had occurred earlier in the church service that day, was a cause for rejoicing ("the ornament and beauty of the church") and "proof of the power which is located in faith."[321] Chrysostom operated on the principle that having access to the word of God in one's native language facilitated the contextual communication of the gospel. Just as divine accommodation occurred through the incarnation and the record of the divine words of Christian Scripture (as originally recorded in Hebrew, Aramaic, and Greek), by extension Chrysostom argued that the divine word was most effectively communicated in the native language of the recipient. Chrysostom cited Pentecost as an illustration of the principle, where the disciples' Spirit-filled ability to proclaim the gospel in the native-non-Greek languages of their hearers, led to around three thousand people being saved that day.[322]

The evangelical commitment to the authority of Scripture has fueled a commitment to Bible translation (e.g., Wycliffe Bible Translators, Bible Society). Translation is itself a contextual process, and has challenged for the translators as they seek to stay faithful to the text while conveying the correct meaning of the text across the cultural and linguistic barriers of the recipient group.[323] Such challenges, however, need to be faced and overcome so that more people can receive the gospel through being able to access the word of God in their native language and in ways that contextually make sense to them.

PRINCIPLE 15: Contextualization of the gospel can only take place in the context of mission. Chrysostom's gospel explanation which was woven

320. *Goth. concin.*; PG 63.501, 8.
321. *Goth. concin.*; PG 63.501, 54–55.
322. *Goth. concin.*; PG 63.501, 34–41.
323. For example, Miller-Naudé and Naudé, "Ideology and Translation Strategy in Muslim-sensitive Bible Translations," 171–90; LeFebvre and Abdulfadi, "A Further Look at Translating 'Son of God,'" 61–74.

through his message highlights an underlying contextual principle: contextualization of the gospel can only take place in the context of mission—affirming the principle of Bruce Nicholls.[324] In this unique cross-cultural sermon, Chrysostom's contextual ability is especially prominent as he masterfully engages the Gothic mindset. Speaking more broadly, Chrysostom viewed all of life as involving mission and took every opportunity he could to explain and apply the gospel to his audiences—whether he was speaking to one of his regular congregations who shared the same cultural heritage as himself, or whether speaking in a cross-cultural context as in *Homilia habita*. It is only as the gospel is proclaimed and incarnationally lived that contextualization can occur.

Conclusion to Homilia habita postquam presbyter Gothus homily

As has previously been argued in chapter four, and demonstrated in the *De Statuis* sermons considered in chapter five, the burden of Chrysostom's preaching to his Antiochene and Constantinopolitan congregations lay not so much in the annunciation of the gospel kerygma as in how the gospel translates into sanctified living. Chrysostom's *Homilia habita* sermon to a Gothic audience therefore is in stark contrast to his regular homiletic approach in at least three ways. First, in *Homilia habita* there is almost no paranesis of an ethical or moral nature, nor rebuke or challenge of the congregation's behavior. Second, the sermon is built on two related themes which make it unique: that the Gothic church service is a legitimate church service and authentic expression of Christianity; and that there is no shame in the church having barbarian Christians in their midst, because barbarians have been proclaimers of the gospel and forerunners of the church since the time of Abraham. The third contrast is that *Homilia habita* contains a significant proportion of content devoted to declaring the gospel. Chrysostom's gospel explanation to his Gothic audience is firmly built on the sinfulness of humanity and the incarnation of the divine Son Jesus, and is consistent with what Chrysostom preached on other occasions. As has been highlighted in chapter four, Chrysostom's theology is that, through the incarnation, the divine Son, Jesus Christ, humbly came to earth in human form in order to rescue humanity from their alienation from God that their sins had wrought.[325] The alienation, according to Chrysostom, was a result of the reality that all of humanity had sinned, had come under God's rightful judgment, and is in need of redemption by and reconciliation to

---

324. See end of 2.2.

325. *In Phil. hom.* 7; PG 62.231, 14–232, 15 (NPNF 01.13, 214–5).

God.³²⁶ Furthermore, Chrysostom's gospel explanation in *Homilia habita* emphasizes the incarnation as God's solution to the sinful state of humanity and as the way of salvation.³²⁷

The explanation for the differences between *Homilia habita* and Chrysostom's other homilies lies in the context. Chrysostom's *Homilia habita* offers a highly contextualized theological response to issues that would have concerned his Gothic audience. The Roman attitude of superiority towards barbarians and barbarian culture in a general sense, as well as Gothic Christianity in a specific sense, would almost certainly have been contentious for those Goths gathered to listen to Chrysostom preach that day. Through both his method and message Chrysostom sought to distance himself from those Greeks who thought themselves superior. Chrysostom sought to identify with his Gothic audience rather than with the Greek-speakers of his day, both in his homiletical style and content. Chrysostom's sermon is almost single-mindedly devoted to affirming the place of barbarians in general (and his Gothic audience in particular) in God's plan of salvation, their value and status as Christians, and the legitimacy of their Gothic services, and to defending his Gothic mission. He does this through exclusively focusing on the 'barbarian' biblical figures (Abraham, Moses, and the wise men) and highlighting them as gospel proclaimers, forerunners of the New Testament church, and examples for all Christians to follow. Chrysostom also contextualized his gospel presentation by emphasizing the incarnation of Jesus rather than his death and resurrection as God's solution to the sinful state of humanity. Chrysostom did this in order to emphasize the ministry of the wise men who came to worship Jesus and who became the first gospel proclaimers of the newborn king (after the angels, Luke 2:13–14).

Chrysostom's approach is both theological and pastoral. Through reminding the Gothic congregation of notable barbarians in the Bible, Chrysostom both affirmed the congregation members in the face of negative societal attitudes towards Goths and pointed them to the one whom not just the wise men but all people must serve and worship.

---

326. *In Rom. hom.* 7; PG 60.442, 60–63; 443, 1–15 (NPNF 01.11, 377); *In Eph. hom.* 4; PG 62.32, 24–37 (NPNF 01.13, 65–66).

327. Cf. *In 1 Cor. hom.* 38; PG 61.324, 10–20 (NPNF 01.12, 227–8); *In 1 Cor. hom.* 38; PG 61.324, 52–326, 13 (NPNF 01.12, 228–9); *In Rom. hom.* 2; PG 60.408, 35–37 (NPNF 01.11, 348).

Conclusion to chapter

This chapter has examined the Chrysostom homilies *De statuis* II, III, VI, XVII, *Adversus Judaeos* 1, and *Homilia habita postquam presbyter Gothus*. Each of the speeches examined has been shown to be a highly contextualized proclamation of the gospel to its audience—both in method and message. While Chrysostom's homiletical method shared some similarities with that of Peter, Stephen, and Paul (such as use of Greco-Roman rhetoric, establishment of common ground, and interaction with their audiences' worldview), the contextual message in each of Chrysostom's homilies was distinct, due to the different contexts, audiences, and settings.

Following the examination and analysis of Chrysostom's homilies, eleven contextual principles have been identified and compared with those previously highlighted in chapters two and three.

Four contextual principles have previously been identified in the sermons in Acts:

i. Principle 1: The early establishment of common ground provides a platform for the gospel to be heard;

ii. Principle 2: For contextualization to be effective, the gospel needs to be explained in ways that engage the worldview of the target audience;

iii. Principle 4: There is no fixed presentation of the gospel as contextual sensitivity requires flexibility;

iv. Principle 5: There is a core content to the gospel, which is for all cultures.

Five additional contextual principles confirmed, critiqued, or nuanced various contextual principles identified in the literature:

i. Principle 9: Contextualization is best achieved in the context of relationship;

ii. Principle 10: Scripture is both the starting point and controlling rubric of contextualization;

iii. Principle 11: Every facet of life and witness needs to be contextualized, not just selected facets;

iv. Principle 12: Practicing the rites and activities of both Christianity and another religion is syncretistic, a denial of the freedom which the death of Christ wrought, and a denial of the gospel itself. Therefore, syncretism is to be avoided by the Christian;

v. Principle 15: Contextualization of the gospel can only take place in the context of mission.

Two further principles were identified, which are original to this research:

i. Principle 13: Contextualization of the gospel leads to transformation in the hearers' self-perception of their identity;

ii. Principle 14: Access to the word of God in one's native language facilitates the contextual communication of the gospel.

This chapter therefore has established contextual principles that are based on a deeper analysis of Christian thought than has been the case in the contextualization debate. In doing so, it has begun to address the deficiency of Christian thought's contribution to the contextualization debate identified in chapter two. Even where the analysis has affirmed previously established principles (whether from the literature or from the thesis research) it has provided a stronger basis for these principles based on the historical tenets of missiology. Furthermore, it has shown not only that the church fathers have the potential to contribute to the contextualization debate, but demonstrated something of what that contribution could look like.

Chapter 6

Conclusion

THE HYPOTHESIS OF THIS research has been that a missiological methodology that is governed by Scripture, while also drawing from the church fathers, the social sciences, and practical theology is not only consistent with the nature of evangelicalism but also consistent with the nature of missiology itself. This has been driven by the critical observation that the contextualization debate has been predominantly informed by insights gained from the social sciences (particularly anthropology), and practical theology, with comparatively few contributions from Scripture or the writings of the church fathers. The purpose of this research therefore has been to test the hypothesis that adding the contribution of Scripture and the church fathers to that of the social sciences and practical theology is both meaningful and consistent with an evangelical approach to missiology, and that it offers new ways of thinking about mission, with implications for future evangelical missiological praxis. This hypothesis, formulated in the context of the discussion about contextualization since its introduction as a neologism in 1972, was tested through an examination of contextualization from missiological, biblical, and historical perspectives, and through identifying and developing contextual principles consistent with the nature of evangelicalism.

The missiological examination of the hypothesis involved an investigation of the literature on contextualization since 1972. Many contextual principles—both stated and implied—were identified, and served as a source of comparison for the biblical and historical sections of the thesis.

The biblical examination of the hypothesis involved an investigation of contextualization in the book of Acts. Four representative passages were selected as recorded examples of the early church engaged in contextualization to both Jewish and Gentile audiences (Acts 2:14–31; 7:1–53; 13:13–47; 17:16–34). The focus was on answering three important questions. First, how did the early church contextualize the gospel to their respective audiences? Second, what contextual principles did the early church use? Third, how do those principles affirm, critique, or add to the contextual principles outlined in the review of the literature on contextualization?

With each of the four speeches, the consistent methodology was designed to evaluate the context, audience, setting, contextual approach, and contextual method. The analysis of the speeches by Peter, Stephen, and Paul in a Jewish context not only revealed each speech to be a highly contextualized address to the respective audiences but also revealed the speakers' largely consistent methodological approach. As each of the three speeches was an occasional address to a Jewish audience, each speaker sought to: quickly establish rapport through their respectful address of their audience; identify common ground; use standard Greco-Roman rhetorical devices; and interact with their audience's worldview—including arguing from the authoritative source for their audiences, the Jewish Scriptures. The consistency of the speakers' method was matched by the consistency in the gospel message they proclaimed. Seven main themes were identified to delineate the contours of their gospel *kerygma*: the centrality of Jesus Christ; the humanity and divinity of Jesus; the unjust crucifixion of Jesus; Jesus' bodily resurrection from the dead; Jesus as the fulfillment and hermeneutical key for interpreting Jewish Scripture; the necessity of repentance; and the opportunity for the forgiveness of sins through faith in Jesus Christ. The analysis of Paul's sermon to a Gentile audience in Athens likewise revealed a highly contextualized address to his audience. Paul's contextual approach to the Athenians was not unlike the contextual approach that Peter, Stephen, and Paul himself used to Jewish audiences, but his contextual message to the Athenians was a more radical departure from that adopted in the speeches in a Jewish context.

From these speeches to Jews and Gentile in Acts, eight contextual principles were outlined which demonstrated how the early church as recorded in Acts went about the task of contextualizing the gospel. These principles were:

Principle 1: The early establishment of common ground provides a platform for the gospel to be heard;

Principle 2: For contextualization to be effective, the gospel needs to be explained in ways that engage the worldview of the target audience;

Principle 3: Faith in Jesus Christ does not necessarily mean social dislocation;

Principle 4: There is no fixed presentation of the gospel as contextual sensitivity requires flexibility;

Principle 5: There is a core content to the gospel, which is for all cultures;

Principle 6: Cultural pressure must not lead to a dampening down of the challenging demands of discipleship;

Principle 7: Existing cultural terms can be used and imbued with new meaning in light of the gospel;

Principle 8: Culture is both positive and flawed and needs redemption through the gospel.

The establishment of these principles is significant because they were developed through a more extensive and rigorous examination of Scripture than has been the case for much of the literature on contextualization.

Each of these principles was compared with those previously outlined in the literature review. In each case the principles were shown to contribute to the contextualization debate:

a. Some of the principles developed from Acts were shown to affirm ones that had been highlighted in the literature review (principles 1, 2, 3, 4, 5, 6, 7, 8).

b. Some of the principles developed from Acts were shown to critique ones that had been highlighted in the literature review ((principles 6, 7).

While these eight principles were illustrative rather than exhaustive they still provided a meaningful contribution to the task of developing an evangelical approach to contextualization.

The historical examination of the hypothesis involved an investigation of contextualization in six homilies of John Chrysostom. The hypothesis underlying an examination of the works of John Chrysostom in relation to contextualization has been that the works of the church fathers can legitimately be used to inform contemporary issues of Christian witness and practice. There is no doubt that the works of the Fathers have significantly contributed to theological discussion and the formation of Christian doctrine over the centuries. It has been an open question, however, as to what degree the works of the Fathers can legitimately contribute to contemporary missiological debates such as contextualization. Consideration was therefore given to this issue.

The issue was approached through first evaluating the works of scholars both negative and positive towards the possibility of the church fathers contributing to contemporary issues of Christian witness and practice. What was revealed was that, while there are many challenges, pitfalls, and caveats identified in the literature in regards to appropriating the works of the Fathers, evangelical scholars not only believe but have already demonstrated that patristic writers could inform twenty-first-century questions of Christian witness and practice. As the focus of this study is contextualization, what was required therefore was the establishment of a set of criteria by which any patristic writer could be evaluated in order to measure the legitimacy of their work potentially being used to inform the contextualization debate. Based on the literature, four criteria were developed:

i. The father must have a theology of Scripture consistent with that of evangelicalism;

ii. The father's understanding of the gospel must be clearly established and must not differ significantly from an evangelical understanding;

iii. The father's cultural milieu and worldview must correspond in some way to mission contexts in the twenty-first century;

iv. The father must demonstrate a significant interest in mission.

John Chrysostom was measured against these four criteria as a potentially valid test case of a church father whose works can inform the contextualization debate, and was determined to fulfill each of these criteria.

Analysis of selected homilies of John Chrysostom followed. Six representative homilies were selected from three different contexts: Homilies II, III, VI and XVII from the *De Statuis* series; *Adversus Judaeos* 1; *Homilia habita postquam presbyter Gothus*. The threefold focus used in the evaluation of the speeches in Acts was adopted for the Chrysostom homilies. A fourth focus was added, being: how do Chrysostom's principles compare with those already outlined in the book of Acts? Again, as for the speeches in Acts, the same methodology evaluating the context, audience, setting, contextual approach, and contextual method was followed for each of the three contexts in which these homilies were delivered.

The analysis of the Chrysostom homilies not only revealed each speech as a highly contextualized address to a particular audience, but also revealed a consistent methodological approach, similar to that adopted by Peter, Stephen, and Paul in Acts. Chrysostom's contextual methodology involved establishing and maintaining rapport with his audience; identifying common ground; using standard Greco-Roman rhetorical devices; and interacting with his audience's worldview (including arguing from Scripture—an authoritative source for many if not most of the audiences he addressed). Both the four *De statuis* homilies and *Adversus Judaeos* 1 were preached in Antioch, within approximately one year of each other, yet their very different contexts meant that there were no consistent themes to tie them together. In light of the sudden crisis that had befallen the Antiochenes, the four *De statuis* homilies evidenced the central themes of God's sovereignty and desire to bring good to the city; the respect and obedience God desired the Antiochenes to display towards their rulers; and the necessity for the congregation to live out their present circumstances in light of their eternal future. In contrast, the looming Jewish feast days which occasioned the delivery of *Adversus Judaeos* 1 determined the two very different themes of Christianity and Judaism being distinct religions and unable to be practiced together, and the inherent responsibility of Chrysostom's congregation to address Judaizing behavior in erring fellow congregants. In comparison, the Gothic context of *Homilia habita* led Chrysostom to focus on the legitimacy of the Gothic mission, and to celebrate Gothic Christianity.

From the Chrysostom homilies, eleven contextual principles were outlined which explained how Chrysostom went about the task of contextualizing the gospel:

Principle 1: The early establishment of common ground provides a platform for the gospel to be heard;

Principle 2: For contextualization to be effective, the gospel needs to be explained in ways that engage the worldview of the target audience;

Principle 4: There is no fixed presentation of the gospel as contextual sensitivity requires flexibility;

Principle 5: There is a core content to the gospel, which is for all cultures;

Principle 9: Contextualization is best acheived in the context of relationship;

Principle 10: Scripture is both the starting point and controlling rubric of contextualization;

Principle 11: Every facet of life and witness needs to be contextualized, not just selected facets;

Principle 12: Practicing the rites and activities of both Christianity and another religion is syncretistic, a denial of the freedom which the death of Christ wrought, and a denial of the gospel itself;

Principle 13: Contextualization leads to transformation in the hearers' self-perception of their identity;

Principle 14: Access to the word of God in one's native language facilitates the contextual communication of the gospel;

Principle 15: Contextualization of the gospel can only take place in the context of mission.

The establishment of these principles is significant because they were developed through an extensive and rigorous examination of one of the church fathers, lacking in the literature on contextualization.

As these contextual principles of Chrysostom were highlighted, each of them was compared with those outlined in the literature review and the speeches in Acts. In each case the principles were shown to contribute to the contextualization debate:

a. Some of the principles were the same as those already noted in Acts (principles 1, 2, 3, 4);

b. Some were shown to affirm principles that had been highlighted in the literature review (principles 5, 6, 7, 9);

c. Some were shown to critique those principles that had been highlighted in the literature review (principle 8);

d. Some of the principles, however, were also found to be unique to Chrysostom (principles 13, 14).

Again, as for the principles noted from Acts, these further principles derived from Chrysostom were illustrative rather than exhaustive, yet still provide a meaningful contribution to an evangelical approach to contextualization.

Therefore, based on the examination of contextualization from missiological, biblical, and historical perspectives conducted in this thesis, it has been established that a missiological methodology that is governed by Scripture, while also drawing from the church fathers, the social sciences and practical theology, is not only consistent with the nature of evangelicalism but also consistent with the nature of missiology itself.

This research is significant in that it has extended and strengthened missiological method in the area of contextualization. Furthermore, it has also demonstrated that the quartet of 1. biblical studies 2. Christian thought

3. The social sciences 4. practical theology should be included in the development of missiological thought and practice not only in the area of contextualization but for any missiological issue. While this research has revealed the marginalization of biblical studies and Christian thought in the area of contextualization, it is quite possible that this has also been the case for other missiological issues. Any issues would benefit from reevaluation in light of the quartet of disciplines above.

There is a significant amount of further research that could be done. First, from a biblical studies perspective, there is much of the Bible that is still yet to be evaluated in any depth for what it might contribute to the contextualization debate. Dean Flemming has pointed the way in *Contextualisation in the New Testament,* but even his book leaves much of the New Testament untouched, let alone the books contained in the Old Testaments. The evangelical tenet of the authority of Scripture, along with biblical studies as a central contributor to the discipline of missiology, should drive further biblical research on contextualization. Second, with almost no published work on contextualization from the perspective of Christian thought, there is significant scope for further research. For a start, only six of Chrysostom's more than one thousand extant homilies were examined in depth here, so there is a substantial amount of material that could be examined for additional contextual principles there alone. Furthermore, the works of other church fathers who fulfill the four criteria established in chapter four could also be examined. Bede and Gregory the Great, for example, are two that offer great potential. Third, while this thesis has examined contextualization from an evangelical perspective, there is scope for contextualization to be examined from the perspective of other theological traditions.

Bibliography

Ahonen, Tina. *Transformation Through Compassionate Mission: David J. Bosch's Theology of Contextualization.* Helsinki: Luther Agricola Society, 2003.

Allen, Pauline. "Challenges in Approaching Patristic Texts from the Perspective of Contemporary Catholic Social Teaching." In *Reading Patristic Texts on Social Ethics: Issues and Challenges for Twenty-First-Century Christian Social Thought,* edited by Johan Leemans et al., 30–42. Washington: Catholic University of America Press, 2011.

———. "John Chrysostom's Homilies on I and II Thessalonians: The Preacher and His Audience." *Studia Patristica* 31 (1997) 3–21.

Allen, Pauline, et al. *Preaching Poverty in Late Antiquity: Perceptions and Realities.* Leipzig: Evangelische Verlagsanstalt, 2009.

Allen, Pauline, and Wendy Mayer. "Computer and Homily: Accessing the Everyday Life of Early Christians." *Vigiliae Christianae* 47 (1993) 260–80.

Anderson, John. "Missionary Approach to Islam: Christian or Cultic?" *Missiology* 4, no. 3 (July 1976) 285–300.

Anderson, Justice. "The Great Century and Beyond." In *Missiology: An Introduction to the Foundations, History, and Strategies of World Missions,* edited by John Mark Terry et al., 199–218. Nashville: Broadman and Holman, 1998.

Anderson, P. J. "The Lessons of 27 Years Gleaning Among Muslims." *EMQ* 20, no. 4 (October 1984) 362–6.

Ariarajah, S. Wesley. *Gospel and Culture: An Ongoing Discussion Within the Ecumenical Movement.* Geneva: WCC, 1994.

Aristotle. *The Art of Rhetoric.* Translated by Hugh C. Lawson-Tancred. Strand: Penguin, 1991.

Arndt, William, F. et al. *A Greek-English Lexicon of the New Testament and Other Early Christian Literature.* 3rd ed. Chicago: University of Chicago Press, 2000.

Arredondo, Arnold. "An Analysis of Missionary Contextualization in the Muslim Evangelism of Phil Parshall." PhD diss., New Orleans Baptist Theological Seminary, 2009.

Athyal, Saphir Phillip. "The Uniqueness and Universality of Christ." In *The New Face of Evangelicalism: An International Symposium on the Lausanne Covenant*, edited by C. Renè Padilla, 49–66. Downers Grove: IVP, 1976.

Ayres, Lewis. *Nicaea and its Legacy: An Approach to Fourth-Century Trinitarian Theology*. Oxford: Oxford University Press, 2004.

Bang, Martin. "Expansion of the Teutons (to A.D. 378)." In *The Cambridge Medieval History Vol.* 1, edited by H. M. Gwatkin and J. P. Whitney, 183–217. Cambridge: Cambridge University Press, 1967.

Barnes, Michel R., and Daniel H. Williams, eds. *Arianism After Arius: Essays on the Development of the Fourth Century Trinitarian Conflicts*. Edinburgh: T & T Clark, 1993.

Barnett, Paul. *1 Corinthians: Holiness and Hope of a Rescued People*. Fearn: Christian Focus, 2000.

Bauer, W. F., et al. *A Greek-English Lexicon of the New Testament and Other Early Christian Literature*. 3rd ed. Chicago: University of Chicago Press, 2000.

Baur, Chrysostomos. *John Chrysostom and his Time*. 2 vols. Translated by M. Gonzaga. London: ET, 1959.

Bavinck, J. H. *An Introduction to the Science of Mission*. Translated by D. H. Freeman. Philadelphia: Presbyterian and Reformed, 1960.

Baynes, Norman H. "The Dynasty of Valentinian and Theodosius the Great." In *The Cambridge Medieval History Vol.* 1, edited by H. M. Gwatkin and J. P. Whitney, 218–49. Cambridge: Cambridge University Press, 1967.

Bebbington, David. *Evangelicalism in Modern Britain: A History from the 1730s to the 1980s*. Grand Rapids: Baker, 1989.

Bediako, Kwame. *Christianity in Africa: The Renewal of Non-Western Religion*. Maryknoll: Orbis, 1995.

———. "Five Theses on the Significance of Modern African Christianity: A Manifesto." *Edinburgh Review of Theology and Religion* 1, no. 1 (1995) 51–67.

———. *Jesus and the Gospel in Africa: History and Experience*. Maryknoll: Orbis, 2004.

Beilby, James, and Paul Eddy, eds. *Divine Foreknowledge: Four Views*. Downers Grove: IVP, 2001.

Betz, Hans Diether. *Galatians: A Commentary on Paul's Letter to the Churches in Galatia*. Hermeneia: Fortress, 1979.

Bevans, Stephen B. *An Introduction to Theology in Global Perspective*. Maryknoll: Orbis, 2009.

———. *Models of Contextual Theology*. Rev. ed. Maryknoll: Orbis, 2009.

———. "Models of Contextual Theology." *Missiology* 13, no. 2 (April 1985) 185–202.

Bevans, Stephen B., and Katalina Tahaafe-Williams, eds. *Contextual Theology for the Twenty-First Century*. Eugene: Wipf and Stock, 2011.

Bevans, Stephen B., and Roger P. Schroeder. *Constants in Context: Theology of Mission for Today*. Maryknoll: Orbis, 2009.

Beyerhaus, Peter, and Henry Lefever. *The Responsible Church and Foreign Missions*. Grand Rapids: Eerdmans, 1964.

Bibliowicz, A. M. *Jews and Gentiles in the Early Jesus Movement*. New York: Palgrave Macmillan, 2013.

Bird, Michael F. *A Birdseye View of Paul*. Nottingham: IVP, 2008.

Black II, C. Clifton. "The Rhetorical Form of the Hellenistic Jewish and Early Christian Sermon: A Response to Lawrence Wills." *HTR* 81, no. 1 (1988) 1–18.

Blowers, Paul M. "Interpreting Scripture." In *The Cambridge History of Christianity Volume 2: Constantine to c.600*, edited by Augustine Casiday and Frederick W. Norris, 618–36. Cambridge: Cambridge University Press, 2007.
Bock, Darrell L. *Acts.* ECNT. Grand Rapids: Baker, 2007.
———. *Luke* 1:1—9:50. ECNT. Grand Rapids: Baker, 1994.
———. *Recovering the Real Lost Gospel: Reclaiming the Gospel as Good News.* Nashville: B & H Publishing, 2010.
Boff, Leonardo and Clodovis Boff. *Introducing Liberation Theology.* Translated by Paul Burns. Tunbridge Wells: Burns and Oates, 1987.
Boin, Douglas. "Hellenistic 'Judaism' and the Social Origins of the 'Pagan-Christian' Debate." *Journal of Early Christian Studies* 22, no. 2 (2014) 167–96.
Bosch, David J. "Evangelism: Theological Currents and Cross-currents Today." *IBMR* 11, no. 3 (July 1987) 98–103.
———. *Transforming Mission.* Maryknoll: Orbis, 1991.
Bowes, Kim. *Private Worship, Public Values, and Religious Change in Late Antiquity.* Cambridge: Cambridge University Press, 2008.
Bowker, J. W. "Speeches in Acts: A Study in Proem and Yelammedenu Forms." *NTS* 14 (1967) 96–111.
Bradshaw, M. "The Gospel, Contextualization and Syncretism Report." In *Let the Earth Hear His Voice*, edited by J. D. Douglas, 1224–37. Minneapolis: World Wide Publications, 1975.
Brändle, Rudolf. *John Chrysostom: Bishop, Reformer, Martyr.* ECS 8. Translated by John Cawte and Silke Trzcionka. Strathfield: St Pauls, 2004.
Bromiley, Geoffrey W. "The Church Fathers and Holy Scripture." In *Scripture and Truth*, edited by D. A. Carson and John D. Woodbridge, 199–220. Leicester: IVP, 1983.
Brottier, Laurence. "Jean Chrysostome. Un pasteur face à des *demi-chrétiens*." In *Antioche de Syrie. Histoire, images et traces de la ville antique*, edited by B. Cabouret, P.-L. Gatier et C. Saliou, 439–57. Colloque organisé par B. Cabouret, P.-L. Gatier et C. Saliou, Lyon, Maison de l'Orient et de la Méditerranée, 4–6 octobre 2001. Topoi supplément 5. Lyon: De Boccard, 2004.
Brown, Dan. "Is Church Planting in the Muslim World 'Mission Impossible?'" *EMQ* 33, no. 2 (April 1997) 156–65.
Brown, Rick. "Biblical Muslims." *IJFM* 24, no. 2 (2007) 65–74.
———. "Brother Jacob and Master Esau: How One Insider Movement Began." *IJFM* 24, no. 1 (2007) 41–42.
———. "Contextualization without Syncretism." *IJFM* 23, no. 3 (2006) 127–33.
Bruce, F. F. *The Book of Acts.* Rev. ed. NICNT. Grand Rapids: Eerdmans, 1988.
Buswell III, James O. "Contextualization: Is it Only a New Word for Indigenization?" *EMQ* 14, no. 1 (January 1978) 13–20.
———. "Contextualization: Theory, Tradition and Method." In *Theology and Mission: Papers Given at Trinity Consultation No. 1*, edited by David J. Hesselgrave, 87–111. Grand Rapids: Baker, 1978.
———. "Reply." In *Theology and Mission: Papers Given at Trinity Consultation No. 1*, edited by David J. Hesselgrave, 124–27. Grand Rapids: Baker, 1978.
Cameron, Alan et al. *Barbarians and the Politics of the Court.* California: University of California Press, 1993.
Cameron, Averil. *The Later Roman Empire.* Cambridge, Massachusetts: Harvard University Press, 1993.

Carey, Christopher. "Rhetorical Means of Persuasion." In *Persuasion: Greek Rhetoric in Action*, edited by Ian Worthington, 26–45. London: Abingdon, 1994.

Carson, D. A. *Christ and Culture Revisited*. Grand Rapids: Eerdmans, 2008.

———. "Church and Mission: Reflections on Contextualization and the Third Horizon." In *The Church in the Bible and the World*, edited by D. A. Carson, 213–57. Grand Rapids: Baker, 1987.

———. *Divine Sovereignty and Human Responsibility: Biblical Perspectives in Tension*. Eugene: Wipf and Stock, 1994.

———. *How Long, O Lord? Reflections on Suffering and Evil*. Grand Rapids: Baker, 1990.

———. *Scandalous: The Cross and Resurrection of Jesus*. Wheaton: Crossway, 2010.

Carter, Craig R. *Rethinking Christ and Culture: A Post-Christendom Perspective*. Grand Rapids: Brazos Press, 2006.

Cate, Pat. "What will it take to reach Muslims?" *EMQ* 28, no. 3 (July 1992) 230–4.

Champion, Craige B. *Cultural Politics in Polybius's Histories*. Berkeley: University of California Press, 2004.

Chan, D. "How to Evaluate Cultural Practices by Biblical Standards in Maintaining Cultural Identity in Asia Report." In *Let the Earth Hear His Voice*, edited by J. D. Douglas, 1249–50. Minneapolis: World Wide, 1975.

Chance, J. Bradley. *Acts*. Macon: Smith & Helwys, 2007.

Chitulescu, Polycarp. "Activitatea misionara a Sf. Ioan Gura de Aur." *Glasul Bisericii* 65/9–12 (2006) 97–105.

Chrysostom, John. PG 48.624 (*De sacer.*); PG 48.701–48 (*De Incomp.*); PG 48.747–56 (*De beato Philogonio*); PG 48.813–38 (*Adv. Iudaeos et Gentiles demonstratio quod Christus sit dues*); PG 48.843–942 (*Adv. Jud*); PG 49.15–222 (*De Statuis*); PG 49.352–62 (*In diem nat.*); PG 50.453–64 (*De s. Pent.*); PG 50.519–526 (*In s. Meletium*); PG 50.533–72 (*De s. Babyla c. Iulianum et Gentiles*); PG 50.579–84 (*De s. Pelagia*); PG 52.435–8 (*Sermo cum iret in exsilium*); PG 52.685–7 (*Epistulae 126*); PG 53.21–385; 54.385–580 (*In Gen.*); PG 56.263–70 (*C. Lud. et theat.*); PG 57.13–472; PG 58.471–794 (*In Matt.*); PG 59.23–482 (*In Joan*); PG 60.13–384 (*In Acta*); PG 60.391–682 (*In Rom.*); PG 61.9–382 (*In 1 Cor.*); PG 61.381–610 (*In 2 Cor.*); PG 61.611–82 (*In Gal.*); PG 62.9–176 (*In Eph.*); PG 62.177–298 (*In Phil.*); PG 62.299–392 (*In Col.*); PG 62.391–468 (*In 1 Thes.*); PG 62.467–500 (*In 2 Thes.*); PG 62.501–600 (*In 1 Tim.*); PG 62.599–662 (*In 2 Tim.*); PG 62.663–700 (*In Titum*); PG 62.701–20 (*In Philm.*); PG 63.9–236 (*In Heb.*); PG 63.467–72 (*dicta post.*); PG 63.499–510 (*Homilia habita*).

Ciampa, Roy E. "Paul's Theology of the Gospel." In *Paul as Missionary: Identity, Activity, Theology, and Practice*, edited by Trevor J. Burke and Brian S. Rosner, 180–91. London: T & T Clark, 2011.

Coe, Shoki. "Contextualizing Theology." In *Mision Trends No. 3: Third World Theologies*, edited by Gerald H. Anderson and Thomas F. Stransky, 19–24. New York: Paulist, 1976.

Coleman, Doug. *A Theological Analysis of the Insider Movement From Four Perspectives: Theology of Religions, Revelation, Soteriology, and Ecclesiology*. Pasadena: William Carey, 2011.

Coleman, M. and P. Verster. "Contextualisation of the Gospel Among Muslims." *Acta Theologica* 26, no. 2 (2006) 94–115.

Conn, Harvey M. "Contextualization: A New Dimension for Cross-Cultural Hermeneutic." *EMQ* 14, no. 1 (January 1978) 39–46.

———. "Contextualization: Where Do We Begin?" In *Evangelicals and Liberation*, edited by Carl E. Armerding, 90–119. Grand Rapids: Baker, 1977.

———. "Culture." In *Evangelical Dictionary of World Missions*, edited by A. Scott Moreau, 252–5. Grand Rapids: Baker, 2000.

———. *Eternal Word and Changing Worlds: Theology, Anthropology, and Mission in Trialogue*. Grand Rapids: Zondervan, 1984.

———. "The Muslim Convert and His Culture." In *The Gospel and Islam: A 1978 Compendium*. Abridged ed., edited by Don Murray, 61–77. Monrovia: MARC, 1979.

Cook, Matthew et al. *Local Theology for the Global Church: Principles for an Evangelical Approach to Contextualization*. Pasadena: William Carey, 2010.

Cortez, Marc. "Context and Concept: Contextual Theology and the Nature of Theological Discourse." *WTJ* 67, no 1 (2005) 85–102.

———. "Creation and Context: A Theological Framework for Contextual Theology." *WTJ* 67, no. 2 (2005) 347–62.

Corwin, Gary. "A Humble Appeal to C5/Insider Movement Muslim Ministry Advocates to Consider Ten Questions (with responses from Brother Yusef, Rick Brown, Kevin Higgins, Rebecca Lewis and John Travis)." *IJFM* 24, no. 1 (2007) 5–20.

———. "Insider Movements and Outsider Theology." *EMQ* 42, no. 1 (January, 2006) 10–1.

———. "Reaching the Resistant." *EMQ* 34, no. 2 (April 1998) 144–45.

———. "A Response to My Respondents." *IJFM* 24, no. 1 (2007) 53–56.

Costanzo, Eric. *Harbor for the Poor: A Missiological Analysis of Almsgiving in the View and Practice of John Chrysostom*. Eugene: Pickwick, 2013.

Costas, Orlando E. *Liberating News: A Theology of Contextual Evangelization*. Eugene: Wipf and Stock, 2002.

Craig, William Lane. *The Only Wise God: The Compatibility of Divine Foreknowledge and Human Freedom*. Eugene: Wipf and Stock, 1999.

Craigie, Peter C. *Psalms 1–50*. WBC 19. Waco: Word, 1983.

Cunningham, Mary B. "Preaching and Community." In *Church and People in Byzantine*, edited by Rosemary Morris, 29–46. Birmingham: University of Birmingham, 1986.

Cunningham, Mary B. and Pauline Allen. "Introduction." In *Preacher and Audience: Studies in Early Christian and Byzantine Homiletics*, A New History of the Sermon 1, edited by Mary B. Cunningham and Pauline Allen, 1–20. Leiden: Brill, 1998.

Cunningham, Scott. *'Through Many Tribulations:' The Theology of Persecution in Luke-Acts*. JSNTSS 142. Sheffield: Sheffield Academic, 1997.

de Wet, Chris L. "John Chrysostom and the Mission to the Goths: Rhetorical and Ethical Perspectives." *Hervormde Teologiese Studies* 68, no. 1 (2012) 1–10.

Dibelius, Martin. *Studies in the Acts of the Apostles*. Edited by H. Greeven. New York: Scribner, 1956.

Dodd, C. H. *The Apostolic Preaching and its Developments*. Grand Rapids: Baker, 1936.

Downey, Glanville. *A History of Antioch in Syria from Seleucus to the Arab Conquest*. Princeton: Princeton University Press, 1961.

Dowsett, Rose, ed. *Global Mission: Reflections and Case Studies in Contextualization for the Whole Church*. Pasadena: William Carey, 2011.

Dowsett, Rose. "Rainbow Faith." In *Global Mission: Reflections and Case Studies in Contextualization for the Whole Church*, edited by Rose Dowsett, 3–10. Pasadena: William Carey, 2011.

Dretke, James P. *A Christian Approach to Muslims: Reflections from West Africa.* Pasadena: William Carey, 1980.

Dupont, J. "La structure oratoire du discours d'Etienne (Actes 7)." *Biblica* 66 (1985) 153–67.

Dumbrell, William J. "The Content of the Gospel and the Implications of that Content for the Christian Community." *RTR* 40, no. 2 (May–August 1981) 33–43.

Dunn, Geoffrey D. "The Roman Response to the Ecclesiastical Crisis in the Antiochene Church in the Late-Fourth and Early-Fifth Centuries." In *Ancient Jewish and Christian Texts as Crisis Management Literature*, edited by David C. Sim and Pauline Allen, 112–128. London: T & T Clarke, 2012.

Dyrness, William A. *Emerging Voices in Global Christian Theology.* Grand Rapids: Zondervan, 1994.

Eckman, James P. *The Truth about Worldviews: A Biblical Understanding of Worldview Alternatives.* Wheaton: Crossway, 2004.

Ecumenical Theological Education. "Contextualization in Theological Education." *Ministerial Formation* 110 (April 2008) 15–17.

———. "The Establishment of the Theological Education Fund (TEF) during the IMC Assembly in Ghana, 1957/1958." *Ministerial Formation* 110 (April 2008) 12–14.

Edwards, James R. *The Gospel According to Mark.* Grand Rapids: Eerdmans, 2002.

Edwards Jr., Otis Carl. *A History of Preaching.* Nashville: Abingdon, 2004.

Eenigenburg, Don. "The Pros and Cons of Islamicized Contextualization." *EMQ* 33, no. 3 (July 1997) 310–5.

Egbunu, Emmanuel. "To Teach, Baptise, and Nurture New Believers." In *Mission in the 21st Century: Exploring the Five Marks of Global Mission*, edited by Andrew Walls and Cathy Ross, 25–36. London: Dartman, Longman and Todd, 2008.

Elliston, Edgar J. *Introduction to Missiological Research Design.* Pasadena: William Carey, 2011.

Ericson, Norman R. "Implications from the New Testament for Contextualization." In *Theology and Mission: Papers Given at Trinity Consultation No. 1*, edited by David J. Hesselgrave, 71–85. Grand Rapids: Baker, 1978.

Escobar, Samuel. "Mission Studies: Past, Present, and Future." *Missiology* 24, no. 1 (January 1996) 3–29.

———. *The New Global Mission: The Gospel from Everywhere to Everyone.* Downers Grove: IVP, 2003.

Esler, Phillip S. *Community and Gospel in Luke–Acts: The Social and Political Motivations of Lucan Theology.* SNTSMS 57. Cambridge: Cambridge University Press, 1987.

Fee, Gordon D. *The First Epistle to the Corinthians.* Grand Rapids: Eerdmans, 1987.

Fee, Gordon D. and Douglas Stuart. *How to Read the Bible for all its Worth.* 3rd ed. Grand Rapids: Zondervan, 2003.

Feinberg, Paul D. "An Evangelical Approach to Contextualization of Theology." *Trinity World Forum* 7, no. 3 (Spring 1982) 7.

Feldman, Louis H. "Proselytism by Jews in the Third, Fourth, and Fifth Centuries." *Journal for the Study of Judaism* 24, no. 1 (1993) 1–58.

Fernando, Ajith. *Acts.* Grand Rapids: Zondervan, 1998.

Fernando, Keith. "Mission: A Problem of Definition." *Themelios* 33, no. 1 (2008) 46–59.

Ferreira, Johan. "The Great Commission: Towards a Biblical Theology of Theological Education." In *Cultivating Wisdom with the Heart: BCV Chinese Department 10th Anniversary Anthology of Essays*, edited by Justin Tan, 15–32. Melbourne: BCV Chinese Department, 2006.

Fitzmyer, Joseph A. *The Acts of the Apostles*. AB 31. New York: Doubleday, 1997.

———. *The Gospel According to Luke (I–IX)*. AB 28. Vol. 1. New York: Doubleday, 1981.

———. *Romans*. New York: Doubleday, 1992.

Fleming, Bruce C. *Contextualization of Theology: An Evangelical Assessment*. Pasadena: William Carey Library, 1980.

Flemming, Dean. *Contextualization in the New Testament: Patterns for Theology and Mission*. Leicester: Apollos, 2005.

———. "Paul the Contextualizer." In *Local Theology for the Global Church*, edited by Matthew Cook, Rob Haskell, Ruth Julian and Natee Tanchanpongs, 1–19. Pasadena: William Carey, 2010.

Flynn, Gabriel, and Paul D. Murray, eds. *Ressourcement: A Movement for Renewal in Twentieth-Century Catholic Theology*. Oxford: Oxford University Press, 2012.

Fonrobert, Charlotte Elisheva. "Jewish Christians, Judaizers, and Christian Anti-Judaism." In *Late Ancient Christianity: A People's History of Christianity*, Vol. 2, edited by Virginia Burrus, 234–54. Minneapolis: Fortress, 2005.

Fornara, Charles W. *The Nature of History in Ancient Greece and Rome*. Eidos: University of California Press, 1983.

Friedrich, Gerhard. "εὐαγγέλιον." In *Theological Dictionary of the New Testament*, Vol. 2. Translated by Geoffrey W. Bromiley, edited by Gerhard Kittel, 721–36. Grand Rapids: Eerdmans, 1964.

Friell, Gerard and Stephen Williams. "Friends, Romans or Countrymen? Barbarians in the Empire." *History Today* 44, no. 7 (1994) 34–40.

Friesen, Duane K. "A Discriminating Engagement of Culture: An Anabaptist Perspective." *Journal of the Society of Christian Ethics* 21 (2003) 145–56.

Gallagher, Michael P. "Inculturation: Some Theological Perspectives." *International Review of Mission* 85 (1996) 171–80.

Gallagher, Robert L. and Paul Hertig. "Introduction: Background to Acts." In *Mission in Acts: Ancient Narratives in Contemporary Context*, edited by Robert L. Gallagher and Paul Hertig, 1–17. Maryknoll: Orbis, 2004.

Gaventa, Beverley Roberts. *Acts*. ANTC. Nashville: Abingdon, 2003.

Geary, Patrick J. "Barbarians and Ethnicity." In *Late Antiquity: A Guide to the Postclassical World*, edited by G. W. Bowersock, Peter Brown, and Oleg Grabar, 107–129. Harvard: Harvard University Press, 1999.

Geerard, M, ed. *Clavis Patrum Graecorum*. II. *Ab Athanasio ad Chrysostomum* (Corpus Christianorum). Turnhout: Brepols, 1974.

Geertz, Clifford. *The Interpretation of Cultures*. New York: Basic, 1973.

Geisler, Norman. *Chosen But Free: A Balanced View of God's Sovereignty and Free Will*. 3rd. ed. Bloomington: Bethany House, 2010.

Gempf, Conrad. "Public Speaking and Published Accounts." In *The Book of Acts in its First Century Setting Vol. I: Ancient Literary Setting*, edited by Bruce W. Winter and Andrew D. Clarke, 259–303. Grand Rapids: Eerdmans, 1993.

Gerstner, John H. "The Theological Boundaries of Evangelical Faith." In *The Evangelicals: What they Believe, Who they are, Why they are Changing*, edited by David F. Wells and John D. Woodbridge, 21–37. Nashville: Abingdon, 1975.

Gibson, Richard. "Paul and the Evangelization of the Stoics." In *The Gospel to the Nations: Perspectives on Paul's Mission*, edited by Peter Bolt and Mark Thompson, 309–26. Leicester: Apollos, 2000.

Gilbert, Greg. *What is the Gospel?* Wheaton: Crossway, 2010.

Gill, David W. J. "Achaia." In *The Book of Acts in its First Century Setting Vol. II: Graeco-Roman Setting*, edited by David W. J. Gill & Conrad Gempf, 433–53. Grand Rapids: Eerdmans, 1994.

Gillett, Andrew. "The Mirror of Jordanes: Concepts of the Barbarian, Then and Now." In *A Companion to Late Antiquity*, edited by Philip Rousseau, 392–408. Chichester: Blackwell Publishing, 2009.

Gilliland, Dean S. "Context is Critical in 'Islampur' Case." *EMQ* 34, no. 4 (October 1998) 415–6.

———. "Contextual Theology as Incarnational Mission." In *The Word Among Us: Contextualizing Theology for Mission Today*, edited by Dean S. Gilliland, 9–31. Eugene: Wipf and Stock, 1989.

———. "The Incarnation as Matrix for Appropriate Theologies." In *Appropriate Christianity*, edited by Charles H. Kraft, 493–519. Pasadena: William Carey Library, 2005.

———. "Introduction." In *The Word Among Us: Contextualizing Theology for Mission Today*, edited by Dean S. Gilliland, 1–5. Eugene: Wipf and Stock, 1989.

———. "New Testament Contextualization: Continuity and Particularity in Paul's Theology." In *The Word Among Us: Contextualizing Theology for Mission Today*, edited by Dean S. Gilliland, 52–73. Eugene: Wipf and Stock, 1989.

———. ed. *The Word Among Us: Contextualizing Theology for Mission Today*. Eugene: Wipf and Stock, 1989.

Glasser, Arthur F. "The Gospel." In *Evangelical Dictionary of World Missions*, edited by A. Scott Moreau, 403–4. Grand Rapids: Baker, 2000.

———. "Old Testament Contextualization: Revelation and Its Environment." In *The Word Among Us: Contextualizing Theology for Mission Today*, edited by Dean. S. Gilliland, 32–51. Eugene: Wipf and Stock, 1989.

Goheen, Michael W. and Craig G. Bartholomew. *Living at the Crossroads: An Introduction to Christian Worldview*. Grand Rapids: Baker, 2008.

Goldsworthy, Graeme. *Christ-Centred Biblical Theology: Hermeneutical Foundations and Principles*. Downers Grove: IVP, 2012.

Goosen, Gideon. "Syncretism and the Development of Doctrine." *Colloquium* 32, no. 2 (2000) 137–50.

Gorday, Peter. *Principles of Patristic Exegesis: Romans 9–11 in Origen, John Chrysostom, and Augustine*. SBEC 4. New York: Edwin Mellen, 1983.

Goss, Edward N. *Is Charles Kraft an Evangelical? A Critique of "Christianity in Culture."* Collingswood: Christian Beacon, 1985.

Green, Joel B. "Learning Theological Interpretation from Luke." In *Reading Luke: Interpretation, Reflection, Formation*. Scripture and Hermeneutics Series Vol. 6, edited by Craig G. Bartholomew, Joel B. Green, and Anthony C. Thistleton, 55–78. Milton Keynes: Paternoster, 2005.

———. *The Gospel of Luke*. NICNT. Grand Rapids: Eerdmans, 1997.

Greenman, Jeffrey P. and Gene L. Green, eds. *Global Theology in Evangelical Perspective: Exploring the Contextual Nature of Theology and Mission.* Downers Grove: IVP, 2012.
Greenspahn, Frederick E. "Syncretism and Idolatry in the Bible." *Vetus Testamentum* LIV 4 (2004) 480–94.
Griffiths, Michael. "The Power of the Holy Spirit." In *The New Face of Evangelicalism: An International Symposium on the Lausanne Covenant*, edited by C. Renè Padilla, 239–53. Downers Grove: IVP, 1976.
Grunlan, Stephen A. and Marvin K. Mayers. *Cultural Anthropology.* 2nd ed. Grand Rapids: Baker, 1988.
Guignebert, C. "Les demi-chrétiens et leur place dans l'Eglise antique." *Revue de l'histoire des religions* 88 (1923) 65–102.
Gutiérrez, Gustavo. *A Theology of Liberation: History, Politics and Salvation.* Translated and edited by Sr. Caridad Inda and John Eagleson. Maryknoll: Orbis, 1971.
Gwatkin, Henry M. G. "Arianism." In *The Cambridge Medieval History Vol. 1*, edited by H. M. G. Gwatkin and J. P. Whitney, 118–42. Cambridge: Cambridge University Press, 1967.
Gwynn, David M. "Episcopal Leadership." In *The Oxford Handbook of Late Antiquity*, edited by Scott Fitzgerald Johnson, 876–915. New York: Oxford University Press, 2012.
Haleblian, Krikor. "The Problem of Contextualization." *Missiology* 11, no. 1 (1983) 95–111.
Hall, Edith. *Inventing the Barbarian: Greek Self Definition Through Tragedy.* Oxford: Oxford University Press, 1989.
Halsall, Guy. *Barbarian Migrations and the Roman West 376–568.* Cambridge: Cambridge University Press, 2007.
Hansen, G. Walter. "The Preaching and Defence of Paul." In *Witness to the Gospel: The Theology of Acts*, edited by I. Howard Marshall and David Peterson, 295–324. Grand Rapids: Eerdmans, 1998.
Hanson, R. P. C. *The Search for the Christian Doctrine of God.* Edinburgh: T & T Clark, 1988.
Harkins, Paul F. "Introduction." In *John Chrysostom: Discourses Against Judaizing Christians.* FOTC series, translated by Paul W. Harkins. Washington: Catholic University Press, 1977.
Harkins, Paul W, trans. *Saint John Chrysostom: Discourses Against Judaizing Christians.* FOTC 68. Washington DC: Catholic University of America Press, 1979.
———. *St John Chrysostom: On the Incomprehensible Nature of God*, FOTC 72. Washington DC: Catholic University of America Press, 1982.
Harrison, Carol, Brouria Bittin Ashkelony, and Théodore De Bruyn, eds. *Patristic Studies in the Twenty-First Century: Proceedings of an International Conference to Mark the 50th Anniversary of the International Association of Patristic Studies.* Turnhout: Brepols, 2015.
Heather, Peter and John Matthews. *The Goths in the Fourth Century.* Liverpool: Liverpool University Press, 1991.
Heintz, Florence. "Magic Tablets and the Games at Antioch." In *Antioch: The Lost Ancient City*, edited by Christine Kondoleon, 163–67. Princeton: Princeton University, 2000.

Heldenbrand, Richard. "Mission to Muslims: Cutting the Nerve." *EMQ* 18, no. 3 (July 1982) 135–9.

Hemer, Colin J. *The Book of Acts in the Setting of Hellenistic History*. Winona Lake: Eisenbrauns, 1990.

Hengel, Martin. *Acts and the History of Earliest Christianity*. London: SCM, 1979.

Henkel, Willi. "German Centres of Christian Research." *IBMR* 21, no. 3 (1997) 103–10.

Hess, Robert. "Book Review: New Paths in Muslim Evangelism." *EMQ* 17, no. 3 (July 1981) 188–9.

Hesselgrave, David J. *Communicating Christ Cross-culturally: An Introduction to Missionary Communication*. 2nd ed. Grand Rapids: Zondervan, 1991.

———. "Contextualization and Revelational Epistemology." In *Hermeneutics, Inerrancy, and the Bible*, edited by Earl D. Radmacher and Robert D. Preus, 691–738. Grand Rapids: Zondervan, 1984.

Hesselgrave, David. J. and Edward Rommen. *Contextualization: Meanings, Methods, and Models*. Pasadena: William Carey Library, 1989.

Hesselgrave, David J., and Ed Stetzer, eds. *Missionshift: Global Mission Issues in the Third Millennium*. Nashville: B & H, 2010.

Hick, John. *Evil and the God of Love*. 2nd ed. New York: Harper and Row, 1978.

Hiebert, Paul. G. *Anthropological Insights for Missionaries*. Grand Rapids: Baker, 1995.

———. "Critical Contextualization." *IBMR* 11, no. 3 (July 1987) 104–11.

———. "The Flaw of the Excluded Middle." *Missiology* 10, no. 1 (January 1982) 35–47.

———. "Form and Meaning in the Contextualization of the Gospel." In *The Word Among Us: Contextualizing Theology for Mission Today*, edited by Dean. S. Gilliland, 101–120. Eugene: Wipf and Stock, 1989.

———. "The Gospel and Culture." In *The Gospel and Islam: A Compendium*. Abridged ed., edited by Don M. McCurry, 22–34. Monrovia: MARC, 1979.

———. *The Gospel in Human Contexts: Anthropological Explorations for Contemporary Missions*. Grand Rapids: Baker, 2009.

———. "Syncretism and Social Paradigms." In *Contextualization and Syncretism: Navigating Cultural Currents*, edited by Gail Van Rheenen, 31–46. Evangelical Missiological Society Series 13. Pasadena: William Carey, 2006.

Higgins, Kevin. "Acts 15 and Insider Movements among Muslims: Questions, Process and Conclusions." *IJFM* 24, no. 1 (2007) 29–40.

———. "Beyond Christianity: Insider Movements and the Place of the Bible and the Body of Christ in New Movements to Jesus." *Mission Frontiers* 32, no. 4 (2010) 12–13.

———. "Identity, Integrity and Insider Movements: A Brief Paper Inspired by Timothy C. Tennant's Critique of C-5 Thinking." *IJFM* 23, no. 3 (2006) 117–23.

———. "Inside What? Church, Culture, Religion and Insider Movements in Biblical Perspective." *St Francis Magazine* 5, no. 4 (2009) 74–91.

———. "The Key to Insider Movements: The 'Devoted's' of Acts." *IJFM* 21, no. 4 (2004) 155–65.

———. "Speaking the Truth about Insider Movements: Addressing the Criticisms of Bill Nikides and 'Phil' relative to the article 'Inside What?'" *St Francis Magazine* 5, no. 6 (2009) 61–86.

Hill, Robert C. *The Homilies on Genesis of St. John Chrysostom*. FOTC 74. Washington: Catholic University of America Press, 1986.

———. *Reading the Old Testament in Antioch*. Bible in Ancient Christianity 5. Leiden: Brill, 2005.
Hoedemaker, Bert. "Contextual Analysis and Unity of Perspective: An Exercise in Missiological Method." In *Popular Religion, Liberation and Contextual Theology: Papers from a Congress* (January 3–7, 1990, Nijmegen, the Netherlands), edited by Jacques Van Nieuwenhove and Berma Klein Goldewijk, 200–9. Kampen: J. H. Kok, 1991.
Hopkins, Keith. "Early Christian Number and its Implications." *Journal of Early Christian Studies* 6 (1998) 185–226.
Horsley, G. H. R. "Speeches and Dialogues in Acts." *NTS* 32 (1986) 609–14.
Hughson, Thomas. "Social Justice in Lactantius's *Divine Institutes*: An Exploration." In *Reading Patristic Texts on Social Ethics: Issues and Challenges for Twenty-First-Century Christian Social Thought*, edited by Johan Leemans, Brian J. Matz, and Johan Verstraeten, 185–205. Washington: Catholic University of America Press, 2011.
Huilin, Yang. "The Contextualization of Chinese Christian Theology and Its Main Concerns." In *Christianity and Chinese Culture*, edited by Miikka Ruokanen and Paulos Huang, 197–204. Grand Rapids: Eerdmans, 2010.
Hunter, David G. "Preaching and Propaganda in Fourth Century Antioch: John Chrysostom's *Homilies on the Statues*." In *Preaching in the Patristic Age: Studies in Honour of Walter J. Burghardt, SJ*, edited by David G. Hunter, 119–138. Mahwah: Paulist, 1989.
Husbands, Mark. "Introduction." In *Ancient Faith for the Church's Future*, edited by Mark Husbands and Jeffrey P. Greenman, 9–23. Downers Grove: IVP, 2008.
Ihssen, Brenda Llewellyn. "'That Which has been Wrung from Tears.' Usury, the Greek Fathers, and Social Catholic Teaching." In *Reading Patristic Texts on Social Ethics: Issues and Challenges for Twenty-First-Century Christian Social Thought*, edited by Johan Leemans, Brian J. Matz, and Johan Verstraeten, 124–160. Washington: Catholic University of America Press, 2011.
Imamura, Yuzo. "A Cambodian Christmas Celebration." In *Global Mission: Reflections and Case Studies in Contextualization for the Whole Church*, edited by Rose Dowsett, 161–63. Pasadena: William Carey, 2011.
Ingleby, Jonathan. "The Hermeneutical Principle in Relation to Contextual Mission Training." In *Contextualisation and Mission Training: Engaging Asias's Religious Worlds*, edited by Jonathan Ingleby, Tan Kang San, and Tan Loun Ling, 17–25. Oxford: Regnum Books, 2013.
Isaac, Benjamin. *The Invention of Racism in Classical Antiquity*. Princeton: Princeton University Press, 2004.
Jenkins, Philip. *The New Faces of Christianity: Believing the Bible in the Global South*. Oxford: Oxford University Press, 2006.
———. *The Next Christendom: The Coming of Global Christianity*. 3rd ed. Oxford: Oxford University Press, 2011.
Jenks, Chris. *Culture*. 2nd ed. New York: Routledge, 2005.
Jipp, Joshua W. "Paul's Areopagus Speech of Acts 17:16–34 as *Both* Critique *and* Propaganda." *JBL* 131, no. 3 (2012) 567–88.
Kalantzis, George. "Crumbs from the Table: Lazarus, the Eucharist and the Banquet of the Poor in the Homilies of John Chrysostom." In *Ancient Faith for the Church's*

Future, edited by Mark Husbands and Jeffrey P. Greenman, 156-68. Downers Grove: IVP, 2008.

Kallon, John. *Contextualization of Christianity in Africa: A Case Study of the Kpelle Tribe in Liberia*. South Carolina: BookSurge, 2007.

Kannengiesser, Charles. *Handbook of Patristic Exegesis*. Vols. 1-2. Leiden: Brill, 2004.

Kato, Byang H. "The Gospel, Cultural Context and Religious Syncretism." In *Let the Earth Hear His Voice*, edited by J. D. Douglas, 1216-23. Minneapolis: World Wide Publications, 1975.

Katos, Demetrios. "Socratic Dialogue or Courtroom Debate? Judicial Rhetoric and Stasis Theory in the *Dialogue on the Life of St John Chrysostom*." *Vigiliae Christianae* 61 (2007) 42-69.

Keener, Craig S. *Acts: An Exegetical Commentary*. 3 vols. Grand Rapids: Baker, 2012-2014.

———. *The IVP Bible Background Commentary: New Testament*. Downer Grove: IVP, 1993.

Kelly, J. N. D. *Golden Mouth: The Story of John Chrysostom: Ascetic, Preacher, Bishop*. Grand Rapids: Baker, 1995.

Kennedy, George A. *Greek Rhetoric Under Christian Emperors: A History of Rhetoric*. Eugene: Wipf and Stock, 1983.

———. *A New History of Classical Rhetoric*. Princeton: Princeton University Press, 1994.

———. *New Testament Interpretation through Rhetorical Criticism*. Chapel Hill: University of North Carolina Press, 1984.

Kim, Hyun Jim. *Ethnicity and Foreigners in Ancient Greece and China*. London: Duckworth, 2009.

Kim, Sebastian C. H., ed. *Christian Theology in Asia*. Cambridge: Cambridge University Press, 2008.

Kinneavy, James L. *Greek Rhetorical Origins of the Christian Faith: An Inquiry*. New York: Oxford University Press, 1987.

Kinsler, F. Ross. "The Current Debate about Contextualization." *EMQ* 14, no. 1 (January 1978) 23-29.

Kinzig, Wolfram. "'Non-Separation': Closeness and Co-operation Between Jews and Christians in the Fourth Century." *Vigiliae Christianae* 45 (1991) 27-53.

Koltun-Fromm, Naomi. "Defining Sacred Boundaries: Jewish–Christian Relations." In *A Companion to Late Antiquity*, edited by Philip Rousseau, 556-71. Malden: Blackwell, 2009.

Kostenberger, Andreas J. and Peter T. O'Brien. *Salvation to the Ends of the Earth: A Biblical Theology of Mission*. Leicester: IVP, 2001.

Kraft, Charles., ed. *Appropriate Christianity*. Pasadena: William Carey, 2005.

———. *Christianity in Culture: A Study in Dynamic Biblical Theologizing in Cross-Cultural Perspective*. Maryknoll: Orbis, 1979.

———. "The Contextualization of Theology." *EMQ* 14, no. 1 (January 1978) 31-6.

———. "The Development of Contextualization Theory in Euroamerican Missiology." In *Appropriate Christianity*, edited by Charles Kraft, 15-34. Pasadena: William Carey Library, 2005.

———. "Dynamic Equivalence Churches in Muslim Society." In *The Gospel and Islam: A Compendium*. Abridged ed., edited by Don M. McCurry, 78-92. Monrovia: MARC, 1979.

———. "Dynamic Equivalence Churches: An Ethnotheological Approach to Indigeneity." *Missiology* 1, no. 1 (January 1973) 39–57.

———. "Meaning Equivalence Contextualization." In *Appropriate Christianity*, edited by Charles Kraft, 155–68. Pasadena: William Carey Library, 2005.

———. "My Distaste for the Combative Approach." *EMQ* 18, no. 3 (July 1982) 139–42.

Kraft, Charles H., and Thomas N. Wisley, eds. *Readings in Dynamic Indigeneity*. Pasadena, William Carey, 1979.

Kreider, Alan. "'They Alone Know the Right Way to Live': The Early Church and Evangelism." In *Ancient Faith for the Church's Future*, edited by Mark Husbands and Jeffrey P. Greenman, 169–86. Downers Grove: IVP, 2008.

Krupp, R. A. *Shepherding the Flock of God: The Pastoral Theology of John Chrysostom*. New York: Lang, 1991.

Kushner, Harold. *When Bad Things Happen to Good People*. New York: Random House, 2001.

Laird, Raymond A. "John Chrysostom and the Anomoeans: Shaping an Antiochene Perspective on Christology." In *Religious Conflict from Early Christianity to the Rise of Islam*, edited by Wendy Mayer and Bronwen Neil, 129–49. Arbeiten zur Kirchengeschichte 121. Berlin: De Gruyter, 2013.

———. *Mindset, Moral Choice and Sin in the Anthropology of John Chrysostom*. ECS 15. Strathfield: St Pauls, 2012.

Lane, William L. *The Gospel of Mark*. Grand Rapids: Eerdmans, 1974.

Larkin Jr., William. *Acts*. IVP. NTCS. Leicester: IVP, 1995.

Lausanne Committee for World Evangelization. "1977: The Pasadena Statement on the Homogenous Unit Principle." In *Making Christ Known: Historic Mission Documents from the Lausanne Movement 1974–1989*, edited by John Stott, 57–72. Carlisle: Paternoster, 1996.

———. "1978: The Willowbank Report on Gospel and Culture." In *Making Christ Known: Historic Mission Documents from the Lausanne Movement 1974–1989*, edited by John Stott, 73–113. Carlisle: Paternoster, 1996.

———. "1978: The Glen Eyrie Report on Muslim Evangelization." In *Making Christ Known: Historic Mission Documents from the Lausanne Movement 1974–1989*, edited by John Stott, 115–38. Carlisle: Paternoster, 1996.

———. *Let the Earth Hear His Voice*, edited by J. D. Douglas. Minneapolis: World Wide, 1975.

Lee, Won Sang. *Pastoral Leadership: A Case Study, including Reference to John Chrysostom*. Eugene: Wipf & Stock, 2015.

Lee, Jung Young. *The Trinity in Asian Perspective*. Nashville: Abingdon, 1999.

Leemans, Johan, Brian J. Matz, and Johan Verstraeten, eds. "Introduction." In *Reading Patristic Texts on Social Ethics: Issues and Challenges for Twenty-First-Century Christian Social Thought*, xi–xviii. Washington: Catholic University of America Press, 2011.

LeFebvre, Michael and Basheer Abdulfadi. "A Further Look at Translating 'Son of God.'" *IJFM* 29 no. 2 (April–June 2012) 61–74.

Lewis, Rebecca. "Insider Movements: Honouring God-Given Identity and Community." *IJFM* 26, no. 1 (2009) 33–36.

———. "Insider Movements: Retaining Identity and Preserving Community." *IJFM* 26, no. 1 (2009) 16–19.

———. "The Integrity of the Gospel and Insider Movements." *IJFM* 27, no. 1 (2010) 44–48.

———. "Promoting Movements to Christ within Natural Communities." *IJFM* 24, no. 2 (2007) 75–76.

Lidório, Ronaldo. "A Biblical Theology of Contextualization." In *Global Mission: Reflections and Case Studies in Contextualization for the Whole Church*, edited by Rose Dowsett, 11–23. Pasadena: William Carey, 2011.

Liebeschuetz, J. H .W. G. *Barbarians and Bishops: Army, Church, and State in the Age of Arcadius and Chrysostom*. Oxford: Clarendon Press, 1990.

Lim, Richard. *Public Disputation, Power and Social Order in Late Antiquity*. The Transformation of the Classical Heritage 23. Berkley: University of California Press, 1995.

Lingenfelter, Sherwood G. and Marvin K. Mayers. *Ministering Cross-Culturally*. Grand Rapids: Baker, 2003.

Luzbetak, Louis J. *The Church and Cultures: New Perspectives in Missiological Anthropology*. Maryknoll: Orbis, 1988.

McCurry, Don M. ed. *The Gospel and Islam: A Compendium*. Abridged ed. Monrovia: MARC Publications, 1979.

———. "A Time for New Beginnings." In *The Gospel and Islam: A Compendium*. Abridged ed., edited by Don M. McCurry, 13–21. Monrovia: MARC Publications, 1979.

McGavran, Donald A. *The Clash Between Christianity and Culture*. Washington: Canon, 1974.

McKnight, Scot. *The King Jesus Gospel: The Original Good News Revisited*. Grand Rapids: Zondervan, 2011.

MacMullen, Ramsay. *Christianity and Paganism in the Fourth to Eighth Centuries*. New Haven: Yale, 1998.

———. "The Preacher's Audience (AD 350–400)." *Journal of Theological Studies* 40, no. 2 (1989) 503–11.

Mack, Burton L. *Rhetoric and the New Testament*. Minneapolis: Fortress, 1990.

Maddox, Robert. *The Purpose of Luke–Acts*. Edinburgh: Clark, 1982.

Manhong Lin, "A Chinese Christian's Reading of Two Ethical Themes of Zhuangzi." In *Christianity and Chinese Culture*, edited by Miikka Ruokanen and Paulos Huang, 355–66. Grand Rapids: Eerdmans, 2010.

Manitius, Max. "The Teutonic Migrations, 378–412." In *The Cambridge Medieval History Vol*. 1, edited by H. M. Gwatkin and J. P. Whitney, 250–76. Cambridge: Cambridge University Press, 1967.

Marshall, I. Howard. "Acts." In *Commentary on the New Testament Use of the Old Testament*, edited by G. K. Beale and D. A. Carson, 513–606. Grand Rapids: Baker, 2007.

Massih, Bashir Abdol. "The Incarnational Witness to the Muslim Heart." In *The Gospel and Islam: A Compendium*. Abridged ed., edited by Don M. McCurry, 49–60. Monrovia: MARC, 1979.

Matheny, Paul Duane. *Contextual Theology: The Drama of Our Times*. Eugene: Wipf and Stock, 2011.

Matz, Brian J. *Patristics and Catholic Social Thought: Hermeneutical Models for a Dialogue*. Notre Dame: University of Notre Dame Press, 2014.

———. "Problematic Uses of Patristic Sources in the Documents of Catholic Social Thought." *Journal of Catholic Social Thought* 4 (2007) 459–85.
Maxwell, Jaclyn L. *Christianization and Communication in Late Antiquity: John Chrysostom and his Congregation in Antioch.* Cambridge: Cambridge University Press, 2006.
———. "Pedagogical Methods in John Chrysostom's Preaching." *Studia Patristica* 41 (2006) 445–50.
May, Stan. "Ugly Americans or Ambassadors of Christ?" *EMQ* 41, no. 3 (July 2005) 346–52.
Mayer, Wendy. "The Audience(s) for Patristic Social Teaching: A Case Study." In *Reading Patristic Texts on Social Ethics: Issues and Challenges for Twenty-First-Century Christian Social Thought*, edited by Johan Leemans, Brian J. Matz, and Johan Verstraeten, 85–99. Washington: Catholic University of America Press, 2011.
———. "Homiletics." In *Oxford Handbook of Early Christian Studies*, edited by S. Ashbrook Harvey and D. Hunter, 565–83. Oxford: Oxford University Press, 2008.
———. *The Homilies of St John Chrysostom—Provenance: Reshaping the Foundations.* OCA 273. Rome: Ponticifio Istituto Orientale, 2005.
———. "The Ins and Outs of the Chrysostom Letter Collection: New Ways of Looking at a Limited Corpus." In *Collecting early Christian Letters: From the Apostle Paul to Late Antiquity*, edited by B. Neil and P. Allen, 129–53. Cambridge: Cambridge University Press, 2015.
———. "John Chrysostom." In *The Wiley Blackwell Companion to Patristics*, edited by K. Parry, 141–54. Oxford: Blackwell, 2015.
———. "John Chrysostom: Extraordinary Preacher, Ordinary Audience." In *Preacher and Audience: Studies in Early Christian and Byzantine Homiletics*, A New History of the Sermon 1, edited by Mary B. Cunningham and Pauline Allen, 105–37. Leiden: Brill, 1998.
———. "John Chrysostom as Bishop: The View from Antioch." *Journal of Ecclesiastical History* 55, no. 3 (2004) 455–66.
———. "John Chrysostom as Crisis Manager: The Years in Constantinople." In *Ancient Jewish and Christian Texts as Crisis Management Literature*, edited by David C. Sim and Pauline Allen, 129–43. London: T & T Clarke, 2012.
———. "John Chrysostom and His Audiences: Distinguishing Different Congregations at Antioch and Constantinople." *Studia Patristica* 31 (1997) 70–75.
———. "Media Manipulation as a Tool in Religious Conflict." In *Religious Conflict from Early Christianity to the Rise of Islam*. Arbeiten zur Kirchengeschichte 121, edited by W. Mayer and B. Neil, 151–66. Berlin: De Gruyter, 2013.
———. "The Persistence in Late Antiquity of Medico-Philosophical Psychic Therapy." *Journal of Late Antiquity* 8, no. 2 (2015) 337–51.
———. "Welcoming the Stranger in the Mediterranean East: Syria and Constantinople." *Journal of the Australian Medieval Association* 5 (2009) 89–106.
———. "What Does It Mean to Say that John Chrysostom was a Monk?" *Studia Patristica* 41 (2006) 451–55.
———. "Who Came to Hear John Chrysostom Preach? Recovering a Late Fourth Century Preacher's Audience." *Ephemerides Theologicae* 76 (2000) 73–87.
Mayer, Wendy and Pauline Allen, trans. *John Chrysostom*. London: Routledge, 2000.

Mayer, Wendy and Bronwen Neil, trans. *The Cult of the Saints: Select Homilies and Letters*. Crestwood, NY: St Vladimir's Seminary, 2006.

Meeks, Wayne A. and Robert L. Wilkin. *Jews and Christians in Antioch in the First Four Centuries of the Common Era*. Missoula: Scholars Press for the Society of Biblical Literature, 1978.

Metzger, Bruce M. *A Textual Commentary on the Greek New Testament*. 2nd ed. Stuttgart: German Bible Society, 1994.

Migne, J.–P., ed. *Patrologiae Cursus Completes (series Graeca)*, vols. 47–64. Paris: Migne, 1857–1866. Thesaurus Linguae Graecae, online, University of California, Irvine.

Miller-Naudé, Cynthia L and Jacobus A. Naudé. "Ideology and Translation Strategy in Muslim-sensitive Bible Translations." *Neotestamentica* 47, no. 1 (2013) 171–90.

Milne, Bruce. *Know the Truth*. 3rd ed. Nottingham: IVP, 2009.

Mitchell, Margaret M. *The Heavenly Trumpet: John Chrysostom and the Art of Pauline Interpretation*. Westminster: John Knox, 2002.

Mitchell, Stephen. *A History of the Later Roman Empire AD 284–641*. Malden: Blackwell Publishing, 2007.

Moo, Douglas. *The Epistle to the Romans*. Grand Rapids: Eerdmans, 1996.

Moore, Peter. "Gold Without Dross: An Assessment of the Debt to John Chrysostom in John Calvin's Oratory." PhD diss., Macquarie University, 2013.

Moreas, Benjamin. "How to Evaluate Cultural Practices by Biblical Standards in Maintaining Cultural Identity in Latin America Report." In *Let the Earth Hear His Voice*, edited by J. D. Douglas, 1263–66. Minneapolis: World Wide, 1975.

Moreau, A. Scott. "Contextualization: From an Adapted Message to an Adapted Life." In *The Changing Face of World Missions*, edited by M. Pocock, G. Van Rheenen, D. McConnell, 321–48. Grand Rapids: Baker, 2005.

———. *Contextualization in World Missions*. Grand Rapids: Kregel, 2012.

———. ed. *Evangelical Dictionary of World Missions*. Grand Rapids: Baker, 2000.

———. "Evangelical Models of Contextualization." In *Local Theology for the Global Church: Principles for an Evangelical Approach to Contextualization*, edited by Matthew Cook, Rob Haskell, Ruth Julian and Natee Tanchanpongs, 165–93. Pasadena: William Carey, 2010.

———. "Missions and Mission." In *Evangelical Dictionary of World Missions*, edited by A. Scott. Moreau, 636–8. Grand Rapids: Baker, 2000.

———. "Syncretism." In *Evangelical Dictionary of World Missions*, edited by A. Scott Moreau, 924–5. Grand Rapids: Baker, 2000.

Moreau, A. Scott et al. *Introducing World Missions: A Biblical, Historical, and Practical Survey*. 2nd ed. Grand Rapids: Baker, 2015.

Myklebust, Olav. *The Study of Missions in Theological Education*. Vols. 1 and 2. Oslo: Olson, 1955.

Naugle, David K. *Worldview: The History of a Concept*. Grand Rapids: Eerdmans, 2002.

Neander, August. *The Life of St. Chrysostom*. Translated by John Charles Stapleton. London: R. B. Seeley and W. Burnside, 1845.

Neely, Alan. "Missiology." In *Evangelical Dictionary of World Missions*, edited by A. Scott Moreau, 633–6. Grand Rapids: Baker, 2000.

Neil, Bronwen. "Towards Defining a Christian Culture: The Christian Transformation of Classical Literature." In *The Cambridge History of Christianity Volume 2: Constantine to c.600*, edited by Augustine Casiday and Frederick W. Norris, 317–42. Cambridge: Cambridge University Press, 2007.

Neil, Stephen. *A History of Christian Mission*. New York: Penguin, 1964.
Newbigin, Lesslie. *Foolishness to the Greeks: The Gospel and Western Culture*. Grand Rapids: Eerdmans, 1986.
———. *The Gospel in a Pluralistic Society*. Grand Rapids: Eerdmans, 1989.
———. "Theological Education in World Perspective." *Ministerial Formation* 110 (April 2008) 18–25.
Nicholls, Bruce. J. *Contextualization: A Theology of Gospel and Culture*. Downers Grove: IVP, 1979.
———. "New Theological Approaches in Muslim Evangelism." In *The Gospel and Islam: A Compendium*. Abridged ed., edited by Don M. McCurry, 119–27. Monrovia: MARC, 1979.
———. "Theological Education and Evangelization." In *Let the Earth Hear His Voice*, edited by J. D. Douglas, 634–48. Minneapolis: World Wide Publications, 1975.
———. "Towards a Theology of Gospel and Culture." In *Down to Earth: Studies in Christianity and Culture*, edited by John R. W. Stott and Robert T. Coote, 49–62. Pasadena: William Carey, 1979.
Nida, Eugene. *Customs and Cultures: Anthropology for Christian Mission*. New York: Harper, 1954.
———. *Message and Mission: The Communication of the Christian Faith*. New York: Harper, 1960.
Niebuhr, H. Richard. *Christ and Culture*. New York: Harper and Row: 1951.
Noll, Mark A. *The Scandal of the Evangelical Mind*. Grand Rapids: Eerdmans, 1994.
Nunez, Emilio. *Liberation Theology*. Chicago: Moody Press, 1985.
O'Brien, Peter T. *Gospel and Mission in the Writings of Paul: An Exegetical and Theological Analysis*. Grand Rapids: Baker, 1995.
Oden, Thomas C, ed. *Ancient Christian Commentary on Scripture*. Downers Grove: IVP, 2001–2005.
Olivar, Alexander. "Reflections on Problems Raised by Early Christian Preaching." Translated by Joiseph Munitiz. In *Preacher and Audience: Studies in Early Christian and Byzantine Homiletics*, edited by Mary B. Cunningham and Pauline Allen, 21–32, Leiden: Brill, 1998.
———. *La Predicación Cristiana Antigua. Sección de Teología y Filosofía*. Vol. 189. Barcelona: Editorial Herder, 1991.
Origen. *Against Celsus*. In Ante-Nicene Fathers series 4. Translated by Alexander Roberts and James Donaldson. Peabody: Hendrickson, 1995.
Osmer, Richard R. *Practical Theology: An Introduction*. Grand Rapids: Eerdmans, 2008.
Oswalt, John N. *The Book of Isaiah: Chapters 40–66*. NICOT. Grand Rapids: Eerdmans, 1998.
Ott, Craig and Harold A. Netland, eds. *Globalizing Theology: Belief and Practice in an Era of World Christianity*. Grand Rapids: Baker, 2006.
Ott, Craig and Stephen J. Strauss. *Encountering Theology of Mission*. Grand Rapids: Baker, 2010.
Packer, James I. "Amsterdam 2000: The Content of the Gospel." *Evangelical Review of Theology* 25, no.1 (2001) 16–17.
———. *Evangelism and the Sovereignty of God*. Downers Grove: IVP, 2008.
Padilla, René. *Bases Biblicas de la Mision: Perspectivas Latinoamericanas*. Buenos Aires: Nueva Creacion, 1998.

———. "The Contextualization of the Gospel." In *Readings in Dynamic Indigeneity*, edited by Charles H. Kraft and Tom N. Wisley, 286–312. Pasadena: William Carey, 1979.

Palladius. *Dialogue on the Life of St. John Chrysostom*. Edited by A.-M. Malingrey and P. Leclercq, *Palladios. Dialogue sur la vie de Jean Chrysostome*, SC 341 and 342. Paris: Cerf, 1988.

Parshall, Phil. "Danger! New Directions in Contextualization." *EMQ* 34, no. 4 (October 1998) 404–10.

———. "I am Really only Asking Questions." *EMQ* 18, no. 3 (July 1982) 142–4.

———. "Lifting the Fatwa." *EMQ* 40, no. 3 (July 2004) 288–93.

———. *Muslim Evangelism: Contemporary Approaches to Contextualization*. Colorado Springs: Biblica Publishing, 2003.

———. *New Paths in Muslim Evangelism: Evangelical Approaches to Contextualization*. Grand Rapids: Baker, 1980.

Parsons, Mikeal C. *Acts*. Paideia. Grand Rapids: Baker, 2008.

Paul VI, Bishop of Rome. *Acta Apostolicae Sedis* 61 (1969) 1–939.

Pears, Angela. *Doing Contextual Theology*. Abingdon: Routledge, 2010.

Pelikan, Jaroslav. *Acts*. Grand Rapids: Brazos Press, 2005.

———. *Divine Rhetoric: The Sermon on the Mount as Message and as Model in Augustine, Chrysostom, and Luther*. Crestwood: St Vladimir's, 2001.

Perelman, Chaïm and L. Olbrechts-Tyteca. *The New Rhetoric: A Treatise on Argumentation*. Translated by John Wilkinson and Purcell Weaver. Notre Dame: University of Notre Dame, 1969.

Pernot, Laurent. *Rhetoric in Antiquity*. Washington: Catholic University of America Press, 2005.

Peterson, David G. *The Acts of the Apostles*. Grand Rapids: Eerdmans, 2009.

———. "The Motif of Fulfilment and Purpose of Luke–Acts." In *The Book of Acts in its First Century Setting Vol. I: Ancient Literary Setting*, edited by Bruce W. Winter and Andrew D. Clarke, 83–104. Grand Rapids: Eerdmans, 1993.

Phillips, Timothy R. and Dennis L. Okholm. *A Family of Faith: An Introduction to Evangelical Christianity*. 2nd ed. Grand Rapids: Baker, 2001.

Pinnock, Clark, ed. *The Grace of God, the Will of Man: A Case for Arminianism*. Minneapolis: Baker House, 1989.

Pivaral, Hector. "Guatemala: A Case Study—The Evangelical Church and the Influential Animistic Mayan Spirituality." In *Global Mission: Reflections and Case Studies in Contextualization for the Whole Church*, edited by Rose Dowsett, 129–39. Pasadena: William Carey, 2011.

Plantinga, Alvin C. *God, Freedom, and Evil*. Grand Rapids: Eerdmans, 1974.

Pocock, Michael. "Introduction: An Appeal for Balance." In *Missiology and the Social Sciences: Contributions, Cautions and Conclusion*. Evangelical Missiological Society Series 4, edited by Edward Rommen and Gary Corwin, 7–18. Pasadena: William Carey, 1996.

Poe, Harry L. *The Gospel and its Meaning: A Theology for Evangelism and Church Growth*. Grand Rapids: Zondervan, 1996.

Polhill, John B. *Acts*. NAC. Nashville: Broadman, 1992.

Porter, Stanley E. *The Paul of Acts: Essays in Literary Criticism, Rhetoric and Theology*. Tubingen: Mohr/Siebeck, 1999.

Porter, Stanley E. and Bryan R. Dyer. "Oral Texts? A Reassessment of the Oral and Rhetorical Nature of Paul's Letters in Light of Recent Studies." *Journal of the Evangelical Theological Society* 55, no. 2 (2012) 323–41.

Poston, Larry. "'You Must not Worship in their Way': When Contextualization Becomes Syncretism." In *Contextualization and Syncretism: Navigating Cultural Currents*, edited by Gail Van Rheenen, 243–63. Evangelical Missiological Society Series 13. Pasadena: William Carey, 2006.

Power, Patricia A. "Blurring the Boundaries: American Messianic Jews and Gentiles." *Nova Religio: The Journal of Alternative and Emergent Religions* 15, no. 1 (2011) 69–91.

Pradels, et al. "The Sequence of Dating the Series of John Chrysostom's Eight Discourses *Adversus Iudaeos*." *Zeitschrift für Antikes Christentum* 6 (2002) 90–116.

Priest, Robert J. and Robert DeGeorge. "Doctoral Dissertations on Mission: Ten Year Update, 2002–2011." *IBMR* 37, no. 4 (October 2013) 195–202.

Ps-Martyrius. *Oratio funebris*. Translated by Timothy D. Barnes and George Bevan. *The Funerary Speech for John Chrysostom*, Liverpool: Liverpool University Press, 2013.

Quasten, Johannes. *Patrology*. Vol. 3. Westminster: Christian Classics, 1983.

Quintilian. *Institutes of Oratory*. http://rhetoric.eserver.org/quintilian/index.html.

Quiroga, Alberto. "From Sophistopolis to Episcopolis: The Case for a Third Sophistic." *Journal for Late Antique Religion and Culture* 1 (2007) 31–41.

Quiroga Puertas, Alberto. "Deflecting attention and shaping reality with rhetoric: the case of the riot of the statues of A.D. 387 in Antioch." *Nova Tellus* 26 (2008) 137–53.

Racey, David. "Contextualisation: How Far is too Far?" *EMQ* 32, no. 3 (July 1996) 304–9.

Raiter, Michael D. "'Sent for This Purpose': 'Mission' and 'Missiology' and their Search for Meaning." In *Ripe for Harvest: Christian Mission in the New Testament and in our World*, edited by R. J. Gibson, 106–49. Carlisle: Paternoster, 2000.

Ranson, C. W. "The Theological Education Fund." *International Review of Mission* 47 (October 1958) 432–8.

Rhee, Helen. *Early Christian Literature: Christ and Culture in the Second and Third Centuries*. London: Routledge, 2005.

Richard, H. L. "Is Extraction Evangelism Still the Way to Go?" *EMQ* 30, no. 2 (April 1994) 170–7.

Richardson, Don. *Peace Child*. Glendale: Regal, 1974.

Ritter, Adolf M. "John Chrysostom and the Jews—A Reconsideration." In *Christianity in the Caucasus*, edited by Tamila Mgaloblishvili, 141–54. Richmond: Curzon, 1998.

Robbins, Joel. "Crypto-Religion and the Study of Cultural Mixtures: Anthropology, Value and the Nature of Syncretism." *Journal of the American Academy of Religion* 79, no. 2 (2011) 408–24.

Rommen, Edward. *Come and See: An Eastern Orthodox Perspective on Contextualization*. Pasadena: William Carey, 2013.

Rommen, Edward and Gary Corwin, eds. *Missiology and the Social Sciences: Contributions, Cautions and Conclusion*. Evangelical Missiological Society Series 4. Pasadena: William Carey, 1996.

Rousseau, Philip. *The Early Christian Centuries*. London: Pearson Education, 2002.

———. "'The Preacher's Audience': A More Optimistic View." In *Ancient History in a Modern University*, Vol. 2, edited by T. W. Hillard and E. A. Judge, 391–400. Grand Rapids: Baker, 1998.

Rylaarsdam, David. *John Chrysostom on Divine Pedagogy: The Coherence of his Theology and Preaching.* Oxford: Oxford University Press, 2014.

———. "Painful Preaching: John Chrysostom and the Philosophical Tradition of Guiding Souls." *Studia Patristica* 41 (2006) 463–8.

Saliou, Catherine. "Les lieux du polythéisme dans l'espace urbain et le paysage mémoriel d'Antioche-sur-l'Oronte, de Libanios à Malalas (IVe–VIe s.)." In *Religious Practices and Christianization of the Late Antique City (4th–7th cent.)*, edited by Aude Busine, 38–70. Leiden-Boston: Brill, 2015.

Sandnes, Paul Olav. "Paul and Socrates: The Aim of Paul's Areopagus Speech." *JSNT* 50 (1993) 13–26.

Sanneh, Lamin. *Translating the Message: The Missionary Impact on Culture.* Maryknoll, Orbis, 2009.

Satterthwaite, Philip E. "Acts Against the Background of Classical Rhetoric." In *The Book of Acts in its First Century Setting Vol. I: Ancient Literary Setting*, edited by Bruce W. Winter and Andrew D. Clarke, 337–79. Grand Rapids: Eerdmans, 1993.

Schaff, Philip, ed. *A Select Library of Nicene and Post Nicene Fathers of the Christian Church*, First Series, vols. 9–14, New York, 1886–1890. Reprint 1975, 1988. Grand Rapids: Eerdmans.

Scherer, James A. "Missiology as a Discipline and What It Includes." In *New Directions in Missions and Evangelization* 2, edited by James A. Scherer and Stephen B. Bevans, 173–87. Maryknoll: Orbis, 1994.

Schineller, Peter. *A Handbook on Inculturation.* New York: Paulist, 1990.

Schlorff, Samuel P. "The Hermeneutical Crisis in Muslim Evangelization." *EMQ* 16, no. 3 (July 1980) 143–51.

Schnabel, Eckhard J. *Acts.* ECNT. Grand Rapids: Zondervan, 2012.

———. *Early Christian Mission Vol. II: Paul and the Early Church.* Downers Grove: IVP, 2004.

———. *Paul the Missionary: Realities, Strategies and Methods.* Downers Grove: IVP, 2008.

Schreiter, Robert J. *Constructing Local Theologies.* Maryknoll: Orbis, 1985.

———. *The New Catholicity: Theology Between the Local and the Global.* Maryknoll: Orbis, 2004.

Schuster, Jürgen. "Karl Hartenstein: Mission with a Focus on the End," *Mission Studies* 19, no. 1 (2002) 53–89.

Schweitzer, E. "Concerning the Speeches in Acts." In *Studies in Luke–Acts: Essays Presented in Honour of Paul Schubert*, edited by L. E. Keck and J. L. Martyn, 208–16. Nashville: Abingdon, 1966.

Shenk, Richard. "The Church Fathers and Catholic Social Thought: Reflections on the Symposium." In *Reading Patristic Texts on Social Ethics: Issues and Challenges for Twenty-First-Century Christian Social Thought*, edited by Johan Leemans, Brian J. Matz, and Johan Verstraeten, 209–21. Washington: Catholic University of America Press, 2011.

Shenk, Wilbert R. "Rufus Anderson and Henry Venn: A Special Relationship?" *IBMR* 5, no. 4 (1981) 168–72.

Shepardson, Christine. *Controlling Contested Spaces: Late Antique Antioch and the Spatial Politics of Religious Controversy*. Berkley: University of California Press, 2014.

Silverstone, Roger. "The Power of the Ordinary: On Cultural Studies and the Sociology of Culture." *Sociology* 28, no. 4 (1994) 991–1001.

Simon, Marcel. *Verus Israel: A Study of the Relations Between Christians and Jews in the Roman Empire (135–425)*. Translated by Henry McKeating. London: Vallentine Mitchell, 1986.

Sire, James. *The Universe Next Door: A Basic Worldview Catalog*. 5th ed. Downers Grove: IVP, 2009.

Snodgrass, Klyne. "The Gospel of Jesus." In *The Written Gospel*, edited by Marcus Bockmuehl, 31–44. Cambridge: Cambridge University Press, 2005.

Soards, Marion L. *The Speeches in Acts: Their Content, Context and Concerns*. Louisville: Westminster, 1994.

Socrates, *Hist. eccl. Sokrates Kirchengeschichte*, edited by G. C. Hansen, GCS NF 1. Berlin: AkademieVerlag, 1995.

Sozomen, *Hist. eccl. Sozomenus Kirchengeschichte*, edited by G. C. Hansen, GCS NF 4. Trans. NPNF 02.02. Berlin: AkademieVerlag, 1995.

Spae, Joseph. "Missiology as Local Theology and Interreligious Encounter." *Missiology* 7 (1979) 479–500.

Speers, John. "Should Missionaries Keep the Muslim Fast?" *EMQ* 27, no. 4 (October 1991) 356–9.

Sproul, R. C. *Willing to Believe: The Controversy over Free Will*. Grand Rapids: Baker, 1997.

Stanfil, Jon. "Embracing the Barbarian: John Chrysostom's Pastoral Care of the Goths." PhD diss., Fordham University, 2015.

———. "John Chrysostom's Gothic Parish and the Politics of Space." *Studia Patristica* 67 (2013) 345–9.

Stanley, Brian. *The World Missionary Conference, Edinburgh 1910*. Grand Rapids: Eerdmans, 2009.

Stark, Rodney. *The Rise of Christianity*. Princeton: Princeton University Press, 1996.

Stein, Robert H. *Luke*. TNAC 24. Nashville: Broadman, 1992.

Sterk, Andrea. *Renouncing the World yet Leading the Church*. Cambridge, Massachussets: Harvard University Press, 2004.

Stewart, Kenneth J. "Evangelical and Patristic Christianity: 1517 to the Present." *Evangelical Quarterly* 80, no. 4 (2008) 307–21.

Stott, John. "1982: The Grand Rapids Report on Evangelism and Social Responsibility: An Evangelical Commitment." In *Making Christ Known: Historic Mission Documents from the Lausanne Movement 1974–1989*, edited by John Stott, 165–213. Carlisle: Paternoster, 1996.

———. "The Authority and Power of the Bible." In *The New Face of Evangelicalism: An International Symposium on the Lausanne Covenant*, edited by C. Renè Padilla, 33–47. Downers Grove: IVP, 1976.

———. "The Biblical Basis of Evangelism." In *Let the Earth Hear His Voice*, edited by J. D. Douglas, 65–78. Minneapolis: World Wide, 1975.

———. "The Lausanne Covenant." In *Let the Earth Hear His Voice*, edited by J. D. Douglas, 3–9. Minneapolis: World Wide, 1975.

———. *What is an Evangelical?* London: Falcon, 1977.

Stuhlmacher, Peter. "The Pauline Gospel." In *The Gospel and the Gospels*, edited by Peter Stuhlmacher, 149–72. Grand Rapids: Eerdmans, 1991.
Tabor, Charles A. "Contextualization: Indigenization and/or Transformation." In *The Gospel and Islam: A Compendium*. Abridged ed., edited by Don M. McCurry, 107–18. Monrovia: MARC, 1979.
Tannerhill, Robert C. *The Narrative Unity of Luke–Acts: A Literary Interpretation*. Vol. 2: *The Acts of the Apostles*. Minneapolis: Fortress, 1990.
TEF Staff. *Ministry in Context: The Third Mandate Program of the Theological Education Fund (1970–1977)*. Bromley: The Theological Education Fund (WCC), 1972.
Tennant, Timothy C. "The Challenge of Churchless Christianity: An Evangelical Assessment." *IBMR* 29, no. 4 (2005) 171–7.
———. "Followers of Jesus (Isa) in Islamic Mosques: A Closer Examination of C5 'High Spectrum' Contextualization." *IJFM* 23, no. 3 (2006) 101–15.
———. *Theology in the Context of World Christianity: How the Global Church is Influencing the Way We Think About and Discuss Theology*. Grand Rapids: Zondervan, 2007.
Terry, John Mark. "Approaches to the Evangelization of Muslims." *EMQ* 32, no. 2 (April 1996) 168–173.
Terry, John Mark, Ebbie Smith, and Justice Anderson. *Missiology: An Introduction to the Foundations, History, and Strategies of World Missions*. Nashville: Broadman and Holman, 1998.
Theodoret, *Hist. eccl.* Edited by G. C. Hanson and L. Parmentier, GCS NF 5. Berlin: AkademieVerlag, 1998.
Thistelton, Anthony C. *Hermeneutics: An Introduction*. Grand Rapids: Eerdmans, 2009.
Thompson, Alan J. *One Lord, One People: The Unity of the Church in Acts in its Literary Setting*. London: T & T Clark, 2008.
Tiplady, Richard. "The Pilgrim Church Needs a New Home." In *Global Mission: Reflections and Case Studies in Contextualization for the Whole Church*, edited by Rose Dowsett, 141–7. Pasadena: William Carey, 2011.
Travis, John [pseud.]. "Appropriate Approaches in Muslim Contexts." In *Appropriate Christianity*, edited by Charles H. Kraft, 397–414. Pasadena: William Carey, 2005.
———. *Messianic Muslim Followers of Isa: A Closer Look at C5 Believers and Congregations*." *IJFM* 17, no. 1 (2000) 53–9.
———. "The C1 to C6 Spectrum." *EMQ* 34, no. 4 (October 1998) 407–8.
———. "Must all Muslims Leave 'Islam' to Follow Jesus?" *EMQ* 34, no.4 (October 1998) 411–15.
Travis, John, Phil Parshall, Herebert Hoefer, and Rebecca Lewis. "Four Responses to Tennant." *IJFM* 23, no. 3 (2006) 124–6.
Trinity Evangelical School, "The Evangelical Affirmations." In *Evangelical Affirmations*, edited by Kenneth S. Kantzer and Carl F. Henry, 27–38. Grand Rapids: Zondervan, 1990.
Trzcionka, Silke. *Magic and the Supernatural in the Fourth Century Syria*. London/New York: Routledge, 2007.
Tylor, Edmund B. *Primitive Cultures: Researches into the Development of Mythology, Philosophy, Religion, Art and Custom*. Vol. 1. New York: H. Holt and Company, 1874.

van Dam, Raymond. "Bishops and Society." In *The Cambridge History of Christianity Volume 2: Constantine to c.600*, edited by Augustine Casiday and Frederick W. Norris, 343-66. Cambridge: Cambridge University Press, 2007.

van de Paverd, Frans. *St John Chrysostom, The Homilies of the Statues: An Introduction*. Orientalia Christiana Analecta 239. Rome: Institutum Studiorum Orientalium, 1991.

van der Horst, Pieter W. "Jews and Christians in Antioch at the End of the Fourth Century." In *Christian-Jewish Relations Through the Centuries*, edited by Stanley E. Porter and Brook R. W. Pearson, 228-38. London: T & T Clark, 2000.

Van Engen, Charles. "Five Perspectives of Contextually Appropriate Missional Theology." In *Appropriate Christianity*, edited by Charles Kraft, 183-202. Pasadena: William Carey Library, 2005.

———. *Mission on the Way*. Grand Rapids: Baker, 1996.

———. "The New Covenant: Knowing God in Context." In *The Word Among Us: Contextualizing Theology for Mission Today*, edited by Dean S. Gilliland, 74-100. Eugene: Wipf and Stock, 1989.

Van Rheenen, Gail. "Syncretism and Contextualization: The Church on a Journey Defining Itself." In *Contextualization and Syncretism: Navigating Cultural Currents*, edited by Gail Van Rheenen, 1-29. Evangelical Missiological Society Series 13. Pasadena: William Carey, 2006.

Van Veller, Courtney Wilson. "Paul's Therapy of the Soul: A New Approach to John Chrysostom and Anti-Judaism." PhD diss., Boston University, 2015.

Verkuyl, Johannes. *Contemporary Missiology*. Translated and edited by Dale Cooper. Grand Rapids: Eerdmans, 1978.

Visser't Hooft, W. A. *No Other Name: The Choice Between Syncretism and Christian Universalism*. London: SCM, 1963.

von Allman, Daniel. "The Birth of Theology." *International Review of Mission* 64 (January 1975) 37-55.

Vroom, Hendrick. "Is not all Contextual Understanding of the Gospel Contextual?" *Journal of Reformed Theology* 3 (2009) 274-87.

Walls, Andrew F. "Alexander Duff." In *Biographical Dictionary of Christian Missions*, edited by Gerald A. Anderson, 187-8. New York: Simon and Schuster, 1998.

———. *The Cross-Cultural Process in Christian History*. Maryknoll: Orbis, 2002.

———. *The Missionary Movement in Christian History: Studies in the Transmission of Faith*. Maryknoll: Orbis, 2009.

Wan, Enoch. "Rethinking Missiological Research Methodology." *Global Missiology* (October 2003) http://www.enochwan.com/english/articles/pdf/Rethinking%20Missiological%20Research%Methodology.pdf.

Warneck, Gustav. *Evangelische Missionslehre: Ein Missionstheoretischer Versuch*. Vol. 1. Gotha: F. A. Berthes, 1897.

Waterman, L. D. [pseud.]. "Contextualization: A Few Basic Questions." *EMQ* 44, no. 2 (April 2008) 166-73.

———. "Do the Roots Affect the Fruits?" *IJFM* 24, no. 2 (2007) 57-63.

Webber, Robert E. *Ancient-Future Evangelism: Making Your Church a Faith-Forming Community*. Grand Rapids: Baker, 2003.

———. *Ancient-Future Faith: Rethinking Evangelicalism for a Postmodern World*. Grand Rapids: Baker, 1999.

———. *Ancient-Future Time: Forming Spirituality through the Christian Year*. Grand Rapids: Baker, 2004.

———. *The Divine Embrace: Recovering the Passionate Spiritual Life*. Grand Rapids: Baker, 2006.

———. *Worship: Old and New*. Rev. ed. Grand Rapids: Zondervan, 1994.

Weinrich, William C. *Revelation*. Ancient Christian Commentary on Scripture: New Testament II. Downers Grove: IVP, 2005.

Wenham, David. "The Purpose of Luke–Acts." In *Reading Luke: Interpretation, Reflection, Formation*. Scripture and Hermeneutics Series 6, edited by Craig G. Bartholomew, Joel B. Green, Anthony C. Thistleton, 79–103. Milton Keynes: Paternoster, 2005.

Werner, Dietrich. "Letter from Staff." *Ministerial Formation* 110 (April 2008) 3–4.

Whiteman, Darrell L. "Contextualization: The Theory, the Gap, the Challenge." *IBMR* 21, no. 1 (1997) 2–7.

Wilder, John. "Some Reflections on Possibilities for People Movements among Muslims." *Missiology* 5, no. 3 (July 1977) 301–20.

Wilde, Robert. *The Treatment of the Jews in the Greek Writers of the First Three Centuries*. Patristic Studies LXXXI. Washington: Catholic University Press, 1949.

Wiles, Maurice. *Archetypal Heresy: Arianism Through the Centuries*. Oxford: Oxford University Press, 1996.

Wilken, Robert L. *John Chrysostom and the Jews: Rhetoric and Reality in the Late Fourth Century*. The Transformation of the Classical Heritage 4. Berkeley: University of California Press, 1983.

Williams, Daniel H. *Evangelicals and Tradition: The Formative Influence of the Early Church*. Grand Rapids: Baker, 2005.

———. *Retrieving the Tradition and Renewing Evangelicalism: A Primer for Suspicious Protestants*. Grand Rapids: Eerdmans, 1999.

———. "Similis et Dissimilis." In *Ancient Faith for the Church's Future*, edited by Mark Husbands and Jeffrey P. Greenman, 69–89. Downers Grove: IVP, 2008.

———. *Tradition, Scripture, and Interpretation: A Sourcebook of the Ancient Church*. Grand Rapids: Baker, 2006.

Williams, David. J. *Acts*. NIBC. Peabody: Hendrickson, 1990.

Wills, Lawrence. "The Form of the Sermon in Hellenistic Judaism and Early Christianity." *HTR* 77 (1984) 277–99.

Witherington III, Ben. *The Acts of the Apostles: A Socio-Rhetorical Commentary*. Grand Rapids: Eerdmans, 1998.

———. *Conflict and Community in Corinth: A Socio-Rhetorical Commentary on 1 and 2 Corinthians*. Grand Rapids: Eerdmans, 1995.

———. *New Testament Rhetoric: An Introductory Guide to the Art of Persuasion in and of the New Testament*. Eugene: Cascade, 2009.

———. *Paul's Letter to the Romans: A Socio-Rhetorical Commentary*. Grand Rapids: Eerdmans, 2004.

———. *What's in the Word: Rethinking the Socio-Rhetorical Character of the New Testament*. Waco: Baylor University Press, 2009.

Wolfe, Henry J. "Insider Movements: An Assessment of the Viability of Retaining Socio-Religious Insider Identity in High Religious Contexts." PhD diss., The Southern Baptist Theological Seminary, 2011.

Woodberry, Dudley J. "Contextualization among Muslims: Reusing Common Pillars." *IJFM* 13, no. 4 (1996) 171–86.

———. "To the Muslim I Became a Muslim?" *IJFM* 24, no. 1 (2007) 23–28.

Wolfram, Herwig. *History of the Goths*. Translated by Thomas J. Dunlap. Berkeley: University of California Press, 1988.

Wright, Christopher J. H. *The Mission of God: Unlocking the Bible's Grand Narrative*. Nottingham: IVP, 2006.

Wright, David F. *Infant Baptism in Historical Perspective*. Milton Keynes: Paternoster, 2007.

Wright, N. T. *What St Paul Really Said*. Oxford: Lion Publishing, 1997.

Wu, Jackson. *One Gospel for All Nations: A Practical Approach to Biblical Contextualization*. Pasadena: William Carey, 2015.

Yego, Josphat P. "Appreciation for and Warnings about Contextualization." *EMQ* 16, no. 3 (July 1980) 153–6.

Yoder, John Howard. "How H. Richard Niebuhr Reasoned: A Critique of Christ and Culture." In *Authentic Transformation: A New Vision of Christ and Culture*, edited by Glenn H. Stassen, D. M. Yeager, and John Howard Yoder, 31–90. Nashville: Abingdon, 1996.

Young, Frances. "The rhetorical schools and their influence on patristic exegesis." In *The Making of Orthodoxy: Essays in Honour of Henry Chadwick*, edited by Rowan Williams, 182–99. Cambridge: Cambridge University Press, 1989.

Yung, Hwa. *Mangoes or Bananas? The Quest for an Authentic Asian Christian Theology*. Oxford: Regnum Books International, 1997.

Zehnle, Richard F. *Peter's Pentecost Discourse: Tradition and Lukan reinterpretation in Peter's speeches of Acts 2 and 3*. SBL 15. Nashville: Abingdon, 1971.

Zhang, Wenxi. *Paul Among Jews: A Study of the Meaning and Significance of Paul's Inaugural Sermon in the Synagogue of Antioch in Pisidia (Acts 13:16–41) for his Missionary Work among the Jews*. Eugene: Wipf and Stock, 2011.

www.ingramcontent.com/pod-product-compliance
Lightning Source LLC
Chambersburg PA
CBHW051633230426
43669CB00013B/2278